Kindly given by

Dr. Gerry McCabe

for the solemn profession of
Sr Joseph of Divine Love.

Please pray for
our benefactors.

THEO-DRAMA
Volume II

THEO-DRAMA

Volumes of the Complete Work:

HANS URS VON BALTHASAR

THEO-DRAMA

THEOLOGICAL
DRAMATIC THEORY

VOLUME II
THE DRAMATIS PERSONAE:
MAN IN GOD

Translated by Graham Harrison

IGNATIUS PRESS   SAN FRANCISCO

Title of the German original:
Theodramatik: Zweiter Band: Die Personen des Spiels
Teil 1: Der Mensch in Gott
© 1976 Johannes Verlag, Einsiedeln

Cover by Roxanne Mei Lum

With ecclesiastical approval
© 1990 Ignatius Press, San Francisco
ISBN 0-89870-283-1
Library of Congress catalogue number 89-83257
Printed in the United States of America

CONTENTS

CONTENTS

II. DRAMATIS PERSONAE (I)

CONTENTS

PREFACE

Here we intend to set forth our theory of "theo-drama", having concluded the predominantly literary prolegomena in volume one, which yielded a whole set of resources for the task. This "theo-drama" is a "theological"[1] undertaking; that is, it reflects upon the dramatic character of existence in the light of biblical revelation. Thus our reflections are themselves *based on* this revelation: they do not merely seek it. This is immediately evident from the fact that our view of God, the world and man will not be developed primarily from below, out of man's "understanding of himself": it will be drawn from that drama which God has already "staged" with the world and with man, in which we find ourselves players. This horizon will prove to be the widest possible horizon (and not a constricting one) inasmuch as it is able to recapitulate and integrate within itself all the ways in which man can possibly view himself.

But this will also apply to all his ways of viewing God. Man's "concepts of God" always swing between two extremes. At one extreme, there is the mythological view in which God (or the gods) is embroiled in the world drama, which, with its own laws of operation, thus constitutes a third level of reality above God and man; at the other extreme, God is seen as dwelling in philosophical sublimity above the vicissitudes of the world, which prevent him from entering the dramatic action. On the basis of biblical revelation, we can say right at the outset that God has involved himself with the creation of the world, particularly in the creation of finite free beings, without thereby succumbing to some superordinate fate. Thus the God of theo-dramatic action is neither "mutable" (as in the mythological view) nor "immutable" (in the terms of philosophy). We shall have to see, as the drama unfolds, how it is impossible for him to be either the one or the other.

[1] "Theological" is used here in its ordinary sense, according to which our entire plan of a trilogy (theo-phany [= aesthetics]—theo-drama—theo-logic [= theology]) is a "theological" one. Naturally, the "Logos", who will be the subject of "methodological" reflection in the third part of the trilogy, is also guiding our way in the first two parts.

We are concerned here with the dramatic character of existence as a whole, as judged by the light of revelation. So we shall not be examining individual, particularly dramatic figures of the Bible or of Christian history—even if Nietzsche says he finds figures of such colossal stature in the Old Testament that Aryan writings have nothing to put beside them and even though it would be tempting to compare what is specific to Old Testament tragedy with what is specifically Greek, on the one hand, and specifically Christian on the other. This topic will not be approached through an examination of individual characters and texts[2] but through a consideration of the various conditions and situations (*status*) of mankind.

What kind of structure can we give to an investigation that encompasses the whole field of "theology", albeit under a formally distinct viewpoint? It would be wearing to take up the methods of theological aesthetics once again; it would mean (1) examining the history of Christian thought according to various theodramatic approaches; (2) elucidating the relationship between "natural" and "supernatural" dramatic action; and (3) illustrating the dramatic action specific to the Old and New Testaments. It would be possible, yet it would have the considerable drawback that the first could only be rendered meaningful on the basis of the third, and the third only on the basis of the second. In other words, one would always have to envisage the whole. It is better, therefore, to choose a structure that has this totality in view right from the start, quite deliberately, but one that leads progressively—a truly "theodramatic" approach—

[2] Adam and Eve, Cain and Abel, the "angels" and the daughters of man, the stories of the Patriarchs (Moriah, Hagar, Jacob-Esau, Rachel-Leah, the story of Joseph), Jephtha, Samson, Israel in Egypt, Moses (committing murder out of a sense of duty, Moses and Aaron, the mediator between God's wrath and human sin), the tragedy of Saul, the tragedy of David, the tragedy of Solomon, Athalia, Elijah, Jeremiah, Ezekiel, Zedekiah, Job, the Suffering Servant, Esther and Judith. John the Baptist, Joseph's suspicion, Herod, the incomprehension of Mary and the brothers, Jesus' temptation, his struggle with the leaders of the nation, his trial, Peter for and against Jesus, Judas between the Old and New Covenants, Magdalen between the world and God, Paul between Judaism and the Gentile world, between authority and humiliation. The world of the Apocalypse. The martyr-tragedies (a favorite theme in Baroque literature), the

from the implicit to the explicit. Our aim is to present the same fundamental themes—God and the creature, the structure and situation of the world and man, the Mediator and his presence (the Church and all that is associated with her) and the movement of history—in three stages. The first stage is the *point of departure* (the "dramatis personae", as it were); the second is the *course of the action*; and the third is the *final play*. This treatment will encompass three volumes.

The present volume therefore has the task of presenting the play's characters, and it immediately comes up against a great difficulty. The spectator reads the list of characters in his theatre program before the curtain goes up; he may try to make a mental note of them; but if he does not already know the play, this list will not tell him anything about the dramatic action; he will glean very little about the play's content. At most, he will get hold of empty relationships. Only the action itself will reveal who each individual is; and it will not reveal, through successive unveilings, primarily who the individual *always was*, but rather who he *is to become* through the action, through his encounter with others and through the decisions he makes. There is at least a reciprocal relationship between the "was" and the "will be". "*Agere sequitur esse*" also requires "*esse sequitur agere*". There is no need to unfold this truth here in philosophical terms,[3] for it is already "dramatically" evident. Christianity, as Newman says, is a supernatural story, practically a stage play. It tells us who the Author is by telling us what he has done.[4] This

stories of heretics, conflicts between the Church and conscience. . . . There is no end to the possibilities for dramatic presentation. Cf. Elisabeth Frenzel, *Stoffe der Weltliteratur, ein Lexikon dichtungsgeschichtlicher Längsschnitte* (Stuttgart: Kröner, 1962). Here the biblical and Christian themes are included among the vast number of other topics found in mythology, world history, etc.

It would be possible, however, to place a theological "reduction" alongside this literary one: all these dramas or tragedies are preliminary sketches or consequences of the central drama of Christ. They all circle around the Cross, at a greater or lesser distance; they are part of the way in which the Cross is "elongated" and expounded, and they are magnetically orientated to that center. Thus they can be interpreted and arranged with reference to the Cross.

[3] Cf. Heinrich Beck, *Der Akt-Charakter des Seins* (Munich: Max Heuber, 1965).

[4] "The Tamworth Reading Room" (1841), in *Discussions and Arguments on Various Subjects* (1872), 296.

applies all the more to man and the world, for they have yet to become what they are. Thus the attempt to adumbrate the play's characters prior to the performance is a profoundly anti-dramatic undertaking; theologically speaking, it is a regression to a static, essentialist theology which, in its doctrine of God, doctrine of man, Christology, and so forth, imagines it can say things about "beings" before the action of these beings is either ascertained (in the case of man) or at least revealed (in the case of God).

In God's case there is a *real* revelation, even if, in this revealing, God remains beyond our comprehension. This paradox is central to the *theologia* of the Greek Fathers; by maintaining it, they went beyond, right from the outset, Gregory Palamas' thesis that God only reveals himself in his "energies", behind which his "being" remains unknowable. If God cannot speak in such a way that he expresses *himself*, if the Word of God, the Son, does not have the power to show us the Father—to make the old maxim *"loquere ut videam te"* come true—then we fall back behind Nicaea and revert to Arianism and Middle Platonism.[5] The Cappadocians were strong enough to hold both sides of the paradox against the Late Arians: they distinguished between "being" and "energy" (thus asserting that God could not be grasped by concepts), while at the same time maintaining that God could be imaged by his Word, his Son, in whom the Father has eternally expressed himself. Maximus the Confessor will give a final form to this paradox, outstripping Palamas in advance.[6] As far as dramatic theory is concerned, however, this implies that the unveiling of the "heart of God", which alone really shows us *who* he is, can only take place through the course of his history with mankind.

If we turn to man, it is even clearer (if possible) that we cannot describe his "essence" from some static vantage point. Theologically speaking, we only know man as he exists in history, participating simultaneously in various *"status"* which he goes through; the succession of these stages implies the dramatic dimension of human life. Something in man must be identical to his original state (*status naturae integrae*), something must be

[5] F. Ricken, "Nikaia als Krisis des altkirchlichen Platonismus" in *Theologie und Philosophie* 44 (1969), 321–41.

[6] On this whole issue: Christoph von Schönborn, O.P., *L'Icône du Christ, fondements théologiques* (thesis, Institut Catholique de Paris, 1974).

identical to his fall from it (*status naturae lapsae*); something in him must correspond to the historical phase of his preparation for redemption in Christ (*status naturae reparandae*), and, finally, something in him must correspond to the effect in him of this transformation wrought by Christ (*status naturae reparatae*). Thus any "static" definition must always take into account the whole drama that takes place between man and God. The condition of fallen nature cannot simply be equated with "the Gentiles", nor can nature on its way toward restoration be equated with Judaism, nor can nature restored be equated with Christianity: each condition participates in all the others,[7] and at most one could say that each of the three theological exponents of mankind predominantly represents one of these conditions.

In this present volume therefore, which outlines the "characters" or the subjective centers of the action, we must face the fact that this initial discussion—for instance, of the roots of finite freedom—cannot be rendered intelligible apart from the ultimate revelation, namely, the mystery of the divine Trinity and the soteriological mystery of the Church.

With regard to the dramatic resources worked out in the Prolegomena, their usefulness will emerge only gradually, particularly in volumes three and four. In the present volume, which deals with the conditions that render action possible, only the concluding part of the Prolegomena, "From Role to Mission", is immediately relevant.

One last thing: a theodramatic theory is not primarily concerned with spectating and evaluating but with acting and the ability to act. As Theodor Haecker told us at the end of volume one, "only the God-man" really identified his person with his role[8]—apart from that identity of both that lies at the heart of his Church and is the indispensable precondition for his growth as

---

[7] At most, one might want to make an exception in cases where (as in Paul) the Gentile is incorporated into the Church of Christ without being obliged to make a detour via the history of the Old Testament; but he too obtains access to the Church through the faith of Abraham. As the Pauline letters show, he cannot share in Christ without affirming the essentials of his prior history in Israel and in a certain sense even recapitulating it.

[8] *Theo-Drama* I: *Prolegomena* (San Francisco: Ignatius Press, 1988) (= TD I), 646.

well as the full answer to his being. J. Maritain has discerned
this:

> The (pure) Church is the only one on earth who carries out the
> role she presents (*le rôle de son personnage*), because, in her, both
> role and person come from God. The world, by contrast, is a
> stage on which the roles and what they embody (*rôles et per-
> sonnages*) are rarely in harmony.[9]

The closer a man comes to this identity, the more perfectly does
he play his part. In other words, the saints are the authentic
interpreters of theo-drama. Their knowledge, lived out in dramatic existence, must be regarded as setting a standard of
interpretation not only for the life-dramas of individuals but
ultimately for the "history of freedom" of all the nations and of
all mankind.

[9] *Religion et culture* (1930), 101.

I. THE APPROACH

In the Introduction to the first volume of *Theo-Drama*, we situated dramatic theory between aesthetics and logic.[1] Thus we understood it to be the center of our appropriation, through reflection, of Christian revelation. We went on to examine the currents of thought that are dominant today in the fields of theology and general *Weltanschauung*[2] and expressed the view that they could only be reconciled by converging on a theological dramatic theory, though as yet, as individual lines of thought, they had not reached this point. The next task of our *Prolegomena* was to study the phenomenon of the theatre—as a metaphor that is closely bound up with life's reality—in order to gather materials (including both form and content) yielding categories and modes of expression for our central venture. Such materials will be of use only if we realize that, in employing them, we need to complement them and go beyond them. God has the chief role in theo-drama: the author's "transcendence" vis-à-vis the play as performed is only a poor metaphor for the part played by God. It is no less inadequate to compare the God-man with the play's hero and the divine Spirit with the director. In theo-drama, furthermore, man is startled out of his spectator's seat and dragged onto the "stage"; the distinction between stage and auditorium becomes fluid, to say the least. The raising of the many-sided intramundane drama to the level of theo-drama, which is essentially transcendent and unique, puts a question mark over even the most interesting dramatic categories, a question mark that must apply, ultimately, to every attempt to present this unique reality in the forms of speech.

Thus we cannot rush blindly into the "performance" but must first try, in this volume, to reach a standpoint from which we can proceed to the dramatic action. *"Dramatis Personae"*: Who will be participating in the action? If we already knew the answer to this, we could do without the present volume. In theo-drama, doubtless, God is the main character; the question is, who else acts, who else *can* act, if God is on stage? On Sinai, we are told, a covenant was concluded "through the hand of an

---

[1] *Theo-Drama* I: *Prolegomena* (San Francisco: Ignatius Press, 1988) (= TD I), 15–23.

[2] TD I, 25–50.

intermediary" who made a bridge between the two parties, between God and the people. "Now an intermediary implies more than one; but God is one" (Gal 3:19–20). Following this line of thought, Christ, in whom God makes his appearance, can only be called a "mediator" by way of analogy: strictly speaking, the term cannot apply to him at all. And if the Church, with her members—Christians—is the "Body of Christ", his "fullness", it follows logically that Christians in turn are "one in Christ Jesus" (Gal 3:28). In that case how can we speak of different actors at all? Do we have God on the one hand and man on the other? Or must we understand it in this way: God is the One, and it is only because man is *not* this One that he is the "other"? Or, putting the same thing differently, from man's perspective: men in the world are individual "ones"; God, however, is not another "one" in this sense: he is incomparably "Other". This being so, how can there be a play, an interplay? Where is there any room for man's "something", if God, by nature, must be "everything" (Sir 43:27) if he is to be God at all?

We must devote ourselves to this apparently "static" problem first, before turning explicitly to the dynamic action. As we have said, however, nothing is purely static in theo-drama; even the theatre program with its list of characters already speaks of action insofar as it implicitly contains the whole play. Reading *Hamlet, Son to the former and Nephew to the present King of Denmark*, we already know something; if we know the play, we look ahead from the encounter with the ghost to the final carnage. Even hearing the word "man", we see him in his undeniable coming-whence and the riddle of his going-hence. Man exists, but how can he? How can he stand, with his precarious freedom, "vis-à-vis" the "One" whose name is God? This is puzzling enough, but what of the One who cannot strictly be called a "mediator" because "God is One"?

We need to establish the standpoints of the "characters", rather as one arranges the pieces before a game of chess and takes account of the way in which each piece "moves". Anyone who knows this can envisage an infinite number of possible sequences within the given field of play, as a result of the players' freedom: yet these different results all come from the same point of departure and are governed by it. We must once again[3] circle around this point of departure, since it makes equally clear the continuity between both points of view and the necessity of the transition from the first to the second. First we shall let the phenomenon speak for itself (A); then we shall attempt a purely intramundane presentation of the drama of existence (B); the ultimate failure of this attempt will legitimately point us toward a transcendent, theological drama (C), which has the power to interpret and expound itself (D).

---

[3] Although we have already discussed it in TD I, 25–50. In *Wahrheit* I (Einsiedeln: Johannes Verlag, 1947), 152ff., I made a first attempt to describe the transition from "image, significance" to "word". There are many references to the same topic in *The Glory of the Lord*, e.g., I (San Francisco: Ignatius Press, 1982), 447ff.; II (1984), 333; III (1986) 247ff., 390ff.; *Herrlichkeit* III/1, part 2, 2d ed. (Einsiedeln: Johannes Verlag, 1975) 710ff.; *Herrlichkeit* III/2, part 1, Alter Bund (1967), 45–68. The ultimate locus of this topic is here: where an aesthetics of form-and-light passes over into a dramatic interplay of dialogical freedom.

A. FORM, WORD, ELECTION

Our *Aesthetics* was concerned with God's epiphany—characterized as the manifestation of his *kabod* (glory)—amid the innumerable other appearances in nature and history, and it also had to discuss the conditions which are required for this glory to be perceived. But insofar as everything was included under the idea of "glory", the formal standpoint remained *purely theocentric*, even where (in "Old Covenant" and "New Covenant") God's glory was manifested as a covenant with *man*, ultimately resulting in the interior response of redeemed man "to the praise of the glory of his grace" (Eph 1:6). We dealt with man's freedom to respond by thus reflecting God's glory only in terms of the gift of grace: in this return to God, grace proved itself victorious and so attained its full stature in creation.

Hasty critics tried to construct the present dramatic theory in its entirety on the basis of our *Aesthetics*; they accused the latter of clinging to aesthetic categories such as *species*, *lumen*, *expressio*, and of operating in an essentialist mode which would cause the picture of Christ to ossify into an icon. That was not the place, however, to offer a vibrant Christology, full of movement (and one that takes account of the historico-critical perspective): it will be developed in the next volume. Even less did the *Aesthetics* present a theological anthropology: we can only turn to it now (in outline).

We inquired into the conditions that make cognition possible (in our "believing in" something that presents itself to us), and we found the answer in the primal, irreducible phenomenon of "seeing the *form*". We can understand this best from the astonished realization we experience in privileged moments and encounters, when something uniquely precious, felicitous and beautiful presents itself to us. The fact "that such things should exist!" elicits that wonder which, according to Plato (*Theatetus* 155d) and Aristotle (*Met* A, 982b, 12f.), is the beginning of all philosophy. The thing of beauty appears in "exemplary identity" (as G. Siewerth[4] says) with Being in its fullness, a fullness

---

[4] *Der Thomismus als Identitätssystem*, 2d ed. (Frankfurt, 1961), chap. 10. For a

21

manifested in this same thing of beauty. For the precious form points toward the ground and origin behind which we cannot go or investigate ("The Rose asks not 'why?'; it blooms because it blooms", that is, its exemplary form takes precedence over the causality that produces it: "The Rose which here thine outer eye doth see, Has bloomed in God for all eternity").[5] It points to the origin that not only conceals itself in the form but also reveals itself in its hidden being. What emerges as self-evident at privileged moments—particularly in erotic and agapeic love—is the all-sustaining, foundational structure of the spirit[6] even within its ordinary activity of judging and deciding. The fact that Being in its totality can be present and reveal itself in individual beings; that—in Augustinian terms—the individual being is illuminated by an absolute light and can be read and interpreted in that light; and that the very uniqueness of the individual being causes the indivisible uniqueness of Being in its totality to shine forth with peculiar clarity—all this, as H. J. Verweyen has shown, provides the basis for God's revelation in the individual form and figure of Christ and for man's transcendental ability to apprehend it.

> Insofar as the reality which thus presents itself erects no barriers against the absolute Ground, the absolute Ground not only has infinite possibilities of manifesting itself to sensory awareness but it becomes free to present and authenticate *itself* in a manner that is *absolute* and *definitive*.[7]

This presupposes that the form can be read as a *meaningful* form and as an *expression*, that is, that the ray of light that comes from Being and communicates itself dynamically to individual beings is apprehended and understood; otherwise (as in Zen) the in-

---

philosophical analysis of wonder and a critical discussion of Siewerth's approach, cf. the discerning book by Hans Jürgen Verweyen, *Ontologische Voraussetzungen des Glaubensaktes. Zum Problem einer transzendental-philosophischen Begründung der Fundamentaltheologie* (Patmos, 1969), esp. 177–84. On the primacy of the Beautiful among the transcendentals, cf. my book *Wahrheit* I, 246ff.

[5] Angelus Silesius, *Der Cherubinischer Wandersmann* I, 289; I, 108.

[6] Silesius loves to generalize here: "No speck of dust's so slight, no merest dot so small; The wise man sees God's glory there, his mighty power withal" IV, 160 passim.

[7] H. J. Verweyen (see n. 4), 184 (my italics).

dividual beings remain unintelligible and void of meaning in their distinction from the unrelated, annihilating Ground of which they are regarded as a part.[8]

Again we must draw the reader's attention to the distinction between "intramundane" beauty and God's absolute self-disclosure in the figure of Jesus Christ (or between beauty in the worldly sense and glory in the theological sense). We have already clarified it in the volumes "Old Covenant" and "New Covenant" of *The Glory of the Lord*, in discussing the whole movement leading from the dialectic of the Sinai epiphany right up to the mystery of the death and Resurrection of Jesus. Now, however, with a view to what follows, it is important to reflect on the way "aesthetics" opens up to and moves across into "dramatics", even in the realm of intramundane phenomena. The fact that this transition only attains its full intelligibility and justification when seen against the background of the divine revelation in Jesus Christ does not in any way alter the phenomenon we are about to describe, nor does it read anything into it; it simply illuminates it and renders it optimally visible. We shall develop it in three stages: form (expression, meaning) —word (freedom)—election. And here we always understand the "beautiful" as a "transcendental" (in the Scholastic sense): the strikingly beautiful thing is only a particularly clear instance, standing for every intramundane meaningful form.

1. *Form, Expression, Meaning*

The beautiful form presents itself to us, it "attests" itself, its character exhibits grace, favor [*Huld*]. In a twofold sense: it is grace on the part of Being that it can produce and sustain such a form, and this grace also attaches to the individual being itself. It

---

[8] Cf. the conclusion of the book by Shizuteru Ueda, *Die Gottesgeburt in der Seele und der Durchbruch zur Gottheit. Die mystische Anthropologie Meister Eckharts und ihre Konfrontation mit der Mystik des Zen-Buddhismus* (Marburg, 1965). Heidegger is in a similar position; for him, individual beings are seen against the background of Being but are not deducible from it: *Herrlichkeit* III/1, part 2, 2d ed., 782ff., 944ff. (*The Glory of the Lord* V: *The Realm of Metaphysics in the Modern Age*).

is attested, and at the same time it attests itself. Thus, despite all the objections of the exegetes, there is a direct path leading from Greek *charis* to the biblical "grace". *Charis* comes from the same root as *chairō*, to rejoice; it delights us because of its objective nature as "gracefulness" [*Anmut*]. But the Greeks immediately experience this in terms of "favor" [*Gunst*], the favor of destiny or of the gods, from whom man also receives direct "proofs of favor". This self-attesting is such a powerful movement toward the observer and receiver, however, that the latter must respond and come to meet it: then *charis* comes to mean the due and duly expressed gratitude. The full significance of *charis* is found in the interplay of these two meanings.[9] As Rilke wrote in his "Archaic Torso of Apollo": "His torso still glows like a candelabra. . . . There is no place in it which does not see you. You must change your life."[10] Here the poet interprets the interplay of grace and gratitude as a demand. The beautiful presents a challenge to all that is mean and common. It does not stand turned in on itself but turned outward, facing all who can grasp it. True, it "seems blissful in itself" (Mörike), but what does "seems" mean here, when the poet is speaking of a lamp? It is precisely beauty's way of seeming [*scheinen*], of "shining in itself", its total lack of ulterior motive, its *gratis* quality, that radiates to all around it. "Who marks it?" Mörike goes on, just as Hölderlin calls out to the declining, "glorious" sun: "Little did they esteem you, Holy One, they knew you not at all. For you rise, effortless and still, above those who toil below." For the poet, however, who "learned to venerate" the sun, Diotima's upward glance to the stars turned the whole universe into grace: "Livelier then grew the streams' chattering; lovingly did dark earth's blossoms breathe toward me, and, smiling over silver clouds, the ether bent over me in blessing." This is the interplay of grace and gratitude: a dialogue. And Hölderlin does not close himself to the challenge of grace.

Where there is dialogue, however, there must be *word*. The word steps forth from the hidden place where form can be

---

[9] Sophocles, *Oedipus on Colonus*, 779; Aristotle, *Nic. Ethics* V, 18, 1133a 3–5. Cf. Conzelmann, article "Charis" in *Th. W.* IX, 363–65. Cf. *The Glory of the Lord* IV, 90ff., on Pindar.

[10] *Der Neuen Gedichte anderer Teil, Sämtliche Werke* I (1955), 557.

understood as expression: as a ground that makes itself known. And such understanding presupposes freedom—not the mere reacting to forms, as in the case of the animal—and in-sight (*intel-lectus*); furthermore, it requires a readiness to accept the message imparted by the form, a "faith" in the genuineness of the ground's expression. It requires an "attentiveness" without which neither the lamp's nor the sun's shining can be grasped as the *gratis* bestowal of a grace—which it truly is. The thing of beauty "speaks to us" from a region in which language operates transcendentally—and "word" here is taken both in its Scholastic and its Kantian sense. Being reveals itself, in its transcendentals, as the Beautiful, the True and the Good, and this very fact is language, at a root level. And the fact that the finite spirit, in its elemental *cogito/sum*, experiences this illumination and follows it through is likewise the birth of language. Where man is concerned, however, this birth of language never takes place in the "purely spiritual" realm above sensory "phenomena" but essentially in his ability to read a form apprehended by his senses. In creation's world of the senses, the word has always become flesh, "the world encompasses me with pointing fingers" (R. Borchardt), "a song lies asleep in all things" (Eichendorff). Respectful attention is a fundamental attitude of the educated man in old civilizations such as Egypt and China. The strange thing is that the "attentive" man, whoever he may be, under-stands the language that operates at the root level of things to be a universal language, although it expresses itself exclusively in particular, fragmentary words; man is aware, in each instance, that the inner meaning is richer than can be expressed by any particular language. A particular language is both poorer and richer than the language "read" from the thing of beauty: it is richer because it formulates and articulates what things of sense can only offer in dumb silence. It is poorer because its gen-eralizing (in order to be understood and used by everyone) necessarily becomes abstract, whereas the inarticulate expression of the thing of beauty utters the Whole in a language that is totally concrete.[11] In his resultant perplexity, man is wont to

[11] Cf. Claude Bruaire, *L'Affirmation de Dieu. Essai sur la logique de l'existence* (Paris: Seuil, 1964), 136ff.

speak of nature's "hieroglyph", of the world's *"chiffre"*, that is, it quite evidently expresses something yet in a language to which we have no key. And on the basis of his human condition, man is right to speak thus, up to a point, as long as the Word himself, who "was in the beginning with God" and "in whom was life" and who "was the light of men", had not so far "come into the world", "to his own", because the world had always been the expression of him ("all things were made through him") yet did not appreciate what he wished to say thereby. When the Word who "was God" "becomes flesh", he steps forth among the figures that surround us and point us in various directions, and now comes the decision (and this is *the* drama, embracing all others): Will "his own" recognize him and "receive" him or not? Will the *chiffres* resolve into the Word, the Logos, ultimate meaning, or shut tight, undecipherable, once and for all?

A further decision is implied here, namely, whether aesthetics (as was the case in classical aesthetics from Plato to Hegel) is *first and foremost* a theory of perception that understands particular beings as *expressions* (Bonaventure) of the self-revealing Ground of Being, going on to develop a doctrine of man, who expresses himself by imitating the divine creative activity; or whether (as in modern aesthetic theories) aesthetics can be transformed into a *primary* doctrine of man's self-expression, whereby man, in this creative activity, explicates the originally *inexplicable* nature of being and existence, causing what is originally dumb and locked to begin to speak. This second, purely anthropological aesthetics might seem to be more apt to provide a preliminary understanding of the theological "appearance" of God in the final form of his revelation, in Jesus Christ's dying, forsaken by God: thus, at the center of the form [*Gestalt*] that is to be interpreted and that provides a key to the whole, there stands the "nonform" [*Ungestalt*] of the Cross; beholding this in faith, the believer can decipher the "superform" [*Übergestalt*] of the trinitarian love that here becomes visible.

This, however, would be a mistake. No human art can create meaningful forms that are really original unless the artist is able or willing first of all to receive a meaning (be it ever so encoded) that comes from beings themselves. Otherwise, using (gradually disintegrating) elements of form that come from a culture that is still receptive to meaning and employing his innate capacity for imaginative creation, he will be engaged in an ultimately destructive project. Naturally, concepts such as "measure", "form" and "light" cannot be absolutized in a classicist manner; but how evident they are in Paul Klee, for example, whose *oeuvre* presupposes and manifests an extraordinary sensory receptivity to the meaning that comes from the primal sources of being!

It is true that, right at the center of our existence in the world, there is the ugly, the grotesque, the demonic, the immoral and ultimately the sinful—all that makes it hard and often impossible for man to believe that the world has a total meaning. At the beginning of the first *Duineser Elegie* we read:

> For the beautiful is naught
> but the start of terrible things we are still learning to endure;
> and we admire it too, for it calmly scorns
> to destroy us.

And when it goes on: "Each angel is terrible", the reader is faced with the question: Does this angel stand for the *shekinah*, the hidden, consuming glory of the Absolute; or is it the personified face of what is ultimately meaningless (as the disconsolate final Elegy suggests)? In pre-Christian times, the boundaries between the two can be very close, as we can see from the grotesque, imposing grimaces on the faces of Chinese or Aztec gods and demons, which suggest that the meaning at the heart of the world is a *mysterium horrendum* and *adorandum*. But after the event of Christ's Cross, man is presented with a choice: hearing the cry of dereliction, he must "discern" either hidden love (shown in the Father's surrender of the Son) or the meaningless void.

We can go even farther here, with regard to the transition from "form" to "word": since the world contains so much horror, it would be pure aestheticism to lock ourselves in a realm of beautiful forms. The hideous form [*Ungestalt*] is part of the world's form [*Gestalt*], and so it must be included, essentially, among the themes and subject matter of artistic creation. Insofar as art is expression, and hence *word*, what is devoid of form [*das Gestaltlose*] can be part of the alphabet with which art puts itself into words, thereby acquiring "form" [*Gestalt*]. This is made clear by Expressionism and Surrealism but equally by the presence of Iago in *Othello* or of Pandarus in *Troilus and Cressida*. What is at stake here is the ultimate, form-imparting word, which can be put together from "nonwords", and the meaning it contains.

That was our intention, in our theological *Aesthetics*, in situating the "nonword" of the Cross at the center of the definitive divine Word. The sole issue in the *Aesthetics* was to show that, on the far side of its collapse and ruin—a collapse that embraces all the world's horror and dissolution of form—there is a Word that is able to enfold this very ruin. To that extent the *Aesthetics* was necessarily "eschatological", but Easter too belongs to eschatology (that is, "concerning the Last Word"), and thus so does everything that is saturated with the interpretative radiance of divine love that streams from Easter. We have stressed often enough that we are only drawing an analogy between the relative success of the artist in dealing with the formless and God's dealing with sin; but the analogy holds here (in the form of an *analogia proportionalitatis*), where the formless is taken up as one element into a higher form, that is, is integrated into expression or word.

Naturally, in both cases—in the language of beauty and of art, as in the language of the Word-made-flesh—what we have is an *already incarnated* language of being and of concrete existence, not a language transcribed—at one remove—in formulas and written documents. How derivative, by comparison, is the interpretation of writings, however sacred! At best such writings can put us in touch with the language of life. Writings are flat, one-dimensional; they indicate and point to something that has depth and dramatic movement: it is an action that steps forth from the primal ground into the foreground, manifesting and displaying itself and, through self-giving, issuing a challenge to us.

2. *Word, Freedom*

This brings us to the second point. The form and the word within it awaken and summon us; they awaken our *freedom* and bid us attend to the call that comes to us from the form. From the standpoint of form and word, these two are a single act, but to the person addressed, because it is a question of freedom, this single act can appear twofold: there can be the Yes of willing attentiveness and the No which deliberately overlooks: "Who marks it?" "Little did they esteem you." The power of aesthetic expression is never an overwhelming power but one that liberates. If we lack receptivity to it, we can blindly pass by the most magnificent work of art. All the same, its power is greater than the kind of power that can put people in chains; it does not fetter, it grants freedom. It illuminates, in itself and in the man who encounters it, the realm of the transcendent word and hence of all meaning, the realm of an infinite dialogue. But again, this dialogue does not consist primarily of formulated words but in the confrontation and communing of lives. What speaks in the work of art cannot, indeed, directly impart this same language to the recipient. But if he does not know this language, it *is* possible for him to learn it through diligence and practice. The work's freedom can educate us to the freedom of seeing and responding. The freedom of the divine Word-made-man who speaks in God's masterpiece is not the form-bound freedom of the work of art: being the Word (in the Holy Spirit), he is also the Word who creates freedom. Whereas the person who is not gifted with regard to art bears no responsibility, the man who is confronted by the Word of God is endowed with freedom through this very encounter and is thus given greater responsibility to enter into the meaning that is being revealed in the Word. Saying No to a work of art has relatively no consequences. But saying No to God's definitive and meaning-full Word can turn into a judgment of the individual who freely ignores it. Thus, again, the transition from aesthetics to dramatic theory is analogical.

Speaking like this may seem equivocal or multi-vocal, and indeed we are deliberately speaking on several levels at once. But the vertical cross section through several levels is precisely what is needed here. We need to make it clear that *"l'art pour l'art"* is a totally derivative and depraved form of the encounter with beauty: the blissful, *gratis*, shining-in-itself of the thing of beauty is not meant for individualistic enjoyment in the experimental retorts of aesthetic seclusion: on the contrary, it is meant to be the communication of a meaning with a view to meaning's totality; it is an invitation to universal communication and also, preeminently, to a shared humanity. It can happen that we fall silent when overwhelmed by some form, perhaps because no one else sees what we have been privileged to see, and we do not know whether or how we can show it to anyone else. But this is a result of the over-fullness of the transcendental word and its revelation, which is too much for the confined and cramped vessels of human communicative skill. No man on earth was lonelier than Christ: "I have yet many things to say to you, but you cannot bear them now" (Jn 16:12).

From this perspective we can gain a preview of what drama can and will be at the various stages. Essentially it is an opening-up or a closing-off to the presence of some light that radiates from existence. Seeing or not-seeing; letting be or violently overpowering, imprisoning, extinguishing. In oneself or in others. Confusing the power of what seems, shines, radiates *gratis* (which equally implies surrender and powerlessness) with the power of possession and the urge to dominate. The confrontation of these two kinds of power, the succumbing of the vulnerable, defenseless power to the force of arms, revealing, as it succumbs, the inseparability within it of power and powerlessness. The vessel shatters, and finite speech with it, thereby opening up to an infinite speech that acts and suffers in it. "And this is the judgment, that the light has come into the world, and men loved darkness rather than light" (Jn 3:19). "He who rejects me and does not receive my sayings has a judge; the word that I have spoken will be his judge on the last day" (Jn 12:48).

3. *Election*

Having spoken of form/expression and word/freedom, we come to a last category that also manifests itself from within in the transition from aesthetics to dramatic theory. When a person is struck by something truly significant, he is not simply placed in a universal perspective from which he can survey the totality: an arrow pierces his heart, at his most personal level. The issue is one that concerns *him*. "*You* must change your life", you must henceforth live in response to this unique and genuine revelation. The man to whom this has happened is marked for life. He has trodden holy ground that is in the world but not of it; he cannot return to the purely worldly world. He bears the brand-mark of his encounter with beauty. An evening at the opera or a concert can be simply relaxation, but the encounter with beauty at a deep level is something else. The myths and fairy tales tell of it. Being touched in this way is *election*. In the *Aesthetics*, we spoke of the interplay of beholding and being enraptured. This was sufficient while the standpoint, as we have said, was theocentric: we only "see" God by being "rapt", "transported" toward him, by being transformed and drawn into his sphere. But where we pass over into the realm of drama, a third element, election, must be added: no one is enraptured without returning, from this encounter, with a personal mission. The third element is latent in the first and second: God only shows himself to someone, only enraptures him, in order to commission him. Where this is not taken seriously, where the aesthetic fails to reveal the ethical that lies within it, such rapture is degraded to a prettifying excuse ("*ravissant*"). Where a thing of beauty is really and radically beheld, freedom too is radically opened up, and decision can take place.[12] But what is ultimate here is not my decision but that I hand myself over to the deciding reality and thus am resolved, decided, to let myself be marked by the unique encounter offered me.

Keeping in mind what we have said about the "word", election—this most personal of all the things that can happen to us—shows its universal character. The elect person has been admitted to the sphere of the transcendent Logos. In this unique event, the Logos has encountered him, the unique individual— *monos pros monon*—yet this Logos is the all-embracing, universal Word that grounds all particular languages. This is what the "rapt" man has tasted, this is the "book" he has devoured—and its taste stays on his tongue. He must proclaim this Logos. In some shape or form, mission will be part of drama. It may be a great, sacred and heroic mission; the mission of faithfulness to one's conscience in the face of empty convention; the tragi-

[12] Verweyen (see n. 4), 140.

comedy of an imaginary mission which, viewed in a concave mirror, does after all demonstrate the presence of genuine mission. In Plato's *Republic*, characteristically, the contemplative ruler, sole and solitary, removed ("transported") from the particular activities of the classes, has the most universal mission, namely, that of directing everything according to the norm of wisdom. The spark of the *"bonum diffusivum sui"* enters into the man who is privileged to glimpse it and makes him, too, a person who is unreservedly "poured out". He becomes the unique point through which the universal Logos wishes to communicate himself to everyone. Nothing but artificial inhibition confines the influence of the beautiful to exclusive circles which alone are supposed to be receptive to it and worthy of it. In itself the thing of transcendent beauty, the miracle of Being (revealing itself in *all* existing things), is a "holy mystery made manifest": of its own essence (as the Good) it tends toward public manifestation, simply by being always public, open to all; in this sense it is the True.

Only in this way can the dramatic "hero"—who in other respects can be as extraordinary or as ordinary as he wants—be of universal interest. His uniqueness is in no way opposed to his universality; rather, each points to the other. Once we have acknowledged the movement from the Beautiful to the Good, we can even go so far as to say this: the greater the uniqueness, the more universal the interest. In such a case, the lens that focuses the universal light is stronger and can disperse this light more effectively. When we speak of uniqueness here, of course, we do not mean the idiosyncratic and freakish, for these too could be found among the universal character-types of Theophrastus and La Bruyère. Seen from the outside, in purely psychological terms, the chosen person can be a solitary, and in aesthetic terms he can be a failure, a tragic figure. But just as the alabaster jar must be broken in order that the scent of the ointment may fill the whole house, so the chosen one *may* have to be shattered so that the universality which was contained in concentrated form in his mission may be manifested. And as for the extent to which this can be grasped by others—if at all—that is quite another question. Here lies the solution of the psychological riddle noted by Augustine and many later writers, namely, why the tears shed in tragedy give us pleasure. Here, it is true, we once more arrive at the point where the spectator's attitude of "enjoyment" becomes ambivalent; Schiller and Brecht demonstrated the paradox in all its acuteness, showing that the stage, though it should not moralize, is a moral institution all the same. Not, let it be said, through "alienation effects" and the various measures employed to prevent the audience becoming involved, but by all the "spectators" being impressed by the explosive nature of election and the scent of their ultimate collapse, in such a way that everyone is obliged to breathe in something of the spirit of his having-been-chosen for the Good. The instance par excellence of this is where absolute Goodness and Beauty choose for themselves an ultimate, definitive shape, a definitively incarnate Word, so that it may appear and pour itself out in the world. In the face of this definitive figure and its victorious ruination, no one who witnesses it can remain unmoved (or moved) on his spectator's seat: he is provoked to step onto the stage and offer his services. "One has died for all; therefore all have died" (2 Cor 5:14).

4. *Liturgy and Slaughter*

The Beautiful, graciously manifesting itself, becomes the incarnated Word, electing those to whom it can communicate itself. But in this progression to the deed, to the drama, it remains what it was at the beginning: the river only flows because the source persists. This simultaneity explains not only the phenomenon of the theatre, that is, that we experience an action in which the Good is striven for as something beautiful, to be enjoyed as such; at a deeper level it explains the phenomenon of existence itself, which, in the face of the Absolute, can be *simultaneously a liturgy of worship and a battlefield*. The best illustration of this is provided by the Book of Revelation, which concludes the corpus of Holy Scripture. We shall have to return to discuss it in detail in our treatment of "theo-drama". According to the Book of Revelation, the stream of life comes from the throne of him who is invisible, on which stands the uniquely Chosen One, the Lamb slain from the foundation of the world. This stream provides refreshment for the myriads of worshippers who surround the throne; it causes the eternal liturgy to blossom, which no earthly terror or horror can disturb. And yet, it is as if this sacred water begins to foam and pour over the world in raging torrents, inundating everything. The Lamb, "as though it had been slain", rides into battle like a warrior, his garment drenched in blood, together with his "called, chosen and faithful ones", to fight against the powers and forces of the world; there seems to be no end to the cries of woe, the slaughter and annihilation. Can this darkness, this wrath that is unleashed from above and from below, these cries of anguish in the face of ever-intensifying plagues, this elegy on the (almost wanton) ruin of all that the world holds precious and enjoyable, be reconciled with the serene, ceaseless hymns of worship before the throne, on the Sea of Glass, beneath the light of the Seven Lamps of the Spirit? How does this carnage fit with the extolling of him who was, and is, and is to come, and who—when the drama is at its climax—"has begun to reign"?

Inevitably, most of the great interpretations of the world had the ambition of bringing the raging world drama into a unity with the divine stillness. So it has been ever since the *Bhagavadgita* and Heraclitus, for whom war was the father of all things and the world a heap of refuse. Yet through all the contradictions, we detect the rhythm of the eternal Logos: in the Stoics, who taught the wise man to be passionless in the midst of the storm of life's passions; via Dante and Milton, to the "Prologue in heaven" of Goethe's *Faust*:

> And battling storms are raging high
> From shore to sea, from sea to shore,
> And radiate currents, as they fly,
> That quicken earth through every pore.
> There blasting lightnings scatter fear,
> And thunders peal; but here they lay
> Their terrors down, and, Lord, revere
> The gentle going of Thy day.[13]

—and to Hegel's "phenomenology of the Spirit", with its vast dramatic canvas, which *has* to be identical with the totally

[13] Goethe, *Faust*, tr. Martin/Bruford (London: Dent, 1954), 9–10.

enlightened repose of his "great logic". But the *Bhagavadgita* remains stuck fast in contradictions, and what we have in Heraclitus is a proud resignation that is already preparing the way for the Stoics' flight from drama. In *Faust* (as in the *Divine Comedy*) the dramatic contradiction is negotiated with the aid of the guiding thread of a self-refining longing for the Absolute or a self-purifying Eros, and in Hegel an ultimate dualism hovers between the struggle of existence and a knowledge that surveys the whole. But neither the simple affirmation of the contradiction nor the flight from it nor man's overcoming of it by "striving and exerting himself" (*Faust*) can explain the mysterious, apocalyptic simultaneity of liturgy and drama. This applies also to the religions of earthly "holy wars" in the name of Yahweh or of Allah: they bring about no reconciliation; they only destroy, creating an empty space where the transcendent God can put forth his power.

Quite different is the holy war conducted in the Book of Revelation by the Lamb, who is also the "Lion of Judah" and the "Logos of God", from whose mouth issues the sharp sword with which he smites the nations and who "treads the winepress of the wrath of God". Here there is no hiatus between worship and service and above all no hiatus between the powerlessness of being slain and the power of conquest—the latter comes by virtue of the former. What we have seen from the background —namely, that the Beautiful never overwhelms those who resist it but, by its grace, makes prisoners of those who are freely convinced—holds true when this background is concentrated in the figure who steps forth from it: it is the power of self-giving love that speaks in the tones of implacable judgment. Just listen to the sound of the "Seven Letters" to the churches in the Book of Revelation.

So our *Aesthetics* has already provided us with something like a criterion for the present theodramatic theory. As the *Aesthetics* developed, grace [*Huld*] showed itself as eternal love's self-giving unto the Cross; there its triumph appeared and its eternal vindication (in the Resurrection). All we need to do is to take what is implicit in our aesthetics and make it explicit in dramatic theory; thus we shall set forth the *problems associated with the various freedoms* in order to arrive at the dimensions of theo-drama. It is equally clear that, where these freedoms unfold, only drama (and nothing else) comes into being, as content and form. In its middle phase, what is generally called "theology" must be "theo-drama".

This can only make its appearance, however, where the genuine freedom of the genuine Absolute reveals itself in order to step into the play—and paradoxically it can only do this in association with a fully unveiled human freedom. But an appearance of this kind is so improbable that we can only focus upon its reality by turning aside from everything that is *more* probable—all the dimensions of purely intramundane drama. And once we have recognized that its paradox will not go away, it will explain itself, of itself; it will be its own interpretation.

B. THE UNFINISHED DRAMA

1. *The Tragedy of Finitude*

A genuinely human figure, developing over the course of a lifetime, is not something given. It has to be built up through free decisions. It is true that human freedom is wrapped in many kinds of conditioning: there is the *élan vital* that carries the young life toward that maturity in which valid decisions are alone possible (but how many decisions are made much earlier, as psychological analysis shows!); there is the weight of heredity, instincts, the milieu; education or lack of education; there is the governing influence of one or several human beings, which, under certain circumstances, can so dominate the freedom of the developing young person (or of the mature adult) that it fails to attain any genuine self-activation. Many people's lives, it seems, rarely rise even as far as half-way above the water level of determinisms. And it is true of every man that really formative, deep-level decisions only occur over long intervals. These determinisms render the intervening periods—in which man thinks that he is no less free—practically homogeneous; at the very least they strongly influence them.

None of this, however, contradicts the statement that man, in his inner, noumenal life-form, is critically shaped by his freedom; and it is only by responding to the personal and impersonal challenges of the world around him that man's freedom is provoked and summoned to realize itself. Accordingly there are degrees in man's free self-determination, but at most this implies that there are also degrees in man's full humanity or—what comes to the same thing—that there is an analogy in the dramatic dimensions of existence. It is very hard (if not impossible) for man, observing the phenomenal unfulfilledness of his existence, to deduce its noumenal un-form [*Ungestalt*] from it: "Judge not". What from the outside may seem to be a tragic obstacle to personal development can be a hidden spur promoting an invisible process of purification. Pictures drawn by the mentally ill often give indications, below the surface confusion, of a deep-laid purity.

37

Just as man is awakened by the call of his fellow man to an awareness of himself and of the world, just as his freedom is awakened by the freedom of others, so his life-form is continually maturing within the field of force he shares with other free human beings: there is work and the release from it; attraction and repulsion; insight and renewed puzzlement; the affirmation and denial of operant norms, views, customs and claims. In this field of force, which is constantly changing shape, ideals are built up and followed through, only to be changed again or replaced or filled out and anchored more firmly. We discern two layers or dimensions of freedom here: one moves toward making a definite Yes or No decision, and the other forms a kind of vast, inexhaustible space within which these definite decisions fall. For, however final a man means any particular decision to be—for instance, the decision to love another human being—it does not constitute a renunciation of the unlimited area within which (without restricting it) he binds himself. This does not contradict what we said earlier about the individual form's exemplary identity with its being in the Absolute; it would only contradict it if the individual form were simply equated with the Absolute. When lovers hand themselves over to each other, they do not renounce the greater, inexhaustible realm of freedom: they simply anchor their mutual bond within it.

We are all well aware of the illusions which Eros dangles before our eyes; we know how far its illusory "eternity" is from a definitive decision in self-renouncing love, a decision that will remain "valid to the end" [end-gültig]. It may be that the latter, if it is to be completely pure, is a boundary concept and that the decisions in favor of other values are similarly ambivalent. Isolated and lifted out of the woof and weft of life values, they can allow us to see through them to what is ultimate; but anyone who thinks that, in the particular value for which he strives, he can hold fast the Absolute itself is grievously deceived.[1] That is why Faust can confidently conclude his pact with Mephistopheles.

---

[1] Cf. *Theo-Drama* I, (San Francisco: Ignatius Press, 1988), 413ff.: "The Good Slips Away".

From this vantage point the drama of human existence can only be tragic. Thus Goethe designates both parts of his *Faust* a tragedy. *Faust* is the tragedy both of this particular individual and of Everyman, insofar as Everyman is he who "strives and exerts himself" and who, "in striving, errs". Ultimately it is the tragedy of every human being in whom freedom's infinite space cannot be filled, given an essentially finite existence, an existence which, externally, is broken off by death. The particular man and Everyman: in each case it is always the concrete human being with his unique personal freedom; and it is solely in the decisions made by this freedom that the drama of existence is acted out. There is no such thing as a collective freedom. Just as everyone is born alone, so he must die alone and, according to Christian teaching, appear alone to account for himself before the throne of the eternal Judge. Even if he was a politician or sociologist, that is, even if his highest aim was the well-being of the community. Surely, we can speak of the tragedy of an oppressed, annihilated people, but this drama too is a drama of the countless individuals who formed this nation and, to a greater or lesser extent, joined in pursuing its ideals. In his *Le Soulier de Satin*, Claudel can cause his main characters to symbolize a particular culture or continent, but (at best) this only allows us to discern their exemplary identity with their mission in God; the decisions of Proeza, Camilo, Rodrigo and Pelajo remain highly personal. And, for the Christian poet, it is precisely because they are personal that they can attain that relative universality which raises their personal interaction into a play of world proportions.

2. *The Overtaking of Tragedy*

For the person who is searching for an overall view and for humanly attainable goals, the utterly personal nature (in each case) of the human drama, in its vast, teeming multiplicity and its essential tragic dimensions, constitutes an unbearable limitation. Thus people set out on spiritual paths that aim to outstrip the freedom of the individual and see it, either from below or from above, as one element within some overarching context.

From below, it is seen in the context of those universal, determining laws of life that we enumerated earlier; here, at best, the element of freedom is embedded as one element among many. From above, the individual appears as one element within the history of a nation or of mankind, within a cosmic evolution. Whether in the terms of Idealism, Naturalism or Socialism, the individual with his tragedy becomes the expression of particular "conditions" that "are not as they should be" and prevent men from being good (Ibsen, Shaw, Brecht); if at all possible, these conditions should be changed. In Shaw's *Man and Superman*, we saw how the projection of these ideals onto the stage—assuming they are intended to be more than a cry of longing for something "different" (as in Brecht)—destroys the drama of existence. Fundamentally, where personal freedom is overtaken in this way, it signals the abdication of drama in favor of a narrative philosophy of history, an epic story of the Spirit or of mankind, however much such an epic development may be pushed forward by means of a dialectic (Hegel, Marx) or an evolution (Teilhard) claiming to be "dramatic". In either case, people claim to know the world's universal law embracing freedom, a priori or a posteriori.

If this has been a constant temptation throughout the course of mankind's history (Gnosticism, for instance, fell victim to it), it also exerts the most characteristic fascination upon the technological age, the age of the "exact sciences". This age has rightly been defined as an age of the new Gnosticism.[2] The tragic side of personal freedom is so absorbed into the overriding interest in mankind's total development that anyone who refuses to surrender his personal drama to the latter is regarded as immoral and ripe for liquidation (Brecht's *The Measures Taken*). There is a basic confusion here between the unfathomable background against which freedom makes its particular decisions and the collective, all-embracing context to which it is supposed to surrender itself. Within its purview, the method of the exact sciences is right to exclude "the God hypothesis" as an efficient factor; it operates on the basis of a "methodological

---

[2] M.-J. Le Guillou, *Das Mysterium des Vaters. Apostolischer Glaube und moderne Gnosis* (1973).

atheism";[3] but this method, emboldened by its technological successes, expands to embrace all the spheres of human existence and includes the latter within its brackets, prefixed by a sign indicating that the world can be synthesized by man.

The attempt is to synthesize human freedom by changing the conditions; first, however, this freedom is supposed to surrender itself so that the synthesis may be achieved. And once it has surrendered itself, it cannot regain itself, for total synthesis, total manipulation, has no room for freedom's impartiality. In such a world, this kind of suffrage must seem dangerously and destructively arbitrary. And as for the infinite realm which is presupposed by freedom of choice, it is bound to be seen simply as a threat to this world.

The deeper question of meaning cannot be held back any longer. The scientific, technological world with its "methodological atheism", provided it is regarded as absolute, that is, seeking the meaning of existence within its closed system, is bound to appear as the negation of any Absolute above the world. In many religions, this Absolute is regarded as the unfathomable mystery or as the Divine; in the religions of the Bible, he is regarded as the living God, the One who ultimately gives meaning to human existence, the fulfillment (to be embraced in hope) of the finite spirit's absolute capacity, a capacity that lies open "at the lower end" of freedom of choice. Thus the Absolute offers the prospect of overcoming the tragedy of individual human existence.

In this context our question becomes twofold. On the one hand, man can understand himself by means of the distinction between existent being (world) and Being (the Absolute, God); on the other hand, he can try to obliterate this distinction by methodologically bracketing out the Absolute (God) and endeavoring to concentrate all meaning in the world's internal realm. But even if he accepts the distinction, the question arises: How, with his tragic life's drama, can he survive in the face of the Absolute?

[3] Klaus Hemmerle, "Fragen nach Gott" in *Botschaft von Gott* (Herder, 1974).

3. Chiffre, Mythic Ritual, Revelation

We need not return to the question of the abolition of the distinction. It necessarily ends by absorbing and suspending the personal drama in the universal drama—be it the universal drama of the absolute Spirit, whose world design has been (gnostically) discerned, or that of the human collective, to which the individual's existence and its tragedy is sacrificed. In the long run it is impossible to go on absolutizing the personal drama of existence, individual in each case, which is "disturbed" (at most) by the existence and proximity of others; this leads to pure absurdity, as can be seen in Sartre's path to Communism and beyond it. The other possibility leads ineluctably to the destruction of the dramatic dimension of human existence: that is, the attempt to break out of the personal freedom of individuals-in-dialogue and move toward a "transcendental dialogics" that is manipulated from the vantage point of Idealism's total subject. (Here a human being arrogantly claims to look—from above, as it were—into another person's area of freedom and calculate whether and how he will respond.) The only legitimate reason for breaking into a person's intimate sphere with techniques such as hypnosis is a therapeutic one: to give him back to his full and free self; and this must be done with care and respect, that is, in the service of genuine dialogue.

But if we accept the distinction, in the drama of existence, between the being of the world and absolute Being, does this distinction guarantee the rights written into the very form of this drama? Can it maintain its specific significance as a "play" in the face of an impersonal (or even a personal) divinity?

The answer must be No, if the concept of the Absolute is taken seriously, and initially this brings atheism (in all its forms, irreligious and quasi-religious) and theism into a paradoxical unity. If the sustaining ground of finitude is the "wholly other", totally distinct from it, what kind of meaning can be claimed for the world's frantic activity? Less meaning, surely, than that of the waves that break above the eternally motionless depths of the sea. For the waves, with their motion, belong to the sea, but the Absolute has no part in the fate of mortals. We can experience or portray finite things against the background of the

Absolute, and it can generate an exciting tension; it is not the tension of drama, however, but of epic narration. It is the tension between the dramatic dimension of existence that indwells worldly events and their insignificance in the face of their motionless ground. "All striving and struggle / Is eternal repose in God the Lord." Initially the epic tension thus created can occupy the foreground entirely, as a chronicle of life in its many-hued diversity, aiming to let the listener or reader share in the experience of its up-and-down motion. Thus it can seem close to the drama. Only the fact that here we have someone telling the whole story from a distance—Homer or the Poet of the *Nibelungenlied* or Turgenev—makes the participant realize that what seems overpoweringly present is at the same time strangely distant. The great epic writer or novelist will not fail, using a thousand techniques, to render the action tangible to us—now near at hand, now remote. In doing so, above all, he can place two accents: he can stress the precious quality of what, in spite of its uniqueness, is doomed to pass away—as if the nothingness of the background shows up even more the semi-relief of the figures. Or he can stress the melancholy that resides in all earthly activity, beyond all its comic and tragic aspects, beyond its pledges of eternity, which time must necessarily break. This melancholy has many gradations, from the resignation of the elegy and the lament, on the one hand, to the burlesque grimace of the dance of death on the other; and again, both can embrace and heighten each other (as in *Death in Venice*, the most beautiful, dreamlike backdrop to transitoriness). In the end, however, in the face of the Absolute, everything finite must be sacrificed; one thinks of Chesterton's *Napoleon of Notting Hill*. Whatever has emerged from the depths of nonbeing, to set itself up in existence or dig itself in, will in the end be leveled, consigned once more to nonbeing. And initially, as we have said, it does not matter which view of the Absolute is being put forward: the nihilistic or materialistic view or the Buddhist or even the Islamic view. For in all these conceptions the Absolute is motionless: in the presence of its stillness, all the noise of becoming and passing away must fall silent.

Only when we have mentioned what is common can we start differentiating. In the face of death, the gesture of renouncing all that is past can have different meanings. It can be an act of homage to what is passing away, under the eye of the God who abides forever—the gesture of the departing characters in Calderon's *Theatre of the World*—and, on the other hand, it can be the mere recognition that the minus sign of nothingness before the brackets that contain finitude robs everything within those brackets of all value. And yet there are mysterious transitions between the two extremes, particularly where the Absolute hovers, indefinably, between Nothing and Everything, as in the concept of Nirvana. Where the latter's whole negativity is interpreted positively, the nothingness of the world's being also acquires a twofold accent: all individual forms are leveled and extinguished as such; but between the vanishing forms a path can be found, implying something positive in the face of the Absolute: a "path of instruction" leading out of the meanders and arabesques of mortal existence. Yet this path too, which already inscribes itself in the living forms, is only recognized by its negativity: it can be traced where finite form is negated and where we see through it to the Absolute that lies beyond. That is an essentially anti-dramatic principle, however, which is why no drama has arisen in India and the Islamic world comparable to Greek or Christian drama. There the epic holds pride of place. And since the Absolute does not come to meet the transitory world on its pilgrim path (for, at most, the latter is governed by the eternal law promulgated by the former), this path lies under the aegis of a "Providence" that appears preeminently in the form of "fate".

Here, on the periphery, something like *chiffres* might come into view, rendering the temporal existence (which has been sacrificed) a sign of the presence of the eternal. A most beautiful example of this would be Wilder's *The Bridge of San Luis Rey*. The man who tries to untie the knot of Providence is burned to death, but the reader has some intimation of the way destinies are interrelated and converge on a common end. Other *chiffres* can be found in Wilder's *Ides of March*, in *Theophilus North*. What they are pointing to is not some form that can be deciphered: they are only suggesting the possibility of a meaning—and this applies to the Absolute as well.

From this point on the periphery, we can go on to ask about

the center: what kind of relationship must there be between the world and the Absolute, between man and God, if the leveling produced by transitoriness and death is not to cripple the dramatic dimension of existence from within? Or, in other words, if the dramatic is not to become a mere defective mode of the epic—a kind of still photograph of existence, cut out of the film which, in showing the ultimate demise of all the characters, will also relativize everything that has passed between them? Man cannot come up with an answer himself; he cannot do it by violently amputating all the factors which extend beyond the framework of the dramatic action—the method employed by Peter Szondi[4]—nor by pointing to the exemplary identity which would be required if a significant action were to be elevated into a manifestation and "deciphering" of the Absolute. At this point the Baroque theatre is right: all human drama contains the element of collapse, implying the leveling of all differences and paying homage to the indifference, impartiality, of the One God. Nonetheless, it is genuine theatre; consequently, for this to be possible, there must be some further factor in the concept of the Absolute.

But if the Greeks also had genuine theatre (leaving aside the somewhat analogous Japanese Noh plays), surely this other factor must have been present in their concept of God too?

It must have been an idea of God which allowed him to take part—an inner, divine, absolute part—in the drama of mortal existence without threatening his absolute nature. Such an idea provides a link between early, *mythic* thought and Christian faith. But the former does not pass without a break into the latter: separating them lies philosophy, which opposes the notion that God can be moved and affected by the human drama. Even the Covenant God of the Old Testament cannot be interpreted as a direct mediation between *mythos* and Christian revelation; even the foreseeing, judging and compassionate God, the God who accompanies his people through history, is impassive vis-à-vis all human tragedy. Christianity alone provides a new approach: God has become man without ceasing to be God.

---

[4] *Theorie des modernen Dramas*, 5th ed. (Edition Suhrkamp 27, 1968).

This is a precise answer to the dreamy babblings of the myths, where Olympus is threatened by Titans and where its inhabitants associate with mankind from time to time and intervene in their plays.

Myth was born of *ritual*. Ritual, however, for primitive man, is

> not an isolated action among all other human or cosmic activities. Rather, rite is essentially the action whereby man feels that he is one with the active axis of the universe and knows that he is in the center of the whole, at the hub of all cosmic phenomena and also of his own existence.[5]

People may use the term "magic" in speaking of this ritualism, which, in the sacral drama, expands individual personal existence into a cosmic and divine drama, or, more cautiously, they may detect at least a naïve, magical element in it. On the other hand, beneath darkness and obscurantisms of all kinds, it is possible to glimpse this primal awareness on the part of the human heart: there would be no world at all, with its problems, if, in some hidden place, in the infinite realm, the planes did not intersect: the plane of man in his pleasure and pain and the plane of a God who knows of it from the inside.

Greek tragedy was erected on the foundation of rite and the myth that articulated it. It brings myth back to its ritual origin as worship. It exhibits human suffering to a divinity who remains in the twilight zone between involvement and noninvolvement. Nor, of its own nature, can it go any farther without departing from its original context, which provides its substance. It will also have the hint of something else in common with Christian drama: it portrays the fate of individuals who fill the whole picture; no generalization is admitted. Neither Orestes nor Oedipus is a particular type of man; it would be simply a mistake to say that they stand for "man as such"; they are just themselves, and the same is true of Prometheus, Ajax, Electra, Heracles, Antigone and the others. The Greek demands to see them fully individualized, both human and superhuman at the

[5] L. Bouyer, *Le Fils éternel* (Cerf, 1974), 74–75, with reference to E. O. James, *Myth and Ritual in the Ancient Near East* (1958), and the major works of Mircea Eliade and Gerhard van der Leeuw.

same time, approaching the sphere of the divine. Accordingly their drama, their tragedy, is utterly unique in each case. From the realm of myth there arises the intimation of the uniqueness of the individual person; first it shines forth only in kings and royal heroes, men of destiny, demi-gods; but it even extends into an age that no longer "believes" in these stage figures, no more than it seriously "believes" in the gods, who occasionally take part in the acting, otherwise they would not be allowed on stage (or would even be laughed at, as in the comedies of Aristophanes). But, drawing on the power of what was once faith in a rite, this age of decline manages to produce a drama the like of which will not be seen again until much later, at high points of the Christian period. For this was the last opportunity meaningfully to enact the unabbreviated drama of existence in the presence of a divinity standing both *above* and *in* this existence, in the presence of the torn and resurrected God of ecstatic love and death. True enough, this was the last play; philosophy already stood at the door, ready to banish the poet of myths from the *polis*. And though these motifs were repeated and recast—for the destinies of these great figures accompanied the history of civilization like *universalia concreta*, they were painted in frescoes, hewn in stone, hymned in poetry—they were no more than literary variations; the theme had gone forever.

Historically speaking, the earnestness and naïveté of myth are unique. Philosophy, with its "refined" picture of God and all that has come in its wake, the scientific and technological age with its "methodological atheism", cannot approach the sacral, ritual action, which was the matrix of ancient tragedy, from any angle. For the same reason it is impossible now to reproduce the idea of the unique, representative hero, whose personal drama, because it touched the divine sphere, could not be relativized either by other destinies or by death (seen as the collapse of all destinies). The fates of Antigone and Achilles were impressive enough to attract all attention to themselves—all holy "fear" and "pity" (*phobos* and *eleos*)—without being mere points of departure for abstract generalizations about human destiny "as such". In fact, they were of no use to philosophy in its search for types and categories, for the latter have to be based, not on such singular destinies as these, but on what is common to all men, in order to shed light on human existence. Humanly speaking, the only way seriously to continue the mythical hero's claim to validity was to go beyond the personal tragic fate. Either, as we have already shown, by absorbing it into the (Idealist) notion of a total subject [*Gesamtsubjekt*] or by inserting it into a Socialist collective destiny; both paths lead, however, to the collapse of genuine drama.

To put it another way: the ancient "hero", when he steps onto the stage, makes a universal, "catholic" claim. He makes this claim on the basis of the catholicity of the mythical rite, which makes man present to God and God to man. So long as this claim remains a living thing, drama is safe from the distancing effect of the narrative epic. Every post-mythical drama will try, again and again, to attain this catholicity. It will take the larger-than-life proportions of the mythical character and try to render them credible in purely anthropological terms, without the intervention of divinity (Hebbel's and Wagner's *Nibelungen*)—an attempt doomed to failure. Or it will try to clothe purely human tragedy in the costumes of the ancient divine-human drama (Kleist's *Amphitryon*), which leads to bitter irony. Or, inspired by ancient drama, it will try to explore the scope of "destiny as such" (Schiller's *Die Braut von Messina*) but, in doing so, will forfeit the catholicity of the heroes (who all become stereotypes). Or else this catholicity of the individual is deduced from his influence on the history of the world and society; this means that the central theme is no longer the hero's dramatic destiny but some (efficient or nonefficient) general social program. In Brecht, the tragedy of the individual person (of *Mutter Courage*, for instance) is not to be presented for its own sake; rather, it is a peg on which to hang the urgent demand for the "conditions" to be "changed". Ultimately, therefore, the drama of both Idealism and Socialism becomes a "puppet theatre". Idealism has exploited this theme ad nauseam from the Enlightenment right up to late Romanticism.[6] Büchner can be regarded as the transition to Socialism; his *Danton* feels himself to be the puppet of the world-spirit [*Weltgeist*]; subsequently the Party program, as the manifesto of the world-spirit (n.b., which has

[6] Cf. TD I, 184ff.

yet to be created!), reduces all personal destiny to that of a puppet.

Now the question must be addressed to *Christianity*: Can it legitimately claim to have found the trail that was lost ever since the demise of ancient tragedy? And can it really follow to the end, with its eyes open, this path along which ancient tragedy tried blindly to feel its way? For that is what it really claims to do. The tragic dimension of personal existence is not softened; in fact, it is wrenched apart to the very limit: in the Cross. In Christianity, this tragic dimension actually touches the sphere of the Divine, yet without swallowing it up (as mythology does) in the tragic destiny: Christian dogma has always rejected "Patripassianism", that is, the idea that God the Father suffered in the same sense as the Son, even if—in the mystery of the Trinity—it directs its attention with hair's-breadth precision to the point of contact between the suffering of the God-man and the nonsuffering of God. Finally Christianity sees it in a Catholic light, because, as an individual and personal tragic dimension— not "typical" or "symbolic"—it brings to light the significance and change of meaning of all intramundane tragedy. Thus the dramatic level becomes ultimate, not to be surpassed; it does not point to some prior "wisdom" or "teaching" or "gnosis" or "theology" that could then be recounted in the epic mode: it remains at the center, as drama, as the action that takes place between God and man, undiminished in its contemporary relevance. Herein, too, lies the meaning of the Catholic sacraments, which continually make the one event present; herein, in a more all-embracing sense, the meaning of the Church insofar as she is the re-presentation of the "drama of salvation" once for all on each particular occasion.

What is meant by "re-presentation"? Does this one drama replace the others or allow them to take their place beside it; or does it make space available within itself so that it can encompass the others and, without doing violence to them, assimilate them to itself? One thing is certain: the path back to the multiplicity of myths, with their way of shedding light on the mystery from the most diverse angles, is cut off. The drama of Christ is the recapitulation and the end of Greek tragedy, just as it recapitulates and bids farewell to the individual tragic figures of the Old Testament. This strikes us as an impoverishment, the result, perhaps, of the abstracting and systematizing activity of philosophy that now straddles the path. This impression disappears, however, when we reflect on the fact, in the first place, that the pluralism of myths and of the rites which underlay them was no longer sustainable for a mankind that was becoming increasingly aware of its unity; Plato himself, the draughtsman of the human *polis*, realized this. In each case, the myth claimed to be a *universale concretum*; but these universals were in conflict, just as the claims of the ancient divinities jarred against each other; they could not be harmonized in any other way than in philosophy's abstract divinity. As Hegel graphically showed in his *Phänomenologie*, their demise was latent in their own starting point.

In the second place, however, we must remember that the drama of Christ is bound to make a universal, catholic claim; and it does this by imparting something of its own catholic and concrete universality to the individual human destiny. This, at any rate, is how the Catholic Church sees herself; how far this is recognized by the Protestant churches is another question. The communication of catholicity, in principle, to every human drama is identical to the mystery of the communion of saints. Within the drama of Christ, every human fate is deprivatized so that its personal range may extend to the whole universe, depending on how far it is prepared to cooperate in being inserted into the normative drama of Christ's life, death and Resurrection. Not only does this gather the unimaginable plurality of human destinies into a concrete, universal point of unity: it actually maintains their plurality within the unity, but as a function of this unity. This is the aim of an organic integration of all individual destinies in Christ (Eph 1:3–10), which is simultaneously the commissioning of the organic fullness of vocations and tasks by the organizing center (Eph 4:7–16). This goes far beyond mere fulfillment of the mythical plurality, but at the same time it goes far beyond mere fulfillment of Idealism's and Socialism's claims to universality. For the latter abandon the sphere of personal drama and integrate the individual destiny into the epic "Odyssey of the Spirit", whereas every destiny that is understood and lived in a Christian way possesses, as such, a universal influence, albeit one that is not subject to calculation.

This justifies our assertion, which is fundamental to the shape of a Christian dogmatics, that, in Christian terms, the dramatic dimension of human existence can only be taken in complete seriousness—and that, accordingly, the Christian revelation can only appear in its full stature—if it is presented as being dramatic *at its very core*.

C. THE UNFOLDING DRAMA

The drama portrayed by the Bible is God's initiative, and so between man's blueprints of existence and God there is not a continuous transition but a leap. The instinctual tendency of ancient rite and myth can do nothing to change this; Old Testament scholarship has recognized more and more clearly that, notwithstanding all the points of contact with the religious myths of the Near East, Israel's approach is independent and asserts itself as such with increasing clarity. And the entire infrastructure we have presented in our *Prolegomena* must not nourish the illusion that we could construct a "theo-drama from below", as a synthesis or as the crowning pinnacle (albeit an utterly transcendent one) of a tower built on earth and reaching into heaven. If the infrastructures prove useful, it is because the created world is oriented toward the world of redeeming grace, and the fragmentary nature of the former receives its unity and wholeness in the latter. And if "the Word becomes flesh" more and more profoundly, unto death on the Cross, it follows that, in the drama God enacts with mankind, not the least particle of the human and its tragic dimension will be lost. If we experience this for what it is and claims to be, we shall find that all the dramatic categories of worldly drama will help us to get a better view of the content, the seriousness and the sublimity of the divine-human drama.

The question now arises as to what, in actual fact, is the distinctively dramatic quality of theo-drama. It is impossible to give a direct answer because it is God who is directing the play, and God cannot be defined. Wherever his traces are seen in the world, mystery is involved. Rationalistic theology continually forgets this when—for example, in Christology and in the doctrine of the Church and the sacraments—it treats God and his grace like some component that can be manipulated by human thought.

However, two preliminary ways of approach are available to us; we can enter into the inner realm only later, when we come to discuss the unfolding drama. The first way is a negative one: we distinguish theo-drama from all "distanced" theological

epic. The second way looks back to the nine basic topics of
modern theology we listed at the start of our *Prolegomena*; they
all converged toward a theodramatic solution without being
able to reach it (because of their one-sidedness). The question is
where to place the point at which the genuine concerns of these
nine tendencies can meet, complement and integrate each other.
Thirdly we shall have to show how, in being traced back to the
one theo-drama, all that is human is lifted beyond itself and
enabled to participate in the unique, concrete reality of this same
theo-drama.

1. *No External Standpoint*

The central issue in theo-drama is that God has made his own
the tragic situation of human existence, right down to its ultimate abysses; thus, without drawing its teeth or imposing an
extrinsic solution on it, he overcomes it. "No sign shall be given
to this generation but the sign of the prophet Jonah . . . and
behold, something greater than Jonah is here" (Mt 12:39ff.).
Jonah is devoured and then vomited out. Jesus goes "down to
hell and back" (cf. Dt 32:39; 1 Sam 2:6; Wis 16:13). The whole
question is this: Is there some standpoint from which we can
observe and report on this dramatic sequence of events? If the
story of Jonah is a real metaphor, there would have to be a
parallel between the "three days" he spends in the monster's
belly and the "three days" Jesus endures in the underworld,
remote from God; in that case we would have to be able to speak
of the turn of events seen in his death on the Cross and his
Resurrection in the same epic terms as the story of Jonah. Then
we would have to regard Pascal's dictum that "Jesus is in mortal
anguish until the end of the world"—a view that also forms the
basis of Bernanos' work—as a pious exaggeration. We smooth
out the folds and say that Jesus' suffering is past history: "now"
he lives in the glory of the Father; we can only speak of his
continued suffering in an indirect sense, insofar as those who
believe in him are referred to, metaphorically, as his members.
Along the same lines we would be bound to interpret the
Eucharist in a minimalist sense, as an anamnesis of Jesus' suf-

fering, as a mere calling to mind of a past event (though significant in its continuing effects). This would bring us to the much-debated clash between spirituality and theology. Spirituality may recall the past life and suffering of Jesus and, entering into it *"lyrically"*, may "pick certain fruits"; theology, on the other hand, will be more sober and, in *"epic"* mode, restrict itself to grasping the historical events as precisely as possible and describing them in their abiding "universal significance". "Lyrical" here means the internal motion of the devout subject, his emotion and submission, the creative outpouring of himself in the face of the vivid re-presentation, in its pristine originality, of what is a past event. "Lyrical" in this sense would correspond to the method recommended in the Ignatian Exercises:

> Let me picture (*imaginando*) Christ our Lord hanging on the Cross before me and speak to him in this way: How has he, the Creator, come to be man? Knowing eternal life, how has he come to this temporal death, this death for my sins? (*Ex* no. 53; cf. 61, 62).

This "lyrical" mode would correspond to the so-called Ignatian method of meditation: once the past event has been awakened by the "memory", the person must proceed to make its content present through "reflection, insight" and bring it alive to such a degree that the "will" can draw consequences from it for today, just as if the event itself were here and now. Ignatius is only cited here as an example who is closer to modern times; naturally the spirituality of the Gothic and Romanesque periods and, indeed, of ancient times, was no different (cf. the *devotio moderna*, Bonaventure, Bernard, the prayers of Anselm, Augustine's *Confessions*, the ancient monastic Rules, Origen and Tertullian). However, strict theology seems unable to rise to this "lyrical" exuberance; it must always try to be as objective as possible, "always ready" to "make a defense to anyone who calls you to account" regarding the Christian faith (1 Pet 3:15)—including pagans and Jews and wavering or wayward Christians, who would gain little from lyrical effusions.

The precision that is rightly demanded of such theology automatically inclines it toward the epic mode of speech. At a very early stage, therefore, the river of Christian utterance splits

into two streams: the lyrical, edifying utterance in the bosom of
the Church, from faith to faith, and the epic mode used for
"external" relations, that is, at councils and in the theological
and polemical treatises dealing with heretics or the threat of
error. Catechesis can form a kind of synthesis between instruction
and edification. In lyrical theology God and Christ are addressed
as "Thou"; in epic theology they are referred to as "He". The
latter seems unavoidable wherever the speaker is addressing his
fellow men (who are then his "thou") and the subject of their
dialogue is the existence or nonexistence, the nature and action
of God. In such cases, perhaps with a certain regret or a kind of
bad conscience, one must speak "about" [über] God, since the
person speaking always stands somehow "over" [über] his subject matter.

While speaking thus, however, we can apply the necessary
correctives. God is unknowable, absolute; he transcends every
concept of him. But these statements too form part of a theological discourse "about" God. Or the theological discourse can
be surrounded by a framework of prayer, as is done at councils;
or it can even be interrupted from time to time, as Anselm does,
by addressing God directly. In itself, however, such alternation
does not yield a valid synthesis. Perhaps we simply cannot get
beyond it? To all appearance this view receives much support
from Holy Scripture: the latter contains a most varied sequence
of stories (or reflections) and prayers. We could use this variety
to reconstruct the three elements of Ignatian contemplation,
first recalling some past event, then constantly reflecting on it
anew and making it real—in *relectures*—and finally causing it to
bear fruit for the believer's life here and now and spurring him
on to make faith decisions. But the more a theology bases itself
on Scripture as essentially the only source—in the *"sola scriptura"*
principle—the more it is brought, consciously or unconsciously,
to see itself as the written, objective account (a book) of something that has taken place; thus it opts for the epic standpoint.
Where the ultimate norm is no longer the revealed action but its
mirroring in Scripture (which is of course inseparable from the
former), epic-narrative theology—accredited by the distanced
attitude of the reporter—will quite logically assume the role of
judge over the events and their actualization. No wonder that

theopraxy voices its protest at such arrogance; such protest, however, is itself no more than a one-sided reaction. We shall discuss this in the next section.

Here we shall simply give a preliminary indication of the way out of these straits. We shall not get beyond the alternatives of "lyrical" and "epic", spirituality (prayer and personal involvement) and theology (the objective discussion of facts), so long as we fail to include the dramatic dimension of revelation, in which alone they can discover their unity. Man can address God, and he can address his fellow man; the Church, too, can speak to those within and to those without. But this tension is resolved in the context of a third dimension that embraces it: in the context of God's action, which challenges the believer, takes him over and appoints him to be a witness. A witness, moreover, in the early Christian sense: a "martyr"—bearing witness with his whole existence. Otherwise he is no real "witness to the truth".

Now we see the way out. The Apostles are witnesses of the Resurrection and of the whole life of Jesus that underlies it: the form of their objectivity coincides with the form of their witness. They are not uninvolved (or even "interested") reporters, but with their lives they vouch for the testimony they must give. Scripture, for its part, testifies to their giving of testimony. The two coincide entirely when Paul writes a letter and, in it, testifies with his whole life to the truth of revelation, putting God's action at the center but including himself (who was taken over by this action, once for all, in Damascus); he pulls out all the stops of his existence in order to convince those to whom he is writing that they too are drawn into this action just as much as he is. Here it is irrelevant whether he is speaking more "lyrically" or more in "epic" terms, for in both respects, above all, he is speaking dramatically: he shows how the drama comes from God, via Christ, to him, and how he hands it on to the community, which is already involved in the action and must bring it into reality. What Paul and the other writers do in the Letters, the evangelists do in their own way: they do not recount stories in which they are not involved; in fact, they know that their only chance of being objective is by being profoundly involved in the event they are describing. They exercise objectivity by giving their witness before the Church and the world, handing on the drama of Jesus' life, the life of the incarnate Word of God, to the catechesis of the primitive Church, a catechesis designed to incorporate the lives of the young Christians into the mystery of Christ's life.

In doing this, the New Testament reaches back to the Old in order to draw it, too, into the dramatic action. For the fathers in the wilderness, "these things happened as a warning . . . they were written down for our instruction, upon whom the end of the ages has come" (1 Cor 10:11). In terms of dramatic technique, we can talk of the analytical method here: the drama that begins with Christ and attains its culmination in him is continually showing us more of its prehistory, to which it belongs, which renders it intelligible and gives it its whole range and ultimate motivation. Thus the New Testament turns back and takes in the Old; it goes back as far as creation (Adam–Eve and Christ–Church throw light on each other: Eph 5), right back to God's plan "before the foundation of the world", which is revealed and unfolded, at the end of the ages, in the Church, to the amazement of the "principalities and powers in the heavenly places" (Eph 3:10). But although this plan has been essentially revealed, it still waits for the ultimate future ("Apocalypse") to develop its full dimensions. It so overarches everything, from the beginning to the end, that there is no standpoint from which we could observe and portray events as if we were uninvolved narrators of an epic. By wanting to find such an external standpoint, allegedly because it will enable us to evaluate the events objectively (*sine ira et studio*), we put ourselves outside the drama, which has already drawn all truth and all objectivity into itself. In this play, all the spectators must eventually become fellow actors, whether they wish to or not.

So we see that citing the objectivity of Holy Scripture will not dispense us from making the dramatic decision. For Scripture mirrors the drama and can only be understood in reference to it; it is part of the drama. It does not stand at some observation post outside revelation. And insofar as it is part of a greater whole, it points beyond itself to its content, and its content is the *pneuma*, which is always more than the *gramma*, the letter; indeed, it contains the letter within it, a vessel that is too small ("the

world itself could not contain the books that would be written"
—Jn 21:25; cf. 20:30f.). The great unwritten acts of God and
Jesus are also part of the drama of world salvation. We shall have
to return to this in connection with the subject of hermeneutics
(D2a–c).

We can approach the question from the other angle, from that of
the attitude of the believing subject. We have already seen that
the epic recounting of dramatic world events speaks against a
background in which the opposites balance out, whether this
background is thought of as Nothingness, Nirvana, Kismet or
life-in-its-totality and evolution. In this background the battling
waves of destiny are neutralized, muted, and the whole attitude
of those listening to the epic narrator will give way, after all the
turmoil occasioned by the foreground destinies, to a kind of
calm, yielding resignation, a lofty benevolence: this is how
things are, have always been and always will be; things must be
accepted as they are; only boys throw stones at heaven. And in
fact, in this calm resignation, this *apatheia*, we can see the subjective common denominator which all religions (apart from
the religion of the Bible) seek to attribute to the man who has
attained maturity. Here, again, they show themselves to be epic
by nature.

   Just as the epic is not abolished by the dramatic but incorporated into it, so the epic attitude of calm resignation is not
rejected by the drama of Christian life—for the tragic nature of
existence in the world, doomed to final ruin, remains a feature
of Christian existence—but drawn into a new, all-embracing
attitude. The latter also calls for the Christian to strike and
maintain a relationship with all that happens in the world, that
is, it calls for a subjective catholicity, and this is no tired
resignation or sage, lofty benevolence, but the readiness to step
into whatever role in the play God has in mind. The Greek
apatheia is transformed into the Ignatian *indiferencia*: a "letting-
go", an availability (and this is where the epic element comes in)
that is ready to accept any commission that comes from God.
This presupposes a certain distancing from immediacy: the
actor does not insist on being identical with a particular role; but
this distancing takes place with a view to being given a particular

and limited role. For, after all, the Eternal Son of God, in whom, through whom and for whom all things were created (Col 1:16), took on the "role" of a particular, limited, human being, demonstrating his catholicity *in* this role.

This subjective demand can seem paradoxical, and it *is*, like much in theo-drama. The paradox is reflected in the New Testament's twofold requirement that, on the one hand, the Christian should be patient and accept everything that happens to him, without resisting; and, on the other hand, that he should fight, albeit with the "shield of faith", with spiritual "weapons" "of divine power" (2 Cor 10:4), so that in the end he will have "fought the good fight" (2 Tim 4:7). It is the same in the Gospels and in an extreme form in the Book of Revelation, where, together with the Lamb, those who are "called, chosen and faithful" wage war against the kings of the earth (Rev 17:14); essentially, however, this war consists in giving a testimony in life and in death. *Martyrium* means both kinds of testimony, and in the Christian life, in the nature of things, there can be no clear distinction between the attacking and the suffering modes of warfare. At its climax, Christ's own active campaign passes over into his Passion so that he may proceed to the most mighty deed of all; thus Christian suffering is at least equally as fruitful for the salvation of the world as external activity. Thus no Christian is obliged to leave the stage and the action: in suffering and dying he is still playing his part in the theo-drama.

In this connection we cannot omit reference to a New Testament theologoumenon to which we shall have to return in more detail later.

> For we are not contending against flesh and blood, but against the principalities, against the powers, against the world rulers of this present darkness, against the spiritual hosts of wickedness in the heavenly places (Eph 6:12).

In the first place, this means that the Christian is not fighting with adversaries of the same order and on the same level as himself: he is part of God's front, bears his weaponry and is fighting alongside God in a campaign against his sworn enemies. But this—seemingly mythical—battle does not take place above men's heads; men do not have to wait in the wings, so to speak, to see which world principle will triumph—the light or the dark. This battle specifically involves men. This did not have to be so in the Old Testament; it was closer to the world of myth than the New, but this particular theodramatic dimension had not yet been revealed in it. It only becomes a present and visible reality at the moment when the Word becomes flesh; when the Abyss, with its "principalities and powers", faces him who has come down in the form of a servant. Jesus' struggle with the demonic Tempter in the wilderness, his continual confronting of him in men who find themselves in the power of the dark realm and his ultimate battle against "the power of darkness" (Lk 22:53) can no more be excised from the gospel through biblical interpretation than can the corresponding passages in the Letters of Paul, Peter, John and Jude. The Book of Revelation, according to its literary genre, depicts these powers as mysterious and somehow superhuman "beasts" coming forth from the Abyss that is hostile to God. They are forms of concentrated wickedness that have attained a terrible vitality, and believers need to be specially "sealed" if they are to withstand them. The "letters to the churches" in the same Book of Revelation show, however, that these powers are not mere fate, merely impersonal occurrences: here, resistance to the powers of the Abyss at "Satan's seat", against the "deep things of Satan" and the "synagogue of Satan", is conceived in highly personal and nuanced terms. Each church and all the individuals in it have to act on their own decision; the phrase "(your) works" recurs eleven times in the seven letters. And these works consist not only in patient endurance or martyrdom but equally in cleansing the community of diverse kinds of offense, in inner conversion and a return to the "former works" (that is, living once again on the basis of perfect love) and also in the external successes that can be granted even to a community that has "but little power" (Rev 3:8f.).

All this together produces a picture of a subjective attitude that, at the level of perfection, would be coextensive with the divine drama that takes place in the cosmos and in history. The center of this drama is in the Lamb "as though it had been slain", which has triumphed as "the Lion of Judah": the Lamb is depicted simultaneously in his eternal triumph, standing on God's throne (and, as Victor, the Lamb breaks the seals of the closed book)—and in his continuing battle, riding out with his garments drenched in blood (Rev 19:13).

With this image, which concludes Holy Scripture, we return to the point at which, according to our expectation, Christian revelation must fulfill the inchoate yearnings of *mythos* and, at the same time, banish its uncertainties. While God is not involved in the drama of destiny in a way that would render the outcome of the struggle uncertain, he does not sit in splendid isolation either, remote from the world's destinies. (If he did, anyone who wanted to adopt God's standpoint would have to raise himself above life's drama and assume an "epic" distance and indifference.) Here we must break off our as yet incomplete analysis of this apocalyptic mystery—God *in* and *above* the world struggle—to return to it elsewhere. It was necessary to focus on it in order to show that, in Christian revelation, there is no standpoint external to theo-drama.

2. *Convergence toward Theo-Drama*

Now that, in principle, we have stepped beyond the plane of epic theology (to say nothing of lyrical theology), we can look back to the nine tendencies of modern theology referred to at the beginning of the *Prolegomena*; at the time, we observed that they converged and pressed toward a theodramatic context but could not reach it. This retrospect can also help us articulate the concrete meaning of theo-drama, enriching it, as it were, by the inflow of these tributary streams. Since the all-embracing context cannot fall under any general concept, theo-drama cannot be defined: it can only be approached from various angles; all the more so because, as we have said, God himself, who escapes all our attempts to define him, appears on stage as the center of the dramatic action.

If there is to be drama, characters must face each other in freedom. If there is to be theo-drama, the first presupposition is that, "beside" or "within" the absolute, divine freedom, there is some other, nondivine, created freedom; a freedom that shares, in a true sense, something of the autonomy of the divine freedom, both in the decision for God and in the decision against him. The question of how such a dialogue is possible if God is the Absolute and the "All" (and nothing can drop out of the Absolute); and moreover of how, even presupposing the biblical view of God, creation can be "good" and yet this created freedom can forfeit God and itself—this question forms the threshold of all that follows. These are mankind's most ancient questions; they are the first questions to confront the reflective heart, and they cause it lifelong unease. We shall not be able to put them behind us, for we cannot deny that we are not nothing, any more than that we are not God; nor can we deny that there exist good and evil and hence created freedom too. We find that we are always in the midst of the most exciting, indeed excruciating, drama; we do no good by inventing theories about God and the world that try to explain away the original fact: the better course would be to accept it and use it as a starting point, so that, subsequently, we can circle around it and reflect upon it.

However, as we proceed from the first presupposition to the second, namely, that God has given this *play of freedoms* a central meaning called Jesus Christ—the climax of the history of the world's salvation, converging on him and radiating from him—that is, as we, as Christian believers, take up the basic dramatic presuppositions and seek to allow the central meaning to illuminate the whole, we find ourselves faced with a confusing wealth of possible aspects. Even in Holy Scripture itself, do not the intelligible units resemble the particles in a kaleidoscope, creating new patterns with even the slightest movement, so that we can never say that any individual pattern is the most important, the normative one, let alone the one which actually or potentially contains all the others?

It is true that the phenomenon of Jesus—the mortal man who died and rose again—floods individual existence and world history with radiant light, but this fullness of light is unbearable to our "moth's eyes" (as Aquinas says, following Aristotle); thus, for Paul, God's wisdom as manifested in the Cross of Jesus seems like "folly"; the Cross emits what Dionysius calls the "bright darkness of God"; his light illuminates both too much and too little. For, in the Cross, God is supposed to have reconciled the world to himself, and those who were afar off are supposed to have come near; but where do we discern even the beginnings or the echo of this profound upheaval and reversal? "Forever since the fathers (that is, the Apostles and the first Christians) fell asleep, all things have continued as they were from the beginning of creation" (2 Pet 3:4). In fact evil, which has supposedly been overcome on the Cross, seems to have become even more virulent. The beasts of the Book of Revelation only step forth after the Messiah has been born.

Or perhaps, on the other hand, nothing decisive is supposed to have happened in the horizontal history of the individual and of mankind? Perhaps everything essential took place at the watershed between time and eternity, on the "line of death", where time is shipwrecked on the shores of eternity? This was the view, in varied forms, which suddenly arose at the end of the nineteenth century (first of all in Franz Overbeck) and which, in the form of *eschatologism*, had so many repercussions right up to the middle of the present century. Is this what Jesus meant? This eschatologism can focus on the immediately imminent arrival of the kingdom of God in glory—as expected by Jesus and the primitive Church—which proved to be an illusion; or it can be spiritualized and become the Church's mode of existence in the "intervening age", which leads up to the advent of the kingdom, or the individual's mode of existence as he looks toward the watershed of eternity. As Kierkegaard put it, "To be spirit is to live as though we have died." But in that case, why should the Word have become flesh, have become man? Simply in order to direct men's attention away from the world and toward the end of time? The Jews may have been strangers and foreigners in the Promised Land, but they did have the promise that they would one day "possess the land"; but what can Christians do (for they too are basically only "pilgrims and strangers" in the world: 1 Pet 2:11; cf. Heb 11:13) but simply wait patiently for the great Sabbath of God (Heb 4:1–10)? It is not by seeing the Cross as the sign that shattered Jesus' illusion (A. Schweitzer) that we grasp the real dramatic peripeteia, but by seeing it as the sign that points to resurrection and eternal life. But again we ask: Why did the Word become flesh? Solely to suffer and bid farewell? Is this the fire Jesus wanted to cast on the earth? Is this the Spirit he promised to send to those who are his?

Both eschatologism and apocalyptic are undeniably present in the New Testament, but other elements are equally plainly present and cannot be dismissed as later adjustments in the face of the nonarrival of the parousia. We must also do justice to the many other currents of thought that have burst into theology since the middle of this century. In themselves, the categories of *event*, in which aspects of the end-time and of eternity burst in, here and now, upon transitory time, and *history*, which removes the Christian phenomenon from the timelessness of speculative theology and returns it to the flow of horizontal time, are insufficient to adumbrate what really takes place at the point of intersection of both dimensions, in Cross and Resurrection, where eternity breaks in to fashion the course of history.

It is certain that, at the beginning of his public ministry, Jesus chose "the Twelve", representing the new and definitive "Israel of God", the original people, of whom only mere traces had remained. It is also certain that, for a trial period, during his actual lifetime, he endowed them with authority and sent them out to proclaim the kingdom. What we have here is not only *event* but also *structure*, even if its place is hard to define. It is clear that this structure is meant to be permanent; there can be no Messiah without a messianic people, no Son of Man (cf. the Book of Daniel) without the "holy ones" of his kingdom (Dan 7:18, 22), no Shepherd as God's representative (Ezek 34:23f.) without his flock. Furthermore, "in the new world, when the Son of Man shall sit on his glorious throne", the Twelve are also to "sit on twelve thrones, judging the twelve tribes of Israel" (Mt 19:28; Lk 22:30). Meanwhile Jesus "appoints" a kingdom for them, for the duration of the world, "as my Father appointed a kingdom for me" (Lk 22:29; cf. 12:32: "Fear not, little flock, for it is your Father's good pleasure to give you the kingdom"); he wishes to build his Church on Peter (Mt 16:18ff.), and anyone who listens to the disciples hears their Lord (Lk 10:16). Finally, the judges he has appointed over Israel will be sent out to all nations, baptizing and teaching; they can do this because: "Lo, I am with you always, to the close of the age" (Mt 28:20). Passages such as these (which we cannot examine critically here) are complemented by those in which Jesus proclaims an ethics that is by no means apocalyptic but rather "creation-based"; these texts complement and support the structural element.

What we have in front of us, then, is a salvation event that is essentially governed by the vertical but which also comprehends an historical, horizontal breadth. In its unrepeatable uniqueness (on the basis of the vertical), it develops a structure that gives it two ways of imprinting its normative character on its surroundings: it can put its mark on the historical dimension (that is, where this structure is, Jesus, with his unique history, will be present) and on the eschatological and supertemporal dimension; for this structure will join with Jesus in judging the people destined for salvation (which now can be the whole of mankind). In addition, the transcendent nature of the history/ event of Jesus of Nazareth not only extends to the world's future by extrapolating the structure of the Twelve (which is guaranteed as permanent by his Resurrection): it also, just as sovereignly, imprints its character on the past. Thus, for God, all that has taken place up to now only has meaning insofar as it was an approach, a heralding of the history that is central: "For all the promises of God find their Yes in him" (2 Cor 1:20); "Everything written about me in the law of Moses and the prophets and the psalms must be fulfilled" (Lk 24:44). So the complex figure is complicated by a further dimension: while everything that belongs to the past has been fulfilled by Jesus' historical (and hence eschatological) presence, he also *becomes present* in an ever-new way in subsequent history, in the present reality of the ecclesial structure he himself established. And in this way he is continually bringing past things to some new fulfillment: the step from the Old to the New and Eternal Covenant is historically unique, and yet, because of Jesus and the Church structure he has instituted, it is of all times.

Here we must anticipate a possible misunderstanding. We can stamp very different papers with the same stamp; accordingly we might imagine that, as a result of the extrapolation of the structure, the history of Jesus of Nazareth—and his death and Resurrection belong to this history; they are essential to the fullness of his figure and to its interpretation—might be transformed into a kind of all-pervading law of world history and of all being-in-the-world whatsoever (that is, that which underlies history). The fact that the center of the Jesus-history reaches out to the alpha and omega of all history would elevate this particular history into a general world law. But as soon as we utter the word "general", we have stepped over the boundary separating theology from philosophy: then the history of Jesus becomes a universal formula, an all-pervading dialectical law ("*Stirb und Werde*": "Die and become"). But in doing so, it either falls to the level of the clearest, most representative instance of the law—just as some particular coin is of the greatest value because of the unique clarity of its minting—or becomes a mere concrete symbol of something that "really" exists beyond this particular history, for example, in the (holy) spirit of the community, of the Church, of the religious "structure". In favor of such a view, one might refer to what Jesus said about the "greater works" (Jn 14:12; cf. 5:20), which seems to suggest that his historical existence is a mere prelude to something that will only subsequently attain its full development.

This view misinterprets the way biblical testimony sees itself. The "Spirit" will not speak on his own account but will "take what is mine and declare it to you" (Jn 16:14); "No one who denies the Son has the Father" (1 Jn 2:23); "Any one who goes ahead and does not abide in the doctrine of Christ does not have God" (2 Jn 9). Such "going ahead", "going beyond" (JB), transforms the historically once-for-all event into a dialectical law; it seems to bring the event nearer to us, but in reality it presents us, not with the unique event, but only with something that, in any case, is everywhere and always there. Furthermore, the structure instituted by Jesus is cut loose from its origin and made into a timeless, generally available abstraction; and, losing its constant uniqueness, the structure's theodramatic element also loses its whole dramatic dimension and gives way to a "structuralism" that has no events. In virtue of Jesus' founding activity, however, the structure instituted by him remains inseparable from the vertical saving event; both aspects, event and structure, are extrapolated, hand-in-hand, into the totality of history. If Jesus' entire historicality is reduced to the level of a mere symbol or type of something universal, both "event" and "structure" become the two sides of a general law of history.

Moreover, if the testimony of Scripture is taken seriously, namely, that God's Word has become flesh in Jesus of Nazareth, we shall be able to do justice to the theological current of

orthopraxy as well as to show its limitations. It only makes sense
to speak of the Word becoming flesh if by this is meant the
central event recounted by the Gospels. But this event is a
horizontal history ("flesh"; "dwelling among us"—living,
struggling, dying and conquering) that is governed by the
vertical ("Word"; "with God"; "became"). Thus this divine
Word of God is a fundamental *act* ("God so loved . . . that he
gave"), and when Jesus, who is God's act, institutes "discipleship"
and "authority", both are modes of participation in his existence
as God's act; but this participation as such presupposes faith,
presupposes "orthodoxy". Such faith is itself described as a
result of God's act (Jn 6:29); it is therefore not a dry holding-as-
true: it means that we allow God's praxis to take effect in us.
That alone, together with Jesus and in our discipleship of him,
and in virtue of the mission with which he has entrusted us,
enables us to perform the right deeds, deeds which are world-
transforming. And insofar as Jesus' here-and-now presence in
every age of the world is inseparable from the extrapolated
structure he has instituted (the ministerial Church), all Christian
orthopraxy is objectively anchored in this form of his "dwelling
among us". But again, this structure is only the visible guarantee
of his immediate presence through grace; illuminated and guided
by this grace, *human* activity is embraced, directed and accompanied by *divine* activity. Thus there is no opposition between
Church structure and Christian orthopraxy, any more than
there was, in that first calling of the Twelve, between authority
and discipleship. Putting it quite simply (since it is not part of
our present task to define the Catholic concept of ministerial
authority): there is no opposition, either, between the call to
discipleship and the gift of fullness of power within it. We can
understand the latter as an ability—a charism—given to the
individual so that he may help bring about the will of God
within the field of action of the christological drama, by playing
his particular "role" within it; thus this gift is a word addressed
to him antecedently to the action: it wants to become flesh in
him, he must receive, affirm it and bring it into reality if he is to
act rightly. This shows us precisely how justified is the demand
for orthopraxy. For in the real Christian life, dramatically lived
out, there is no moment of pure orthodoxy distinct from and

prior to orthopraxy. "Doxy", rather, is simply an internal
factor in the transition from divine to human "praxis", in the
realm of christological dramatic action. Living faith, which is
always discipleship, arising out of grace's personal call (charis
and charisma), is the commitment of the whole person, and thus
it is "praxy", on the basis of an attitude of homage and receptivity
("doxy") vis-à-vis the preeminent divine activity in the drama
of Jesus Christ. Within this drama, however, people are called
to exercise discipleship with full authority; so the person thus
called does not need to wait until the drama of Christ has been
played to the last act: he can and must begin to join in, in the
very midst of the action. More precisely—lest there be any
misunderstanding—if God, acting in his Son, is "preeminent in
everything" (Col 1:18), that is, needs no one's assistance in
playing his drama to the very end (Cross, descent into hell and
Resurrection), the Son also has preeminence in that he is "the
head of the body, the church" (*ibid.*). He does not exist apart
from her; he makes room for the Church to play her part in his
all-embracing drama. Uniquely, God "makes room" in the case
of the Virgin: her (orthodox and "orthopractical") Yes contributes to making the Word's Incarnation possible; subsequently
he also makes room, in a qualitatively different way (but which,
from the outside, cannot be clearly distinguished from the
former) for the others who share in her readiness and suffering
by being drawn, through grace, into the conflicts and sufferings
of Christ. And here we must include those who are called to
discipleship during Jesus' lifetime but neglect to "watch and
pray" when the hour of the Passion comes and so take flight or
deny him: in spite of this, on the basis of the Eucharist they have
already received—the mode of suffering adopted by Christ's
body and blood—they have been drawn sacramentally into the
drama of salvation. These differing degrees of participation
show that, without affecting the preeminence of God's action in
Christ at any point, we cannot say that the Christian life is only
possible *after* Christ's personal drama has been accomplished.[1]

If we did this, we would have to assume that mere theoretical

---

[1] Cf. the balanced treatment by Wolfgang Beinert, "Orthodoxie und Ortho-
praxie" in *Catholica* 48 (1974), 257–70.

belief (that is, "dead faith") comes before "living faith". (This is theologically inadmissible, since "dead" faith can only be understood as the empty shell of a living faith.) We would have to conceive Christianity primarily as a "teaching" and an orthodoxy and in all seriousness give this preeminence over its concrete realization (theopraxy and Christian orthopraxy). This in turn would mean that we were mistaken in placing theodrama before theology. Here, however, we discern the radical difference between Catholic and Protestant "teaching". Orthodox Protestant theology treats us as believers and agents only *in actu secundo*, in order to "give Christ preeminence in all things"; thus "faith" can be cleanly separated from "works" and given priority over the latter. Liberal Protestantism tries to insert us into the Christ-event *in actu primo*; but by doing so it degrades this event and makes it merely a type, or the highest symbol, of some generalized salvific action on God's part.

The remaining three trends of modern theology can be fitted into this same context: the political, the futuristic and the dialogic. (For the present we do not need to discuss "role" in any detail, since it will have its place in the central problems of Christology and the resultant issues of Christian vocations and charisms.)

What we have called the "extrapolation" of the structure of Christ's existence beyond its confined historical limits and into every period of history also shows its public and *political* relevance. The fact that, initially, it puts the accent on the individual's call to follow Christ does not mean that Christ's work is always a private matter, concerned only with saving the individual's "soul". Jesus is concerned to fashion a new and definitive People of Israel, the eschatological "Israel of God" (Gal 6:16). As Paul shows, part of its "mysterium" is that the "nations" can belong to it with equal rights (Eph 1:13f.; 3:6); it is the "leaven" that works through the entire dough "till it is all leavened" (Mt 13:33). There is no limit to this mission, in terms either of place, time or substance. We are not told that this mission is to combat only the results of injustice and not also its causes: we are simply told that this must be done with the weapons of the kingdom, "genuinely spiritual weapons". This once again shows where the realm of the political fits into the total context. Quantifiable external success cannot provide a standard by which to measure Christian conduct, nor can it yield categories for evaluating the meaning of God's action in Christ, which underlies such conduct. To elevate political success to a central position and a goal-in-itself is to shift the drama's center of gravity away from Cross and Resurrection and toward the allegedly Messianic (and perhaps even Zealot) activity of Jesus. This would be an error of historical judgment and would fail to hear the testimony of Scripture. The only course left open to us is to take seriously the fact that we have been commissioned to *act*, without reading into it any promise of success. In the parable, the weeds are not to be rooted up: "Let the two grow together until harvest"; there can be no "chemically pure" field of wheat—or else the wheat itself would suffer. Similarly, the good and bad fish are to stay together in the net until they are sorted out at the end of time. The Church's mode of presence, with her explicit, all-embracing task in the world, corresponds to the presence of the individual man Jesus, with his superhuman task of "taking away all the sin of the world" (Jn 1:29 = Is 53). This task stretches Christ—and, analogously, his Church—beyond the limit: this is one of the most profound aspects of the theo-dramatic situation. For what we have in Christianity is an initiative undertaken by God on behalf of the world ("God desires all men to be saved": 1 Tim 2:4), not an initiative on man's part by which he escapes from the world and clings to God. This initiative involves exposing oneself to the enemy (a decidedly dramatic element); it is not done by immunizing oneself, through meditative, philosophical or mystical techniques, against the world. That would be the death of drama.

Here the aspect of *dialogue* comes to the fore. In the Christian drama God does not speak in monologues. He engages in conversation, shared speech (*dia-logos*). This shows once again that Christianity is not (like the Koran, for example) a "teaching" that has fallen from heaven but an interaction, a kind of negotiation between two parties; nor can the Church look toward issuing a statement, in the form of Scripture, tradition and theology, at the "end" of these negotiations. For, of his very nature, the one dialogue partner is affected "through and through" (*dia*) by the standpoint of the other partner. In Christianity, God himself is quite fundamentally a partner of this kind. In contrast to the world, which is closed in on itself, does not want to listen to him and distorts all his words even as he utters them, God is the One who allows himself to be most profoundly affected by this partner so unfit for speech. His willingness to be thus affected goes to the extreme of the "wondrous exchange" (*admirabile commercium*) of standpoints and situations on the Cross. And only on the basis of the Cross is faith given to the disciples and all subsequent believers, rendering them capable of dialogue with God; thus they are given the childlike prayer to their Abba, Father, inspired by the Holy Spirit, who finds in the hearts of believers that unutterable word which they themselves are incapable of formulating.

Thus an even deeper layer of the dialogue dimension is opened up: we must ask—again—how God, the Absolute, the essentially Perfect and All-knowing One, can allow himself to be affected by some other standpoint. It is not enough to point to the humanity of Jesus who, as a man, is necessarily dependent on, necessarily interacts with other men and necessarily listens, questions, enters into conversation or avoids it and can even confess his ignorance (Mk 13:32). This Jesus is only the Father's Word. Through Jesus' human capacity for dialogue, the Father reveals his divine capacity for dialogue. He already began to do this in the Old Covenant, when, through the mouth of the prophets and other mediators, many dialogic words were spoken to the people, words which receive their answer in the Psalms or Wisdom literature; even here, in the Covenant—whether it was kept, endangered or broken—the field is wide open for the most diverse kinds of speech. The presupposition for God's speaking in this way is uncovered in the New Covenant: if the Word was "in the beginning" "in the bosom of the Father", this points to a source of dialogue in the Absolute himself, existing from before all time. And if the procession of the Second divine Hypostasis out of the First is simultaneously interpreted as "generation" and "utterance" (since the Son is the Word), and not only as the silent outpouring of love; and if Love, in turn, is grasped as the Third Hypostasis, proceeding from both the One who generates/utters and from the Word, it becomes clear how profoundly rooted the dialogic principle is in God. Can we imagine any greater self-expropriation than that which takes place in the process of generation, particularly here, in the realm of perfect Spirit?

If man—like everything—is created in the Word, it follows that the word-dimension is part of man's being, not only the interpersonal word but also the answer to the Word who was in the beginning. The latter can be an unarticulated cry, resounding in the inexhaustible realm of possibility, so that man does not know how to formulate any intelligible answering word: all the same (as we began by demonstrating) man stands within the enchanted circle of expression, word and even election. Guilt can becloud and suppress his awareness of this, but it can never totally obscure it. He can become hardened and stubbornly silent, he can refuse to answer; but he cannot banish from his spiritual ear the sound of the words that address him. He exists within this sound. "The word is very near you; it is in your mouth and in your heart" (Dt 30:14 = Rom 10:8). In Jesus Christ this word is addressed to us articulately and in a way we simply cannot avoid hearing, and it also liberates us and empowers us to give answer—provided that, through the mediation of "preaching" (Rom 10:14ff.), the word of Jesus penetrates to man's hearing in such a way that he can believe.

The easiest way to approach the last great trend of modern theology, the *futuristic*, is by way of the dialogic, although, of course, it is connected with all the other attempts or at least needs to be brought into relationship with them all. Where there is dialogue, it is incomplete unless and until both speakers have stated that they have said their last word. And so long as mankind endures through history, its word is inconclusive. We can indeed say that "objective revelation came to an end with the death of the Apostles", but we also know how limited this assertion is. For, from God's side, "came to an end" can only mean that, in his unique Word, he has uttered all that can be uttered, to the very last syllable—blood and water from the pierced heart—and that beyond it, objectively speaking, no earthly word remains to be spoken, since God himself has taken up and resolved the final objection raised by his sworn enemy. And this last, definitive Word causes a fountain of speech to well up into eternity. "*Verbum Dei non est alligatum.*"

Arising from God's revelation, two connected elements are to be kept in mind: first, the once-for-all, temporal history of Christ is mysteriously rendered present to all times; constantly transposed into the ever-new present, it yet remains wholly operative, actual and open to development in all its parts. *Now* Jesus promises water to the thirsty, water which will become a spring welling up from within him; *now* he cleanses the Temple; *now* Peter finds the coin in the fish's mouth . . . "Again he sets a certain day, 'Today' . . ." (Heb 4:7), "Behold, now is the acceptable time; behold, now is the day of salvation" (2 Cor 6:2). As a result of the extrapolation of Jesus' existence and, together with it (and not apart from it!), the Church's structure instituted by him, something takes place which Kierkegaard calls "simultaneity": today's disciple is rendered "simultaneous" with the Master of long ago. The seal of this simultaneity (which is also substantially conditioned by the Church's structure and ministerial authority) is the real presence of Christ in the eucharistic action, which—as Odo Casel emphasized—is drama: it is a re-presentation, each time, of the once-for-all divine action.

The second element is the sending of the Holy Spirit at the exact moment when the Word of God utters his last; the sending of the Spirit who initiates believers into the unfathomable depths of the divine Word and who will tell them what to say when the time of testing comes (Mk 13:11). This applies to the Church as a whole. She does not need to perfect her "theology" so that in future there will be nothing left to do, or practically nothing. If there *is* a growth in the understanding of revelation (although it is questionable whether the concept of "growth" is appropriate here), it is primarily in the awareness of how inexhaustible it is. For revelation shows us how God is always greater than we thought. This does not mean that the Church, on the basis of the understanding vouchsafed her, cannot set up certain normative affirmations as signposts for our understanding, affirmations which will never prove to have been will-o'-the-wisps. But a signpost only sets us on the right path; it does not replace either the path or our proceeding along it.

The futuristic dimension, however, is concerned not only with insight but also with Christian action. No Christian can regard his work as finished prior to his death. "Not that I have already obtained this or am already perfect; but I press on to make it my own, because Christ Jesus has made me his own" (Phil 3:12). What the Apostle is saying here is true not only of his own life but of the Church as a whole. Her tradition is not so much a link with the past as a marathon relay race in which one runner hands on the torch to the next. The last parables in Matthew all refer to working or preparing for the Lord's future. "When you have done all that is commanded you, say, 'We are unworthy servants' ": the Church is prevented from ever resting on any past achievement; she is continually being spurred on to make a better response. And in doing so she does not have to worry that she is walking toward a future that has two sides, namely, the historical future in which she has to exercise her mission and God's future, which brings the course of history to a conclusion and gathers God's harvest into the Father's kingdom. For the Church is running toward God's future side by side with the world, only with more vision and more hope than the latter. The Lord's parousia is a parousia not for the Church alone but for all. Even in the Old Testament it was spoken of as the "Day of the Lord". But, in contrast to this and to all the world's vague hopes, the Church's hope has a special, distinctive shape and intensity. The concept and the word "parousia" contain both the future and the hidden presence of the Lord: the Lord is "He who is to come" (Rev 1:4, 8; 4:8) because he indwells everything in a hidden manner and can announce a "coming" and an appearing in the midst of history (Rev 2:5, 16). His "I am coming soon" (Rev 3:11) can refer both to an advent within history and an advent at the end of history. And as for the final call of the Spirit and the Bride: "Come!" (22:17) and the last dialogue: "Surely, I am coming soon. Amen. Come, Lord Jesus!" (22:20)—they are both so futuristic, in an absolute sense, that they do not need to refer exclusively to the last coming but can include all forms of advent, even those within history.

This means that the mode of time operating in theo-drama is so unique that it enables us to discern the uniqueness of the theodramatic action as a whole. As soon as Jesus appears, the kingdom of God is "about to arrive", it stands knocking "at the door" (Rev 3:20), it is about to step over the threshold (Mt 24:33; *prope est in ianuis*; James 5:9: *ante ianuam assistit*). It has not merely *started* to come, but, in virtue of his presence, *in* his presence, its coming is in full course, it is actually arriving, inchoately (which is expressed by Luke's phrase: "the kingdom of God is *entòs hymon*", 17:21). In virtue of the "pledge of the Spirit", man's attitude of believing, loving hope also participates in this inchoate presence of the future; but great care must be taken lest this inchoate aspect be overridden in favor of a secret (Gnostic) vision or prescience that would rob it of its dramatic tension. "For we walk by faith, not by sight" (2 Cor 5:7), and "hope that is seen is not hope" (Rom 8:24). All the same, Christian hope is substantially different from any other, pagan or Jewish,[2] because it rests on the inchoate presence of the Jesus-event, which—unlike God's great deeds in the Old Testament—not only guarantees things to come but actually *contains* them in fullness: "Be of good cheer, I *have* overcome the world" (Jn 16:33).

The first Christian generations expected the imminent coming of the Lord in chronological time: this enabled them to realize much of this paradox of Christian hope, which has since lost its power and waits to be revitalized. But we must not conceal the fact that they too, by putting the accent on the chronological coming, did not perfectly preserve the balance of the entire phenomenon. There was an unresolved tension between the "soon", which left everything open, and its interpretation in terms of imminent temporal proximity, which may have failed to direct the attention of Christians sufficiently to mankind's temporal future and to their sharing in responsibility for it. Later on, the chronological element became misleadingly obtrusive when, on the basis of contemporary interpretations of the Book of Revelation, people started calculating when the end of the world was to come: once more an alleged knowledge claimed to go behind the unitary structure of hope, thereby robbing it of its inner tension: the "soon" could always arrive *before* the point in time that had been calculated.

In reality, the futuristic is not a cosmic but a christological category. Just as the Logos, as Alpha, is not a chronological

---

[2] Cf. "The three forms of hope" in *Truth Is Symphonic* (San Francisco: Ignatius Press, 1987), 170ff.

starting point but the "origin", so, as Omega, he is not the chronological end but the goal toward which everything is pressing, not outwardly, but inwardly. This means, again, that we may not transmute the "soon" into a timeless existential dimension of Christian life; it affects this life *in* its temporal nature, and it does so on the basis of the equally temporal history of Jesus of Nazareth. In his existence the futuristic has its exemplary, primal shape.[3]

3. *A Single Drama*

In the foregoing we attempted to show that the substantial efforts of modern theology are concentric, converging on a theo-drama, and that it is only in relation to this center that they can reciprocally complement each other. Divorced from this center, they largely cancel each other out. Thus the structural dimension stands opposed to the dimensions of event, history, future, and so forth. Now, however, the question arises: Can we still hold this center, toward which all the theological trends transcend and converge, in our spiritual gaze as a *single "shape"* [*Gestalt*]; or are the lines so confused that the most we can do is to postulate a convergence point, but one that lacks all visibility?

If this were the case, it would also place a question mark over the point of departure of our *Aesthetics*, for in the first section of the present volume we endeavored to show that, by an inner necessity, the "aesthetic" form tends directly toward the dramatic. Assuming that our point of departure was not a mistake, the only reason why it is so difficult to see all the different lines together is that the Christian and the theologian are being required to do something to which, initially, they are unaccustomed: for so long they have been used to "epic theology", and now they have to adapt to a new way of seeing—but there is nothing arbitrary about this requirement. What used to be viewed from "epic" distance, and thus was relatively immobile, now has to be experienced in act, in the succession of acts that

[3] Cf. "Glaube und Naherwartung" in *Zuerst Gottes Reich* (Benziger, 1966), 7–24.

constitute its inner dynamism. Thus Christian contemplation
would be challenged to leave the auditorium, step onto the stage
and resolutely join in the action. "Action", of course, means
far more than worldly busy-ness: the concept itself is drawn
primarily from God's action in Christ's life, death and Resurrection. What is required is the surrender of attitudes that are
seen as hostile to one another, in favor of a new center; the epic,
contemplative attitude would be summoned out of its distance
and brought into the drama, whereas the emphases on orthopraxy and the futuristic would have to ponder the fact that it is
God, not man, who is the prime determinant of the course of
theo-drama; this reflection would draw attention to a forgotten
aspect, namely, the aspect of listening and receptivity in faith.

For the moment let it suffice that we have raised the hope that
it is possible to move from the periphery formed by the various
aspects toward a single center (that has yet to be rendered
visible). Now, however, another perspective is pressing for
attention, demanding priority: the *testimony of Scripture*, which
asserts the uniqueness of the drama enacted by God with his
creation. Scripture always presupposes that very reduction
toward which, starting from the diverse theological standpoints, we have toiled. In Scripture it is already attained. Indeed, we cannot really speak of a "reduction", because from
the scriptural standpoint everything is always regarded from the
point of view of God's action—man's action is drawn into the
latter—and, however manifold and wide-ranging God's action
is, however much it may be beyond our grasp, it is at all events
one single action (assuming that it really is God's action, proceeding from his initiative and drawing the world into it). So
my spiritual eye does not need any overview of the dramatic
"shape"—which it cannot have in any case. It suffices to have
evidence that God (in Jesus Christ and in the Holy Spirit) is
guiding the action; in this way it is also given evidence of the
play's unity and of the convergence of the disparate theological
trends which are so pressing today. Scripture is sufficient to give
us such a testimony, and thus it sheds adequate light for guiding
the individual in making concrete ethical decisions.

We should not be too quick to counter the foregoing with the
oft-quoted theological pluralism of the Bible. Naturally the

standpoint of the word of God must be so total and so rich that it mocks every attempt to tie it down to particular schemata. All we can do is to circle around it, approaching it from countless perspectives. That is evidently why the Spirit inspired the variety of biblical writings. Neither in the forward march of the Old Testament nor in the great synthetic utterances of the New can these writings be "systematically" shown to coincide, if by "system" we mean some totality that can be cited, surveyed and evaluated before the judgment seat of human reason. On the other hand, their convergence is so evident that every new contribution is gratefully accepted as complementing our understanding of the totality, which is always richer than we thought. Where there are gaps, we need to ask ourselves whether something is missing that is essential for our apprehension of the whole, or whether in fact an area has been left open for that dramatic movement without which the entire event would be doomed to ossify and to be truncated into a Gnostic system.

Let us take up one of the synthetic passages and complement what it implies by referring to other such passages. The *beginning of the Letter to the Ephesians* opens with a hymn in praise of the glory of God's grace, revealing his plan for the world, which is dependent on no necessity but solely on his free will and decision. The standpoint here is the highest possible, the most all-embracing: before the foundation of the world, we were chosen to become adopted sons, and that "in Christ" (that is, the Son-made-man) and "through Jesus Christ", who is designated simply "the Beloved". The goal of our being chosen "in him" is that we "should be holy and blameless before him" (God the Father), and we can only do this by "finding redemption through his blood, the forgiveness of sins". In God's gracious decision, therefore, when we fall as a result of our freedom, we are caught up by the safety net of the Beloved's redeeming act on the Cross. This plan is described as a plan of "love", of "every spiritual blessing", of "his glorious grace"; but this love is not blind: it is a love that encompasses "wisdom and enlightenment"; freely bestowed love, grace, is identical with the Logos embracing the world and its history. God's divine purpose, which initially remains a secret, is this: to bring about the "fullness of time" by means of Christ's active stewardship (*oikonomia*); in this fullness of time, evidently after various preceding periods, "everything" will be "united in Christ, the head".

Let us pause here. Initially it might seem that, in this hymn of praise (*berakah*) of Ephesians 1:3–10, we are being presented with a lofty, epic, undramatic portrayal of the world plan, from its beginnings prior to the world's existence right up to its final end; a framework into which everything else can be fitted. Indeed, the whole picture, after the repeated references to God's glory and in particular to the glory of his grace (1:6, 12, 14), seems almost to sink to the level of a monologue process in which God uses the cosmos, men and even Christ himself only to radiate the glory of his grace, to acquire an increase of glory (1:11–12). To counter this impression, we must first recall the *Sitz im Leben* of the hymn (and of similar ones): it is not a theological treatise but the community's hymn in praise of its Redeemer. Thus "there is no need for long-winded explanations of all the phases of salvation history"—we are speaking only of the Cross, not of the Fall—"since ultimately what is at the center is not salvation history but Christ, . . . the living Christ who is at work in the Church. The crucial question posed by the hymn is not, therefore, who or what is redeemed but who is the Redeemer. And that is not a theoretical question but a question of flesh and blood, a question that affects every fiber of one's own existence."[4] The perspective expands "from the experience of the community that has come to salvation in Christ through baptism"[5] backward to the origins and forward to the end-time; both lie, not in contemplative remoteness, but, in concrete immediacy, in the event of transformation. The fact that "the Resurrection was the theological cradle of Christology"[6] is only the first step; it is also, as Ephesians in particular does not tire of showing, the cradle of ecclesiology: the community lives, in all immediacy, at the same dramatic turning point of death to life, as a result of "the immeasurable greatness of his power . . . according to the working of his great might, which he ac-

---

[4] Wolfgang Beinert, *Christus und der Kosmos, Perspektiven zu einer Theologie der Schöpfung* (Herder, 1974), 32.

[5] *Ibid.*, 38.

[6] R. Schnackenburg in *Mysterium Salutis* III/1, 238.

complished in Christ when he raised him from the dead and made him sit at his right hand in the heavenly places" (1:19–20). If it is to do justice to the event, which could oppress us by its tremendous power, the hymn of praise must unfold, in word, the event's dimensions in history and its dramatic structure.

As we look back from the "fullness of time", two things strike us: men's election, in the Beloved who is to give "his blood" for them, entails the whole heart-rending drama that "God did not spare his only Son but gave him up for us all" (Rom 8:32). John too says that "God so loved the world that he gave his only Son", adding, "so that everyone who believes in him should not perish but have eternal life" (Jn 3:16). But does "everyone" believe in him? That is a question we shall have to ask as we look forward. But as we continue to look backward, we come to the second point: as a result of Christ's stewardship, all things are united under him as head. They were not so from the first, not in everyday reality at any rate; and in those ages when they lacked the one, concrete Head, they were subject to powers or authorities which, contrasted with the true Head, can be termed "abstract". The next section (Eph 1:11–12) shows that this period of "abstractness" was also a period when Jew and Gentile went their own separate ways, either subject to a law (mediated by "angels": Gal 3:19) or, through conscience, a law unto themselves (Rom 2:14). Elsewhere this time prior to the appearance of the concrete Head is called a time of "immaturity", of "slavery to the elemental spirits of the universe", a time of "submission to guardians and trustees" (Gal 4:2–4): this provides the theme of a drama that is not heavenly but earthly and one that is bound to become a tragedy "in the fullness of time", when the abstract law, in all its forms, is confronted with the concrete Head and will not agree to abdicate in his favor.

It follows that if, from the fullness of time, we look ahead and contemplate God's plan, we shall see that by no means has everything been decided (as in the "epic" mode). It is very characteristic that the Letter to the Ephesians, which begins so serenely, ends with the portrayal of a battle of almost mythical proportions, in which those on the side of the Head are contending, "not against flesh and blood, but against the principalities, against the powers, against the world rulers of this present darkness, against the spiritual hosts of wickedness in the heavenly places" (6:12); it speaks of the "wrath of God" (5:6), of the "evil day" (6:13), and of a plurality of these present "evil days" (5:15). At all events Christ's victory "in itself" is not yet a victory "for us": "For he must reign until he has put all his enemies under his feet" (1 Cor 15:25). We too are involved in this dramatic campaign, so much so that the "evil day" leaves us no time to speculate about the necessarily favorable outcome: all of us must transform the graces we have received from God into a divine armor (Eph 6:13) and use it as such. The image of the superhuman, quasi-mythical battle is heightened in the Book of Revelation and given a twofold outcome: either victory with the Lamb or being thrown alive, together with the beasts, into the lake of fire (Rev 19:20; 20:9f., 15). All human life presses toward the lonely scene in which each individual must appear personally before the judgment seat of God and Christ and give an account of himself (Rom 14:10; 2 Cor 5:10).

Whether we look backward or forward from the appearance of the "Head" in the "fullness of time", the Head is seen to "unite all things in himself" and thus gives ultimate, concrete meaning to all the dramatic episodes of mankind. As Paul and John repeatedly stress, the Father has handed over everything to the Son, so that he represents the ultimate norm in all worldly processes. This also applies to the ages prior to his Incarnation, when he was already in office as God's plenipotentiary. Paul distinguishes between the Jews who "first hoped in the Anointed One . . . destined and appointed" and the Gentiles who have now "heard the word of truth, the gospel of your salvation", who were once "far off" but now "have been brought near" in the blood of Christ (Eph 1:12f.; 2:13). Once all things have been subjected to Christ, the entire distinction, which goes right through the Old Testament at its deepest level—Israel is chosen from among the other nations, who are *not* chosen—remains operative solely in him: "Christ became a servant to the cir-cumcised to show God's truthfulness, in order to confirm the promises given to the patriarchs", whereas the Gentiles are to "glorify God for his mercy" (Rom 15:8f.); and precisely in this manner, by being taken into Christ, this distinction is obliterated in his one, crucified body (Eph 2:14–18). The consequences of this obliteration of the greatest distinction in world history—

even taking post-Christian history into account—are enormous. For now, under the banner of a Judaism that sets itself up as absolute, the God-given "Law" (in all its forms) will be put forward as the presence of the divine in the world, and people will attempt to subject man's freedoms to its abstract omnipotence. And, on the other hand, under the banner of a self-absolutizing pagan culture, people will play off the "lawless" (*anomos*, 1 Cor 9:21) and "godless" (*atheos*, Eph 2:12) freedom of the "autonomous individual" against the abstract Law. Often enough the one will change into the other, because neither of them can free itself from its abstract nature except by being lifted up into the concrete Head. Both forms of existence, in their separateness, remain "typical" and symbolic (cf. 1 Cor 10:11), pointing beyond their relative selves. Law must prove obsolete in the person who fulfills it from within, out of the love of Christ (Gal 5:23; 1 Tim 1:9), and freedom must hand itself over as a prisoner to Christ, so that it can now truly receive itself back from him (Gal 5:1).

Thus Jesus Christ, the Beloved before all worlds, "born of a woman, born under the law" (Gal 4:4), who became obedient to the Father for us unto death on the Cross and so was exalted above everything in heaven, on earth and under the earth (Phil 2:9f.)—this Jesus Christ, in his dramatic role, which encompasses all dimensions of the world and of history, becomes the norm of every real and possible drama in the personal and public domains. Insofar as every individual drama must first be lifted up to him, the Head, in order to discover its meaning, the conflicts that exist within the world are, at best, *provisionally* soluble. Thus, comedy has a happy ending because the tensions which create it are not pressed too far, and tragedy can give the relatively satisfying appearance of a certain immanent justice, even when the hero is doomed: it summons us to face up to the abiding tragic dimension of all existence, while leaving it an open question whether this is a sign of the dignity or of the meaninglessness of all existence. In comedy, the "gracious" good fortune prevails which, in tragedy, could equally well be denied and, one day, *will* be denied—in death, "the last enemy". To that extent, tragedy is the deeper truth of existence that underlies every comedy.

If the once-for-all drama of Christ is to be exalted as the norm of the entire dramatic dimension of human life, two things must happen simultaneously: the abyss of all tragedy must be plumbed to the very bottom (which no purely human tragedy can do); and, in it and transcending it, we must discern the element of gracious destiny that genuinely touches human existence (and not merely *seems* to touch it). Thus the dramatic aspect of existence yields postulates addressed to Christology, although they can only be meaningful if they have already encountered the revelation concerning Christ. First, there is the postulate that Christ's being is of such a kind that he is able to descend into the abyss of all that is tragic—far beyond the ability of any tragic hero (who only bears his *own* destiny)—and hence that the tragic overstretching of his person must be absolute, that is, divine. (For "demi-gods" are self-contradictory.) The other postulate is that, precisely in this abyss of unsurpassable tragedy, the element of grace asserts itself, that grace which encompasses existence and can persist and penetrate into the conciliatory aspect of tragedy. Both together lead to the absolute christological paradox: in the horror of dissolution—under the weight of the world's guilt and of forsakenness by God—we are delivered from the meaninglessness of the world's suffering, and grace and reconciliation carry the day. John brings both aspects together in his concept of "exaltation" (exaltation on the Cross and exaltation to God's presence) and "glory". "Glory" is the manifestation of the Father's love for the world in the Son's bearing of the world's sin: by an inner necessity, this pure obedience to the Father calls for the Father to glorify the Son and announces it in advance ("If God is glorified in him, God will also glorify him in himself, and glorify him at once": Jn 13:32).

In Christ, therefore, penetrating the whole doomed predicament of human existence and being obedient to the Father's directions are simply one and the same. The movement of Incarnation, according to the Father's purpose, does not come to an end until all man's remoteness from God, all his guilt and pain, have been endured and undergone in performance of this obedience. The obedience is freely given, but the monstrous content laden upon Christ—which could not be imagined, in all its concreteness, from outside—is positively explosive. While the world's tragedy "oppresses" the Suffering Servant under its weight, the prophecy of Isaiah 53 is fulfilled: he has "humbled *himself*"; "he makes himself an offering for sin"; "he shall see the fruit of the travail of his soul and be satisfied; . . . my servant (shall) make many to be accounted righteous." All norms, ultimately, come down to the Son's (unlimited) capacity for obedience: the Father asks him to give tangible proof of the divine love for the world and loads upon him the totality of men's free turning away from God.

All the gospel instruction addressed to later believers is uttered on the basis of this ultimate, sole norm. It radiates from it and so leads toward it. To that extent it presupposes a realm, an (ante-)room in which human freedom makes decisions about values according to criteria that are largely drawn from the world itself. This realm of free preference, which is part of human existence in the world and among other men, is by no means overwhelmed or narrowed by the norm of Christ. Yet it is thoroughly affected by it, for in the light of the gospel it is clear that all things were created in the Word that was eventually to become flesh; that is, from the very outset, everyone is already *within* the norm that is to appear definitively in Christ. Furthermore, from the very outset, our shared humanity is permeated by a christological element on the basis of Christ's consummating act on behalf of all: "What you have done to the least of these my brethren. . . ." If we take it seriously that we are "within" Christ's norm, the call of conscience, which urges us to give preference to the higher value in any situation, is also—latently—subordinate to the norm of Christ's obedience to the Father; conscience does not address itself to an absolute freedom that is its own starting point but to a freedom that is indebted and responsible; indebted and responsible, namely, to that Word who is the "life" and the "light" of the men who were created in him (Jn 1:4). Thus, in this anteroom, prior to revealed Christology, man the agent can establish certain "general" norms of action, abstracted from human existence, and these may be relatively correct. But once the absolute norm has appeared on the scene, as we have said, they must be understood as rays emitted from it or approaches toward it. "One of the multitude said to him, 'Teacher, bid my brother divide the inheritance with me.' But he said to him, 'Man, who made me a judge or divider over you?' " (Lk 12:13f.): the gospel does not replace human decisions and arrangements. Immediately after this, however, Jesus tells the parable of the rich man who decides to store up his goods and dies the following night: according to this advice, each of the two brothers ought to try to settle his dispute: the one by sharing, the other, perhaps, by renouncing his part or, having inwardly renounced it, by accepting the proffered share in gratitude. So the concrete norm has universal application, but it leaves the person free to decide; and even as it leaves him free, it points to the source of all true freedom: the Son's readiness to perform the Father's will.

As for the Father's will, it never has merely one meaning (as if its utter concreteness could be changed into a general, abstract law of permanent validity). This is the place for us to listen to the profound words of the psalm: "*Once* God has spoken; *twice* have I heard this: that power belongs to God; and that to thee, O Lord, belongs steadfast love" (Ps 62:11f.). God's word is one: it does not sway this way and that between righteousness and love. But when, in the world, is this One to be understood as (loving) righteousness, and when as (righteous) love, so that man can act in accordance with the norm? When is it time for Jesus to hide from his enemies and avoid them, and when is it time to confront them and surrender into their hands? He knows these times by always looking to the Father: "Truly, truly, I say to you, the Son can do nothing of his own accord, but only what he sees the Father doing" (Jn 5:19). In making the decisions required by the needs of the hour, the Christian and the Church must ponder and reflect, of course: but at the same time they must look up to the obedient Son with humble entreaty, so that, through him, they may find the will of God here and now.

How far, in the anteroom of the "law" and of "lawlessness" (where conscience sets forth the fundamental purpose of the law: Rom 2:15), can the individual dramas of Jews and Gentiles be incorporated into the drama of Christ as aspects of it? Only Christ's judgment will tell us. It will show whether a life was built on the "foundation" of Christ or not, for "no other foundation can any one lay" (1 Cor 3:11). And the Christian will continue to feel the gap between worldly existence with its many relative norms and the ground and goal which is Christ, the absolute norm. But, while he feels this—and it is part and parcel of existence in the world—he must not lose the faith-knowledge that Christ was on a journey, together with his disciples, both before and after his Resurrection, and that he explicitly designated himself as the "Way", that is, the communication with the Father. This is also a consequence of his power to "extrapolate" the temporal existence he lived and render it present to all times.

As the perfect man with his peerless drama, he is the living framework within which every human destiny is acted out; every human destiny is judged by his perfection and saved by his redeeming meaning. Thus the individual's own drama can be either crossed out, rejected and "burned" (while the actor himself "will be saved only as through fire": 1 Cor 3:15), or, by grace, it can be recognized as a dramatic action within the dramatic action of Christ, in which case the actor becomes a "fellow actor", a "fellow worker" with God (1 Cor 3:9).

From this vantage point, once more, we can ask the question we asked at the beginning: Are our "eyes of faith" able to see the normative form, now unfolded into a drama, as a form? The answer can now be in the affirmative. Form is a meaningful unity in a multiplicity of organs; in its fundamental articulations —his Incarnation, his preaching of the kingdom and preparing of the Church, his suffering, his solidarity with the dead and reunion with the Father, his return at the end of history—Christ's dramatic form is the simple self-presentation of a single attitude, which is the effective expression of God's love for the world. The attitude itself is no arbitrarily accepted "role", no fortuitous "avatar", but the free expression of the free person who, as the Father's Son, receives himself from him and owes his being to him. Thus, obediently walking the path of human nature and undergoing his atoning death, he also demonstrates—with power—the Father's loving self-surrender for the world. Everything fits organically into this center with that supernatural logic that infallibly characterizes the deeds of the Logos: in and through the "dia-logos" between the Father and the incarnate Son in the unity of the Spirit, the world—which is created

free—is allotted its space where the Son is (for he is its prototype, fashioner and goal: Col 1:14-16). The fact that the world is
in God means that when men, with their finite freedom, stray
from the path, the Son has to go to the most extreme form of
self-surrender—Eucharist, Cross, the descent to hell. Thus the
trinitarian mystery translates into a cosmic mystery, both in
terms of an event here and now and as an ever-expanding
history. Because of our shared humanity, which is implicated in
the redemptive event, and the establishment of a Church structure
for which our shared humanity calls, this mystery acquires both
political relevance and a future thrust. For what has been accomplished "in itself" has also yet to come "for us" (and "with
us", as we must say in the context of the Church); we must wait
for it in prayer and right faith—"orthodoxy"—and help to
bring it about, in faith, by right deeds—"orthopraxy". This
entire, central world drama is of such importance that it automatically attracts every power hostile to God (none can remain
"by itself"); and as for the man who has been "liberated for
freedom" and joins in the action, he is put in a much more
exposed position, between God and the anti-God forces, than
he ever imagined. For what has been accomplished "in itself"
(in the Resurrection and exaltation of Jesus) becomes the starting
point of the outpouring of the trinitarian Spirit of the—now
manifest—love between Father and Son: this Spirit makes what
has been accomplished present as a saving event and a stumbling
block to the world in every age and thus dramatizes world
history and the history of the Church as a struggle between
"Jerusalem" and "Babylon", as Augustine depicted it. But since
the whole intramundane drama, set in motion by God's intervention, can never ultimately be enacted on any other stage but
that of the Trinity, in the area that has been made available there,
its final destination can be nothing other than the glory of God.
This is the goal toward which all the "praise of the glory of his
grace" (Eph 1:6) tends. This glory is identical with the "selflessness" of the reciprocal self-surrender of the divine hypostases; thus, by seeing God's glory as the goal of everything that
happens, all things are opened up to the *gratis* of love.

This is another condensation of what we have already set
forth on a broader canvas: if it is to be fully rounded, the

theodramatic form needs all the aspects: they all come from it and all return to its unity. The totality, however, rooted in and resting on the Father's eternal decision, is expressly called "mystery" (Eph 1:9; 3:9; and so forth); and this mystery, even when it has been revealed (*apocalypsis*), is not some configuration that can be grasped in its totality by earthly understanding. It remains a mystery of faith. The deeper our knowledge of it, the more unfathomable (Eph 3:8) the divine love becomes (*gnōnai te tēn hyperballousan tēs gnoseōs agapēn:* Eph 3:9). And for this knowledge, as we showed at the beginning of the *Aesthetics*, we need the "eyes of faith". Lest the object of our beholding should turn into an "absolute knowledge", however, it was necessary to distinguish our endeavor from that of Hegel in particular. This we did at the start of the present work (*Theo-Drama* I, 54–70). "Absolute knowledge" is the death of all theo-drama, but God's "love which surpasses all gnosis" is the death of "absolute knowledge".

From this point we can go on to discover what *hermeneutics* can tell us within the context of theo-drama, which is understood as the central aspect of the Christian revelation.

D. THEODRAMATIC HERMENEUTICS

All theology is an interpretation of divine revelation. Thus, in its totality, it can only be hermeneutics. But, in revealing himself in Jesus Christ, God interprets himself—and this must involve his giving an interpretation, in broad outline and in detail, of his plan for the world—and this too is hermeneutics. The first hermeneutics has to be oriented to and regulated by the second. The second hermeneutics, however, cannot seal itself off and ignore man's freedom and his free understanding; so it, in turn, is open to the first hermeneutics. For God does not play the world drama all on his own; he makes room for man to join in the acting. In other words: when God, acting in Jesus Christ, utters, expresses himself, his language must be intelligible to the world, or at least *become* intelligible through the divine Spirit, who teaches men's hearts to listen and to speak so that they can utter a word in reply. God's word is always "in the process of interpreting", and "the resultant word is articulated in the interpreting and answering word of those who hear it (God's language)". And only through the Spirit of God in man, who explodes his narrow, anthropocentric horizon of interpretation and causes him to adopt God's standpoint, can man understand this language; only thus can there be an "adequate response" to God's self-disclosure, a response which, because it is adequate, is in turn the "express word of the event of God".[1]

It is not enough, however, for God to involve himself with the world and with man. If there is to be an integrated interplay, man too must involve himself with God's drama. In principle he already has "access" to it, for God has opened up the play to him, but he must go on freely to accept this fact and act on it. This is the overall situation of a theodramatic hermeneutics. The substance of it has in part already been formulated in the foregoing and in part must now in various elements be brought together. We shall discuss

1. the fundamental law according to which (for the person

---

[1] Heinrich Schlier, "Was heisst Auslegung der Heiligen Schrift?" in *Besinnung auf das Neue Testament* (Herder, 1964), 42f.

who has access and allows himself to be involved) the phenomenon is self-illuminating;

2. the relationship between the apparently uninvolved word
of testimony (Holy Scripture) and the Word who dramatically
illuminates himself;

3. the structure of what is called theological "evidence".

1. *Self-Illumination*

a. The General Human Horizon of
Interpretation Is Transcended

We go to the theatre to share in the experience of an action which
interprets itself as it unfolds. Similarly, when listening to a
symphony, we must listen to it in its progress through time if
we are to "understand" it. By allowing music or the stage to
have its effect on us (and this, of course, requires our active, alert
attention), we come to appreciate what they want to say to us. It
is surely not normal—in the intention of the playwright or
composer—that I should read the play or the score prior to the
performance. We must remember that the Greek plays were not
published and that many authors or directors are of the opinion
that stage plays should not be printed. The advance knowledge
this gives can help me to grasp the event as it moves forward and
passes on—otherwise I might fail to appreciate it in its whole
significance—but it can also slacken my attention and diminish
my spontaneity. On the other hand, the performance, be it of a
stage play or music, is addressed to a spectator, a listener who is
not entirely uneducated in human and artistic terms: he must be
able at least to laugh and weep at the right places, he must have
sufficient knowledge of life's laws and its role-playing, sufficient
awareness of the proportions of melody, harmony and rhythm,
to be able to appreciate what he is experiencing and evaluate
what it is saying and its expressive power.

But this is, as it were, only the external, material presupposition, allowing the internal, formal process to unfold
unhindered: the work must interpret itself. When the curtain
rises on the first act, a situation is revealed, like an inner space

into which we must enter (the "ex-position"). A field of tension is built up, riveting the spectator's attention, all the more as fragments of meaning emerge which demand to be amplified, to be mutually complemented and interrelated, although for the present this seems inconceivable and perhaps threatening or impossible. As the performance unfolds we see how, after much shaking of the kaleidoscope, after the accumulation of many new elements—characters or simply situations—the final shape emerges. The action moves forward with its vicissitudes, dragging the spectator along with it; if the tension is correctly introduced, he will gladly enter into these changes and reversals. A destiny is operating through the entire complex of events, working through characters who are decidedly free; it unites the action, unites the players, unites stage and auditorium; it stands at the center. It is more than a fortuitous instance of something long familiar: it is a kind of center of the world, around which the sun, moon and stars all revolve.

(This must not, and cannot, happen in Brecht's "epic theatre": on the one hand, the unfolding action is only an "instance" of "universal conditions", and these conditions are not really metaphysical but merely economic; once I have read Marx's *Das Kapital* I can grasp them completely and judge the particular case on that basis. On the other hand, the characters' story must never become so engrossing as to acquire a significance of its own, cut loose from and transcending the "conditions". This, at least, is the theory; fortunately Brecht the poet does not always follow it.)

In theo-drama, the individual aspect must be of absolute relevance. Here, individual destiny cannot be observed with the indifference of the spectator who "knows how things are", in general or under particular circumstances. Moreover, this in-dividual aspect must be relevant to *all*, not only (as in *mythos*) to individuals, that is, demi-gods, kings and heroes, while the others, as it were, look over the fence with "pity" and "fear". "Relevant to all": this was Plato's objection to the poets; this was why he banished *mythos* from the *polis*. But how can an individual destiny show itself to be thus absolute and relevant to all, without being downgraded, within the universal human horizon of understanding, to a mere "instance"? Only by unrolling this horizon (that is, explicitly the horizon which is common to all men) and simultaneously transcending it. The universal horizon, beyond all particular "solutions" (in terms of *Weltanschauung*) proposed for the riddles of existence, is constituted by these very riddles, such as injustice, crime, suffering, death, on the one side, and joy, compassion, self-sacrifice on the other. No one can penetrate beyond these frontier mountain-chains of negative and positive values; behind them the sun of every man's understanding sinks and goes down. No one can produce a synthesis of these values and nonvalues. Here, therefore, in the sphere of ultimate values and nonvalues which simply *are*—even if people try to explain them away—there can be no transposing of horizons from one culture to another, from one age to another. In the case of theo-drama, this will simplify things. This horizon—and not just any particular horizon—has been unrolled in the life and death of the man Jesus of Nazareth: it is manifest for all to see; all can follow the action. But, thus manifest, this horizon is transcended, in a movement that comes from God and goes to God, not by some particular *Weltanschauung* or doctrine, for and against which arguments can be adduced, but by the ultimate lines of human destiny being drawn to a transcendental point of convergence. This point, which lies below man's horizon but is brought into unique visibility here, is called "resurrection on the third day", and it results in a thorough interpretation and clarification of the horizon of human destiny. Initially, it is true, the transcendental point toward which the lines converge, untangling the confusions of destiny, is a point purely within the individual drama of Jesus of Nazareth: only as such, individual, does it become universal, relevant to all men.

Immediately this raises the question: If the transcendental point solves the riddles of human destiny, how can man's ordinary horizon of understanding—where we wrestle with injustice, crime, suffering, death, and so forth—be preserved as such and not be simply overridden? Applying this specifically to the drama of Jesus: How (within the ordinary horizon of existence) can he die in "ultimate" abandonment by God and yet be raised in a union with God that is equally "ultimate"? Initially the only reply we can give is this: what seems ultimate within the human horizon, and is experienced as such (Jesus does not experience some kind of ideological "transfiguration" in his death), is taken seriously in theo-drama—indeed, it is treated more "absolutely" than in any other drama—and precisely in this way it is transcended. It is transcended in the action of God, *as* the action of God, who, using the hieroglyphs of human destiny, writes his own, definitive word, a word which cannot be guessed in advance. And he writes it in such a way that, within the unity, the distinction remains: the convergence point that unravels man's fate does not become a universally available human horizon but is "witnessed to" (by witnesses like the heralds in ancient tragedy, like the "eyewitness" who tells Atossa of the defeat of her son, Xerxes, and of the victory of the Greeks)[2] and, accordingly, "believed". However, while the eyewitness is distinct from those who are only believers, in the case of the drama of Jesus, he is not dispensed from faith; he is in many ways dependent on faith in the very midst of his "beholding";[3] strangely enough, in fact, sight that is apparently direct yields no greater understanding than faith. The reverse is the case:[4] Jesus regards it as an advantage that he will vanish from his disciples' sight ("It is good for you that I go away") and that they will be given that inner insight which the Holy Spirit imparts to believers.[5] It is the Spirit who perfects the self-illumination that takes place in theo-drama; he reveals its meaning retrospectively, from the end, and at the same time proclaims its universal scope forward, into an ever-new future.

---

[2] "An eyewitness, not taught by others' words": Aeschylus, *The Persians*, 267.

[3] Cf. the risen (and vanished) Jesus is only "indirectly" recognized by the disciples on the Emmaus road: Lk 24:31. It is possible to doubt even in the midst of beholding: Mt 28:17. As Jesus says to Thomas: "Blessed are they who do not see and yet believe": Jn 20:29. Cf. also the way the women run away and disobey the angel of Resurrection: Mk 16:8. On the "eyewitness", cf. Markus Barth, *Der Augenzeuge* (EVZ, 1946), and *The Glory of the Lord* I, 311, 316, 324.

[4] Cf. the questions the disciples address to the transfigured Lord on the way to the Mount of Olives: Acts 1:6. On this topic, cf. Fernand Guimet, *Existenz und Ewigkeit* (Johannes Verlag, 1973), 39–49.

[5] Jn 16:7, 12ff.

b. The Transposition of Horizons and
the Theological Laws Governing It

On the basis of what we have already said, it will be clear that, for theo-drama, the problem of transposing historically limited horizons into other, equally limited horizons remains secondary. It is solely a case of different perspectives on the same universally human horizon; often, too, it involves the illusory hope that things which are part of man's ultimate horizon (like death, suffering and injustice) can be removed or at least regarded as themselves illusory and be transcended. In each case, deeper insight restores the horizon. This happens, for instance, when man realizes that he must combat moral and physical evil with all available means and yet will never banish it. (Man's triumphs are always offset by new evils; the fundamental nonvalues become immune to man's "medicines".)

No one can deny the necessity of undertaking certain trans-positions, for example, from the spiritual horizon of Jesus' time to that of our own. We only need to think of the geocentric model of the world; of the historical consciousness, limited to a few millennia; of the cosmological dress worn by theological relationships ("heaven"—"earth"—"hades"); and of the apocalyptic ideas promoted by all this. All the same, several laws must be observed when undertaking such transpositions.

1. Every transposition embarked upon by man has a theological a priori: the Holy Spirit, whose task is to universalize the drama of Christ; as a symbol of this, at Pentecost, he translates every language into every other language. "Are not all these who are speaking Galileans (and men of the first century)? And how is it that we hear, each of us in his own native language (including that of the twentieth century, and so forth)?" (Acts 2:7f.). And it is typical that this a priori transposition, which is of the substance of the theo-drama itself, still calls for faith (or at least something like it); for it is always possible to cast irony on the phenomenon: "They are filled with new wine".

2. Where there is no faith, there will be a tendency to con-centrate on the secondary, time-bound elements within a par-ticular horizon of understanding and to elevate them into primary ones; thus they will seem to be untranslatable and will have to be

abandoned. Examples of this are the apocalyptic, imminent expectation of the kingdom of God, the miracles of Jesus and the Virginal Birth. These are abandoned, but people still regard them as valid expressions *for their time*, expressions which, "unfortunately", are no longer realizable according to the contemporary world model; thus they must be "demythologized" and replaced by a mode of expression that is generally intelligible to the modern world. In such a substitution, however, the question is this: Are not these *chiffres*, which seem to belong to a world model of the past rather than of the present, constituted precisely in such a way that, through them, God was able to express a uniquely divine element of this unique drama, something that cannot be replaced by the categories of the universally human and the existential? In other words, should we not recognize this apparently secondary aspect (once familiar and no longer so) as the organic expression of something primary that imprints its primary character on what is alleged to be secondary? Karl Barth, for instance, has discovered this kind of primary character in the case of the Virgin Birth, and we must doubtless acknowledge the same to be true of the substance of the miracles of Jesus—"Even though you do not believe me, believe the works" (Jn 10:38). Where apocalyptic is concerned, we must be very careful not to set aside the primary elements that are (visibly) invested in what is visibly secondary. This is a test case, for the rejection of apocalyptic confronts us with the ultimate question: Was not Jesus deluded with regard to the details of his world view and with regard to his raison d'être as a whole?—in which case all transposition into modern terms is superfluous anyway. The neutral study of world models has the legitimate task of examining the vitality and fragility of the framework provided by a particular *Weltanschauung*; it is not the business of such study, however, but the business of faith alone, to ascertain how far primary revelation has been expressed in secondary and time-bound forms. Were this kind of combination of primary and secondary to be discovered, there would be two ways of resolving the difficulty. Either what is apparently secondary must be raised to the primary level, in which case the very thing that seems to be time-bound is not part of an obsolete framework but remains an adequate and supertemporal expression of the living revelation, as can be proved with certainty, in our view, in the case of the Virgin Birth. Or else we must say that revealed truths are expressed in an obsolete terminology or conceptual world (as in the apocalyptic terminology—in the narrower sense—of the apocryphal apocalypses of the time); and that, even then, at least in the mouth of Jesus and in the intention of the Spirit who inspires Scripture (even if the horizon of the hagiographers is restricted to that of their time, cf. 2 Pet, Jude, 2 Th), these utterances are intending to express *greater and different things* than can be contained in the limited concepts of the period. No doubt this can be applied to the texts referring to Jesus' expectation of the imminent coming of the kingdom.[6] We shall return to these questions in the context of Christology (in *Theo-Drama*, volume III).

3. If transpositions are to succeed, however, they must not be bought at the cost of losing any of revelation's substance or weight. The light that streams forth in the self-illumination of the dramatic action must be neither obscured nor trivialized, that is, robbed of its divine uniqueness. Naturally, therefore, the aim of "greater intelligibility for modern man" cannot be an ultimate criterion, particularly as what Jesus *really* meant then, even clothed in the conceptual garb of the time, cannot be limited to these concepts; furthermore, even when his words were understood, they caused the same offense then as they do today. When a translation has been made, it is often not clear at first glance whether there has been a loss of substance; it requires deeper reflection upon the organic interconnections of revelation. So, for instance, when attempting to "explain" the Virgin Birth in purely "modern" categories, we must take into account the consequences for Christology: if Joseph is the physical father of Jesus, how does he experience the Fourth Commandment— proclaimed by Yahweh—and how does the implied father-child relationship affect Jesus' relationship with his heavenly Father? Can this relationship still be regarded as qualitatively different from "adoption in place of a child", for instance, as practiced by the Old Testament kings? Is it any different from the new stage

[6] Cf. the brief summary (which calls for further expansion) in our study "Glaube und Naherwartung" in *Zuerst Gottes Reich*, Theologische Meditationen 13 (Benziger, 1966).

attained in the New Testament, where believers are "adopted as sons" (Gal 4:5), "born (again) of God" (Jn 1:13; 3:4), and are thus "children of God" (Rom 8:17)?

Plenty of other examples could be cited, for example, concerning the mode of continuance of the apostolic office (and hence, in particular, of the office of Peter) in the history of the Church: the loss of significance in the understanding of the pneumatic plenitude of power, of its origin and scope, has immediate and far-reaching consequences for those who seek to follow Christ in his obedience to the Father, an obedience that reconciles the world to God—though here too theological and spiritual reflection will not make any hastily drawn equations. In this context, for instance, we can take 2 Corinthians as our point of reference, a piece of writing from apostolic times that surely has the greatest dramatic tension within it, and we can ask: Is the full dramatic spectrum of this spiritual struggle between Paul and his community still to be found in the Church of today, and, if so, how can it be properly conducted? Or, arising from the view that apostolic authority cannot be transmitted (or only in a very limited manner) to successors, has not the real tension of this struggle and its inner theological content been reduced to something that is past, historical, archaeological and hence irrelevant to us? This would be a clear case of loss of substance.

Of course, the concept of "loss of substance" or of "weight" is not immediately obvious. "Weight" cannot be measured externally by the number of "propositions to be believed" or "commandments to be kept". As new dogmas and instructions are formulated down the centuries on the basis of revelation, this weight can become a burden "which neither our fathers nor we have been able to bear" (Acts 15:10). The "weight" we are speaking of is both qualitative and spiritual; it must not be interpreted in an integralist or fundamentalist manner; it itself calls for a "spiritual judgment" (1 Cor 2:15) on the part of the man who has a living faith. In framing its verdict, this spiritual judgment has regard to a totality or fullness which the believer can discern through the Holy Spirit, at least to the extent that, while he can never attain an overview of it, he can detect every substantial omission from it as a violation of the law of the whole, of inner proportion, or, rather, of the law of God's self-giving, which is "always more". We shall not go astray if we designate faith's sense of the whole, its sense of the "always more" of revelation—handed on in the Church in all its vitality —as the *"regula fidei"* of the early Fathers, which coincides neither with the objective substance of the *"Credo"* nor with the subjective act of faith on the part of the individual but is superior to both and mediates both.

c. The Regulating Church

Let us bear in mind that the self-illumination of the divine drama that involves the world remains constantly present and actual throughout the course of history. What takes place today is not the reverberating thunder following a lightning flash that occurred two thousand years ago but the Spirit of God manifesting himself here and now in "tongues of fire" over and in the Church of believers. Let us realize, furthermore, what an amazing thing it is for a great and diverse multitude of people —believers—to have a lively sense of the aforementioned totality of revelation down through the changing periods of history, even granted, as we have said, that the individual endowed with faith is also given a faculty enabling him to discern this totality (1 Jn 2:20). In the light of this it will seem not only appropriate but necessary for the entire community of the Church to be equipped with a special organ to serve as a regulatory principle for maintaining the integrity of revelation; its function is to indicate any serious interference with the balance of the Church's organism, any loss of substance or weight. Such an organ would be the embodiment of the *regula fidei* within the community of the Church as a whole.

Here lies the importance of what we are accustomed to call the *Church's teaching office*. Initially we observed that theology can only be a hermeneutics of revelation and that revelation, in turn, as God's self-interpretation in Christ to and for the Church, is also hermeneutics; the former is oriented to the latter, whereas the latter must explicate itself in terms of the former. Hence, theologically speaking, the "teaching office" can only be situated within the area of the latter hermeneutics (which is naturally the fundamental one). Its task is to preserve, for believers, the totality of God's self-interpretation in Christ, through the Spirit, in and for the Church. Certainly this includes a relationship with theology, but it is no longer concerned with putting the events of revelation into theological concepts, let alone "systems". The "teaching office" will react—like a seismographical instrument—when some substantial underground tremor threatens the totality or catholicity of revelation. When a theological proposition, for instance, which is correct within the total context, is emphasized so one-sidedly, or is so wrenched from its organic place in the heart of the organism, that the organism's inner harmony, expressed by the *regula fidei*, seems to be upset. Such displacement can occur in the area of theological formulations, but here too, of course, the individual propositions have to fit into a balanced totality; the same proposition can bear a different charge in the mouth of Augustine and in that of Jansen. The "teaching office" is not primarily concerned with the formulation but with the charge it bears. Its particular definitions and condemnations are always made with a view to reestablishing the endangered totality. The theologian strives toward this totality; the "teaching office" pronounces on the basis of it. The latter's role need not always be a negative one; it can also consist in examining some element which the Church's (theological or more spiritual) reflection has come to regard as part of revelation's organic center and in expressly setting it forth as part of the totality. Here the essential thing is not so much that the specific content can be shown to have been there all down the centuries, right back to its origin, as something consciously possessed; it is much more important to show that the organism of truth must have carried this particular organ within it in order to function healthily, whether or not it was clearly or less clearly conscious of the organ itself. What is crucial is that, when the truth is seen from within, the same balance is always maintained. (Seen from the outside, supplementary definitions will always look like "papistical innovations".)

These observations will serve as a preface to our explicit discussion of Holy Scripture. When it speaks on its own account, the "teaching office" will have to base itself on Scripture. However, what we are concerned with here is God's living, ever-present and ever-relevant self-interpretation in what he does for and with men; so, whenever it is a case of the laws of transposition, we can and must also speak directly about this regulatory function. First of all the "teaching office" is a reality here and now because the event that has taken place between God and man is to be proclaimed to the world as something that is *always taking place in an ever-new "now"*. Not as a mere (epic) report of some past dramatic happening; it must always refer to the fact that this historical phenomenon, as such, is of all times, always "today". So the Apostles preached, and so it must be preached through all ages. Here too the "teaching office" has a regulatory role. Every Christian has the task of proclamation through his life and his words, but this message must first be proclaimed to him, and with authority. For revelation not only interprets itself authoritatively in and to the Church; *as* revelation it also explicitly and officially imparts authority. Thus, for every age, revelation is both a proclaimed revelation and at the same time a self-interpreting revelation: "As the Father sent me, so I send you"; "Whoever hears you, hears me"; "We also thank God constantly for this, that when you received the word of God which you heard from us, you accepted it not as the word of men but as what it really is, the word of God, which is at work in you believers" (1 Th 2:13).

Without denying that theological study enjoys the help of the Holy Spirit or wanting to represent theology as of no consequence to the Church—for, as we have shown, God's self-interpretation takes place essentially in the medium of man and his receptivity to it—the foregoing does bring to light the difference between teaching office (that is, official proclamation) and theology.

2. *The Place of Scripture in Theo-Drama*

a. A Word That Journeys with Us

The tremendous role of the Bible in the Christian religion seems to throw doubt on the latter's dramatic dimension. Are we not presented with an epic account of what has taken place, and is not all subsequent and future history subjected to this final, immovable word? According to this view of things, hermeneutics would limit itself to establishing as securely as possible the meaning found in the document; it would then go on to confront the meaning, thus attained, with the contemporary understanding of existence and critically assess the former by the latter or vice versa—depending on whether the biblical horizon were seen merely as one among others, "of its time", or whether the possibility were entertained that (in addition?) the Bible might go one crucial dimension further than any and every particular cultural era (cf. Mt 24:35). Speaking of Scripture as the *"norma normans"*—but what for?—heightens the impression that everything that takes place in the dramatic mode proceeds under the aegis and according to the rules of a fixed, written text that determines everything in advance, even if these rules leave room for free decisions.

Scripture's real position as related to theo-drama is in fact much more complex; so complex, indeed, that it cannot be reduced to any comprehensive formula.

First of all it is clear that Scripture is by no means the finished stage text governing the enacting of real history; evidently, the scriptural text becomes fixed at the end of events rather than at the beginning. To say nothing of the earliest history: we know nothing of things that were written at the time of the history of the Patriarchs; oral tradition on this subject and on the Exodus and the period of the Judges reaches back for centuries, to be collected at the time of the Kings and—in a process that, in terms of salvation history, does not adopt a high profile—is unified, formulated and fixed in a rough-and-ready fashion. Similarly, in the age of the Prophets, it remains relatively unimportant whether they deliver their oracles purely orally or put them down in writing or have them written down by their disciples. Furthermore, this totality, even in its written form, is continually moving. What is written is continually being reread and reinterpreted; as its deeper meaning comes to light or its current relevance comes into focus, it is reformulated, interpolated, brought up to date, heedless of anachronisms; this is done with the consciousness that the same, onward-rolling history permits and demands it. So it often happens that the most diverse layers of tradition are found in a single text, resulting in the difficult problem of deciding which layer contains the "authentic" meaning. This applies by no means only in the case of the Old Testament but equally, in a certain respect, to the New. Christ himself is so much the incarnate Deed and Word of God that it would be quite inappropriate for him to write anything. When, nonetheless, his history comes to be written down, the writing of it shows, not (as in the Old Testament) progress in revelation itself, but progress in understanding and reflection upon it. Concern for the transmission of what "really happened" goes hand in hand with concern that these past events shall be represented, not as naked facts (which would be merely the surface level), but in the fullness of what was "really intended" and which is only now, in the wake of Easter, being understood. These different layers of reflection upon the profound meaning of the Word that is made flesh in Jesus can be recognized everywhere in the text of the New Testament; again, it is impossible to say whether an earlier or a later stage is closer to what is really meant, nearer to the center of the fullness of the Word. Since it is a case of God's final Word, its truth cannot be equated with naked historical facts, now less than ever; similarly, this truth's self-interpretation in terms of an ecclesial understanding cannot be regarded as a secondary process, neatly separable from "history". Jesus always possessed the fullness of the Spirit (Jn 3:34); what he said and did could not be understood by the disciples until the Spirit came upon them (Jn 7:39); only in the light of the exalted Lord who pours forth the Pneuma do they become able to put into words something of what has really taken place.[7] So the word of the New Testament is equally a word that journeys, proceeding once for

[7] Indeed, we may wonder whether the radiance of Easter, shining on past events, did not shed light preeminently on those words and deeds of Jesus that the disciples had not understood and which stuck in their memories as such. This could explain, in part, the problem of the difference between the Synoptic and the Johannine picture of Jesus: the mind of the Fourth Evangelist, with his deeper grasp, retained things that the others largely missed. No one has yet explained the source of the "meteor from the Johannine heaven" in Matthew and Luke, which does not appear in the same form in John (Mt 11:24ff.; Lk 10:12ff.). It argues for the historicity of an entire layer, which otherwise is only spotlighted with the same explicitness in John.

all along the path from the earthly Jesus to the exalted Christ—
and yet, in the Holy Spirit, it is new at every moment for
everyone who hears it. It is the path through death to resurrection, and every Christian, in his discipleship, must take this
path. In the New Testament also, therefore, we should hesitate
to prefer an older "layer" to a younger one; here too each layer
retains its own inalienable value, which must not be sacrificed to
a "forward-moving" integration. (One thinks of the layers
constituting the development of christological reflection.) Thus
we can risk making the general proposition that the meaning of
Scripture (where it is in process of development) journeys along
with history, and this journeying is attested to not merely
externally but in the details of its text. Of course, this raises the
problem of how this journeying of the word is related to the
closing of objective revelation at the end of the apostolic age and
to the completeness of the canon of Scripture. The "closing" as
such arises from the definitive and unsurpassable character of
the divine Word uttered in Jesus; but the fact that the Word is
henceforth present in world history in this fullest form, capable
of infinite assimilation and interpretation, is in truth not a
"closing" at all but the widest imaginable "opening". One sign
of this is that this form of presence in world history will
provoke far more dramatic reactions than the progressive form
in the preparatory epoch of the Old Covenant. "My words will
never pass away", says Jesus, and preeminent among these
"words" is the effectual word of his Cross and his Resurrection;
until the end of the world this word will present the human
spirit with a fundamental choice.

    Another problem connected with the "closing" of the scrip-
tural corpus is that of the relationship between the words and
deeds of the historical Jesus and the formulations of post-Easter
prophecy within the Church. The final redaction of Scripture
does not need to coincide absolutely, in a *material* sense, with the
actual spoken words of Jesus, with the actual shape of his deeds
and movements. "I have yet many things to say to you, but you
cannot bear them now" (Jn 16:12): this cannot refer only to
those unsaid words of Jesus that can be formulated by "the
Spirit of truth, who will guide you into all the truth" (16:13) for
the benefit of the Church in her deepening understanding; it

must also refer to words actually uttered but formulated in an inchoate and preliminary manner, which are now fleshed out in a linguistic form appropriate to the new understanding. The disciples' words at the end of the farewell discourses: "Ah, now you are speaking plainly, not in any figure! Now we know that you know all things . . . , by this we believe . . ." (Jn 16:29f.) can be regarded as a post-Easter profession of faith. The Spirit who interprets Jesus' deeds and words—his own Spirit— guarantees the objectively appropriate form of expression, which is in that sense a final, "closing" form. The same thing applies to post-Easter accounts (such as the account of Pentecost): through the inspiration of the Spirit, the writers find appropriate images and symbols in which to express the historical events in a way that can speak to men. They cannot be reduced to something "underlying" them, nor can they be distilled into some general abstract truth. They are limbs of the living body of Scripture and can only participate in the life of the whole if they are left intact. It is the final form that is normative. Its definite and definitive quality is all of a piece with the decisiveness and resoluteness of God's offer of salvation. And God's last word has not been said until the "word" "resurrection" has been developed and formulated in such a way that its whole range is made visible. God's final word is so vast, however, that it makes room for us to hear his silence too, just as the stars reveal the night sky.

b. A Word That Is Both
Attested and Generative

On the other hand, the testimony of Scripture is not external to the events, insofar as the latter are themselves understood, in biblical terms, as "words", "utterances", "judgments" of God. The unity of word and event is expressed both in the Old Testament *dabar* and in the New Testament *rhēma*. It can happen that the "utterance" precedes the "historical event", so that, when the word "comes to pass", Israel may acknowledge Yahweh's might and infallibility (Is 42:9); but the utterance refers to the event, it does not remain "empty" or without result (Is 55:11): "I the Lord have spoken, and I will do it" (Ezek

17:24).[8] The antecedent word is sovereign, but it also has a dialogue character: it is superior to Israel's reaction to it, yet ultimately such a reaction is precisely what it is aiming at. Indeed, it is always proclaimed by a spokesman of God within Israel, someone who has understood it and affirms it. It is a word within the "Covenant", that is, a word journeying toward incarnation. Hence it is a word that goes step by step with the people, although we cannot speak of continuous progress. It is hard to decide whether the particular step forward consists more in the initiative of the word of God or more in the response of Israel (and subsequently of the primitive Church) to God's effectual word. Even if it is successful, Israel's response must be ascribed to the deed character of the word: it is ascribed to the Spirit—*ruach*—of God. In this category are the development and formulation of the chief commandment (the *Shema*, Dt 6:4ff.) on the basis of existing covenant law, or the step from the suffering of Job to that of the Suffering Servant. At the same time we must remember that, corresponding to the nature of God's word, each step contains something ultimate within it, something that is not "superseded" by the next step. (Thus in the gospel the tables of the Ten Commandments are just as much in evidence as the Shema, and on the Cross the words of Job become real just as much as the silent sufferings of the Suffering Servant.) So what Scripture subsequently (and yet throughout its "journeying") embraces as the word of God and puts into human words has an inner continuity with the word of God that is always active in history: at times it is the latter itself, at others it is its reflection.

As for this reflection, it too cannot be separated from the word itself with total clarity. Since God's word [*Wort*] always involves dialogue and creates some kind of hearing faculty in its dialogue partner, it already contains an answer [*Antwort*] within it. Under certain circumstances, this can be a negative answer: the hardhearted or stiff-necked reaction, the turning away; but this too, as the shape of the answer [*Antwort*], is inscribed within the word [*Wort*]. On the other hand, the answer which the word seeks to elicit always implies that the person answering has (in

---

[8] Cf. Ezek 22:14; 24:14; 36:36; 37:14.

one way or another) *heard*, that is, it presupposes the word. And the more adequate the answer, the more it itself becomes a (dialogic) word. A psalm can be a meditation on the word or a hymn in praise of the God who speaks or a cry of entreaty to him: overshadowed by the Spirit, this answer is so adequate that it can be taken over by the word. The same is true of the Wisdom books as a whole and of the prophetical word (and here it does not matter whether this word is directly infused or has undergone a process of reflection in the prophet's mind). Thus we can understand the continuity between the answering believer and the hagiographer: the scriptural word that attests [*bezeugend*] is not external to the word of God that is attested [*bezeugt*] (or, to put it more profoundly, that "implants and generates itself" [*sich einzeugend*]), and, although the two are not simply identical, the generative [*zeugend*] word can make constant use of the attesting [*bezeugend*] word in order to make itself present, in the latter, for the individual believer. For although, in one respect, the written word *as such* can never contain the "breadth and length and height and depth" of the incarnate Word—as Scripture itself clearly testifies (Jn 20:30; 21:25)—this testimony, since it is inspired by the Spirit, is always more than itself: what seems on the surface to be a book is inwardly "spirit and life"; it is always ready to be used and interpreted by the living God according to his design, to be disclosed to the individual who loves him, or the group or the epoch, as a word that is new and ever-new beyond all imagining.

The externally fragmentary and unsystematic character of the biblical books in itself provides a useful instrument for this purpose. "*Biblia*" is a collection of writings of every possible literary genre, including occasional writings (the apostolic letters), poems, prayers, proverbs, laws, chronicles, oracles, secret revelations, laments, sober instruction for the Christian life. . . . This apparent confusion is crisscrossed by threads, open and hidden, linking everything with everything else; thus a kind of vast net is created (with a coarse mesh or a fine one?) within which the attested and generative word of God can traverse unhindered. The net embraces the contents, and yet it does not hold them fast: it is so loose and broad that, in principle, it loses nothing of the contents, but it does not claim to be itself the whole content. On the other hand it is not vague, because the word always has a specific content—nothing is more specific than the infinite God—and, if Scripture "leaves things open", it only does so in the sense that it makes room for the incarnate Word of God who attests himself in and through the same Scripture.

There is one more thing that we must not forget: Jesus knows that he is the Word uttered by and testifying to the Father, but at the same time he himself can refer to the Father as the one who speaks: "As I hear, I judge" (Jn 5:30), "What I say, therefore, I say as the Father has bidden me" (Jn 12:50), "I speak thus as the Father taught me" (Jn 8:28). But Jesus can also hear this infinitely specific word of the Father resounding from the iron finality of the Old Testament words of God: "It is written, 'You shall worship the Lord your God and him only shall you serve' " (Mt 4:10). For him, the fixed, written word radiates with all the fullness of divine power and decision; thus he replies to the Sadducees: "Is not this why you are wrong, that you know neither the Scriptures nor the power of God?" (Mk 12:24; Mt 22:29). But at the same time—in all the Gospels—he sees this fixed word moving toward himself: Moses wrote of him (Jn 5:46; cf. Lk 24:27), and the prophecy of salvation is fulfilled in him (Lk 4:21).

c. Gramma and Pneuma

All this is further confirmed by the stark opposition, frequently made by Paul, between "gramma" and "pneuma", which, in view of the contexts (Rom 2:27f.; 6:7; 2 Cor 3:6f., 14ff.), can only be interpreted as an opposition between the "Old Covenant" (2 Cor 3:14) insofar as it is "fading away" (v. 11) and "obsolete" (Rom 7:6: *palaiotēs grammatos*: the obsolete written word), and the "new" Covenant prophesied by Jeremiah (31:33), in which God will put his law within them and will write it upon their hearts. At its core, this opposition is not between "the letter" and "the spirit"; "the letter" ("tablets of stone", 2 Cor 3:3) refers to a merely external aspect; the negative side of the old "written word" (*graphē*), the side that must be transcended, is not the fact that it was written down: it lies in the "fleshly" character of the old Mosaic law. It is characteristic that, in Romans, "flesh" (together with "law", "circumcision" and "letter") is opposed to "heart" (Rom 2:25–29); but "heart" does not denote spiritual inwardness as contrasted with physical outwardness, otherwise Paul could not tell the Corinthians that they themselves were a letter of recommendation "written with the Spirit of the living God, not on tablets of stone but on tablets of the human heart" (2 Cor 3:3). To the transitory fleshly institution ("circumcision" as a sign of belonging to the "Old Covenant") there corresponds a quite different, much more profound, incarnational fleshly reality in which, through the Holy Spirit, God's law is inwardly "enfleshed" in the human heart. When Paul says, abruptly, that "the written code kills, but the Spirit gives life" (2 Cor 3:6), he is thinking not so much of the Scripture which consists of written characters but of the "prescriptions of the law",[9] which must remain unfulfilled— with regard to God's deepest purpose—until the coming of Christ and which thus emphasize the chasm between God's requirement and human weakness and guilt.

For Paul, therefore, as for all the other New Testament writers, the ancient Scripture (*graphē*) remains most definitely inspired by the Holy Spirit of God,[10] but this Spirit is already (covertly) the Spirit of Christ, as is said explicitly in 1 Peter 1:11.[11] The view similarly found throughout the whole of the New Testament, that the entire Old Covenant (and hence the entire Old Testament) is "fulfilled" (*plērōthēnai*) and has "reached perfection" (*teleiōthēnai*) in Christ's life, death and Resurrection, is simply another expression of the same thing. Objectively

---

[9] *Th. W.* I, 763 (Schrenk).

[10] Mt 22:43 = Mk 12:36; Acts 1:16 (all three passages are concerned with David's inspiration by the Spirit); Acts 28:25 (Isaiah's inspiration by the Spirit); 2 Pet 1:21: "men moved by the Holy Spirit spoke from God"; 2 Tim 3:16: "All Scripture is inspired by God". There are numerous other places showing clearly that it is God who speaks in the ancient Scriptures.

[11] The prophets "inquired what person or time was indicated by the Spirit of Christ within them when predicting the sufferings of Christ and the subsequent glory"; thus, ultimately, they were ministering, not to themselves (i.e., to their own time) but to the believers of the New Covenant, "in the things which have now been announced to you by those who preached the good news to you through the Holy Spirit sent from heaven" (1 Pet 1:12).

speaking, this could only be understood properly in a proleptic sense, and in the Old Covenant this was subjectively impossible; even less could there be a response to it in terms of deeds; this hiatus and deficiency result in "gramma", unfulfillable prescription. All searching of the Scriptures is in vain if Christ is not sought and found there, for they speak of him (Jn 5:46). Insofar as "gramma" signifies deficiency, therefore, it simply cannot be fulfilled; it *must* "kill", for only the incarnational Spirit can give life.

This shows us the ontologically different characters of Old and New Testament Scripture. Origen had a particularly fine sensitivity to this.[12] Insofar as the ancient Scriptures are only journeying toward the Incarnation of the Word, there is something "abstract" about them, in spite of their proleptic intent and their accompanying forward movement. Scripture is a "pre-scription" in more than one sense: it is a written preliminary to what will be the concrete existence of the Word; it is a regulation or decree, anterior to the possibility of its fulfillment; to that extent it has a recognizable and circumscribed meaning which, in its fixed, written form, can only contain a small particle of the full reality, which—in the Incarnation of the Word of God—will flatten all the barriers of meaning, empowering us "to comprehend what is the breadth and length and height and depth" of "the love of Christ which surpasses knowledge" (Eph 3:18f.). Whenever, in the New Testament, anything is said about this fullness—orally or in the written

---

[12] Texts in H. de Lubac, *Histoire et Esprit* (Paris, 1950) [*Geist aus der Geschichte. Das Schriftverständnis des Origenes* (1968)]. The changed character of New Testament Scripture is shown in that "flesh" and "pneuma" are brought center-stage, whereas the written word acquires an almost incidental character. This provides a basis for ideas such as that of Irenaeus: "If the Apostles had left no writings behind them, we should have had to follow the order of the tradition they handed on to those to whom they entrusted the Church" (*Adv. Haer.* III, 4, 1–2). This is not the case, as most commentators say, of a mere "irrealis" (Von Campenhausen, *Kirchliches Amt und geistliche Vollmacht*, 2d ed. [1963], 187), for in IV, 16, 3, with regard to the Patriarchs, Irenaeus says that they needed no Decalogue because it was written into their God-fearing souls: "They needed no Scripture to admonish them, for they possessed within themselves the righteousness of the law." Cf. III, 4, 2: the barbarians who, on the basis of "tradition" "sine litteris", received and followed the faith.

word—it is always an expression of the fullness itself. The christological paradox, that is, that "the whole fullness of deity dwells bodily" in the individual man, Christ (Col 2:9; cf. 1:19), also governs the shape of the new Scripture, with the result that it cannot be compared to any other book. This fact, that the New Testament is governed by Christology, moved Origen to designate Scripture as *one* mode of the enfleshing of the Logos (in addition to the enfleshing in his physical body and in his eucharistic-ecclesial Body).[13] This way of speaking can be approved provided we keep in mind that one form of the Body is able to pass over into another, that is, if we maintain the integration of all aspects into the total incarnational form. The physical body would be inarticulate, and hence not the body of the Word, if this Word were not also enfleshed in human language (which is documented by so-called "Scripture"), and if this Word (both the physical and the uttered Word) did not give rise, in the believers who receive it, through Eucharist and preaching, to the Body of the Church. Once we have seen this, we can regard the ancient Scripture (*graphē*) as part of this Incarnation event in the way the New Testament writers and subsequent tradition held it to be. The coming-into-being of the Incarnation is rooted in the faith of Abraham, who looked forward to the Day of Christ (Jn 8:56), in the faith of Moses, who "considered abuse suffered for the Christ greater wealth than the treasures of Egypt" (Heb 11:26), and in the faith of the prophets who were inspired by the Spirit of Christ (1 Pet 1:11). All that is seen proleptically, however, is only incorporated in the fulfillment when the latter eventually arrives.

The purpose of these remarks has been to refute the superficial idea that, in theo-drama, Scripture plays the part of a somehow uninvolved spectator and reporter who can survey the whole process and can "tell in advance who the murderer is". In all its aspects, Scripture is something quite different: it is part of the drama itself, moving along with it. We have seen how rich it is in perspectives not only in the unimaginable wealth of its

---

[13] Texts in H. de Lubac (see preceding note), 393ff.; also H. de Lubac, "Textes alexandrins et bouddhiques", *RSR* 27 (1937), 336–51.

interrelated utterances but in the various layers found in each individual utterance, as modern exegesis is increasingly discovering. We have also seen that we cannot make an absolute distinction between the attesting (and generative) Word and the attested Word. We cannot say that Scripture is the Holy Spirit's testimony [*Bezeugung*] to the fact that God's Logos has borne witness to himself by his power of generation [*sich zeugend bezeugt habe*], for the Logos himself speaks in the Holy Spirit, and the Spirit "will take what is mine and declare it to you" and interpret it (Jn 16:14). And Jesus adds: "All that the Father has is mine; therefore I said that he will take what is mine and declare it to you." The Father testifies to himself through the Son and the Spirit; the fact that he is the abundant Source is made manifest through all the aspects of the Incarnation event.

With regard to scriptural hermeneutics, we can also see that it is a precarious undertaking to try to distinguish several "senses of Scripture". Of course, since it is a question of incarnation (and the "prologue" to it found in the Old Testament), the fundamental meaning will be the "historical", the directly human meaning and the meaning intended by the writer. But on the basis of all we have said, it is clear that the "spiritual" sense is not some second meaning above or behind it: the "spiritual" sense is the central, christological sense that is always contained in the "historical". This "spiritual", christological and pneumatic meaning can inwardly unfold itself as the Good News of God-given grace, which as such wants to incarnate itself in the faith and life of the man who hears it (the "moral" or "tropological" sense) and directs his gaze ahead to a fulfillment (the "anagogical" or eschatological sense), which is made plain in the Risen Christ and is as yet hidden in the believer, as a present reality embraced in hope. All these aspects are interrelated and merge into one another; the four classical senses to which we have referred are not fixed stopping places: there are many intermediate points. Nor is the sequence itself irreversible: thus the moral appeal issued by God's gracious action can presuppose the eschatological aspect of perfection, containing it as one of its elements.

If we let the "gramma/pneuma" antithesis stand in all its

radical contrast, as the watershed between the old and the new
aeon,[14] it is clear that the only really Christian interpretation of
Scripture is a pneumatic one, that is, one which reads the
(ancient) Scripture (*graphē*) with a view to the Incarnation of the
entire divine Word and all subsequent Scripture in the light of
that Incarnation; furthermore, it will seek to interpret what it
reads by the Pneuma of Christ. However, insofar as Scripture
as a whole is only one aspect of the Word's total Incarnation
event, not separable from the others, Scripture shares in the
theodramatic character of this totality.

This has two consequences for the interpretation of Scripture.
First, since God's entire purpose for the world is present in
every phase of theo-drama—although human freedom is not
thereby upstaged, even when God utters his final and unsurpassable Word in Christ—the entirety of the word must also be
present, at all times, in the individual books and words of
Scripture, however much they may characterize one particular
aspect, one particular phase. God's word can reveal itself anew
from an infinite number of sides, but it cannot be parcelled out.
Therefore, if we are to proceed theologically, the individual
passage can only be properly interpreted within the total context of Scripture, however much effort we must first invest in
ascertaining its particular meaning, its special significance, and
so forth.

Second, insofar as Scripture is one aspect of the ongoing
theo-drama (and we, as believers, are involved in its unfolding
course), Scripture cannot and will not communicate to us some
kind of dispassionate knowledge or set us on some lofty vantage
point—not even when it comes to uttering God's final and
definitive Word. Precisely because this Word is a total word of
salvation—a Yes that has no No (2 Cor 1:19)—we are faced,
more dramatically than ever, with a decision: Shall we respond
with an adequate Amen (2 Cor 1:20) or not? It is on the basis of
this paradox, namely, that the decision has been both made and
not yet made—the paradox that will occupy us throughout our
study of theo-drama—that Scripture as a whole remains the word

---

[14] E. Käsemann, *Geist und Buchstabe. Paulinische Perspektiven*, 2d ed. (1972),
236–85 [*Perpectives on Paul* (Fortress)]; cf. also his *An die Römer* (Tübingen:
Mohr, 1973), 68, 71 [*Romans* (SCM)].

of God, "living and active, sharper than any two-edged sword, piercing to the division of soul and spirit, of joints and marrow" (Heb 4:12). This paradox is what makes Scripture a dramatic instrument in the hand of the saving and judging Word. Thus active and operative, Scripture interprets its meaning and so performs its own hermeneutics. And in doing so it also outlines the form of theological proof.

3. On the Structure of Theological Proof

a. The Self-Attesting Fact

The question of the structure of theological proof—a question that belongs in a "theo-logic"—cannot be answered systematically here. We must restrict ourselves to drawing the relevant consequences from what we have already said, in anticipation of the theodramatic theory to be set forth. This very word, "theo-drama", gives a valuable clue as to the direction in which theological proof should be developed and tested. A method of proof that diminished the dramatic character of the Christian event would automatically show itself to be a failure. Such are all the attempts to separate knowledge from faith and from testimony or which allow the latter to sink to the level of mere subordinate elements. In such cases the history that involves God and man is eviscerated, absorbed into a "system" that can be viewed and grasped as a whole, and in particular the dramatic climax of the biblical end-time is obliterated in a "nontime", a twilight in which Minerva's owl can fly.

The historical fact remains not only the point of departure of all theological proof but also its permanent point of reference. The final and unavoidable paradox is that, precisely in this contingent fact, the ultimate Logos (who embraces all that is both factual and ideal) has appeared on the scene. With that single "point" of fact, the sphere of the eternal touches the temporal sphere, and this point alone can spread meaning that is ultimate [*end-gültig*, that is, that will "hold good at the end"] to the whole realm of fact, the whole history of the world and of humanity. What is unique in history must also be unique as far as God is concerned, otherwise the allegedly historical unique will sink back into myth or the realm of the mere symbol. This means that the theological proof—circling round the One reality —can only move simultaneously in two directions: on the one hand, seeking firmly to establish the historical fact in its uniqueness and, on the other, endeavoring to show that this fact contains a meaning that embraces, consummates and transcends every other projected meaning. So it is not only that the historical fact presents us with one impressive interpretation of the world, capable of holding its ground among others: here, quite explicitly, we are presented with a total meaning which—in spite of its historical, a posteriori character—cannot be surpassed; it is "always more" than we can imagine, and this is something we can read from it a priori.

Subsequent reflection can lead us to separate the two aspects and give a natural priority to the first, developing it into a distinct science ("exegesis", "fundamental theology"—however that may be conceived); the "credibility" of the chief witnesses will have to be assessed, next that of the supporting witnesses and finally the credibility of the Scriptures that testify to the witnesses; only then, after this has proved sufficiently reliable, can reflection go on, in a second science ("theology", "dogmatics") to ponder the momentous meaning contained in the testimony. Clearly, there is something wrong with this analytical process: the Witness who proclaims the fact, or rather, the Fact who witnesses to Himself, also—inseparably—bears witness to his eternal, a priori unsurpassable meaning; thus the reflecting person is faced with a choice: either he rejects the supporting testimony (for example, by accusing the supporting witnesses, Paul and John, of a faulty or excessive interpretation of Christ, the chief witness), or else he must acknowledge the integrity of the foundational testimony to be part of the Fact (in which case he is acting as a "dogmatician" as well as an "exegete" or "fundamental theologian").

In other words, there is an initial and basically human appeal about the fact's testimony, allowing us to weigh the seriousness and reliability of the witness with a degree of certainty. The limits of this criterion become visible, however, in the martyr (the development of the word *martyr* and *martyrion* from simple oral testimony to the testimony of blood is significant, though difficult to demonstrate),[15] for many a man has gone to his death for the sake of an opinion, a teaching, a *Weltanschauung*, and that in itself does not prove the objective correctness of these ideas; why should not Jesus of Nazareth have been such a man? If this were the case, the blood-martyrdom of the secondary witness, assimilating him to the prime witness, would be of little value. It must be the other way round: the entire testimony of Jesus must allow us to discern that his Passion, in particular, forms a part of its meaning; it is by no means a mere confirmation, at the level of ordinary human meaningfulness, of the truth of his teaching (cf. Socrates) but an integrating element of his unique truth. Only on this basis can Christian martyrdom serve as a kind of proof of (or pointer toward) the truth of the Christian fact. Before Pilate, Jesus testifies to his kingship (or his office as Messiah and fulfiller of all God's promises), but it is a kingship that consists in bearing witness to the truth; ultimately this witness is his Passion, which proves the truth of the Father's love in surrendering his Son to the world for the world's sake. His kingdom is "not of this world", but it does not transcend history either, because "for this I have come into the world": it is the suprahistorical kingdom of God which, through *this particular* history, incarnates itself in *all* history (Jn 18:33–37).

A posteriori and a priori are inseparable here. This means that we are always presented with the *entire* phenomenon of Christian revelation within history: only the Whole can bear witness to itself and prove itself to be the unsurpassable reality it *must* be, if God himself, the Unique One, is involved in this unique train of events. God, "than whom nothing greater can be thought", must demonstrate his presence in the unfolding history of

---

[15] Norbert Brox, *Zeuge und Märtyrer, Untersuchungen zur frühchristlichen Zeugnis-Terminologie*, Studien zum Alten und Neuen Testament V (Munich: Kösel, 1961). Brox denies that there is a direct transition from the biblical word-testimony to the second-century blood-testimony. He denies, in other words, that the latter is directly dependent on the former. He finds the theological cause leading to the later concept of martyrdom in the anti-Docetic tendency of Ignatius of Antioch (blood-martyrdom "proves" that Christ really suffered). He sees the philological cause in the presence of a secular Greek concept of deed-testimony alongside the word-testimony, unconnected with the latter's biblical form.

revelation in such a way that it too, the drama of God and man, shows itself to be something "than which nothing greater can be thought". The crucial question for the problem of theological proof is whether there can be such a demonstration and what shape it might take.

b. Pointers to the (Ever-Greater) Totality

A single proof concerning one aspect of revealed truth can only be conducted, therefore, if this aspect is evaluated on the basis of the totality and its place within it. This always presupposes that the totality can only come into view where there is acceptance of (that is, faith in) the One who is bearing witness to himself. This is because the God who, in the testimony, is bearing witness to himself—for he is the prime Witness—remains sovereignly free, even when revealing himself; but he is so free that he is able to create beings who are themselves free, whose freedom he can bring to perfection by his own free self-revelation and self-giving. Thus we can indeed express this totality in the words "*Soli Deo Gloria*", provided we add that God's grace glorifies itself in his creation and revelation (Eph 1:6, 12, 14), that "the God of love did not need man, but man needed the glory of God",[16] that it is "the glory of man to abide in the service of God",[17] because "the glory of man is God";[18] and for that very reason the "living man" who has been led to perfect freedom "is the glory of God".[19] Thus the starting point for beholding this (ever-greater) totality is that primal relationship between God and the world (man) that leaves God, the Creator and Redeemer (through his self-communication), free to allow free, created beings to exist. They come into existence out of him, exist in his presence, they are in him and oriented toward him. We can speak of the "*analogia entis*" here, insofar as, on the one side, this relationship is distinguished from a pantheism or theopanism which dissolves God into the world or the world into God (and hence, dissolving the interplay of divine and created freedoms,

---

[16] Irenaeus, *Adv. Haer.* IV, 16, 6.
[17] *Ibid.*, IV, 14, 1.
[18] *Ibid.*, III, 20, 2.
[19] *Ibid.*, IV, 20, 7.

abolishes theo-drama). On the other side, it must be distinguished from every form of pure dualism, which either isolates God's divinity from the world and closes it in on itself (Deism) or isolates the world's secularity from God (resulting in sin being seen as a fall from the divine realm, secularism and the God-is-dead theology). The possibility of distinguishing between God —who "is all" (Sir 43:27) and thus needs nothing—and a world of finite beings who need God remains the fundamental mystery. It grounds everything that comes after, while not being deducible from anything. To it there is no "greater" alternative. It can only be illuminated by the infinite freedom of God, who shows himself, *in* (but not of necessity *through*) the existence of what is not God, to be "He-who-is-always-greater": we can never catch up with him. We must keep the field free for this "ever-greater" God if we wish to guarantee the possibility of the theodramatic dimension: we must assert that unconditional (divine) freedom in no way threatens the existence of conditional (creaturely) freedom, at whatever historical stage the latter may find itself—whether it is close to the former, alienated from it or coming back to its real self.

A corollary follows from this: in the primal Creator/creature relationship, the Creator (who is "ever-greater") remains superior to all attempts on the part of the creature to grasp him; all the same, he cannot be simply unknown to the creature, even if initially this only means that the creature knows of its creaturely, wholly conditional nature and can thus conclude that it must owe its origin to some primal ground. But even when God goes on to give his creature a new, deeper knowledge and participation, such revelation only causes the Revealer's freedom to shine forth even more brightly; it makes it impossible for man to turn this gift he has received into a possession of his own, impossible for him to dissolve the faith which trusts (and the insight which he gains *within* such faith) into some kind of autonomous knowledge. There is nothing obscure or contradictory about the constant assertion of Christian theology and spirituality that, as our insight into God's marvels increases and as our familiarity (*familiaritas*) with him grows, our reverence (*timor filialis*) is also heightened, as we can clearly see from Jesus' own attitude toward his Father. The analogy of interpersonal drama can help our understanding here: where there is genuine personal love between two people, there is a simultaneous growth in intimacy and in respect for the other person's freedom. So God cannot be simply the "Wholly Other" (and hence the Unknowable), but neither can the "revealed [*geoffenbart*] religion" become "religion unveiled" [*offenbar*], transmuted into some kind of absolute information about God.

This yields a *second* feature, namely, a fundamental realism vis-à-vis the world, which, with its bottomless suffering, its dubious aspect and its positive meaninglessness, resists all Idealism's attempts to interpret it away. But it also resists every future-oriented utopianism on the part of Socialism. And, at a deeper level, it resists all mere "doctrine" and all the personal techniques designed to overcome suffering. Neither words nor techniques nor consolation drawn from the future can match up to the reality of suffering, which overtakes us all, every day. All these futile attempts had to be superseded by a deed that was able, from within, to reverse the value of suffering and endow it with meaning, a deed only God could perform. Here, taking us by surprise, a perspective is opened up on the central Christian synthesis that lies in the divinity of the crucified Jesus of Nazareth. Biblical theology itself, and the patristic theology that continued it, saw the solution of the riddle of human existence in the possibility, in the God-man, of God sharing man's suffering, indeed of his suffering for man. All meaning hangs on the fact that, in Jesus, the God who "cannot suffer" is able to experience death and futility, without ceasing to be himself. Every suggestion that underplays the genuine humanity of Christ (Gnosticism) and his genuine divinity (Arianism), as expressed by the formula of Chalcedon, threatens and actually destroys the full meaning of the "pro nobis" upon which all Christian theology depends. God alone can forgive sins, and so only he can "bear sins"; and the way in which he actually bears them cannot be discovered through speculation but must be presented, for our belief, in the mystery of the Cross—which is a stumbling block to Jews and folly to Gentiles.

Third, from this central point, conclusions can be followed in two directions, toward God and toward man. Toward God, insofar as the realism of God's suffering with the world in Jesus of Nazareth points in the direction of the mystery of the Trinity, in the direction of the distinction between the One who sends and the One sent, the One who utters and the One uttered, the One who surrenders and the One who is surrendered and (even) the One who forsakes and the One who is forsaken. However, this duality cannot be ultimate, it expresses a unity of the Spirit, of disposition, a unity which also emerges directly from the way Jesus and his witnesses understand God. This unity of the Spirit is indispensable if the world is to be given an inner participation in God's sphere. These affirmations are set forth without any defense whatsoever, yet they are essential if we are to render intelligible Christianity's claim to be, a priori, the "ever-greater".

This same realism of God's suffering with the world in Jesus of Nazareth points simultaneously in the direction of a perfection of man; for man is only human by being an ensouled body, and his death, in the natural realm, puts an end to the possibility of giving meaning to his temporal existence. In the mystery of Jesus' Resurrection not only does suffering acquire a fulfillment of meaning but man is given a hope of personal perfection—as a physical existence in time and space—which is incomparably superior to every other speculation (immortality of the soul, reincarnation, the absorption of the finite in the Absolute). This hope of man's perfection is bound up with his hope for the perfection of the cosmos that is centered on man. God's affirmation of his world—demonstrated in the death and Resurrection of Jesus—empowers man "to keep faith with the earth" without getting enmeshed in doctrines of "eternal recurrence" or ever-ascending evolution. In this third "pointer", where, centered on the crucified and risen Jesus of Nazareth, the fullness of divine life (Trinity) is bound up with man's perfectibility (resurrection), theology and anthropology interact to produce a dimension that can be claimed to be unsurpassable. Proving this in detail is the task of a painstaking theology; we shall say something shortly about the way in which such a proof can be approached.

A *fourth* aspect consists in what Paul likes to term "the mystery of Christ". On the basis of the three preceding aspects, this refers to the infrahistorical synthesis of the particular and

the universal, of the "chosen" people and the other peoples who
are not chosen, a synthesis which, in Paul's mind (Eph 3), is
clearly unrivalled. For on the one hand, this unity embraces all
the particular salvific measures (positive and negative) which
God took to educate Israel for the coming fulfillment; they are
included in the unity on condition that these particular forms
transcend themselves and become universal, otherwise they are
"broken off" (Rom 11:17)—although this does not mean that
they will not attain the promised fulfillment (11:26), since they
constituted, and still constitute, the particular historical "root"
(11:18) of the process of universalization. On the other hand, all
national boundaries are obliterated in the face of Christ's Incarnation, death and Resurrection: if God's particular Word
addressed to Israel becomes flesh, that is, becomes a human
being, and if this man loads all human guilt upon himself and
atones for it, it follows that every human being is affected, both
personally and socially, by this Man-Word. And since—the
third aspect—the individual and mankind are here being offered
the promise of ultimate salvation, it also follows that this
"mysterion" (Col 1:26; Eph 3:4–9), this *Gestalt* that manifests
itself in history, theologically discerned, is a priori without
rival. It is a variant of the second aspect, according to which the
universality of salvation remains linked to the particular, concrete figure of Jesus of Nazareth; only thus can it be a reality, not
an idea or a utopia.

This gives us a further conclusion, namely, that, after Jesus,
the presence of this salvation (which is both concrete and universal) had to be entrusted to a community that would preserve,
proclaim and administer it, that is, the "Church of Jews and
Gentiles" that concretely realized the original plan for Israel.
Thus it is called the "Israel of God" (Gal 6:16). But it also
transcends its concrete form, becoming universal; this constitutes its special, abiding paradox,[20] which can only be resolved christologically: thus, in her own way and according to

[20] This is the locus of the whole dialectic concerning there being "no
salvation outside the Church", which is concerned with two things: first, that
the Church is the authentic steward and executor of Christ's legacy; and second,
that, nonetheless, there must be ways of belonging to the Church that are not
bound to the Church's visible form.

her own proper rank, the Church works and suffers together with Christ on behalf of mankind as a whole (*"sacramentum mundi"*). The presence of this concrete element within universal history (and for its sake) is the indispensable means whereby the concrete and unique "now" of the saving event in Christ can be present at every historical moment without vanishing into the realm of the abstract. It is not for nothing that Paul sees the Church's structural element in particular, the apostolic office, to be uniquely irradiated by, and reflecting, the glory of God and Christ (2 Cor 3).

The *fifth* aspect closes the series by returning to the first. The basic presupposition for all understanding of existing things and of Being is the relationship between uncreated and created freedom; it is the creature's freedom that causes him to be termed the "image and likeness of God"—and this likewise is the concrete thrust of the *"analogia entis"*. On the other hand, the whole point of this distinction between the created and the uncreated is that, in it, the glory of God shall fulfill itself "superabundantly"[21] in the freedom of the creature. It follows, then, that the self-fulfilling Word of God, that is, his perfect self-giving, must elicit a perfect answer from and in the free creature; absolute freedom must not force or overpower the creature's freedom. In affirming this, we must maintain the whole span of tension: for, on the one hand, the full Word (*Wort*) both presupposes and effects the full answer (*Antwort*)—otherwise it does not really reach man, does not really become "flesh"; and, on the other hand, the presence of perfect self-giving, which is now the definitive model of ethical human action, faces man with a far more acute decision than all previous forms of ethics. Only after God has uttered his absolute Yes to man can man utter his absolute No to God: genuine atheism is a post-Christian phenomenon. This wide range in freedom, from a full human Yes and (at least the intention of) a full No, brings

---

[21] Paul insists on this word (*hyperballōn, hyperbolē*): 2 Cor 3:10; 4:7, 17; 9:14; 11:23; Eph 1:19; 2:7; 3:19; cf. the numerous other compounds with *hyper-*, esp. *hyperauxanein*: 2 Th 1:3; *hyperekperissou* (*-ōs*): Eph 3:20; 1 Th 3:10; 5:13; *hyperexein* (*-ōn*): Phil 3:8; 4:7; *hyperperisseuein*: Rom 5:20; 2 Cor 7:4; *hyperpleonazein*: 1 Tim 1:14. Expressions such as these clearly denote the "ever-greater", unsurpassable nature of divine revelation and divine grace.

the tension of theo-drama to its peak; more than anything else, it forbids us to dissolve man's ultimate attitude of faith, loving hope and solidarity into the all-knowing attitude of one who thinks he knows how the play will end and who is "above" divine judgment.

We have listed these five aspects as pointers toward a totality to which they look, "than which nothing greater can be thought". Of course, they can be regarded as a naïve outline of Christian doctrine, lacking in nuance, in which every statement needs to be thoroughly substantiated. No doubt. But our intention was only to present a kind of formal framework for the claims of totality (or catholicity), a framework which must always be part of our consciousness when we are attempting theological proof of the truth of any particular aspect. Proof can only proceed by showing that the aspect belongs to this totality and is indispensable to it. This raises the question of whether and how we can glimpse this totality (for, as we have said, we cannot have a total survey of it) in such a way that our theological judgment can aspire to be valid.

c. Inclusion and Exclusion

First of all we must refer back to the self-interpretation of God's revelation,[22] which does not throw partial, unconnected rays of light on individual truths but is intended to communicate a complete orientation concerning God's guiding action and man's response. To that extent, all revelation also has its point of unity in the definitive Word of God, Christ—*omnis scriptura divina unus liber est, et ille unus liber Christus est*[23]—and since Christ is the definitive revelation, the "sealed book" opens of itself—*liber ipse aperit seipsum*.[24] In Christ, God speaks a final Word (*eschaton logon*), albeit in the midst of the ongoing drama of the world. This gives the believer an authentic grasp of God's attitude toward him and shows him what his attitude should be toward

[22] Cf. section D 1 a (pp. 92 ff.) above and *The Glory of the Lord* I (Ignatius Press, 1982), 429ff.

[23] Hugh of St. Victor, *De arca Dei morali* II, 8 (PL 196, 642C).

[24] Bernard, *In die s. Paschae, sermo de septem signaculis* (PL 183, 280C). Quoted in de Lubac, *Exégèse médiévale* I (1959), 322–23.

God. Each illuminates the other: the ethical teaching of Jesus and the Apostles is so clear that our gaze passes smoothly from authoritative discipleship to the authorizing prototype, Jesus. The reliable interpretation of the latter (the meaning of his life, death and Resurrection) shows the fundamental ethical demands made of Christians to be internally evident.

If this view of things is to be imparted to us, we must allow ourselves to be led by the word. Theologians have the bad habit of interrupting the word before it has finished speaking; on the basis of some fragment they begin putting forward their own speculations, importing principles which may *seem* evident to man but which, from the perspective of God's word, are by no means evident. Such, for instance, are the ideas man cultivates concerning God's perfection and hence of the perfection of Christ (and of Mary and the saints); such ideas, however, do not come from God's self-revelation. There are theories which assert that God is not affected by the world's pain and sin or which speculate about the nature of Christ's knowledge or the limits of his abandonment by God in his Passion or about the painlessness of Mary's childbirth, and so forth. These theories do not take into account the fundamental biblical assertions that God is moved by world events,[25] nor do they pay any real attention to the passages that refer to the Son being delivered up by the Father (Jn 3:16; Rom 8:32); they cannot let even the clearest words of Jesus stand intact (such as Mk 13:32; 15:34; cf. Heb 5:7). Perhaps the contemporary theologian has an easier task here, looking at biblical revelation from the point of view of "modern man's self-understanding", that is, of his bankruptcy in the face of the question of ultimate meaning: it may be that he has a somewhat less obstructed view of the whole depth of the mystery of the Cross.

However, allowing oneself to be led is essentially the attitude of humility and simplicity in Christian faith, making room for God's self-disclosure, opening up the whole area, in purity of heart (Mt 5:8), to the light of God. Thus we discern that simple totality which belongs to it insofar as it is the light of God, who

---

[25] Cf. *Herrlichkeit* III/2, part 1, Alter Bund (Einsiedeln: Johannes Verlag, 1967), 147ff. (*The Glory of the Lord* VI, *Theology: The Old Covenant*).

himself is simple and "one-fold".[26] Pure hearts are promised
that they shall "see God", and this makes it easier for them to
arrange peripheral things around the center of gravity, integrate
the particular into the intended totality and perceive the "unsurpassable" quality of the divine self-giving. Instead of possessing
a "proof", they "are" a reflection of it in their lives. As they
respond to the glory of God and reflect it, it shines forth not
only for them but for others. For, according to the Spirit of
revelation, the really holy person—in the sense of Leviticus
11:44f.: "For I am the Lord your God; consecrate yourselves,
therefore, and be holy, for I am holy"—is the best "proof" of
the truth of revelation.

Theological proof cannot live in total isolation from this. It
must try to approximate to it in spirit, in the one Holy Spirit of
the many sanctifying gifts, which include wisdom and knowledge
and divine utterance (prophecy). But it will only be able to do
this if it moves and thinks within the context of the primal
mystery where absolute and finite freedom are distinguished, in
the worship and wonder of infinite love, which, since it needed
no created being, took the "unmotivated" decision, in utter
freedom, to create a world and lead it to God. Theological proof
must go even farther back, to the eternal generation of the Son;
this is not something that results simply from the Father's
"nature" as the One who pours himself out (otherwise we could
have grasped the "law" of Being in the *bonum diffusivum sui* and
so have mastered it). Nor does it express some *need* on the part
of the Father, that is, the need to translate himself into his
antithesis, the Son, in order to show himself to be really and
truly the Father. (For in this case the law of dialectic would be
higher than the freedom of self-giving love, and man, having
deduced this law, would have gained power over God and the
world in the form of "absolute knowledge".) No proof may
attempt to take us any farther than faith's contemplation of the
Father who surrenders his Son: any allegedly overall view
would destroy both this contemplation and its object; as we
have already said, it would take all the drama out of the history

---

[26] Cf. on this topic, *Convergences: To the Source of Christian Mystery* (San
Francisco: Ignatius Press, 1983), 17–45; Conny Edlund, *Das Auge der Einfalt*
(1952).

of God's dealings with the world. We would be mere spectators, following the action but not involved in it, excluded from the salvation that takes the form of happening and letting happen.

So the method of proof is indivisibly twofold: it excludes all the one-sided views that refuse to accept that all things can be integrated into the free God/world totality, as interpreted by Christian revelation; and it includes everything that allows itself to be thus integrated. Thus it operates simultaneously by exclusion and inclusion. If, according to God's "gracious purpose", the totality presses toward *communio*, *koinonia* between God and man, this method "ex-communicates" everything that opposes this *communio*, at whatever level, and "in-communicates" everything that promotes it. *Communio*, however, is the primal mystery, namely, that God, out of his freely bestowed love, allows that which is not God to participate in all the treasures of his love; and this comes about in a reciprocity which, in Christian revelation, has again to be grounded in God (in the Trinity), yet without abolishing the creatureliness of the creature. This gives us a foretaste of the daring integrations embraced by Catholic faith: God's power is manifest in Christ's lowliness, his wealth in his poverty; all is free "grace", which, as such, elicits man's "works" by way of response; the Church, as Christ's presence in the world, is both herself and more than herself—and more paradoxes of the same kind. These daring concepts are the very opposite of the human speculation that attempts at all costs to bring contraries together under one heading and that is therefore bound, in its syntheses, to regard the opposition of thesis and antithesis as ultimately insignificant. The Son is not the antithesis of the Father, nor is the world the antithesis of God; thus the Holy Spirit is not the synthesis to be deduced by speculation, either in the internal or in the "economic" Trinity. Rather, in Jesus, the believer is to see the Father; indeed, he is to discern the Father's most distinctive gesture of love in the abandonment of his Son on the Cross. In fact these daring efforts on the part of faith are simply obedience to the God who shows himself, who is able to unite things which man regards as incapable of union. The typically theological disobedience questions the *"magnalia"* worked by the power of God's love, questions its divine integrative power. Even where this disobedience adopts a biblicist or fideist garb, it is ultimately the self-righteousness of rationalism.

Again: theological proof cannot produce its own ideal of *communio* and then try to build enthusiastic syntheses on it. The model of union is established by God and carried out in detail by him; the task of theology is to follow, step by step, going through all the stages of the divine path, all the aspects of the divine model, and—on the basis of the given unity and with a view to the ultimate unity—reflecting upon it. The unity is God's trinitarian, salvific decision, which manifests itself as the "mystery" of the Son in the unifying power of the Spirit, and always in such a way that it addresses man's freedom and solicits the latter's most distinctive commitment. Here, therefore, the whole intramundane dialogue of standpoints, world views and perspectives is overtaken by an ultimate dramatic dialogue, which, while it lets God have the first and last word in all things, acknowledges that this same God has determined to send his Word into the world and leave it there. Thus, not only can the world hear this "key word", this "cue": it is also prompted to respond to it, well or ill; the world is obliged to step forth from the wings and act, in freedom, on the stage. This response consists not only in man's praxis but also in his *epignosis*, his theology.

We could sum up all this by referring to the principle of the "ever-greater", which applies to all that concerns God and his revelation. Ignatius of Loyola (whose life's rhythm it is) is not the first to elevate it into a principle, nor is Anselm (whose *id quo maius cogitari nequit* constitutes the fundamental rhythm of his thought): we find it in the Johannine writings, which allow us to speak of a specifically *Johannine comparative*. In John we find two things at the same time: a relentlessness, which, just where the highest point seems to have been reached, directs our attention to an even higher region; and a great calm, which regards this "greater" dimension (capable of infinite upward expansion) as the natural presupposition of the manifested *Gestalt*, indeed, as the latter's own inner form. Just when Nathanael thinks he has experienced the greatest revelation possible for a Jew, Jesus says: "You shall see *greater* things than these" (Jn 1:50). When the testimony of John, a "burning and shining lamp", seemed the greatest testimony that could be borne to Jesus, the latter says: "The testimony which I have is *greater* than that of John . . .", a testimony whereby the Father witnesses to himself in the works of Jesus as the One who has sent him (5:36). And even these works are not superlatives: "*Greater* works than these will he show him, that you may marvel" (5:20). And even these greater works will be surpassed by the one who believes that the Son is going to the Father and that the God of the entire Trinity will be at work in the Church: "He who believes in me will also do the works that I do; and *greater* works than these will he do" (14:12). In his conversations with the Samaritan woman and with the Jews, the phenomenon of Jesus always goes beyond every comparison they can adduce: "Where do you get that living water? Are you *greater* than our father Jacob?" (4:11f.). "Are you *greater* than our father Abraham? . . . Who do you claim to be?" (8:53). But Jesus replies that he is not glorifying himself; he points to the ever-greater mystery of his origin, open above him: "The Father is *greater* than I" (14:28). The First Letter of John applies this comparative three times to the Christian life (and hence to theology also): man must receive truth, and such truth is based on the truthfulness of the testimony; but the divine truthfulness infinitely surpasses the truthfulness that exists between men: "If we receive the testimony of men, the testimony of God is *greater*, for this is the testimony of God that he has borne witness to his Son" (1 Jn 5:9). But he has borne witness not only *to* believers but explicitly *in* them, so that they participate in the world-transcending truth of God: "He who is in you is *greater* than he who is in the world" (4:4). The Christian is indwelt by the God who is ever-greater—and this is no mere transcendence on man's part!—and this indwelling, in some indefinable manner, surpasses the believer's consciousness and conscience: "God is *greater* than our hearts, and he knows everything" (3:20). The only apparent exception to this ever-open comparative is the Gospel's superlative: "*Greater* love has no man than this, that a man lay down his life for his friends" (Jn 15:13): what is and remains the highest possible work of love among men opens out into an unfathomably greater work: God himself, out of love for us, surrenders his only Son to death, thereby making himself the peerless prototype of love (1 Jn 4:9).

The Johannine comparative can exclude everything that refuses to submit to it. Everything that calls a halt at any point belongs to the "world" and is excluded, because in doing so it has already excluded itself ("If they had been of us, they would have continued with us", 1 Jn 2:19). But such exclusion only serves to highlight and do justice to the stronger, inclusive power of God's truth, which, when it is lifted up from the earth, draws all men to it (Jn 12:32).

4. *The Freedom of Faith*

We have spoken of "pointers toward the ever-greater totality": there must be no overwhelming proofs, lest the freedom of the act of faith be overridden in a rationalistic way. We have no overall view of the totality as such, and the contradictions to be reconciled are so acute that there are many who refuse even to look in the direction of totality. The problem that arises here, namely, how the convergence of pointers (which is not absolutely compelling in itself) can harmonize with the certainty of faith on the basis of a substantiated personal "assent", occupied *John Henry Newman* all his life. Although he does not discuss the "freedom" of the act of faith in those terms, the issue itself is most definitely at the heart of everything he writes concerning our personal responsibility to "realize" something we have grasped notionally. Let us take him as our guide for a moment.

The problem's roots lie in the controversy with Abbé Jager in 1834. This is what brought Newman from the idea of a totality consisting of apparently disparate faith propositions to the recognition of a totality that is alive here and now, a totality that both has a definite profile and is also freely unfolding.[27] Newman had taken this notion, that is, that there is a canon of a limited number of explicit faith propositions, from the Caroline Divines of the seventeenth century. This revealed truth stands "in-

[27] Described with great clarity by Jean Stern, "La Controverse de Newman avec l'Abbé Jager et la théorie du développement", *Newman-Studien* (= NS) VI (Nuremberg: Glock und Lutz, 1964), 123–42.

dependent and objective" over against the Church; it does not lie "hidden in the womb of the Church, as if, together, they constitute a single unity". But in Tract 73 Newman goes on to propose that revelation is not a revealed *system* but consists of a certain number of separate and incomplete truths that belong to it; but the system itself, mighty though it be, is not revealed. All the same, secondary truths can be deduced from the revealed propositions, and they clarify them by developing them; Newman is prepared to admit this even in the case of the ancient creeds. Indeed, in the second letter to Jager, he acknowledges a "prophetic tradition" within the Church, which (as envisaged in 1 Cor 12:28) is both an interpretation of Scripture and a supplement to it.[28] Jager attacks Newman's starting point, the limited number of fundamental propositions. For his part, Newman is unsure whether he is to see the *"regula fidei"* simply in Scripture or in the creed or in the totality of Christian teaching. Finally, in 1839, he is "alarmed", when studying the acts of Chalcedon, to find that he has been clinging to the ancient "classical texts" like Eutyches, who refused to accept the interpretation of the christological mystery as set forth by Leo I and the Council.[29] Now he sees the unity that exists between revelation and legitimate Church interpretation. In the last "University Sermons" he realizes that it is not a number of propositions but the living Christ who stands at the center of revelation, whose deeds, words and veiled hints "constitute a germ to be developed". In the end (in the fifteenth Sermon) he catches sight of the *totality* of divine revelation and refers faith directly to this totality, which is unfolded through history and yields the aspects of particular dogmas, yet, in its totality, is not altered or enlarged.

> The question, then, is not whether this or that proposition of the Catholic doctrine is in *terminis* in Scripture, unless we would be slaves to the letter, but whether that one view of the Mystery, of which all such are the exponents, be not there; . . . Those propositions imply each other, as being parts of one whole. . . .

[28] This view is developed further later on, in *The Prophetical Office of the Church* (1837).
[29] Tract 90 (*Via Media* II, 277).

One thing alone has been impressed on us by Scripture, the
Catholic idea, and in it they are all included.[30]

In 1844 he notes: "How relatively insignificant is the question
whether Scripture contains the entirety of the faith. The real
question is this: Can the Church decide what is in Scripture and
what is not?"[31]

Now, however, the crucial question presents itself: Is a believer
able to grasp the mystery in a single view in such a way that he
can interpret the individual dogmas as integral parts of a totality?
Right up to the *Grammar of Assent* (1870), Newman holds to the
view that a "real" (that is, "existential") assent can only be given
to individual propositions, not to a system of propositions such
as theology—rightly, according to Newman—attempts to construct.[32] How does the totality become recognizable in the
partial aspects? Newman's answer is: in the convergence of the
indicators.[33] However, not only must they exist objectively,
they must also be subjectively discernible, and the organ for this
is the "illative sense". We can see how broadly Newman con-
ceives this organ from the ten approximations to it which J. Artz
has described.[34] In brief, we can say that it is the ability, inherent
in every natural and scientific exercise of thought, to home in on
the totality that is being sought. It is the ability to anticipate, the
instinct to go beyond partial and half-truths, to go beyond the
merely conceptual to the underlying reality which it intends.
Although Newman sometimes compares this spiritual instinct
to imagination, to a "smelling of the truth",[35] to a "sense of

[30] 15th University Sermon: *Newman's University Sermons*, (London: SPCK,
1970), 336.

[31] Cited from J. Stern, *op. cit.*, 138, 142.

[32] *Grammar of Assent*, new edition, edited with a preface and introduction by
C. F. Harrold (New York, 1947), 170, 171 (= GA).

[33] Newman more frequently speaks of the "convergence of probabilities".
On the replacement of "probability" by "indication", "pointer", cf. Johannes
Artz, "Der Ansatz des Newmanschen Glaubensbegründung" in *NS* IV (1960),
261f. Newman's "converging probabilities" (*GA* 273) is also more explicit than
his "cumulation" (*GA* 219, passim), although the legal model (see below)
would have us understand the latter in terms of the former.

[34] "Der 'Folgerungssinn' (illative sense) in Newmans 'Zustimmungslehre'
(Grammar of Assent)" in *NS* II (1954), 219–45.

[35] *GA* 160.

touch",[36] he does not mean anything sensory, let alone anything irrational, but the total person's concrete faculty of judgment, which is more than a mere conceptual inferring of conclusions. This is "implicit reasoning", where "implicit" expresses the fact that the process is both spontaneous and unobserved, that is, a psychological immediacy, which does not necessarily imply any ontological intuition.[37] All the same, the mind must have before it some "image" of the whole, a "concrete, unique *Gestalt*";[38] "image" is contrasted here with "notion",[39] but this is only intended to indicate the concreteness of the process and of the object of perception, not of the total view attained, but rather a "single grasp".[40] This is, as we have said, the dowry of every natural process of thought ("natural inference"), which does not need to proceed by explicit logic ("formal inference"). Thus the Fathers of the Church always saw the Christian faith as analogical to the natural phenomenon

---

[36] University Sermon, January 13, 1834.

[37] Although the word "intuition" is sometimes used (*GA* 252, 254). Cf. E. Przywara, *Religionsbegründung, Max Scheler—J. H. Newman* (Herder, 1923), esp. 93f., 149ff.

[38] As formulated by Franz Wiedmann, "Theorie des realen Denkens nach J. H. Newman", *NS* IV, 178.

[39] *GA* 27.

[40] "Grasp . . . per modum unius", *GA* 229, "by a mental comprehension", *GA* 222. One can see how close Newman comes, in these formulations, to Romantic hermeneutics. This is natural; they are both engaged in polemics against Enlightenment rationalism in philosophy and theology. In Schleiermacher, in particular, the presuppositions of understanding are found in the anticipatory "feeling" for the totality of meaning but also for the object's concrete individuality. In the Idealist manner, however (cf. Schelling's "Imagination"), the object is ultimately graspable by a transcendental preconstruction or reconstruction. (Thus Friedrich Schlegel believes that the one who understands can awaken within himself the primal language of all things and on this basis understand the particular language of all things.) The "spirit of the nation" can become the medium (Savigny, Niebuhr). Dilthey (and his school) links up with Schleiermacher: the interior (psychological) experience contains the conditions that facilitate historical understanding: life can only be understood on the basis of life. This whole line of hermeneutics leads far away from Newman's central concern, which is to find a rational basis for the free act of faith in the face of an ever-greater divine revelation (that can never be systematized). Cf. J. E. Hasso Jaeger, *Origines et destinées de la notion de l'Herméneutique*. Conférences données au Centre de Philosophie du Droit, 1971 (typescript).

of belief that every rational human being must engage in; Newman too assures us that initially he is speaking of "belief" in general, not specifically of "faith".[41] Only where it is a case of ultimate, fully responsible, personal decisions about objective truths do these two modes of thought combine in the "informal inference", responding to the truth-appeal of the thing itself, which calls the whole man to make a decision regarding the whole meaning. At this point we are far away from an *aesthetic* (in the narrower sense) perceiving of *Gestalt*; we would have to speak, with Newman, of an *ethically demanded* perception of form, involving both the person's sense of responsibility and his *freedom*.[42]

Newman uses several analogies to illustrate what he means. The first one, more negative in character, is the parallel between the mode of knowing in modern mathematical physics and that in theology. At the age of twenty, Newman wrote an article showing that even exact science only arrives "notionally" at probabilities; it is only possible to get beyond these probabilities by a principle that is "analogous to faith".[43] Secondly, he takes up the thought of the Benedictine, Eusebius Amort (d. 1775), who had worked out an argument from the "greater probability" but which does not go as far as Newman's idea of convergence.[44] The juridical analogy is substantially more important: according to the celebrated treatise on evidence by the jurist S. M. Philipps,[45] the judge (or jury) is able to use the convergence of "circumstantial evidence" (that is, pointers) to exclude "all reasonable probability of the innocence" of the accused and thus attain certainty; similarly, in theology, it is possible to sum up the total weight of evidence. Newman quotes the case of a judge who has explained to the jury the quality of the evidence it is to attain: it

[41] GA 76.

[42] On the aesthetic and ethical total view, cf. H.-J. Walgrave, O.P., *Newman, Le développement du dogme* (Casterman, 1957), 120.

[43] For an analysis of the 1821 essay, see F. M. Willam, "Die philosophischen Grundpositionen Newmans" in *NS* III (1957), 111–56, esp. 135–48.

[44] W. Bartz, "Die Demonstratio Catholica des Eusebius Amort und der Konvergenzbeweis J. H. Newmans" in *Trier. Theol. Zeitschrift* (64), 81ff.

[45] *Treatise on the Law of Evidence* (London, 1814). Cf. Hasso Jaeger, "La Preuve rabbinique et patristique" in *La Preuve* I, *Recueil de la Societé de Jean Bodin pour l'histoire comparative des institutions*, XVI (1965), 584–89.

is reached by that same conscientiousness and responsibility that a man devotes to personal matters of the highest importance. In such a case, the conclusions drawn will be just as worthy of belief as the available facts themselves.[46] By "a mental comprehension of the whole case" one attains a "discernment of its upshot . . . by a clear and rapid act of the intellect".[47]

Such an act, however, is free. And the more responsible it is, the more it proceeds from the whole person, the freer it is. Newman's distinction between "inference" (the conditional acceptance of a proposition) and "assent" (its unconditional acceptance)[48] is designed particularly to shed light on freedom. Certainty is reached by "placing oneself mentally . . . in this middle point. . . . One is free to see or not to see."[49] But the center upon which the theological pointers converge is nothing other than the majesty and infinite love of God, who, in his revelation, offers himself to man and calls for his response.[50] It is the nature of this "center", then, to elicit a reaction from man's innermost freedom. If he wishes to refuse, he will find a thousand reasons for considering the pointers toward this totality to be too weak, quite apart from the fact that, objectively, they may present themselves to him in a form that is obscured and unworthy of belief. Moreover, Newman suggests that it may be a law of Providence that God speaks more softly, the more he promises . . . so that our faith is lifted high above reason by its Object, just as, in the obscurity of its origins, it sinks below the same reason. Divine truth, he says, is grasped by a subtle and indirect method, which is less tangible than other methods, and this exposes it to contradiction and contempt.[51] This passage shows how grace starts to work in the area of psychology, using

[46] GA (1901 ed., 324ff.).

[47] GA 222.

[48] GA 119.

[49] August Brunner, Glaube und Erkenntnis, 175f., quoted by Artz, NS IV, 268.

[50] It is well known that, as far as Newman is concerned, the really convincing proof of the existence of God is the creature's inner, personal encounter with the Creator in the phenomenon of conscience. By contrast, the mere sight of the world, with its contradictions, its suffering and guilt, would have made an atheist of him, as he himself says in the Apologia, 241ff.

[51] University Sermon, January 13, 1834.

its light to open up a path whereby freedom may advance to the center; we can also see why Newman gives the uneducated man just as much opportunity as the learned theologian of seeing and affirming the convergence of pointers that results in certainty, if he wishes to. The good man and the bad man will regard very different things as probable.[52] "It is clear how much room there is here for the intervention of the will. None are so deaf as those who do not want to hear."[53]

First Excursus: The Approaches Adopted by Early Christian Apologists

What we have said about hermeneutics can be illustrated by reference to the first defenders of Christian truth. However unsystematic and clumsy their efforts may appear, they all aim at the very point that concerns us here. That is, they attempt to show, in the historical fact of Christian revelation (articulated over time in the Old and New Covenants), the presence and self-manifestation of the primal mystery, a mystery which, a priori, goes beyond every religio-philosophical solution invented by man, existing or possible. All of them, right from the start or as they unfold, go back to the mystery of the *"analogia entis"*, showing that this can only retain its authentically mysterious character if Christian revelation is presupposed. From the point of view of methodology, it is quite correct for them to come into contact here with non-Christian "philosophy", for ancient "philosophy" is identical with "theology" or the doctrine of the divine (*theion*). On the other hand, the apologists do not simply philosophize: they defend the truth of Christian teaching both in a positivist, biblical manner (whereby, for men of ancient times, the theme of the greater antiquity of biblical revelation has a logical significance) and in a practical and ethical manner, for to them, theologically speaking, the existence of Christian holiness (as contrasted with pagan decadence) is just as convincing as the historical demonstration of the source of this new way of living. Here we shall focus on a few salient points.

[52] *Oxford University Sermons*, 191 (quoted in Harrold, n. 30 above, introduction, XVII). "The religious mind sees much which is invisible to the irreligious mind. They have not the same evidence before them."

[53] To Harry Wilberforce, Summer 1868 (in vol. 8 of Laros' [German] edition of Newman's works, 161). From this it would be possible to show how indispensable the Church's infallibility is for Newman, particularly in her teaching office. R. A. Dibble, *J. H. Newman: The Concept of Infallible Doctrinal Authority* (Washington, 1955); Jean Stern, "L'Infaillibilité de l'Eglise dans la pensée de J. H. Newman" in *RSR* (1973), 161–85.

It is characteristic that *Aristides* begins his Apology to Hadrian with a presentation of the *"analogia entis"*. He speaks of the distinction between the Mover and the moved; God is "incomprehensible", yet we can have intimations of him through his works; he lacks nothing ("he does not call for sacrifices of food or drink. . . . He does not look to anyone for anything, but all living beings look to him": I, 5; he is "without any need": XIII, 3). He created the world for man's sake, and "it seems to me that the only important thing is to honor God and not to harm one's fellow men". God is all in all: "Heaven cannot hold him, rather it is He who embraces heaven and all that is visible and invisible. He has no opponent, for there is no one more powerful than he" (I, 5–6). Whereas Barbarians, Greeks, and Jews too, either did not know God or failed to give him the right response, Christians have "acknowledged God's benefactions", and thus "on their account blessings pour forth upon the world" (XVI, 1). Here, already, we find the idea that "it is only through the intercession of Christians that the world continues in existence" (XVI, 6)—an initial form of the notion that the Church is the *sacramentum mundi*. Here God's imperishable word is kept alive and in the prayers of mankind (XVII, 7–8).

In *Tatian*'s "Address", again, God is without beginning, the Creator and Origin of all things; he is invisible yet can be recognized in and through creation (IV, 3f.). He needs nothing outside of him (IV, 5); his Logos is the "foundation of the universe", "light of light", not a declension from God. The notions of emanation and dialectic are rejected right from the outset.

On many occasions *Justin* emphasizes that God lacks nothing (*Ap* I, 10; I, 13), that he creates out of his goodness and that man is free (I, 10, 43, 44). Every man participates in God's Logos (and, to that extent, is a "Christian": I, 46). But only the man who knows the "hidden mysteries" of the crucifixion of the Logos will grasp the whole Logos; otherwise he will only get hold of fragments (II, 10, seed-traces of the Logos: II, 7)—which is why the pagan philosophers so often contradict each other. It is this presence of the totality of the Logos that makes "our religion evidently more sublime than all human teaching" (II, 10). Here we can discern the inclusive aspect, which Tertullian will describe as the "testimony of the naturally Christian soul" (*Apology* 17:6), and the exclusive side, which is expressed in the rejection of the self-contradictory pagan teaching on the divine. *Hermias*, in his "Ridiculing of other philosophers", carries out this negative task exclusively: the philosophers get lost in their own endless, abstruse researches, their results are "unsubstantiated and profitless, unsupported by any firm fact and any clear reasoning" (10). In contrast to Hermias, and complementing him, we have *Minucius Felix*. In his *Octavius*, he first

presents the "*analogia entis*": God cannot be measured or seen; he is the
Father of all things (XVIII, 7–8), filling heaven and earth, so that we
"live with him" (XXXII, 9) and discern his presence in his works
(XXXII, 4). Then he goes on to emphasize and demonstrate the
convergence of the partial *logoi* of the philosophers upon the Christian
total *Logos* (XIX, 3). Human freedom is a fundamental concern of his,
too (XXXIV; XXXVI, 1): God tests it; and (as Seneca said)[1] God finds
it a "glorious spectacle" to see how man struggles and proves himself
(XXXVII, 1).

In the first part of his Apology, *Athenagoras* first proves, positively,
that Christians are not atheists by believing in one God: there are
suggestions and hints of this in the philosophers, but they contradict
each other. The principle is carried through on the basis of Christian
revelation: looking back to ancient philosophy, it can be shown that
two gods could not exist in parallel or the one within the other (8),
whereas the biblical concept of God matches God's sublimity. Moreover, through the Trinity, it demonstrates how God was able to create
a world external to himself. Then, negatively, he shows that Christians,
because they are monotheists, cannot sacrifice to gods, for their God
essentially lacks nothing (13). "Yet the sacrifice which is most dear to
him is that we should seek to know him. . . ."

Theophilus (in his *Ad Autolycum*) gives us variations on the same
theme: God's glory is beyond our grasp, he is above any heights we
may attain (I, 3), he is without beginning, the Lord of all, who created
all things from nothing and can be recognized in his works (I, 4); but
though we can discern God in his Providence, this does not mean that
we can see him (I, 5). Man is the image of God (I, 4), he lives and
breathes in him (I, 7), he is free (II, 27) and can freely choose between
mortality and immortality (II, 24). God is self-sufficient, has no need of
anything, whereas man needs God (II, 10). If he is to approach God, he
must make himself into a pure mirror in which God can spiritually
reflect and echo himself (I, 2).

The *Epistle to Diognetus*, like Aristides and like the *Epistle of Barnabas*,
emphasizes the futility of the (Jewish) sacrifices, since God "lacks
nothing". "For he who created heaven and earth and all that is in them,
and who gives us all that we need, surely lacks nothing himself" (3).
But in sending his Word to men (7), God, who is invisible to men, has
rendered himself recognizable to faith: this happens both by a participation in God's good things and by insight (8). God's "superabundant kindness and love toward men" desires to effect a "tender

[1] Cf. *Theo-Drama* I, Part 2: *Dramatic Resources* (San Francisco: Ignatius Press,
1988), 135.

exchange" between God and man on the basis of his Son's self-surrender (9). Only now does God reveal himself as the Father who "first loved men and for their sake created the world . . . as his image" and, in his Son, summoned them to his "heavenly kingdom". Now there can be the giving and receiving of love and that "imitation of God" whereby a person can selflessly take his neighbor's burden upon himself (10).

We can conclude this excursus with a glance at Tertullian's turbulent "Apology". Not until its seventeenth chapter does it begin to unfold the Christian concept of God: God is immeasurably great, and so "he is known only to himself; through his overwhelming greatness he is equally near to man and remote from him". By his Word he creates the world from nothing, a world which is ordered in such a way that "he, the invisible One, is seen; he, the incomprehensible One, is made graciously present; he who is beyond all evaluation is appreciated by human senses." Then he takes up Justin's analogy of the Logos indwelling every rational soul (which will become so important in Origen); only in positive revelation does the Logos become explicit and genuinely intelligible. There follow considerations of the formal unity of salvation history (20: prophecies from the past are fulfilled here and now, which gives us good reason to trust the promises referring to the future, as in the Epistle of Barnabas 5, 3; cf. 1, 7; 7, 1) and also the material unity of salvation history (21), which is grounded in Christ's preexistence. Christ's divinity is attested not only by revelation but also by its effects in the world: "Look and see whether this divinity of Christ is true and real, whether it is something which, when known, refashions men in goodness . . ." (21, 31). It ends (46ff.) by refuting the view that Christianity is merely one philosophy among others. The counterproof is conducted on all fronts at the same time, theoretically, practically and ethically, and above all eschatologically: only the power of God, which was manifested in the dead Christ, can perfect man by raising him from the dead.

Behind the concentric approaches of the Apologists stands the unexpressed idea not only that the Christian religion is in fact the transcending totality of all the *logoi spermatikoi* in the speculations and ethics of both pagans and Jews but also that this totality is and remains unsurpassable. This is because it has been fashioned by a God who does not need the world he has made and who, in his economy of salvation, has perfected his creative work by freely surrendering himself to it. This implicit idea first becomes explicit in Irenaeus.

Second Excursus: Truth Vindicates Itself (Irenaeus)

In arguing against the unreal fantasies of false gnosis, Irenaeus takes his stand on the historical and factual totality of the divine self-revelation that constitutes the world's foundation and completion. In the second book of his *Adversus Haereses*, against the background of a reason that has been set free through revelation, false gnosis is shown to be baseless; in the third book, on the basis of Scripture, he demonstrates the unity of God and of the economy of his Word (from the creation to the Incarnation); the fourth book is concerned with the unity of history (as a unity of both Testaments); and in the fifth he discusses the unity of mankind that has been achieved by Christ's Resurrection and the perfection of the world in and through God. In all the books Irenaeus speaks of the unity of the individual human being, the unity of the human race and the (pneumatic and institutional) unity of the Church, in dependence upon Christ. These unities are interdependent; or rather, there is a single unity that manifests itself in all these aspects, and this is the "true gnosis", which has such internal cohesion that no part of it can be isolated from the rest nor can anything be added to it (cf. *Ad. Haer.* IV, 33, 7–8). Ultimately it is the economic unity of the Trinity (IV, 33, 15), which embraces beginning and ending (IV, 12, 4) and "constitutes a single head at the center"—the head of him who, "by stretching out his hands gathered both peoples unto the one God", who "is above all and through all and for us all" (V, 17, 4). This reveals the universal dimensions of the Cross (*Epid.* 34). This unity, however, is received in faith "by the Church, and we preserve this faith carefully, for the Holy Spirit has, as it were, poured this excellent inheritance into a precious vessel, where it keeps its pristine freshness, as well as constantly renewing the vessel that contains it" (III, 24, 1). In IV, 6, 5–7, Irenaeus is positively inebriated by the superabundant totality: twenty-six times he repeats the words "all" and "everything", showing and establishing this fullness from all sides.[2] Throughout, it is the real, the factual, not the speculative, that is the locus of proof. Three times he sets forth the maxim (which Justin had already adopted in *Apol.* I, 22, 4): "The better man proves himself by his works" (II, 30, 2; II, 30, 5; III, 12, 11). In the face of this, Gnostic speculation is mere "theatre" (I, 10, 5), a mythologizing "tragedy" (II, 12, 3) or, indeed, a "comedy" (II, 14, 1; II, 18, 5). It sounds like a victory chant when, in a masterful passage, Irenaeus applies Paul's dictum, "The spiritual man judges all things but is himself judged by no one", to the Catholic position vis-à-vis all forms of heresy, including paganism and Judaism (IV, 33,

[2] Cf. also IV, 22, 2.

1–11): it must be so, for all these conceptions are partial, whereas only that of Irenaeus embodies the all-inclusive unity (IV, 33, 15).

The foundation and background of everything remains the *"analogia entis"*: God, who is ever-greater, who, "according to his greatness and his ineffable glory . . . is incomprehensible, and who, according to his loving-kindness to men and his almighty power, even grants the divine vision to those who love him" (IV, 20, 5), remains the leitmotif of the entire work.[3] Both aspects are necessary, neither renders the other superfluous. The Father must remain invisible, "lest man should come to despise God, and so that he always sees space ahead of him for his further progress"; but he must not remain so invisible "that man, totally deprived of God, should cease to be himself" (IV, 20, 7). The invisible Father renders himself visible in his Word and Son, who reveals him to us as the loving Father and Creator of all things (V, 17, 1), so that all created things and historical ordinances can be traced back to God's beneficent decree (*eudokia*).[4] This divine decision is perfectly free, for if God were not totally free of all necessity, he would not be God (III, 8, 3).[5] But if God, who is incomprehensible in his majesty, reveals himself in his Word and makes himself accessible, this Word must not be subordinate to him but must be capable of "traversing" him (IV, 4, 2), must be equally eternal (II, 30, 9) and hence preexistent (III, 18, 1; *Epid.* 51), Co-Creator of the world (V, 18, 3), and must have proceeded from the Father by being born, within the Godhead, in a way that is beyond anyone's knowing or deducing (II, 28, 6). When the Son is described as *"polys"*, "manifold and rich" (IV, 20, 11), this is not because his manifold riches place him one step lower than the unity of the Father, for the Father too is equally termed *"polys"*, "manifold and rich" (II, 35, 3).[6] The Son "ministers to the rich and manifold will of the Father by being the Savior of those who are to be saved, the Lord of those who are to be ruled, the God of created beings, the only Son of the Father, the prophesied Messiah, the incarnate Word of God" (III, 16, 7). Irenaeus habitually refers to the Spirit, the "Wisdom of God" (*Epid.* 4), as of equal rank with the Word; Word and Spirit are the "hands" with which the Father fashions the world, and just as the Son will ground the *communio* between God and men (V, 1, 1; V, 14, 2–3), so the Spirit establishes the *communio* between men and the Son (III, 24, 1); the "communion of the Spirit" (V, 8, 1; V, 12, 2; V, 11, 1) completes God's work, which the Son has entrusted to the Spirit for that purpose

---

[3] II, 6, 1; II, 13, 4; III, 11, 5; III, 24, 2; IV, 19, 4; IV, 20, 4–6.
[4] II, 11, 1; III, 11, 9; III, 23, 1; IV, 6, 3; IV, 7, 3; IV, 20, 1; IV, 26, 2; V, 1, 3.
[5] Also IV, 13, 4–14, 1; IV, 17, 1; IV, 18, 6; *Epid.* 9.
[6] Also III, 10, 6; III, 16, 7.

(III, 17, 3; *Epid.* 5). This does not affect the "simplicity of God", which the Gnostics had dissected (III, 13, 3); God's insight is one with his Word (III, 13, 9). Thus, as Creator, he is infinitely free (II, 1, 1), and the world has no other ground but his pure goodness (IV, 14, 2),[7] which is, of course, the goodness of the absolute majesty of God, who by his very nature must also be and must remain the just Judge (III, 25, 2–3). It is absurd, therefore, to tear apart these two aspects of God and allot them to two different "Gods".[8] Furthermore, all created reality must bear the imprint of its "source"; Irenaeus uses the term *ousia* to bring out the relationship of "being" between God and his creature (IV, 2, 4; IV, 9, 1; IV, 11, 2), which persists despite the radical opposition between the Creator-being and the created being. The world belongs to God (V, 24, 1).

In man, once again, we find the tension that Justin and Tertullian had already encountered. Before all else, because man is free (IV, 15, 2; IV,

[7] Which also means that God does not need a world of ideas as a blueprint for his creative activity. He draws from himself the being, the model and the idea of all things: IV, 20, 1; II, 16, 3): "The being of all things can be traced back to his will": II, 30, 9; he "invents" the world: *ipse adinvenit*: II, 10, 4—out of nothing: II, 10, 3.

[8] The refutation of pseudo-Gnosis proceeds according to the principles of theodramatic totality. In the first place, Gnostic man is not free, no more than the "emanations" of the primal origin (the pleroma) are free; thus the entire confused, mythological "drama" is naturalistic. The possibility of "emanations" from God is refuted; the concept itself is contradictory (II, 13; II, 17). There can be nothing divine outside God, otherwise God is restricted and we have to seek (ad infinitum) for some overall totality embracing both principles (II, 1–3). Furthermore, the rationalistic attempt to deduce God is both self-contradictory and blasphemous (I, 16, 3; II, 25, 1; II, 28, 6–7), and such irreverence, even if it talks in terms of the "unfathomable" and of "keeping silence", is doomed to fail to recognize God: "For your Creator cannot be plumbed by reason, nor should you seek to think up some other Father beside him." The construction of a supramundane sphere can only be regarded as an ideological superstructure erected on top of human conditions (II, 28, 4); the splitting of God into several divine potencies occurs because people lack a higher vantage point and cannot grasp the contrary realities within the world as a symphony and harmony of opposites (II, 25, 2). The notion that an "ideal world" played a role in creation explains nothing (II, 7–8); in Christian terms the world is not a "shadow" of the pleroma, but the latter is a "shadow" (an ideological superstructure) of the real world (II, 15, 3).

With his refutation of pseudo-Gnosis, Irenaeus counters in advance all the Neoplatonic tendencies of later Church Fathers, particularly trinitarian subordinationism. Theo-drama takes place between the free, loving God of creation and redemption and the free human being who is to be led to perfect freedom.

37, 1–4; IV, 39, 3; *Epid.* 11), he is God's image and likeness (IV, 37, 4; V, 12, 4). "By nature" he has in him something of the Logos,[9] and hence he has a relationship to the God who reveals himself, although it is only in the successive revelations of the Word, up to his Incarnation, that man learns who God really is. Man can only be perfected by God himself (III, 20, 1), which means that he can only fully be the image of God when God's eternal Image, his Son, becomes man and enters into fellowship with mankind (IV, 33, 4; V, 2, 1; V, 16, 2; *Epid.* 22). Between the inchoate image and the perfected image stretches the whole drama of man's coming to himself, which, for Irenaeus, can only be understood as a drama between God and man. A measuring rod (*metron*) is held up to finite freedom, identical with the requirement of obedience to infinite freedom (IV, 37, 4), which, both for itself and for the creature, is the epitome of the Good (IV, 38, 4; II, 25, 3–4; II, 28, 1–9). It is precisely this "measure" that the pseudo-Gnostics fail to observe, whereas the Son of God observes it in his economy of salvation and in his Incarnation. God's entire plan cannot be anticipated: God's word must reveal it to him step by step, so that man matures into a genuine knowledge (V, 1, 1). Irenaeus' particular insight into this drama lies in his view that human freedom, which is essentially a developing one (IV, 9, 3; IV, 38, 1) must undergo the testing experience (*peira*)[10] of the unnatural "alienation" from God (V, 1, 1) in order to reach an inner understanding of the Good, that is, of the love of God. The experience of suffering which, if man's freedom is to attain an inner maturity, is indispensable to him—although he freely turns away from God—can become his salvation: God's Word, uttered by the Father and obedient to him, endures this suffering of alienation on the Cross in a completely real way, to the utmost; for since God is free in every respect, it is not in the power of the sinner who has turned away to reestablish a right relationship with God by his own efforts.

Here we begin to discern the significance of an anti-Gnostic anthropology: man is spirit, soul and body in a unity (II, 29, 3), and all these three elements belong to the image of God (V, 6, 1; V, 12, 1f.), so that even the flesh must be described as *capax Dei* when God reveals himself to man. The whole man is always involved, and suffering and death belong to him. Hence, in Christology, the emphatic realism of Christ's becoming man, becoming flesh (III, 10, 4; III, 11, 3; III, 16; V, 1, 2), of his lowliness (*Epid.* 73) and of his genuine Passion. (For the fact

---

[9] II, 6, 1; IV, 13, 3; IV, 15, 1; IV, 16, 5: *Epid.* 8. Men are sons of the Father "by nature, so to speak, because they are created by God". At a deeper level they only become such through obedience: IV, 41, 2.

[10] III, 20, 2; III, 23, 1; IV, 39, 1; V, 3, 1.

that Christ has suffered is greater and better and more effective than if
he had merely taught, for example: III, 18, 5–6; II, 20, 3.) Hence the
stress on a genuine recapitulation of human death, too, for without it
the Incarnation would not have been complete (V, 23, 2; V, 31, 2). The
Son's suffering and dying are real: he undergoes them not only *with* us
but expressly "for us" (III, 20, 2; *Epid*. 72), bearing our sins (IV, 33, 11)
out of pure love (V, Prol.) and in atoning obedience to the Father: here,
for the first time, God reveals the entire scope of his fatherly care for us;
there is no other way we would have become aware of its depth.

In God's plan of salvation, the redemption that comes through the
Son is intended for all men (IV, 6, 5), for mankind is a unity (III, 12, 9).
All men share the same nature and are free (IV, 37, 2)—an emphatically
anti-Gnostic feature—and all stand in need of being saved by the
perfected Logos if they are to attain perfect freedom. Jesus' deed is
man's liberation (IV, 11, 4; IV, 18, 2); he comes "in the fullness of
freedom's time" (IV, 22, 1), bringing the "New Covenant of freedom"
(III, 12, 14; IV, 33, 14). The "new" thing he brings—and which he
himself *is*—consists in the gift of freedom (IV, 34, 1), the proclamation
of the "glad tidings of freedom" (IV, 34, 3); those who "preach the
truth" in the Church are "apostles of freedom" (III, 15, 3). However,
this act of liberation cannot be a forcible overpowering of man that
comes from outside, for God always acts, like light, by "persuasion",[11]
never by "compulsion" (IV, 39, 3; V, 1, 1; V, 19, 1). Freedom,
particularly as a result of the Holy Spirit's operation, is our assimilation
to the Son's attitude toward the Father, namely, elasticity in his hands
(IV, 39, 2–3), childlikeness (III, 15, 2), simplicity (II, 26, 1), which
progresses much further in the knowledge of God than the pre-
sumptuous Gnostic theology (V, 20, 2). As a result of its whole
approach (and in accordance with its idea of God as "the Abyss" and
"the Silence"), pseudo-Gnosis is bound to condemn man "always to
seek and never to find",[12] whereas, even when he is found,[13] the
Christian God is so rich that we can go on seeking and finding him for
all eternity (II, 28, 3; IV, 28, 2; V, 36, 1); he is rich enough to share with
us his inexhaustible treasures of life (IV, 20, 5–7).

However, since our redeeming God does not overpower our freedom, man retains freedom to decide for or against grace: he can refuse it

---

[11] *Suadela*: persuading, i.e., suggesting something by showing its plausibility;
leading someone toward conviction. In using this expression, Irenaeus by no
means intends to question the objectivity of Christ's justifying act.

[12] I, 1, 4; III, 24, 2; IV, 9, 3; IV, 19, 1; V, 20, 2.

[13] The Father (or rather, his glory) is "grasped" (*chōrein*): III, 20, 2; V, 35, 2.

(IV, 28, 3; V, 27, 1–2), in which case he himself "freely chooses separation from God, that is, death". Thus, with the advent of the grace of Christ, there is a heightening of the danger implied in freedom; in other words, the severity of judgment is increased. Now what is at stake is an eternal Yes or No (IV, 28, 2; IV, 36, 4; *Epid.* 56). Only after Christ does there arise that concentration of satanic and anti-Christian powers in world history (V, 25, 1; V, 26, 2; V, 27, 1–2; V, 29, 2). Thus the eschatological saving events do not overtake and supersede the drama of existence: they actually raise it to its real stature. If Christ, in his own temptation, "recapitulated the warfare we wage with our enemy" (V, 21, 1), he has not dispensed us from fighting our own battle. Here the Judgment seems to be (dualistically) open, but ultimately Irenaeus is convinced that Adam, the first father and representative of all mankind, will be saved (III, 23, 3–8; cf. the Fall came about through inattention, not through wickedness: IV, 40, 3).

In Irenaeus' intuition of the totality, the latter only attains full actuality, at every present moment of history, in the context of his doctrine of the Church, of her *"archaion systēma"* (IV, 33, 8—this can mean both "structure" and "epitome") that comes from Christ. The Church is both things at the same time: as a "structure" that has been fashioned by him, she contains, preserves and proclaims the totality hitherto described, but as "epitome" she also constitutes an aspect of that totality itself. Here again we see that the Church is both herself and more than herself and that, therefore, we cannot distinguish between what she "is" and what she "has". As far as the "structure" is concerned, we can distinguish between its founders, who received from Christ the totality of God's work in order to hand it on, and the officially authorized succession of those who subsequently transmitted it (III, 3, 2); we can distinguish between Holy Scripture (of the Old Covenant, supplemented by the writings of the Apostles), which contains all knowledge essential for salvation (II, 28, 1) and which is the "body of truth" (II, 27, 1)—and the living transmission of this truth (III, 4, 1), the apostolic "office", which, having "received the sure charisma of truth" (IV, 26, 2; cf. IV, 32, 1), has the task of maintaining the proper interpretation of Scripture within the tradition. It would not be right, however, to set these aspects against one another, for example, to see a contradiction in the affirmation of the sufficiency of Scripture, on the one hand, and the necessity of its being authentically interpreted and of the traditions of the presbyters on the other;[14] similarly it would

---

[14] E.g., Norbert Brox, *Offenbarung, Gnosis und gnostischer Mythos bei Irenäus*

be a mistake to ask which of these aspects is "superior" to the other.[15] For the Church is not only a structure but an aspect of the one Epitome who indwells her as her greater Self; he does not live in her as in a neutral container but as in a living organism, which is fashioned, organized and animated by this totality. This is the context for Irenaeus' teaching (which is difficult to categorize) on the *"regula veritatis"*, which, on the one hand, is the epitome of revealed truth (imparted to us in baptism: I, 9, 4) and, on the other hand (as we have already said), is a kind of "organ of balance", maintaining the authenticity of this epitome. To that extent the word "canon" also means "plumbline"; but, humanly speaking, the "epitome" can only be grasped in a particular form, which means that the *"regula veritatis"* can be equated with those shorter (III, 11, 1) or longer (I, 10, 1; III, 4, 2) credal formulas that sum up and "epitomize" revealed truth. The very fact that Irenaeus envisages a variety of such formulas shows that he does not imagine that the totality can be imprisoned within them. Truth is organized (I, 8, 1), but this organism is so living and transcendent—since God's ever-greater love is its core[16]—that words and formulas can never master it. It is significant, however, that the short formula contains the *"analogia entis"*, understood theologically: "A single almighty God, who by his Word has made all things, visible and invisible . . . , and through this Word by which he perfected the creation, he has also given salvation to the men within it" (III, 11, 1).[17] This core (similarly defined by the Apologists), according to the deposit of revelation and the Church's sense of faith, yields the individual structural elements which all bear the mark of totality, of the ever-greater.

We have already discussed the most important of these characteristics in listing the "pointers to the totality". Let us highlight three of them, showing the anti-Gnostic emphasis typical of Irenaeus:

First there is the continuity between creation and redemption. We have already seen that creation took place through the same Logos as the redemption and that man, by nature, participates in the same Logos who, appearing in perfected form as a human being in Christ, dies and rises again. It is characteristic, therefore, that Jesus uses the things of

---

von Lyon, Salzburger Patristische Studien I (1966): "Two notions . . . are juxtaposed but not brought into harmony with one another": 96.

[15] *Ibid.*, 101.

[16] "Quanto autem *plus* eum dilexerimus, hoc *majorem* ab eo gloriam accipiemus": IV, 13, 3.

[17] If it is the mark of false gnosis to pull the Father apart from the Son (the Creator and the Redeemer) and make them two Gods, the error of the Jews is that they want to know the Father apart from the Son: IV, 7, 4.

creation in his miracles in order to work redemption: water, transforming it into wine, and bread and wine, to be fashioned into his
Eucharist (III, 11, 5); he makes clay from the dust, putting it on the eyes
of the man born blind—a reference to the way the Father made Adam
from the earth (V, 15, 2–3). Similarly, the example of the Jews, who
took the spoils of Egypt with them at their exodus, is a model for us:
we are right to make use of natural things in order to carry out our
Christian ministry (IV, 30, 1–3). The Christian totality does not throw
a dark shadow over the world and the things within it, as do all the
other world-denying religions and the Christian sects, for this world is
the work of the God who is the highest Good, destined for the greatest
possible participation in him.

Then there is the continuity of the historical ages. The apparent
break between the Old and the New Covenant simply gives Irenaeus
an opportunity of demonstrating most emphatically how the two
belong together and how the New logically follows from the Old. In
the first place, the Old Covenant as a whole is a prophecy looking
toward Jesus Christ: it ratifies him and is itself ratified by the prophecy's
fulfillment (V, Prol.). The underlying diversity of the two Covenants
becomes visible at the same time as their harmony (III, 12, 12); the New
is anticipated (IV, 32, 2) and heralded (IV, 9, 1) in the Old: "We only
speak of less and more with regard to things which have something in
common, whose natures do not contradict each other." Thus the "law
of slavery" was given to a single nation, whereas the "grace of freedom
was poured out over the whole world" (IV, 9, 2). Naturally the Pauline
idea of the Law as a pedagogue preparing for Christ is strongly
emphasized (IV, 2, 7; IV, 12, 5; IV, 13, 1) with love appearing as the
fulfillment of the whole Law (IV, 12, 2). All the same, on the other
hand, there is no abridgement of Paul's teaching that the law convicts
of sin: III, 18, 7, and that justification (for example, of Abraham,
without circumcision) is on the basis of faith alone: IV, 16, 2; IV, 25, 1;
V, 22, 1. Thus, while God's Word will be present everywhere in the
Old Covenant (IV, 5, 3ff.; IV, 10, 1), partially glimpsed by the
prophets (IV, 20, 10; IV, 33, 10),[18] the entire economy of the Old
Covenant will only become intelligible through Christ's Cross (IV,
26, 1). The Old Covenant could not attain perfection (which is why the
fathers must wait in the *infernum*), but Christ overcomes this by
descending there, for he has come not only for his contemporaries but
for all men, including those who lived before him (IV, 22, 1; IV, 31, 1;

---

[18] On one occasion Irenaeus says that God is seen in the Old Covenant by the
Spirit, in the New by the Son and in the kingdom of heaven by the Father
himself: IV, 20, 5.

IV, 33, 12).[19] This all-embracing doctrine of history emphasizes the "temporal appropriateness" of everything that happens; the "right moments" (*kairoi*) constitute an ordered series (III, 16, 7), a "well-constructed, articulated melody" (IV, 20, 7). Our gaze goes back beyond the time of the Law, right back to the beginning, and we discern that the latter is in harmony with the perfecting (recapitulating) end: Adam–Christ, Eve–Mary; for woman too must utter the obedient consent that makes the Incarnation possible and accompanies it, that consent which the first woman refused.[20]

Finally there is the continuity between Christ–Spirit and the Church, perfecting the *communio* of mankind and creation with the Father. In Mary, the Spirit elicited the perfect response to the Word; in the life of the Church he also produces a proportional response to the demands of Jesus' perfect ethics; this can go to the lengths of martyrdom for the truth of the total Incarnation and Passion of Jesus (III, 12, 13; IV, 33, 9). Irenaeus can only see the Church as a unity: through the succession of those who are called to witness to the truth (III, 3, 2), she and her doctrine of faith are always the same in all ages and in all places (I, 10, 1; V, 20, 2).[21] Similarly, succession (apostolic office), sound teaching and holiness in the Church cannot be separated (IV, 26, 4–5). The fullness attained in Christ is not a past that is forever fixed, it is always continuing in the Church here and now: "He has filled everything with his advent, and in the Church he continues to fulfill the New Covenant prophesied by the Law until the prophesied end shall come" (IV, 34, 2).

We have set forth the theology of Irenaeus[22] here simply as one

---

[19] In *Mysterium Salutis* III/2 (1969), 249, I misinterpreted Irenaeus' *id quod erat inoperatum conditionis visurus oculis* (*Adv. Haer.* IV, 22, 1) as the "vision of chaos"; in fact it refers to the righteous men who lived before Jesus, whose imperfection he removed by his descent *ad inferos*.

[20] It will suffice merely to indicate the theme, which has such a central place in Irenaeus: Eve–Mary: III, 22, 4; V, 19, 1; *Epid.* 33; the role of Mary: III, 19, 2; III, 21, 10; III, 22, 2; IV, 23, 1; IV, 33, 4 (with the commentary of the critical edition in *Sources chrétiennes* IV, 296ff.), IV, 33, 11; V, 1, 3; V, 21, 1.

[21] "The path of those who belong to the Church runs through the entire world and has the firm apostolic tradition, showing us that the faith of all is one and the same. All confess one and the same Father, all believe in the same economy of the Incarnation of the Son of God, acknowledge the same gift of the Spirit, observe the same commandments, maintain the same form of Church order, expect the same advent of the Lord, hope for the same sanctification of the whole man, that is, of soul and of body. Thus the Church's message is true and assured, since she teaches one and the same path of salvation throughout the whole world. God's own light has been entrusted to her."

[22] Irenaeus is well able to distinguish theology from the revealed truth

example of the totality principle of theodramatic hermeneutics of which we have spoken in outline. In the central fact of the Incarnation of the Word, the greatest thing possible is achieved: the total glorification of God and of man in God (IV, 17, 6).

---

ordinarily believed, but it is the latter which constitutes its foundation and its permanent starting point. On this basis theology "endeavors to discover" how the divine meaning is contained in the historical facts: I, 10, 3.

E. THE THEMES OF DRAMATIC THEOLOGY

Theology has always been aware that it has to do with a drama between God and man, and this awareness is expressed down the centuries in the various forms theology has taken. It was less clearly aware, however, that it was bound to adapt its form to this dramatic content, particularly where theology understood its task to be, not to enter into and reproduce the normative, given drama, but to explain its meaning—just as countless studies attempt to elucidate the meaning of *Faust*. For theology is not an adjunct to the drama itself: if it understands itself correctly, it is an aspect of it and thus has an inner participation in the nature of the drama (where content and form are inseparable). Secondly, theology has at its disposal various degrees of intensity of such participation as well as various literary themes and patterns, enabling it to represent revelation's dramatic character, and each of these embraces one aspect of the unique, archetypal and inexhaustible drama. Of course, this presupposes that theology understands itself to be involved in and committed to the drama which—according to the Bible—is taking place.

What we said about the Gospel of John is applicable to the other Gospels, and it also applies to the Old Testament as a whole: "Constructed in the manner of a drama, it enables us to take part in the conflict between darkness and light and compels us to choose the light while there is still time (Jn 12:30)."[1] The Old Testament part of the drama moves toward a catastrophe (the rejection of the nation, cf. Jeremiah), which is followed by a highly equivocal reconciliation;[2] this is rendered unequivocal in the New Testament part and is expressed in a reciprocal heightening: of the nation's rejection of God's offer, on the one hand, and of a superabundant granting of salvation on the other —which comes at the very climax of rejection. Objectively, that

[1] Cothenet, in *Dict. Spir.*, article "Imitation du Christ", col. 1556. Cf. C. M. Cornick, "The Dramatic Character of the Fourth Gospel" in *JBL* 67 (1948), 159–67; A. Feuillet, in Robert-Feuillet, *Introduction à la Bible* II (1959), 625.

[2] Cf. *Herrlichkeit* III/2, part 1: Alter Bund, "Das lange Zwielicht" (Einsiedeln: Johannes Verlag, 1967), 285–336 (*The Glory of the Lord* VI).

is, from God's perspective, this result must be regarded as (eschatologically) final and definitive, while, in the dramatic dimension of the Church's history, it is always present, here and now, unresolved, polarized, involving all of us, as a community and as individuals, in the biblical drama.

The whole drama, with Jesus Christ at its center, but drawing the world, from its beginning to its end, into the action, has from time to time been the object of theological portrayal. For the most part this portrayal has been partial, that is, theology was presented from the point of view of a particular dramatic theme. Here we shall mention four such themes; two of them will be illustrated by one author apiece.

1. *God's Lawsuit*

God's lawsuit against his chosen but unfaithful people, threatened and yearned for by the Old Testament prophets, reaches its climax in the life, death and Resurrection of Jesus. Its background is the "Covenant" and the "Law" enshrined in it. Fundamentally it is a law of grace, manifesting an essential attribute of the God who freely reveals and gives himself and summoning the chosen people to respond with gratitude; as the gracious events unfold, it is seen to have an unmistakably juridical component.[3] This is connected with both God's divine nature and man's responsibility, deemed worthy, as he is, of the Covenant with God. The juridical component has an abiding and legitimate place within theo-drama and its theological presentation. No theology is to be rejected as unbiblical or unspiritual because it employs juridical categories (for example, Anselm's teaching on redemption). For as long as the New Covenant of grace stands, "judgment" will remain an indispensable, basic articulation of revelation, something that belongs to its language.

Against the background of the law of grace enshrined in the Covenant between God and man (initially Israel), any infringe-

---

[3] *Herrlichkeit* III/2, the chapter on Hesed, Sedeq and Mizpat, 147–60 (*The Glory of the Lord* VI).

ment of the law by sinful man draws down God's judgment against him.[4] This judgment in the Old Covenant can be called "fictive", but the fact that it is ultimately carried out, to the very letter, in the case of Jesus, shows its whole gravity and realism. "Hear the word of the Lord, O people of Israel; for the Lord has a controversy with the inhabitants of the land. There is no faithfulness or kindness and no knowledge of God in the land" (Hos 4:1f.). Isaiah makes the same proclamation (3:13–14), Jeremiah (2:9), Micah (6:2, recalling God's proven faithfulness: 6:3–5).[5] Yahweh's case for the prosecution (with the announcement of the relevant penalties) can also turn into a direct pronouncement of judgment, as in Psalm 50 and similar psalms. On the other hand, a desperate man such as Job can attempt to construct a case against God when he can no longer discern the latter's justice.[6] Thus, darkly, Job points ahead to the Cross of Jesus, where God seems to have lost his case against mankind.

In the New Testament, God's lawsuit against the Covenant people becomes utterly concrete in the most paradoxical way: just when, in the fate of Jesus, God seems to have lost his lawsuit, he resoundingly wins it in Jesus' Resurrection, as Paul shows in the Letter to the Romans (3:4) and John explains in some depth (16:7–11). Terms and expressions from the law courts pile up all around this lawsuit of world-historical, eschatological proportions. Thus, most of all, the terms "witness" and "testimony":[7] Jesus receives "testimony" from John the Baptist, from God; he refuses to accept the "testimony" of man; he appoints the Twelve to be "witnesses", and so forth. Then come the terms "convince", "convict" (*elenchein*),

---

[4] J. Guillet, article "Procès" in *Vocabulaire de théologie biblique* (1962), 858–63. We have adopted the presentation of the biblical theme of judgment given by Hasso Jaeger in *La Preuve* (see n. 45 above), 415–594.

[5] J. Harwey, "Le 'Rib-Pattern', requisitoire prophétique sur la rupture de l'alliance": *Bibl.* 43 (1962), 172–96. Further references in H. Wildberger, *Jesaja* I (1972), 8 and 10; also H. Jaeger, *La Preuve*, 434.

[6] H. Richter, *Studien zu Hiob. Der Aufbau des Hiobbuches, dargestellt an den Gattungen des Rechtslebens* (Berlin, 1959).

[7] I. de la Potterie, "La Notion de témoignage dans s. Jean" in *Sacra Pagina* = Bibl. Eph. Theol. Lovanens. XIII (Paris-Gembloux, 1959), 193–208. Also H. Jaeger, *La Preuve*, 462.

"accuse" (*katēgorein*), "Advocate" (*paraklētos*), "to judge", "Judge", "judgment" (*krinein, kritēs, krisis*).[8] The "eyewitness" plays a special role in the post-apostolic age.[9] In all these terms, which are drawn from the language of human jurisprudence in order to denote a transcendent "law (of grace)" in the Covenant between God and man, the historical and factual nature of divine revelation is most strongly stressed: Jesus himself, this historical human being, is witness to the divine truth, as he tells Pilate (Jn 18:37). Other testimony, true and false, is brought for and against his testimony; false testimony collapses when confronted with him, the divinely appointed Judge (5:22); yet he himself does not judge: his very existence brings about a separation among men (9:39; 3:18ff.).[10] Some are able to read his words, his works, himself as "signs" (*sēmeia*) of divine truth written in history; others cannot; the blind can acquire sight, and those who see can become blind, particularly if they have the capacity to see and yet do not want to (9:41). In this whole process, truth is not simply something ready at hand: it is something that unveils itself in and through men's attitude, so much so that God's truth itself is veiled through the false witness and false judgment of men. So when the Spirit, as the Witness of the Risen Son, "convinces the world of sin and of righteousness and of judgment", God's truth will reveal itself only—again—to those who (in faith) can "see", just as they alone will understand the judgment on the "world" to be what it really is.

This initially limited picture of God's lawsuit against man—and ultimately *with* man—can thus be broadened into an all-embracing interpretation of revelation, since it not only points back to the concluding of the Covenant in the Old Testament but also points ahead to the relationship between the God who creates, manifests himself, redeems man and judges him, and the free creature who has freely "fallen" and yet to whom God can give healing and new sight. Here the theme of the "lawsuit" opens out into a universal theodramatic dimension.

[8] Cf. the articles in *Th. W.* and in *Bauer*.
[9] Cf. the too little known work by Markus Barth: *Der Augenzeuge* (Evangel. Verlag Zollikon, 1946).
[10] D. Mollat, article "Jugement" in *Suppl. Dict. Bibl.* IV, 180.

2. *The Total Drama as Lawsuit*

In his short work, *Justification*,[11] Markus Barth has shown how the "lawsuit" theme opens out in this way. Starting from the Pauline doctrine of justification, he seeks to embrace the entirety of the scriptural meaning, not least the Old Testament substratum —which enables him to leave behind the rooted Protestant "dialectic" alternating between irreconcilable poles[12]—for instance, "sacrifice and faith (or obedience), judgment and love",[13] God's "righteousness and" his "love and faithfulness". "Forensic" does not actually mean external but simply in the manner "of a legal process before a court",[14] and of course the earthly law court is only an image, not a model that we can use to assess and read God's action.[15] And when M. Barth presents the whole court process as a drama in five acts, he has to admit right from the outset that Paul also uses metaphors that are quite different from the legal ones[16] and that at least in one place—where he speaks of Christ's justification by God and God's justification by Christ in the act of Resurrection—God's pronouncement of justice has no analogy,[17] which also applies to "the glory of his judgment".[18]

Everything rests on the Old Testament identity of God's "righteousness" and his "grace", which "signifies firm faithfulness to the Covenant",[19] so that even justification, which is "the attribution of faith as righteousness", is not a fiction and does not need to be distinguished from the inner imparting of new life:[20] in the Resurrection of Christ, evidently, the two are one. This fundamental equation grants us an immediate glimpse of the ultimate reality: "God's anger is the heat of his love",[21] and so his judgment (that is, the implementation of his justice)

---

[11] *Rechtfertigung. Versuch einer Auslegung paulinischer Texte im Rahmen des Alten und Neuen Testaments.* Theolog. Studien 90 (EVZ-Verlag, 1969). [American edition: *Justification* (Grand Rapids, Michigan: Eerdmans, 1971).] References are to the original German text.

[12] 36.   [13] 11, 44.   [14] 5.

[15] So much so that in Israel every earthly court sentence was delivered "in the Name of God", who was seen as the only One possessing and handing out justice: Barth 14; H. Jaeger, *La Preuve*, 446 passim.

[16] 8.   [17] 42.   [18] 52.   [19] 33.   [20] 57, 60.

[21] 17.

will cause "annihilation and resuscitation, curse and blessing, to follow one another in a strange sequence",[22] but in each case the first is brought about only with a view to the second. Nor is it as if God is conducting a monologue in this twofold act: "The manifestation of God's righteousness . . . aims to elicit reciprocity: man too should and shall show righteousness and faithfulness".[23]

> It is precisely the forensic character of the Covenant agreement that calls for a real response on the part of the nation and for a change in its manner of life. The responsibility expected of the People of God and accepted by it runs quite counter to the assumption that this People can only, and should only, act "as if" it were chosen and sanctified.[24]

Consequently M. Barth sees no ultimate contradiction in the two assertions of Paul, that is, that man is justified by faith but will be judged according to his works.[25]

Here we give merely a brief sketch of the five acts of the drama. The first is the court of judgment of God's wrath (announced with increasing urgency and with ever-widening scope by the prophets); according to the beginning of the Letter to the Romans, neither Gentiles nor Jews (particularly the latter!) nor proselytes will escape it: "There is no righteous man, no not one"; all fall short of the standard and the demand of God's holiness. But "does that constitute a juridical victory on God's part? . . . In that case God's triumph would be bought simply at man's expense"; he would have "failed as Creator".[26] So in the second act God sends his Son as the Advocate ("witness") of the accused. "He pleads on behalf of sinful men, not saints in disguise." The Son is "the divinely appointed representative of men",[27] he makes intercession. (He does not ask that grace should take precedence over justice, for with God they are one and the same, namely, his covenant faithfulness.) And, as the Old Testament supplicants, from Abraham and Moses right up to the Suffering Servant, did in some anticipatory fashion, he interposes his life ("blood") for sinners. The "sacrifice" of his life, like every sacrifice, is "an act of justice".[28] It is an act of justice in his total obedience to God, his keeping of the Law,

[22] 13.   [23] 12.   [24] 55.   [25] 64 n.   [26] 25.
[27] 48.   [28] 35.

which calls for the love of God and of neighbor. God accepts the Advocate's offer of himself. He does not spare his Son, makes him "to be sin"; God's curse lies upon the Crucified. Insofar as he is a representative of men—Jews and Gentiles—all those whom he represents are "crucified with him". "His death is their death".[29] But insofar as the Crucified is God's Son, the "tension" that comes to the surface here "between fulfillment and failure" is "taken into God himself. . . . Here, plainly, God stands against God." With Jesus' last cry, "the terrible idea of the death of God becomes thinkable".[30] An absolute abyss opens up: "in burying the body of Christ, all hope has to be buried too".[31]

The third act, the Resurrection of Jesus from the dead, introduces a completely new turn in the court process, something that has no analogy. But we always knew that the Lord of the Covenant has the power "to go down to hell and to return from there". And there is nothing arbitrary here, for in the "inner-trinitarian event" of the Resurrection, God the Father proves his faithfulness toward his obedient Son. The latter's death was both a total confession of sin[32] and a prayer;[33] so his Resurrection is both his absolution and the granting of his intercession on behalf of sinners. At this point M. Barth rejects the metaphor of "redemption" ("payment") as belonging to a different context of images, particularly since it resulted in "the legal-mercantile satisfaction theory, which involved belief in Christ's vicarious function and the application of his merits".[34] "Only the personal love between Father and Son and God's own faithfulness to men . . . won the day." Because the Son is our representative, his justification has also "totally changed our legal status".[35]

The fourth act, the sending and work of the Spirit, finally shows that our justification (our "having been raised with Christ") means that we have been inserted into the life of the Son: we have been made coheirs with him. On the basis of the Resurrection event, the Apostles are sent out not only to make known the fact of God's gracious judgment (the cognitive

[29] 38.   [30] 38–39.   [31] 41.   [32] 31.   [33] 45.
[34] 45–46 n.   [35] 47.

aspect) but "through proof of the Spirit and of power", by reflecting the suffering and Resurrection of Christ, to make the event present in the life of the Apostles and then in the life of the community too. Four themes come together here, not without further significance in the background. First there is the trial of Jesus; then the announcement that the Apostles will give their testimony, inspired by the Spirit, before governors and kings; next the portrayal of the Acts of the Apostles, according to which the preaching of the gospel will lead from one court proceeding to another but will not be hindered by this—in fact it will be powerfully promoted as a result; and finally the reference to the coming Last Judgment.[36] Thus the Old Testament theme (righteousness-judgment-lawsuit) retains its vitality throughout, coming to a climax in the "doxology of judgment" (which also has its roots in the Old Testament) in which the Judge is acclaimed after he has pronounced sentence: "Yes, you are right!" (literally: "Thou art justified in thy sentence and blameless in thy judgment": Ps 51:4). In Paul, this act of approving God's justice, which is the fundamental attitude of the man who has been reconciled, is simply: faith. It is the Covenant response to God, now made possible through Christ, namely, faithfulness in return for faithfulness. "First of all faith is God's and his Son's attribute and gift."[37] Through the Spirit, all this remains constant, here and now; justification does not remain a merely past or present event but always a future event too (Gal 5:5). For, prior to the last act, we live in hope.

The fifth act is the visible manifestation of salvation—in the form of the Last Judgment. Now the powers of the cosmos (of which M. Barth has already taken due account) bow to Christ; "they are not simply annihilated but are finally brought into that order which corresponds to their place in God's good creation".[38] Man, however, irradiated by the light of Christ, reveals what is hidden in him, things unknown even to himself. Both what is evil and what is good in him (of which, no doubt, he is "hardly or not at all aware") must "go through the fire of Christ's judgment". Thus it is clear that "nothing is good or evil in itself"; "a thing is only good and just when God regards and

[36] 54 n.   [37] 58.   [38] 66–67.

accepts it as such. He who alone is good is the only One who can determine what is good." But since our Judge is also our Advocate with God, "our case simply cannot be utterly lost". "God is well pleased with his Son, and this overflows onto those whom his Son represents."[39]

M. Barth develops his dramatic outline in seventy pages, almost in the style of a telegram. Naturally many questions remain open. Is it not necessary, if we are fully to understand the biblical dramatic perspective, to engage in explicit reflection on the nature of human freedom and its powers and on what is implied by the powerlessness which characterizes our fallen state? Surely a little more must be said about the Mediator and how, on the one hand, he is able to keep the Covenant with God up to the very last, while, on the other hand, he is able to show such ontological solidarity with sinners that his justification (his Resurrection) becomes theirs? How is it possible to reject the notion of "vicarious" action while accepting the idea of "representation"? And how can the gift of life through the Spirit make man inwardly good, if goodness is always dependent on God's decision? Is the danger of theo-panism (or Christo-panism) totally banished, as M. Barth most explicitly wishes? And does a genuine drama come into being between divine and human freedom?

3. Christ's Dramatic Struggle

M. Barth's sketch, from the Reformed tradition, had already been preceded by that of the Lutheran, Gustaf Aulén, whose *Christus Victor*[40] attracted much attention when it appeared in English in 1931. In 1968, replying to objections, he published his *Das Drama und die Symbole*.[41] Once again soteriology is at the center, but (especially in the second work) it expands to a comprehensive theology. Three types of atonement doctrine

---

[39] 71.

[40] *Christus Victor*, an Historical Study of Three Main Types of the Idea of Atonement (SPCK, 1931) = V.

[41] *Das Drama und die Symbole. Die Problematik des heutigen Gottesbildes* (Göttingen: Vandenhoeck & Ruprecht, 1964) = D.

are sharply differentiated: the biblical and patristic type (taken up by Luther), which is termed "dramatic" and hence "classical"; the "objective" type (actually it *objectifies* in a rationalist spirit), which is also called "Latin", which was begun by Tertullian and finds its clearest expression in Anselm; and the "subjective" type, developed by Abelard in reaction to Anselm[42] and asserting itself in Pietism, Enlightenment and Idealism. Rather than engaging in the often hair-splitting distinction between "dramatic" and "objective", it is better first of all to inquire about Aulén's overall perspective, which corresponds to his presentation of the "classical" type.

Two (related) intuitions are dominant: first, the overwhelming power of evil in the world, stronger than any human power. God alone is a match for it, but it cannot be defeated by an external act of power on God's part.[43] It may be the case today that this truth can no longer be expressed in biblical categories (for example, Paul speaks of the "elemental powers" of "death" that are the fruit of "sin") or in the patristic (often mythological) metaphors according to which Satan has some right over man: nonetheless, this truth is no less current in the world's dominant atmosphere.[44] People no longer speak of sin because the concept has been narrowed and "rationalized" by legalism. They no longer speak of "the wrath of God"; instead there is the phenomenon of the *homme révolté* who opposes a cruel God or an anonymous fate, and people feel overwhelmed by life's emptiness and meaninglessness; the world is a world without grace. Behind it all, therefore, Luther's question, "How can I find a gracious God?" is today just as relevant as formerly.[45] The only one who can deal with these "powers" is he who is mightier than man: God must enter the lists against them.

[42] V 150, 155.

[43] V 43, 44.

[44] Aulén takes up an analysis of Tillich's in which he distinguishes "three types of anxiety according to the three directions in which nonbeing threatens being. Nonbeing threatens man's ontic self-affirmation, relatively in terms of fate, absolutely in terms of death. It threatens man's spiritual self-affirmation, relatively in terms of emptiness, absolutely in terms of meaninglessness. It threatens man's moral self-affirmation, relatively in terms of guilt, absolutely in terms of condemnation", *The Courage to Be* (London: Nisbet, 1952), 38. But Aulén criticizes this stance from a theological point of view.

[45] D 83ff.

The second intuition transposes a "double-sidedness" into the picture of God itself.[46] For, on the one hand, as we have said, evil cannot be overcome from outside; God's opposition to the powers of evil must be carried on from within, on the stage of world history. On the other hand, this opposition must not lead to a Manichaean dichotomy, for God alone is absolute, and even the hostile powers must finally serve his all-embracing design for the world. We can even put it this way (with M. Barth): there is a conflict between "wrath" and "love" in God himself, but love is deeper than wrath, and the latter is overcome by the divine self-surrender in Jesus Christ.

From this perspective we can understand Aulén's polemic stance vis-à-vis Anselm's "rational" system; we can discern his Lutheran manifesto: "God was in Christ reconciling the world to himself" (2 Cor 5:19); that is, God alone, the only One who can deal with the vast might of evil, acts in and through Christ, through his Incarnation, his life and teaching, his dying and rising, and thus God is both the Reconciler and the Reconciled in an action that is one and continuous.[47] Christ (who is truly man!)[48] is, as such, solely God's action in history. Not only does this show the dramatic dimension to be an ultimate category for interpreting world events: it is the very key to the picture of God. In Christ, God personally steps onto the stage, to engage in "close combat" and vanquish the powers that enslave man.[49] Furthermore, the drama of Christ—which is "not a mere tragedy",[50] because through the Cross the victory of the Resurrection is achieved—is the only valid picture of what God is in himself: the One who conquers by total self-surrender.

This preempts any stress on a "work" performed by man that might be thought to rise up to God and influence him in any way or change his mind. The terms "satisfaction", "expiation", "merit", which were introduced by Tertullian and were employed much by Gregory I, gained the upper hand in Anselm: Christ's death reconciles God with the world according to the legal pattern of restored justice—though Aulén readily admits that, according to Anselm, God does not change; indeed, it is the Father who causes the Son to become man and to die—so that (allegedly) continuity is no longer maintained by the grace of

46 V 170f.   47 V 162.   48 D 272ff.   49 D 294.   50 D 276.

God but comes to rest[51] in a rationally perspicuous system of justice (that is, in the Old Testament "Law" instead of the Gospel).[52] In addition, the death of Jesus (which now becomes the only significant soteriological act of his Incarnation) no longer confronts and wars against the "elemental powers of this world" but is addressed to God the Father.[53] The thrust of Aulén's theory lies in this opposition of legalism and rationalism (or *"dogmatics"* and *"drama"*).

By contrast, the third, "subjective" type plays a role that, though historically important, is of little significance for theology. It moves the continuity from God (the classical type) or the *ratio* (second type) to the moral condition of the subject. Thus, for Schleiermacher (in spite of the Enlightenment inheritance), "redemption" means the transformation of a life, the dawning awareness of God; and "reconciliation" is the result, being reconciled with the universe. Even in Ritschl there is no essential change from this position, although he reintroduces the old, objective-sounding term "justification" (instead of "salvation").[54] The subjective type is Idealist and monist, and so it excludes any genuinely dramatic dimension. And whereas for Anselm it is solely the death of Jesus that is soteriologically relevant, for the "subjectivists" Jesus is only important as a human teacher and model.

Aulén's main historical difficulty seems to be that the biblical and patristic, "classical", view is so full of mythologizing elements: what are these "powers", who is this "prince of this world", who, according to Paul and John, rule the world and mankind? Who is this "devil" who, according to the Church Fathers, has been given power over men, either a legal power (so that he has to be paid a "ransom") or a power he has arrogated to himself (Gregory of Nazienzen), so that he must be overthrown by cunning (Christ incognito as God: Gregory of Nyssa), swallowing the hook along with the bait like a fish, or being taken in the mousetrap of the Cross (Augustine)? It is out of the question to revamp these and other symbols today.[55]

[51] Again and again the Lutheran dialectic of Law versus Gospel is emphasized as one of the fundamental antinomies (D 8; V 84f.), along with "judgment/redemption" (D 102).

[52] V 97–109.   [53] V 105.   [54] V 154.   [55] V 176.

Aulén calls for new forms so that the abiding, fundamental conflict between God and the hostile powers can be expressed, not purely monistically nor purely dualistically, but *dramatically*. John Macquarrie says of Aulén's demand: "It seems to me to offer the most promising basis for a contemporary statement of the work of Christ", but he also observes that one of Aulén's weaknesses "was his failure to come to grips with the mythological background of the principalities and powers".[56]

We can leave it an open question whether, as with Macquarrie (and in fact with Aulén himself),[57] the demonic can be regarded as the primal sin of idolatry, which ultimately destroys the person. But Macquarrie is right when he says that Aulén's "subjective" and "objective" types are indispensable components as far as man is concerned;[58] he thus removes the Lutheran dialectic from our image of God and from the doctrine of redemption.[59]

Later on we shall have to consider how "theo-drama" can be "theo-logic" and, in its own way, "theology". Aulén is surely right when he says that the unfathomable nature of God's love and his covenant with mankind is shown forth in Christ's life, and most particularly in his Cross and his abandonment by God;[60] that this covenant is fulfilled in the God-man, who at the same time was totally obedient to the Father and showed total solidarity with men;[61] and that God's victory, sealed in the Resurrection of Christ, was implicit in it.[62]

[56] *Principles of Christian Theology* (New York, 1966), 286f.

[57] Ultimately Aulén leaves it open whether the "devil" is to be imagined as a personal or an impersonal being. The only important thing is the "overwhelming power of the demonic" and its "destructive power in man's innermost self": D 235.

[58] *Principles of Christian Theology*, 289.

[59] Aulén himself resists the suggestion that the dramatic interplay of what cannot be rationally systematized should be seen in terms of "logical contradiction": "The classic type is characterized by a whole series of contrasts of opposites, which defy rational systematization, while the other two find rational solutions of the antinomies along theological or psychological lines": V 172.

[60] D 243.   [61] D 253.

[62] Consequently Aulén resists all attempts to isolate the Cross from the Resurrection; he rejects all one-sided Passion-mysticism (of which even Bultmann seems to be in awe), as well as the tendency to reduce the picture of God to a

4. The Drama of Discipleship

The scope of this heading is so vast that a few indications will have to suffice. If, according to the Christian understanding, there is at the center of history a drama that determines it in its entirety (whether it is seen more as a lawsuit or as a battle or in other categories), human life, both personally and socially, will also be shaped by it.

In the Old Testament this theme is not prominent, for here it is primarily God who conducts his lawsuit against his people, whereas Israel's external wars make no significant contribution to the topic. In its original form, Job's dictum, subsequently much quoted in its LXX version (7:1), that "man's life on earth is a warfare", is simply a reference to the exhausting toil of the hired laborer who works in the fields. It is Origen who first applies the wars of Israel's desert wanderings to the spiritual warfare of Christians.

The idea of life as military service was common in pre-Christian antiquity, at least from Plato on (but no doubt it had roots in Pythagoras), and particularly among the later Stoics (Seneca and Epictetus);[63] but there is a basic difference between the innumerable passages that could be quoted and the Christian understanding: the "warrior" of antiquity had to remain "at his post" in the face of an unalterable power (fate) and thus prove himself worthy of the divine mission allotted to him, whereas the Christian disciple somehow has to fight shoulder to shoulder with Christ against God's enemies.

Thus Socrates, for instance, who had fought in several actual battles (as he mentions in his valedictory speech), was called to

---

one-sided and (merely) "suffering God", as, for instance, in William Temple's *Christus Veritas* (1924), which comes very near to Patripassianism. Cf. A. M. Ramsey, *From Gore to Temple* (1960). For Aulén, however, the fundamental battle remains that between God and hell. Thus those Church Fathers are nearest to his heart who portray this battle in images which, while admittedly mythical, are all the more vivid and eloquent. In his *Gott und Hölle* (Leipzig: Studien der Bibl. Warburg, 1932), Josef Kroll has assembled a wealth of documents on this subject.

[63] Hilarius Emonds, "Geistlicher Kriegsdienst. Der Topos der militia spiritualis in der antiken Philosophie" in *Heilige Überlieferung*, Festgabe für Abt Ildefons Herwegen (Münster, 1938), 21–50.

his post by God; he must hold on there even if death is the result
(*Apol.* 28d).[64] In a similar vein the dying Socrates (*Phaid.* 62b)
rejects suicide (with a reference to esoteric teachings): man must
stand fast at the post at which the gods have placed him. In the
Laws (626e) "self-conquest" appears as the preeminent conquest,
a view that will be taken up by every Idealist philosophy and
dramatic theory (Kant, Schiller). The Stoics use the image of life
as warfare in broad and manifold ways; thus we meet the notion
that God hardens, proves and tests the man he values: this is an
honor for the man concerned.[65] Or the unique "vocation" of
Socrates can be extended to all men.[66]

Jesus too is aware that he is conducting a war. Thus he is the
one who "enters a strong man's house and plunders his goods"
after having "first bound the strong man"—Beelzebub—(Mt
12:29). And in the next verse we read: "He who is not with me is
against me." He is aware of the direction his commission must
and will take, if it is to be carried out right to the end.[67] He sends
his disciples into the very same situation (Mt 10:16ff.; Jn 15:20ff.,
and so on). This quite transforms every Jewish understanding of
war, even if warlike metaphors are adopted from the prophets
and apocalyptic writings, as we find frequently in Paul; precisely
where he speaks in some detail of the Christian's armor (Eph
6:10–18), he is referring to the spiritual battle against demons,
for the sake of the "gospel of peace".[68] The enemy against

[64] On the translation of *phroura* as "guard-post", cf. Emonds, "Geistlicher
Kriegsdienst", 26ff.

[65] E.g., Seneca, *De prov.* 4, 6.

[66] In Epictetus it is the philosopher, in the first place, who is thus called (*Diss.*
3, 24, 31) and then every man (*Diss.* 3, 24, 100).

[67] H. Schürmann, "Wie hat Jesus seinen Tod bestanden und verstanden? Eine
methodenkritische Besinnung" in *Jesu ureigener Tod* (Herder, 1975), 16–65.

[68] A. von Harnack, *Militia Christi* (Tübingen, 1905). Harnack's second
theme, the Christian's refusal of military service, does not concern us here.
Other references in Paul: 1 Th 5:8; 2 Cor 6:7; 10:3–6; Rom 6:13f., 23; 13:12; Phil
2:25; Col 4:10; 1 Tim 1:18; 2 Tim 2:3ff. In the passages of the early Fathers
quoted by Harnack, it is noteworthy that the Christian awareness of fighting for
and with Christ often appears in the garb of antiquity; that is, the Christian
warrior is urged to exercise the office and rank to which he has been appointed
(1 Clem 37), not to desert (Ignatius to Polycarp 6) and not to leave his *post*
(Clem. Alex., *Strom.* VII, 16, 100; Hermas, *Simil.* V, 1; Tertullian, *De or.* 19).
Cyprian's image (cf. Harnack 42) of the Christian's warfare as a magnificent

whom Jesus has to do battle could not even be identified in the Old Covenant; he is only startled into the open with the advent of Jesus, filled with the Spirit of God—hence Jesus' many encounters with demons, his temptation, hence the hour of darkness[69]—and hence the Christian disciple's committed involvement. It is normal for this discipleship to be initially an individual matter; thus, down through the history of the Church, most exhortations on "spiritual warfare" are addressed to the individual warrior, and such instructions are tirelessly repeated and reformulated through the centuries and millennia.[70] However, they move toward the periphery of dogmatics and actually migrate into the area of "spirituality", where they lead a special life and thus (once again) "de-dramatize" dogmatics.

Just as Christ's spiritual battle took place in order to reconcile the world with God, however, the battle that features in the life of the disciple must also have its essentially social dimensions. Origen is well aware of this.[71] But it is Augustine who establishes the connection most impressively, in a twofold way: particularly in his Commentary on the Psalms, he never isolates the drama of Christ, the Head, from that of the Church, his Body; accordingly the battle he portrays (particularly in the *City of God*) takes place in world history between the two *civitates*, that of God and that of this world. Often the two bodies are locked together indistinguishably like those of two warriors wrestling

---

spectacle watched by God and the angels may be influenced equally by Paul and Seneca. Tertullian (*Apol.* 50) links the motifs of lawsuit and warfare: "We are engaged in a battle when, summoned before the court, we have to fight for the truth there at the risk of our lives."

[69] J. Jeremias, *Ntl. Theologie*, 2d ed., I (1973), 96–99.

[70] The article "Combat spirituel" in *Dict. Spir.* only manages to give a few illustrations in view of the vast wealth of material.

[71] Anyone who has to fight a hard battle not only against flesh and blood like the Corinthians—1 Cor 10:13—but also against demons, like the Ephesians—Eph 6:12—(*Peri Arch*. III, 2, 3 and 4), does so essentially in service of the Church and the world. For texts, cf. W. Völker, *Das Vollkommenheitsideal des Origenes* (1931), 175ff. Cf. also the symbolism in the story of Moses, who prays with uplifted arms during the battle with the Amalekites (Ex 17:8–16): *Hom in Ex*. XI, 4: "Origen describes this battle against sin with a vividness that leads us to believe that it is based on personal experience; it is full of dramatic movement, which never isolates the individual but situates him in the great cosmic context" (Völker 42).

in the heat of battle; only at the Last Day shall we actually see them separated. While Augustine, like his predecessors and successors, often speaks of the individual's "Christian *agôn*"— since the boundaries of both *civitates* pass right through every heart—he also always sees the whole soteriological scope of the individual's particular struggle.[72]

The theme continues to exert its influence down the centuries[73] (with various political slants too);[74] the heart of the Ignatian Exercises (in the meditations "The call [to arms] of the earthly king helps in the contemplation of the life of the Eternal King" and "The Two Standards [banners]") radiates a profound influence even on much modern spirituality; again, it embraces the individual and the social dimensions in a unity. The individual dimension is outlined in the complex of "Rules for distinguishing between different spiritual influences", which looks back to a weighty biblical, patristic and medieval tradition;[75] the social dimension consists, as in the Fathers, in fighting side by side with Christ within the Church (*Exercises* nos. 170, 353); it is a matter of the kingdom of Christ asserting itself in time (nos. 95, 145). The "choice" that is central to the *Exercises* signifies the individual's discovery of the particular mission God has intended

[72] B. Roland-Gosselin, "Le Combat chrétien selon s. Augustin" in *Vie Spir.* (1930), 71ff.

[73] F. Tournier, "Les Deux cités dans la littérature chrétienne" in *Etudes* (1910), 644–65. The author identifies a striking link between Augustine and Ignatius in Werner II von Küssenberg (d. 1174), 8th Abbot of St. Blasius and his work, the *Liber deflorationum* (PL 157, 722–1256). (He points to *Similitudines* 46 and 80 of the Pseudo-Anselm, PL 159, 625, 651, as a parallel to Ignatius' meditations on the "call".) Werner's book influences the *Miscellanea* from St. Victor (PL 177, 496) and other authors like Alain of Lille (*Sent.* PL 210, 248). We can recognize the direct influence of Augustine's teaching on the "two states" in many writers, e.g., Rupert, Hugh, Richard, Gerhoh, Hildegard, etc. (cf. Tournier 656). For work which may have influenced Ignatius, see the critical edition of the *Exercises* in *Mon. Hist. S. J.* 100 (1969), 34–60.

[74] Cf. E. Troeltsch, *Augustin, die chr. Antike und das MA* (1915). A revival of this has taken place in the entire theology of Reinhold Niebuhr.

[75] Cf. Peter Vogt, *Die Exerzitien des hl. Ignatius ausführlich dargelegt in Aussprüchen der hl. Kirchenväter* III (Regensburg: Kösel-Pustet, 1914), part 2 (1925), 107–248; for the whole history, cf. the splendid article "Discernement des esprits" in *Dict. Spir.* III (1957), 1222–91. Some useful material in Leo Bakker, *Freiheit und Erfahrung* (Würzburg, 1970).

for him within the work of redemption (no. 135). There is an evident continuity between this subjective/objective, or individual/
social program and that of the Fathers.[76] However, in continuing the patristic tradition that embraces all Christians,
Ignatius also takes up the particular tradition that sees the
ascetic, the pneumatic man (Origen), then the monk (the Desert
Fathers, Evagrius, Pseudo-Makarius) and every person living
according to the evangelical counsels as the warrior of Christ
par excellence.[77] Erasmus, in his *Enchiridion militis christiani*
(1503), tries to liberate the theme from its restriction to the
religious life; the Theatine, Scupoli, in his *Combattimento spirituale*
(1589), sets forth the rules of battle in detail.

We have only mentioned a few of the peaks rising up out of
endless mountain ranges. This must suffice here, since our sole
aim was to show that the sense of the drama of a life lived in
discipleship of Christ has remained alive down the centuries,
even if it was excessively isolated from the manuals of dogmatics.

One observation by way of an appendix: when it is poetically
presented, of course, the theodramatic dimension does not have
to be clothed in the external form of the drama. It can just as well
be expressed in epic form (Milton) or in that of the novel
(Dostoyevsky's *The Devils*). There is also a close relationship
between the so-called "drama of stages" (for example Strindberg's
After Damascus) and the account of a pilgrimage like Dante's,
through hell and purgatory to heaven, or Bunyan's in *The
Pilgrim's Progress* (1678)—where the action is decidedly warlike
in places.[78] Two continuations of Bunyan's epic show how
narrative can pass over into drama: first, the bitter satire of
N. Hawthorne's *The Celestial Railroad* (1843),[79] where the

[76] Cf. Peter Vogt, *Die Exerzitien* . . . II, 7–125; 205–68.

[77] The very beginning of the *Rule of St. Benedict* speaks of military service
under the true King, the Lord Christ (Prol. 3; Prol. 40; c 1, 2; c 2, 20; c 61, 10, as
enumerated by Vogüé). The passage is undoubtedly influenced by the (Pseudo?)-
Basilian *Admonitio* used as an introduction to the Rule of St. Basil. Cf. Vogüé, *La
Règle de saint Bénoit, Sources chrétiennes* (1972), 1:412–13; 4 (commentary), 83ff.

[78] On the sources, cf. Henri Talon, *John Bunyan, the Man and His Works*
(London, 1951), 166ff. Bunyan's last work is entitled *The Holy War* (1682), in
which man's conversion is situated in the cosmic and apocalyptic war between
God and the devil.

[79] In *Mosses from an Old Manse* (1846).

Bunyanesque pathos, rendered obsolete in the industrialized world, challenges the reader to come to a deeper decision; and then C. S. Lewis' *The Great Divorce* (1946),[80] where the inter-play between hell and heaven is openly portrayed in terms of a dramatic decision on man's part. This brings us to the topic of the "stage", with which the main part of this book begins.

---

[80] Earlier, Lewis had already written *The Pilgrim's Regress*, taking up Bunyan's theme.

II. DRAMATIS PERSONAE (I)

A. THE STAGE: HEAVEN AND EARTH

It is a characteristic of theo-drama that its stage is not a neutral area on which any tragic or comic action whatsoever can be played: its stage has been designed for the *one* drama that is to be played on it; it is determined in part by the action that is to take place there. The drama, too, can only be played on this stage and on no other. That is why we must speak of the stage before we come to the actors themselves. But it also shows us why this nonneutral stage cannot be exhaustively described from outside the play: in fact, starting from an apparently uninvolved "outside" realm—the cosmological—it invites us to penetrate into ever more recondite "inside" realms, which are determined by the essential vantage point of the characters, by the action that moves to and fro between them and indeed by the nature of the characters themselves.

"In the beginning God created the heavens and the earth" (Gen 1:1): thus the Bible begins, epitomizing everything that God has made.[1] Note, right at the outset, that this picture of the world has two levels, not three: God did not, for instance, create the heavens, the earth and the underworld (let alone hell); the underworld, the realm of the dead, and hell, the place of the damned, only come into the focus of consciousness as a result of sin. This third dimension belongs only accidentally to the two substantial poles of creation. The same applies, in a manner of speaking, to the sea: it comes into being in the wake of the horizontal separation of heaven from the world that lies below it (Gen 1:9f.), insofar as it is imagined to be a place of the lost, inhabited by monsters hostile to God.[2] In this sense it will have

---

[1] It is clear that the Hebrews had no word to describe the cosmos as a whole (as the Greeks had). But this pair of terms remains dominant in the New Testament, where the word *"kosmos"*, too, was both available and frequently used.

[2] The Babylonian myth of the overthrow of the primeval sea in connection with creation is used in the Bible only as a poetic image: Job 3:8; 7:12; 9:13; 26:12; 40:25ff.; Ps 68:8; 74:13f.; 77:17; 89:10f.; 93:3f.; 104:7, 26; 107:29; 148:7; Is 27:1; 51:9f.

disappeared in the eschatological world.[3] Generally, however, the sea and its denizens, like all other creatures, are summoned to join in the praise of the Creator.[4] Even on cosmological grounds, therefore, it is wrong to speak of the "three-decker model of the world" as a central biblical idea.

In Genesis 1–11, the special history of salvation that begins with Abraham is preceded by an account of the creation of the world and of primeval history, in concepts and ideas consciously borrowed from a store of human tradition—even with regard to the portrayal of the divine creative activity[5]—but which just as deliberately drops all mythical elements, that is, asserting that heaven is "created" just as much as the earth is. Initially God, the almighty Creator, is equally remote from either; an almost endless series of passages in Scripture, up to and including the New Testament, tirelessly celebrates him as the One who "has

[3] Rev 21:1. But God had already made a way for his people to pass through the dried-up sea (in the passing of the Sea of Reeds) and through "the waters of the great deep": Is 51:10; cf. Ps 74:13; Is 27:1.

[4] Ps 69:35; cf. Acts 4:24; 14:15; Rev 14:7.

[5] Cf. the introduction to the great commentary on Genesis by Claus Westermann (*Bibl. Komm. AT*, 1966–1974 [English translation, SPCK, 3 vols.]), where it is demonstrated that the biblical creation has nothing to do with a primal drama concerned with vanquishing chaos (contrary to Gunkel, *Schöpfung und Chaos in Urzeit und Endzeit*, 1895) and that, on the other hand, many elements that are common not only to eastern religion but also to mankind in general are incorporated into the biblical text without further ado. Thus the account of creation contains traces of the various ideas on the process that were current at the time. It is seen as a birth, or rather the offspring of a birth (Gen 2:4a, at least, still speaks of the *toledōth*, the "generations" of heaven and earth); as the result of a battle (a faint shadow of this in Gen 1:2); as activity and creativity, primarily as a work of separation (Babylonian, but also Sumerian and Egyptian); as the fashioning of man out of clay (a view found all over the world; associated with his fashioning of men is a special decision on God's part; God discusses the matter with himself); as the forming of man in the image of God (another widespread idea, cf. H. Wildberger, "Das Abbild Gottes" in *Th. Z.* 21 [1965], 245–59, 481–501); and finally it is seen as creation through mere utterance (even in primitive cultures, for example, Memphis—Ptah creates the world out of his heart [= spirit] and by his tongue—and Mesopotamia). On the one hand, God speaks "and it is so", on the other hand, he works (he "separates", "makes"), and finally he causes things (plants, for instance) to "spring forth" from the earth. There is even a precedent for God's resting after his work of creation (Westermann 36–57). On the question of the narrative form of this "creation out of nothing" and how it *can* be "narrated", see Westermann 60–64.

made heaven and earth".[6] Just as frequently it is emphasized—
in deliberate opposition to all mythology—that God "created
heaven (or the heavens) and the earth".[7] Thus God's glory is
"above the heavens" (Ps 113:4), "above heaven and earth" (Ps
148:13); he has to bend down in order to see them both (Ps
113:6), he is omnipresent in both (Ps 139), fills both (Jer 23:24),
but is lifted up above them, because the Creator's immanence
presupposes his transcendence; hence the call: "Be exalted, O
God, above the heavens! Let thy glory be over all the earth!" (Ps
57:6).[8] Both are creatures, which is why it is forbidden to swear
by either of them.[9] Both are required to extol their Creator,
praise his righteousness, pay their homage to his majesty.[10]
Both of them can only tremble before him,[11] and both mourn
for the laying waste of Israel.[12] The people are warned not to
worship the heavens (that is, the heavenly host or the "Queen
of heaven").[13] Both heaven and earth belong to God (Ps 89:12;
1 Chron 29:11); he is the "God of heaven and earth" (Ezra 5:11).

Without departing from the foregoing in the least, the Bible
goes one step further. Basically it is a single step, but it can be
interpreted in two directions. It is the step taken by man living

---

[6] Gen 14:19, 22 (Melchizedek!); 24:3; Ex 20:11; 31:17; 2 Kings 19:15; 2 Chron
2:11; Neh 9:6; Judith 13:18; Ps 102:26; 121:2; 124:8; 134:3; cf. 135:6; 146:6; Is 37:16;
Jer 32:17; Dan 14:5; Jonah 1:9; 2 Macc 7:28.

[7] 1 Chron 16:26; Job 9:8; Ps 33:6; Ps 96:5; Ps 136:5; Prov 3:19; Is 40:22; 45:12,
18; 48:13; 51:13, 16; Jer 10:12; cf. 31:35.

[8] Cf. also Ps 108:5.

[9] But they can be called as witnesses: Dt 4:26; 30:19; 31:28; cf. 32:1, 40;
1 Macc 2:37; God himself does this: Ps 50:4. For the prohibition on swearing:
Mt 5:34 (cf. the further reason in 23:10–22); James 5:12.

[10] Ps 19:2; 50:6; 69:35; 85:12; 89:6; 97:6; 136:26; 1 Chron 16:31; (= Ps 96:11).
Is 44:23; 49:13; Tob 8:5. In Ps 148:1–6 everything connected with heaven is
individually summoned to join in praising God, because everything in heaven
has been created.

[11] Joel 2:10; 4:16.

[12] Jer 4:28; cf. the covering of the heavens, Ezek 32:7. Then there are the
eschatological texts in which heaven passes away, just like the earth, e.g., Is 34:4
(Rev 6:14); Mt 24:35 (5:18); Lk 16:17; 21:33; 2 Pet 3:7–12; Rev 20:11.

[13] 2 Kings 17:16; 21:3, 5; 23:4, 5; Zeph 1:5; 2 Chron 33:3, 5; Jer 7:18; 8:2;
44:17ff. On the Day of Judgment Yahweh will punish the host of heaven: Is
24:21f. He continually watches over the hosts: Sir 17:32 (cf. 16:28).

within a natural world model, to whom the world presents
itself, in all immediacy, as an "above": the heavens, and a
"below": the earth, just as Yahweh promises his blessing to his
people "as long as the heavens are *above* the earth" (Dt 11:21);
everything earthly is described, in countless passages, as lying
"under heaven". Initially we can see this "above" as a symbol of
God's being eternally "above" all things: "For as the heavens are
higher than the earth, so are my ways higher than your ways
and my thoughts than your thoughts" (Is 55:9). There is a
similar metaphor in the affirmation that God's "steadfast love
extends to the heavens, (his) faithfulness to the clouds" (Ps
36:6),[14] or that his faithfulness is "firm as the heavens".[15]
Accordingly, the laws and mysteries of heaven are inaccessible
to earthly man, who is essentially "under" heaven.[16] On the
other hand, man is dependent for his existence on the gifts that
come from above: the sun and its dependability (Ps 19:5–7), rain
(Dt 11:14; 28:22; 1 Kings 8:36) and dew (Dt 33:28; Zech 8:12)—
although there is an awareness that the fullness of blessing
comes both from *above* and from *below* (Gen 27:28; 49:25).[17] In
the context of this dependence on what comes from above—
which also indicates man's limitations—man's hubris, his stub-
born endeavor to overstep the appointed limits, is seen as an
attempt to "climb, storm and conquer heaven". This is what
happens, collectively, in the building of the Tower of Babel
(Gen 11:1–9),[18] and individual sins of pride are frequently seen
in the same terms.[19]

[14] Also Ps 57:11; 108:5; similarly Ps 103:11.

[15] Ps 89:2; cf. 89:29, 36, 37.

[16] Gen 6:17; Ex 17:14 and very frequently. In Ecclesiastes (3:1, 1:14; 4:3:
"under the sun", etc.), this "under" is the characteristic of transitoriness and
futility. On this aspect of hiddenness and inaccessibility: Prov 30:4 ("Who has
ascended to heaven?"); Is 40:12 ("Who has marked off the heavens with a
span?"); Jer 31:37; Bar 3:29; Job 38.

[17] Cf. Dt 33:13; Neh 9:15. And Ps 85:12: "Faithfulness will spring up from
the ground, and righteousness will look down from the sky. Yea, the Lord will
give what is good, and our land will yield its increase." But the "blessing from
below" is still a blessing, a gift freely granted, and hence in a higher sense it too
comes "from above". So the Letter of James can have the last word here: "Every
good endowment and every perfect gift is from above" (James 1:17).

[18] Cf. C. Westermann on the dangers of overinterpreting this passage.

[19] Is 14:13; Jer 49:16; 51:53; Dan 4:7, 8, 10; cf. Ps 139:8. Conversely there is
the theme of the proud man's being thrown down: Ezek 28:16 passim.

This means that the natural model of the world, where man looks up in limitation and dependence, contains an implicit religious element which, as we have said, can be interpreted in two directions: either what is "above" is divinized (in whatever way and to whatever degree), as happened in most if not all prebiblical religions,[20] or else it leads to a recognition of the grace that comes from the Creator of heaven and earth, that is, from "above"—from "heaven"! Israel resolutely chooses the second way (heaven is a created reality), and so it must walk along a difficult path: having adopted this point of departure, logic dictates that the concept of "heaven" migrate from its relative (cosmological) visibility to become the invisible (yet still worldly) point of departure (and hence point of destination) of God's saving activity.[21]

The biblical rejection of the divinization of heaven—and to that extent the account of creation and all that follows from it signifies a process of "demythologization" (which does not imply, however, an abolition of religion)—indicates the difficult path of seeing the earth/heaven distinction not only as a (dispensable) metaphor for the man/God distinction but also as an (indispensable) *sacrament* of the latter. As Karl Barth says, "There is in the one cosmos an 'above' and a 'below'. . . . They only reflect, but they do reflect, the true and proper and strict above and below of Creator and creature, of God and man. . . . We cannot try to go behind this likeness to a true reality that can be detached from it. We cannot treat this likeness as a cipher that can be dispensed with once it has been solved. . . . (In this case) all that is left is a little morality and mysticism, a little psychology or existential philosophy."[22] In biblical terms, heaven is "the place in the world from which God acts to and for and with man . . . from which He may really come to man and have real dealings with him". Without this "distance thus posited between himself and man", there could be "no genuine

[20] In the Greek world: "Heaven is the . . . sky, vaulting itself over the earth; at the same time it is that which totally embraces everything, a *theion* . . . (this) duality is indissoluble and unchanging" (H. Traub, Th.W.N.T. V, 497).

[21] Cf. on this subject the cautious but compelling steps in Karl Barth's *Church Dogmatics* III/3 (Edinburgh: T. & T. Clark, 1950), 418–99; from 450 onward, Barth discusses angelology).

[22] CD 421–22.

intercourse", "no dialogue" and hence "no drama" between God and man.[23] Thus the heaven/earth tension is the presupposition of all theodramatic action, both from God's side and from man's, and the more this realm of tension manifests its religious and revealed background behind and in the cosmological foreground, the more (as we began by saying) it constitutes one element of the drama itself.

Thus, prior to all action whatsoever, we discern the outlines of a picture of man and a picture of God. We discern the picture of a man who is placed on the earth to be "fruitful" there, to develop various technologies (Gen 4:17–22), to carry out his daily work (Ps 104:23), but all the same he remains essentially dependent on a blessing from a realm far above him that is inaccessible and cannot be manipulated by him. This is the paradox of a being which knows that it can only fulfill itself through grateful dependence on a grace on which it has no claim.

And we also discern the picture of a God who, despite his superiority to every creature (including heaven), wishes to be concretely present to man; so much so that, having chosen a particular place in this world, having filled it and set his mark upon it, God sets out to enter into a relationship with man, with the result that the shared history of God and man becomes an ever more concrete shared history of heaven and earth, right up to the proclamation of the "kingdom of heaven" on earth and the "ascent into heaven" of the incarnate Word of God.

Thus, seen from the end, the sacramental aspect of the field of tension becomes evident. But it was always there from the beginning, in the difficult, tentative way Israel had to go if it was to see God and heaven in a unity, neither divinizing heaven nor binding God to a single, created place.

It is impossible to ascertain when and under what influences Israel began to designate the "God of heaven and earth" as the "God of heaven": initially there must have been some Canaanite and, toward the end, some Persian influence. And even when this second denotation (and all it implies) becomes dominant, it is clear that he is God "in heaven above and on the earth

---

[23] CD 432.

beneath".[24] But he is also the One whose "steadfast love toward those who fear him" is "as high as the heavens are above the earth" (Ps 103:11). The elementary awareness of God's superiority automatically translates into the cosmological dimension: "The heavens are the Lord's heavens, but the earth he has given to the sons of men" (Ps 115:16). Or, with a certain bitterness, "God is in heaven, and you upon earth" (Eccles 5:2). And the natural blessing from above is translated into a divine and personal blessing: it becomes the miraculous feeding in the desert,[25] just as, conversely, heaven is "shut" and becomes "iron" (Lev 26:19) and "brass" (Dt 28:23) as God's punishment for sin.[26] Fire from heaven can mean two things: God's consuming answer in response to the offered sacrifice[27] or his judicial punishment.[28] The Covenant on Sinai is thus made visibly: God descends to the mountain[29] (or at any rate is present on its peak), while Moses climbs to the top. Even in Genesis, God is the God who "comes down".[30] And even at this early stage, the designation of God as the "Creator of heaven and earth" (Gen 14:19, 22) or as "God of heaven and of the earth" (24:3) passes over imperceptibly into the term "God of heaven" (24:7). Perhaps it is the natural attributes of God, who is "above", which assert and insert themselves in front of the name, so that the latter follows, as it were, automatically. God looks down from heaven, proclaims his judgment from heaven, listens from heaven,[31] sends his wisdom from heaven (Wis 9:10), but also sends brimstone from heaven as a punishment (Gen 19:24) and hailstones (Jos 10:11), thunder (1 Sam 2:10) and fire (2 Kings 1:10ff.). He calls from heaven and speaks from heaven.[32] Then (in later, more reflective passages) he hears *in* heaven.[33] For he has his dwelling in

---

[24] Dt 4:39; Jos 2:11; 1 Kings 8:23.

[25] Ex 16:4; Neh 9:15; Ps 78:23ff.; 105:40; Wis 16:20.

[26] Dt 11:6; 28:24; 1 Kings 8:35; 17–18; 2 Chron 6:26; 7:13; Ps 147:8; Haggai 1:10. It is not the (physical) heaven that sends the rain, but God: Jer 14:22.

[27] Lev 9:24; 1 Kings 18:38; 2 Macc 2:10; 1 Chron 21:26; 2 Chron 7:1.

[28] 2 Kings 1:10, 12, 14; Sir 48:3.

[29] Ex 19:18, 20; Neh 9:13.

[30] Gen 11:5; 18:21.

[31] Ps 14:2; 20:7; 53:3; 76:9; 80:15; 102:20; Is 63:15; Lam 3:50.

[32] Gen 21:17; 22:11, 15; Ex 20:22; Dt 4:36; Neh 9:13.

[33] 1 Kings 8:34, 36, 39, 43, 45, 49; similarly 2 Chron 6:14, 23, 25, 27, 30, 33, 35, 39; 7:14; Neh 9:27, 28.

heaven[34] and is therefore the "God of heaven",[35] the "Lord of heaven",[36] the "King of heaven".[37] For the most part these are late designations; in the Books of the Maccabees, "heaven" becomes a reverential term for "God".[38]

But while the name becomes established—and a tradition of relevant poetical imagery is handed on[39]—the concept of "heaven" is more and more decosmologized (as we can see in the observation that the heaven of heavens cannot contain God [1 Kings 8:27] and that he is supreme above them [Ps 113:4; 148:13]). At the same time, the interrelationship between heaven and earth becomes more and more strongly religious, or, more precisely, it is understood according to the events of revelation. This begins in prehistorical time with the rainbow as a sign of God's covenant with creation (although here, as yet, heaven is not explicitly thought of as God's dwelling place), and it proceeds in the reference to the stars of heaven in the blessing of Abraham;[40] in the ladder from earth to heaven in Jacob's dream, where the angels go up and down (Gen 28:10ff.); in the making of the Covenant on Sinai, sealed by the meal of the Seventy with Moses and Aaron before the face of God (Ex 24:10f.); and where God is understood to dwell simultaneously in heaven above and in the Israelites' camp beneath, so that Moses builds the earthly tabernacle in accordance with the heavenly prototype; thus the "tent of meeting" (Ex 40:34) comes into existence. Thus God's commandment is not "beyond your reach" but "very near you" (Dt 30:11); this means that Isaiah's tremendous affirmation portrays not only future events but things that are present here

[34] Dt 26:15; 1 Kings 8:30 (but 8:27!); 2 Chron 6:21; 30:27; Ps 2:4; 11:4; God builds his "upper chambers in the heavens": Amos 9:6.

[35] Ezra 1:2; 5:12; 6:9, 10; 7:12, 21, 23; Neh 1:4, 5; 2:20; Dan 2:19, 37, 44; 2 Chron 36:23. For Job, God is "high in the heavens" (22:12).

[36] Tob 7:17; Dan 2:28; Judith 5:8; 6:19.

[37] Dan 4:37.

[38] 2 Macc 7:11. "Let the will of heaven be done" (1 Macc 3:60). Heaven is praised (1 Macc 4:24, 55); it is called upon (2 Macc 3:15); heaven helps us (1 Macc 12:15; 16:3; 2 Macc 8:20); the judgment of heaven (2 Macc 9:4).

[39] The images of God's "traveling" through the heavens or above them are borrowed from mythology, but they are only used as poetical accompaniment: Dt 33:26; Ps 68:33; Job 22:14, and the whole gamut of epiphanies through atmospheric conditions.

[40] Gen 15:5; 22:17; Ex 32:13; in later texts the promise is seen as already fulfilled: Dt 1:10; 10:22; 28:62; Neh 9:23; 1 Chron 27:23.

and now: "For as the rain and the snow come down from heaven and return not thither but water the earth, making it bring forth and sprout, giving seed to the sower and bread to the eater, so shall my word be that goes forth from my mouth; it shall not return to me empty, but it shall accomplish that which I purpose and prosper in the thing for which I sent it" (Is 55:10–11).

So heaven really has "windows";[41] the request that God will "rend his heavens and come down" (Is 64:1) has a genuine point, particularly in view of the unprecedented event of Elijah's being caught up into heaven.[42] This event, which for the first time elevates an earthly man into God's realm,[43] and the somehow correlative vision at Isaiah's "call", where he beholds the (heavenly) glory of God in the (earthly) Temple (Is 6),[44] totally subsumes the cosmological aspect of the distance between heaven and earth in the religious and revealed dimension. Both events relativize the spatial distance and, in doing so, intensify man's fear and trembling before the majesty of God. Elijah's life, which has been consumed for God, is transported to this same God in a stormy wind and on a chariot of fire; and Isaiah's life, which is henceforth to be consumed for God, is prepared for its mission by fiery coals, in the presence of God—both in heaven and in the Temple.

While, in such events, the dramatic relationship between heaven and earth approaches its zenith, man can in no way release himself from the limits of his earthly standpoint. His humble posture at prayer, "stretching forth hands to heaven"[45] —or lifting "heart and hands"[46] and looking to heaven[47]—only

[41] They can open to release woe, as in the case of the great Flood (Gen 7:11; Is 24:18), but also to pour out blessing (Malachi 3:10); the ironic remark in 2 Kings 7:2, 19 is inappropriate and unseemly.

[42] 2 Kings 2:1, 11; 1 Macc 2:58; Sir 48:10; this event becomes the basis of eschatological hope.

[43] By contrast, the translation of Enoch (Gen 5:24) remains "primeval", unintelligible within Israel's historical experience.

[44] Its antecedent is the heavenly vision of Micaiah, 1 Kings 22:19ff., and it is followed by Ezekiel's great vision of God's "chariot", for which "the heavens were opened" (Ezek 1:1); the latter leads into the apocalyptic visions of Daniel and the apocryphal writings.

[45] Ex 9:22f.; 10:21; 1 Kings 8:22, 54; 2 Chron 6:13; 2 Macc 3:20.

[46] Lam 3:41.

[47] Job 35:5; Dan 12:7.

shows that he wishes his pleading to reach up to God in
heaven.[48] As well as this cry of prayer there is also sin that cries
to heaven,[49] so that, at all events, man stands before God's open
eye and ear. In many respects the noncanonical, late Jewish and
apocalyptic literature forms a literary transition to the New
Testament; but insofar as it is concerned with inquisitive journeys to heaven, delving into the upper world and that which is
to be revealed in the future, it has no business in genuine
revelation. What really traverses and fills the stage between
heaven and earth comes from God alone: his wisdom (Prov
8:1ff.), his Word, which is sent out to traverse the earth, yet
touching heaven (Wis 18:16).

One final thing: the more heaven is decosmologized, the
more it would be bound to become an empty concept, ultimately
identical with God, were it not taken over by a creaturely reality
that initially appears in the Bible as God's "host". (Thus God is
termed "Yahweh Sabaoth": Lord of Hosts.) From our point of
view it makes no difference whether the religio-cultural background points to former pagan (and now insubstantial) gods or
to a cult of the stars: in the Bible both of them are totally
repudiated, and every cult of the "host of heaven" is severely
forbidden. In the great Old Testament visions of the heavenly
reality, this divine entourage is not lacking, from the vision of
the prophet Micaiah Ben Simlah (1 Kings 22:19; 2 Chron 18:18)
to the vision of Isaiah with the seraphim and that of Ezekiel with
the cherubim, quite apart from the Psalms (82:1; 89:8). It is also
quite possible that, in the "we" of the account of creation ("Let
us make man . . ."), God is addressing his heavenly court
("sons of God", "angels"). In the New Testament, when this
heavenly reality is spoken of as the "Jerusalem which is above"
(Gal 4:26), it is densely populated: "myriads of angels" inhabit
"the city of the living God" (Heb 12:22). And when, in the
Book of Revelation, the "Word of God" rides forth to the final
battle on a white horse, we read (Rev 19:14) that "the armies of
heaven, arrayed in fine linen, white and pure, followed him on
white horses." Heaven and earth are thus in a theodramatic

---

[48] 2 Chron 30:27; Sir 35:17; Job 20:6; 1 Macc 3:50; 4:10, 40; 9:46.
[49] Gen 4:10; Ps 73:3, 9; 2 Chron 28:9.

relationship with each other, and these "armies" of God are not uninvolved: they are attendants, servants, figures endowed with a mission (Heb 1:7). "Are they not all ministering spirits sent forth to serve, for the sake of those who are to obtain salvation?" (Heb 1:14). We shall have to return to them later.

What happened to Elijah and Isaiah—a mission comes from heaven to earth, and the recipient is transported from earth to heaven—was an anticipatory outline: it acquires flesh and blood, and definitive form, in the *New Covenant*. In the Incarnation of the Word and Son of God, in his "humiliation" and "exaltation" (Phil 2), the dimensions of the stage are marked out; indeed, only now can its real area be ascertained. For now that third dimension, which only comes into being through sin and death, emerges into full view: the "underworld", *sheol, hades, infernum*. Its role in salvation history had remained uncertain in the Old Testament. Through the perfect Incarnation of the Word and Son, this "place", which was not envisaged at the creation, which "entered in" subsequently, actually acquires a central significance: it is drawn into theo-drama as man's ultimate possibility and condition.

As a result of the "humiliation" and "exaltation" found in the New Testament, the poles which, in the Old Covenant, are relatively statically opposed to each other acquire a motion; while this motion does not simply abolish the poles or confuse them, it does aim at an interpenetration of the spheres—which no externally applied analogy can adequately clarify. The cosmological dimension retreats entirely before the theodramatic, without any surrendering of the created nature of the heavenly pole; Old Testament formulas are taken over without alteration: "heaven and earth" is used for the universe,[50] God is spoken of as the Creator of heaven and earth,[51] heaven as God's dwelling

[50] Mt 5:18, 34f.; 11:25; 24:35; Lk 12:56 passim. The person praying lifts eyes and hands to heaven: Mt 14:19; Mk 6:41 par; 7:34; Lk 9:16; 18:13; Jn 17:1; Acts 1:11; 7:55; Rev 10:5.

[51] Acts 4:24; 14:15; 17:24; Rev 10:6; 14:7. Since it is created, heaven too will "pass away" at the end of time: Mk 13:31 par, passim, often in order to emphasize the permanence of the Law (Mt 5:18 par) or of the words of Christ (Lk 16:17).

and throne;[52] revelation still comes from heaven,[53] and God is now called the "Father in heaven".[54] The Father initiates the movement which, when consummated, is the arrival of the "kingdom of heaven" or the "kingdom of God" on earth.[55]

If "every spiritual blessing in the heavenly places" (Eph 1:3) has come down to earth in the Incarnation of the divine Word, we must also reflect on Genesis and the fact that heaven and *earth* were created and the latter was endowed with its own manifold power of conception and fruitfulness; this is why the blessing (which, ultimately, always comes from above) is often described as coming from below just as much as from above. Thus, for instance, the forsaken Jerusalem is graciously lifted up and adorned by God: "For as the earth brings forth its shoots, and as a garden causes what is sown in it to spring up, so the Lord God will cause righteousness . . . to spring forth . . ." (Is 61:11). If ultimately everything comes from God, if only heaven is active and earth is merely passive, there can never be a drama. Without this presupposition all Christology would dissolve in Monophysitism, and the doctrine of grace would dissolve in extreme Predestinationism. In its higher potency, grace endows the one who receives it with a special receptivity: he is enabled to conceive, to be a womb; he is enabled to bring to maturity the fruit he has been given; so much so that heaven becomes dependent on earth, earth seems to give birth to heaven. Later we shall have to reflect on how this self-emptying ("poverty": 2 Cor 8:9; "kenosis": Phil 2:7) on the part of heaven is in accord with its nature; that is, it does not betray a weakness but rather manifests its fullness and its freedom to be itself, even on earth and *in* earth.

[52] Mt 5:34; Acts 7:49; Heb 8:1; Rev 4.

[53] Mt 3:17; 11:27; 16:17; God's anger also comes from heaven: Lk 17:29; Rom 1:18. The blessing of rain and fruitfulness continues to be regarded as coming from heaven: Acts 26:13; heaven is "shut": Lk 4:25; James 5:17f.; Rev 11:6.

[54] Mt 5:16, 45; 6:1, 9; 7:11, 21; 10:32f.; 12:50, etc.

[55] Almost exclusively "kingdom of heaven" in Mt (apart from 2 Tim 4:18), but Matthew is also acquainted with the term "kingdom of God" (12:28; 21:31, 43) and "kingdom of the Father" (13:43; 26:29). Most probably "kingdom of heaven" is primarily a reverential term instead of "kingdom of God". For parallels to the Lord's Prayer petition, "on earth as it is in heaven", in Jewish prayers cf. Billerbeck I, 419ff.

But the closest possible interaction between the poles does not abolish the field of primal tension, however paradoxical the affirmations may be in the final stage. We have paradoxes of this kind in Paul's terminology, where he speaks of Christ as the "heavenly man" (1 Cor 15:45ff.)—which by no means undermines the fact that Jesus was "born of a woman, born under the law" (Gal 4:4).[56] Similarly there is the Johannine antithesis: only one has come down from heaven, whereas all the others are "from below" (Jn 3:13; 8:23); and yet the criterion of genuine faith lies in confessing that "Jesus Christ has come in the flesh" (1 Jn 4:2). Christology has the task of holding firm in and through these tensions; but not only Christology: it follows that the whole doctrine of salvation must do the same. Every "Christology from below" presupposes a "Christology from above": "No one has ascended into heaven but he who descended from heaven, the Son of man" (Jn 3:13)—which is not an invitation to undervalue the ascent of Christ, still bearing the scars of his earthly suffering. Christology will have to be the touchstone of all statements about the stage of ecclesiology and of the individual Christian life: What does it mean to say that our Mother (the Church) is in heaven (Gal 4:26); that, at the end of time, Jerusalem will come down from heaven to the earth (Rev 21:2); and that, when we die, God will provide for us an "eternal house" (or garment; Paul is referring to the glorified body)? What is meant by the words of Jesus which speak of our having "treasure in heaven" (Mk 10:21), a "heavenly reward" (Mt 5:12 par), and that the names of the disciples are written there (Lk 10:20; cf. Heb 12:23)? And what can it mean to say that, by way of anticipation, we have been "made to sit with him in the heavenly places" (Eph 2:6), that we have our home (that is, our citizenship) in heaven (Phil 3:20), and to that extent are strangers and pilgrims on earth (1 Pet 2:11)?

Before dealing with this question we must head off two interpretations. The New Testament relationship between heaven and earth can only be illuminated *dramatically*, not aesthetically or in a Gnostic and structuralist manner.

---

[56] In Paul there is an anti-Gnostic point in his discussing the "earthly man" *before* the "heavenly man". L. Bouyer, *Le Fils éternel* (Cerf, 1974), 102.

Augustine, it seems, does not entirely escape the danger of an aesthetic interpretation when, arguing against the Manichees, he addresses God in these terms in his famous prayer: "Deus, per quem universitas etiam cum sinistra parte perfecta est, . . . cum deteriora melioribus concinunt":[57] here the "lower" is applied to the earth and the "better" to heaven, and the two together—despite all the individual clashes—yield a whole, a perfect harmony, in such a way that the unity between the higher and the lower is better than the higher on its own.[58]

The danger of a Gnostic and structuralist interpretation lurks in the late Jewish apocalyptic, which has its roots in the wisdom literature. According to this, everything that is to come forth at the end of time has already existed, hiddenly, in God (thus privileged seers were able to behold it); history consists simply in drawing back the curtain that conceals what is only provisionally veiled. In such a case anthropology would be merely the realization of a correspondence that already exists between the eternal and the temporal man: *Leben im Diesseits und Jenseits* ["Living here and now in the Beyond"].[59]

Nor is it possible to take up a standpoint (in salvation history) prior to or subsequent to the earth/heaven dichotomy, as Ephrem the Syrian attempts to do, with naïve boldness, in his *Hymns on Paradise*.[60] He portrays a perfect existence that is simultaneously entirely sensual (earthly) and entirely spiritual (heavenly), the existence of Adam prior to the Fall; yet the latter is at the same

[57] *Soliloquia* lib I, 1, 3. "O God, through whom the universe, even in its evil part, is made perfect, . . . as the lower things make harmony with the better."

[58] *De ord.* I, 2, 2; *De mus.* VI, 11, 30; *De Civ. Dei* XI, 22. Cf. Scotus Erigena, *De Div. Nat.* III, 20 (PL 122, 684B): How can God proceed "usque ad extremas hujus mundi visibiles turpitudines et corruptiones"? Answer: we forget that "nullam turpitudinem in universitate totius creaturae posse esse. . . . Quod enim partim contigit, in toto Deus fieri non sinit, cujus universitati nec turpitudo turpis est, nec malitia nocet, nec error errat."—On the influence of this idea right up to Thomas and Descartes, cf. E. Gilson, *La Liberté chez Descartes et la théologie* (Alcan, 1913), 211–35.

[59] The title of a book by Friedrich Weinreb (Zurich: Origo, 1974), in which, as in earlier works, he tries to harmonize a Jewish-Gnostic-Cabbalist view of the world and of man with the great affirmations of the Bible (in both the Old and New Covenants). Despite astonishingly profound insights, the whole project is not dramatic but structuralist. Cf. also *Die Rolle Esther* (Zurich, 1968).

[60] Ephrem de Nisibe, *Hymnes sur le Paradis*, *Sources chrétiennes* 137 (1968).

time the eschatological Adam dependent on Christ's saving act. This is a life in perfect freedom,[61] of which we who are redeemed by Christ already have an anticipatory taste and smell[62] on earth, through the Holy Spirit and the Church—for Ephrem's highest image for paradise is that of perfume. True, the poet integrates the whole of salvation history in his protological/ eschatological standpoint, but in doing so he adopts a perspective within which all development, all coming-to-be has already been absorbed into Being. He is perhaps the greatest theological lyricist, approached by many mystics, who take up their positions in the unmoving "un-ground" [*Ungrund*], in the "exemplary identity", and thus overstep the dramatic dimension.

On the contrary, we must hold fast to the fact that heaven and earth have been created as distinct realms with a view to a drama in which each pole has its own, proper, positive role to play. The two roles cannot be compared quantitatively with each other; the older theology used to speak of the angels being superior to men in one respect, and of man being superior to the angels in another. We cannot know in advance what the stage will look like at the end of the play. On the one hand, we have the prospect of heaven and earth "passing away" (Mk 13:31 par) and being "no more found" (Rev 20:11);[63] on the other hand, there is the great promise expressed by Isaiah, that God will create a new heaven and a new earth (65:17; 66:22; cf. Rev 21:1). Is this the language of the Old Covenant, which had no comprehensive word for "world" and so was obliged to speak in *dual* terms of the one cosmos in which "God is all in all" (1 Cor 15:28)? This might be suggested by the fact that on the final stage there is neither sea (Rev 21:1) nor sun and moon (21:23); the alien, treacherous sea is replaced by the eternally solid crystal (21:21; cf. 4:6; 15:2; and a text as early as Ex 24:10). These images, too, do not signify any mutilation of creation but its thoroughgoing *transformation*.

This expression embraces the Pauline hope for man and

---

[61] *Hymn*. VII, 31; cf. XII, 19–20; XIV, where the passing through slavery and the desert to freedom is portrayed.

[62] *Hymn*. XI.

[63] Of course this refers to heaven and earth in the "cosmological" sense. The heaven mentioned in Revelation 4–5 (etc.) naturally cannot pass away.

cosmos. Paul looks forward to his own "transformation" (Phil 3:21) and that of everyone at the Last Day (1 Cor 15:51–52). And this transformation, this metamorphosis, is always going on, even during the earthly life of the Christian who follows Christ (2 Cor 3:18). It is described as a refashioning (not a dismantling, 2 Cor 5:4), resulting in death being "swallowed up" in victory (1 Cor 15:54) and "what is mortal" being "swallowed up by life" (2 Cor 5:4).

We bring our preparation of the dramatic stage to a close by noting once again, on the one hand, that the stage is set exclusively for this one play and will be involved and modified by the play itself as it unfolds; and on the other hand, that much has already been decided, on the basis of the fundamental heaven/earth distinction—matters such as the relationship between God and the world, man's specific constitution, matters of Christology and ecclesiology and the doctrine of the Last Things. Anyone who wishes to be led by God's word into God's truth must open himself to the heaven/earth dimension —which is a better expression than "the beyond" and "the here-and-now".[64] But he must not fail to realize that, while he finds himself on the stage as soon as he comes into the world, he also has a part in shaping it. He does this through the measure of his receptivity, which enables him in an earthly way to receive heavenly things and give birth to them, and through the measure of his freedom to keep the kingdom of heaven away from the earth or, conversely, to cause it to come nearer. Ultimately, therefore, the stage is entirely assimilated into the spiritual dimensions of the actors themselves.

---

[64] On the current relevance of this topic: G. Martelet, *L'Au-delà retrouvé. Christologie des fins dernières* (Desclée, 1975).

B. INFINITE AND FINITE FREEDOM

1. *The Theme Defined*

Theo-drama (as distinct from merely human drama) is only possible where "God", or "a God", or some accredited representative of God, steps onto the stage of life's play as "a person" in the action, separate from the other characters. Anyone who has pondered philosophically over God will be immediately suspicious at the mention of this "person". In this connection we have already shown, in our *Prolegomena*, that the high periods of religious drama—and in fact of all drama, for it shrivels and dies where it lacks religious roots—are to be found, on the one hand, in the prephilosophical, mythical realm of the Greek (and oriental)[1] drama and, on the other hand, in the post-philosophical, Christian realm of the mystery play (which unfolds in Shakespeare and Calderon). In other words, these high points are found where God was able to appear on stage as a free Someone over against free worldly beings (Titans, humans, angelic powers). The philosophical epoch, from Socrates and Plato, via the Stoics, to Late Platonism, could not produce any theo-drama in the real sense, because here God was the "sun of the good", the all-embracing "Nature", the unapproachable "One", sublimely superior to all the oppositions found in the world: consequently he could not step forth onto the world stage as a particular and special character vis-à-vis other particular and special characters.

Now it is clear that the mythical drama, which split the divine into individual, personal figures and presented it on stage as such, cannot be brought back to life. The question is, therefore: Can Christian theo-drama still assert itself in the aftermath of philosophical reflection? (Quite definitely it cannot do this by simply ignoring the latter.) In fact it can only assert itself on the basis of a careful evaluation of all philosophical postulates that

---

[1] On the oriental forms of drama, which we did not discuss in detail in the *Prolegomena*, cf. Heinz Kindermann, ed., *Fernöstliches Theater* (Stuttgart: Kröner, 1966).

have to do with a notion of God that can be commended to human thought. But biblical, Christian theology will have to confront these philosophical postulates with an unalterable, twofold postulate of its own, arising from its fundamental nature: first, that the "Absolute" is free (which the philosopher can concede, in a limited sense); and second, that the "Absolute" has a sovereign ability, out of its own freedom, to create and send forth finite but genuinely free beings (which is bound to cause the philosopher the greatest embarrassment) in such a way that, without vitiating the infinite nature of God's freedom, a genuine opposition of freedoms can come about.

It is one of the fundamental assertions of the Bible and of theology that such opposition exists and that it works itself out dramatically in a variety of forms.[2] It can be argued that this shows the biblical idea of God to be unphilosophical because it limits the infinity of the Absolute by the existence of finite freedom. In fact, in a Stoic or Islamic view of the world this infinity can always be upheld, since finite freedom (that of the wise man) simply consists in making room for, or not opposing, the absolute law, or *logos*, or "will", which takes effect in any case. Leaving aside the question of whether the foolish man's ability to resist this law does not also imply genuine freedom, let us restrict ourselves to the philosophical objection to the sequence

---

[2] Characteristically, the insight that God freely created the world and endowed it with freedom forms the turning point of Chesterton's conversion, resulting in a change to a dramatic view of existence. Having tried the modern immanentist world views—materialism, idealism, evolutionism—which caused him to swing back and forth like a pendulum from extreme optimism to extreme pessimism, he experienced this illumination: "According to most philosophers, God in making the world enslaved it. According to Christianity, in making it, He set it free. God had written, not so much a poem, but rather a play; a play he had planned as perfect, but which necessarily had been left to human actors and stage-managers, who had since made a great mess of it" *Orthodoxy* in *Collected Works of G. K. Chesterton*, I (San Francisco: Ignatius Press, 1986), 281–82. Quite similar is P. Claudel (cf. the passage in *Theo-Drama* I, 268ff., "The Author") or M. Blondel, who describes the constellation of forces and situations surrounding every human being as the thickening of a plot: it can only be solved by each person "going through the point of decision" for or against God's absolute freedom (*Lettre sur les exigences de la pensée contemporaine en matière d'apologétique* in *Les Premiers Ecrits* [P.U.F., 1956], 44). The same thing could be demonstrated in Kierkegaard's *oeuvre*.

narrated in the Bible, in which, as a result of his creatures' freedom, God seems to be confined to the role of a partner or antagonist. He is the One, and the creature stands over against him as the "Other", and between the two something like a "covenant" is actually concluded, which seems (ultimately, in the "New Covenant") to seal and confirm the notion of two sides confronting each other. It could be said in reply that, precisely in the New Covenant, the implied reciprocal limitation is overcome in that God infuses his own Spirit into the hearts of those devoted to him (Jer 31:31–33; Rom 5:5); but this, in turn, could be countered by observing that the relationship between Jesus Christ and his Father maintains a sharper-than-ever distinction between "My will" and "thy will" (Lk 22:42). Will it ever be possible for this kind of view of God, where he seems to be fundamentally restricted by the opposing freedom of his creature, to be reconciled with the philosophical view?

In the first place, we must remember two matters of history. First, the fact that, as a result of intensive work by the Fathers and High Scholasticism, the biblical picture of God was harmonized with the philosophical view. It is foolish for theologians to reproach the Fathers and Scholastics with this and speak of an alienation and "Hellenization" of the biblical view of God. We can admit that in this process, by accident, some of the sharp contours of the biblical drama have been smoothed out (the eschatological element, for instance); this should not have been done; but the process itself was essential if the biblical message was to be presented to and accepted by thinking people. In the event, the Christian postulates triumphed over the philosophical ones—integrating and at the same time relativizing them—in all the crucial issues. In the Christian framework, the Platonic-Plotinian "Good" and "One", which by its very nature pours itself out in radiating waves, becomes the absolutely free (and thus personal) God who is under no compulsion, not even from his own nature, and who freely sends forth from himself the world of finite spirits, created to be free. However, the christological opposition of the two wills becomes the expression of two dimensions, of which philosophy could have no inkling: that between God and the sinfully fallen will, and that within God himself, that is, within infinity, characterizing the distinction between various divine modes of being. But does this not lead us to theological subtleties that can no longer be appreciated by an average Christian (or Jewish) consciousness? Is it not a fact that the majority of people continue to entertain an understanding of God that is anthropomorphic and close to mythology, where God is one among many; where God is in one place and the world in another; where God is in heaven and man is on earth; where God is one existing thing among other existing things, even if he is elevated to the level of the "*ens perfectissimum*"?

This "popular", philosophically unrefined view of God is actually current in many places, as is shown by modern atheism. For when the latter protests against God—whether in the name of science or of the world or of human freedom—it becomes clear "that every form of rejection of God is directed against a specific, distorted and grotesque notion of God", but also that in this process the last two centuries (roughly) have seen a gradual dissolution of the "common understanding".[3] Here the adoption of the biblical events and affirmations as part of a total, humane, religio-philosophical world of thought—which is itself an historical phenomenon—is not even taken into consideration, mostly because all such reflection is rejected as superfluous and alienating. Consequently there is no awareness of the biblical paradox that God can be "everything" (Sir 43:27) and yet man can be "something"; and that God can be absolutely free without robbing man of his genuine freedom; and that, in fact, God shows his almighty power particularly by imparting authentic selfhood to his creatures.

Thus the first requirement for the project—which is essentially a theological one—is *that theology should take seriously and that it should cherish the explicit or implicit philosophy man employs when thinking about the meaning of the world and of existence and that it should pursue its own reflection upon the biblical revelation in association with this mediating philosophical reflection*. It can do two things in the process: reflecting on revelation—which, after all, endeavors to shed light on the ultimate roots of the meaning of all being— it can bring out the philosophy that is immanent in theology;

[3] E. Coreth, *Grundfragen der Hermeneutik* (Herder, 1969), 202.

but at the same time it can make use of the accumulated reflections of non-Christian humanity, which will help it, at least, to avoid restrictive and distorting anthropomorphisms (that is, hidden mythological elements) in its interpretation of revelation. It will require a great effort, in terms of both thought and living, if, in this process, what is specific to the biblical facts is to be maintained without any watering-down. A simple mental experiment will demonstrate this: if God is "everything", when we add the world to him we do not have any "more": finite reality, even if it is free, cannot constitute any opposition to him, for the latter can only be conceived in connection with the existence of some limit. God is absolute unity, and thus he cannot be designated as the "Other" (or even as the "Wholly Other") over against any finite thing; rather, we must agree with Nicholas Cusanus when he calls God the *Non-aliud*, the "Non-Other". We, for our part, with our finite freedom, must indeed designate ourselves as the "others" when we think of our relation to God; but we cannot draw the conclusion that we are the "others" as far as God himself is concerned. The question we ought rather to ask is this: Since we owe everything (including our freedom) to the "everything" that God's freedom represents, can we be the "others" when seen from God's vantage point? Does he not recognize and affirm us *in him* and not outside him? These are unavoidable paradoxes, terrifying and enrapturing us, and the Christian must keep them in mind when he addresses God as "Thou", as Old and New Testaments commend him to do— albeit in the "fear of the Lord", which reminds him that God is greater (both more remote and yet closer at hand) than man can ever appreciate.

Let us listen to C. S. Lewis:

> . . . The man who does not regard God as other than himself cannot be said to have a religion at all. On the other hand, if I think God other than myself in the same way in which my fellow-men, and objects in general, are other than myself, I am beginning to make Him an idol. I am daring to treat His existence as somehow *parallel* to my own. But He is the ground of our being. He is always both within us and over against us. Our reality is so much from His reality as He, moment by moment, projects into us. The deeper the level within ourselves from which our prayer, or any

other act, wells up, the more it is His, but not at all the less ours.
Rather, most ours when most His.[4]

The second requirement is this: anyone who reflects on the
revelation in Jesus Christ must take this inherent philosophical
thinking beyond itself, in two directions: he must heighten the
contrast between infinite and finite freedom and reveal the abyss
that opens up between the holiness of infinite freedom and the
plight of finite freedom that has fallen into sin, which can only
be redeemed by the healing succor of God's holy freedom. (This
is the problem to which Paul addressed himself and, later,
Augustine.) Then he must deepen philosophy's "the Other as
non-Other" in the direction of the trinitarian mystery of "the
Other in the non-Other", that is, in the One divine Being.

These two dimensions only open up, ultimately, in the Cross
of Christ, where—putting it in a nutshell—God himself is
forsaken by God because of man's godlessness. Here the nub of
the theo-drama must lie: God himself brings it to this point so
delicately that, on the one hand, nothing godless is imported
into God and, on the other hand, man's freedom is not overridden by a drama within the Godhead that seems to have
nothing to do with him.

By laying bare these two abysses, that which opposes God
and that which is internal to him, we are already in the very
midst of the *action* of theo-drama. This, however, is the subject
of volume four. Here we see the methodological difficulty we
have to meet in this present volume and volume three, namely,
that of describing the "characters of the play" before the play is
actually in progress. We have already referred to this difficulty
in the Preface. If we are to master it without falling back into a
static theology of essences, there is only one middle path we can
take: our portrayal must stick close to the sources; the contrasted
"characters" are never grasped prior to the action or outside it; it
is as though they are stopped just for a moment in the midst of
their acting and asked who they are. They will answer in the
context of the action, which reveals their nature; but we cannot
say that their nature only emerges through the action (*essentia
sequitur existentiam*), nor even that it coincides with the action.

[4] C. S. Lewis, *Letters to Malcolm*, 1964 (Collins, 1977), 71.

(To speak with and against Gregory Palamas: God's "essence" is not identical with his "energies", although it *really* manifests itself in them.) Every moment of the action's horizontal course can and must raise profound vertical questions: Who is this God who, without undergoing alteration, is able to create and send forth, out of himself, beings possessing finite freedom? What is he like? Who and what is the bearer of this kind of finite freedom? Who and what is man, this baffling hybrid, originating both from below, from matter, and from above, from God? How can such a being actually exist, behave and act as an integrated unity? And, finally, who and what is the Mediator who will recapitulate in himself the conflict between God's "everything" and man's "something" and, by so doing, sublimate and abolish it? And when, at some moment that is both in time and timeless, he has played his part and accomplished his mission, what will be his legacy—ever present, here and now, whether acknowledged or not? What will be the real bone of contention of world history, heightening its dramatic vista to apocalyptic proportions, with the result that the whole scale of personal initiative and decision in the Mediator's work is only fully unveiled in what, with the Bible, we may call the "principalities and powers"? Who and what are they?

Admittedly all these questions remain somehow abstract when divorced from the play which gives rise to them and which will be discussed later. But they arise from something extremely concrete, indeed, from the sole *concretum*, they remain a part of it and can only be understood as such. Moreover, we must not fail to see that the centers of action portrayed here are of unequal dignity, so much so that, once again, we realize that this whole drama has no analogy. God himself is here—in Calderon he is not one of the actors but the "Master" of the play—and he is more than a mere spectator. He is the One responsible for the play, and yet he is not responsible when man, in freedom, acts inappropriately; all the same, he stands by his original responsibility. Here we have man, both singular and plural, thrown onto the stage, endowed with freedom, condemned to freedom and given grace to exercise it, with the power of becoming what he can on the basis of his own nature and constitution and yet unable to do this outside the divine freedom but only in it and with it. How sublime and yet how needy man is! And then we have the Mediator: indispensable and yet beyond all human calculation, in a pact with both warring parties and yet not a traitor to either; epitomizing the living drama in the very "composition" of his being, torn asunder by his tragic situation and yet, thus torn, healing divisions. All else simply follows, beyond our wildest hopes, from the principle he has established; for, while he is the play's *peripeteia*, reversal, the whole play by no means runs its course mechanically from then on: it continually reveals new, exciting, unforeseeable aspects of this reversal, and it goes on intensifying right up to the last scene.

2. *The Interrelationship*

a. The Ancient World

It follows from what we have just said that, in lifting the "dramatis personae" out of the ongoing play, we cannot begin with a pure anthropology or a pure theology ("God in himself"). For a purely philosophical anthropology does not unveil finite freedom in its full dimensions, as—illuminated by the light of revelation—seems appropriate to man; and equally, a purely theological doctrine of God that did not arise out of a theology of God-made-man would fail to present the full dimensions of the divine freedom: it would not set forth the true relationship between God and created freedom. The nature of both of them is only revealed in their dramatic interplay (for or against each other), which comes within our grasp in the Christ-event. It is quite legitimate, however, to abstract from the concrete dramatic conditions and inquire as to their "nature", that is, the presupposition of there being such a dramatic situation in the first place.[1]

---

[1] This is also recognized by the Protestant, Paul Ricoeur (*Philosophie de la volonté* I, "Le Volontaire et l'involontaire" [Paris: Aubier, 1949]), when he endeavors to reach an "understanding of the voluntary" by a twofold abstraction: first, from guilt (the condition of fallen man, of the *servum arbitrium*) and then from the "transcendence" of "liberating grace". Man's fallenness cannot be

This is immediately confirmed if we take a look at the pre-Christian views on human and divine freedom. (Post-Christian philosophy, even if it claims to be pure philosophy, like Kant's thought on freedom, is directly influenced by Christian revelation.) In the ancient world it is clear that the socio-political perspective is fundamental to an understanding of human freedom; here the first question is, not how the "free" human being understands himself within the *polis* (by contrast with the "unfree" slave),[2] but how the *polis* understands itself to be indivisible and hence free; here "free" and "slave" are final terms in a spectrum of status categories within this freedom.[3] The free citizen has a direct relation to the divine *nomos* (not to the whim of a ruler). Of course, from Socrates and Plato on, the individual's soul is regarded as free from social and natural compulsion; its relation to the divine *nomos* (the epitome of what is meant by "home") becomes immediate;[4] this is in reaction to a Sophist libertinism which criticized both *mythos* and *nomos*.[5] A transition between the two can be seen in the borderline case portrayed several times by Euripides (we referred to this in an earlier work),[6] in which an individual dies for the freedom of the *polis*: "In the sacrificial death of the individual for what is evidently right, the individual's freedom and the freedom of the *polis* once more coincide in an exemplary manner, resulting simultaneously in the salvation of both."[7] Then the individual's subjection to the divine law becomes more and more the hub of freedom; from Aristotle on, only the wise man is the "free"

some prime given but logically presupposes a more pristine state. Thus he allows the legitimacy, and indeed the necessity, of a philosophical approach to finite freedom within theology. Cf. on this subject, Paul Vignaux, "Christianisme et philosophie de la liberté" in *Les Quatres fleuves* 3 (Seuil, 1974), 103–4.

[2] H. Schlier, *"eleutheros"*, etc. in *Th. W.* II (1935), 484ff. K. Niederwimmer, *Der Begriff der Freiheit im Neuen Testament* (Berlin, 1966).

[3] D. Nestle, art. "Freiheit" in *RAC* VIII (1972), 269–306; cf. also his *Eleutheria, Studien zum Wesen der Freiheit bei den Griechen und im Neuen Testament*, part 1: "Die Griechen" (Tübingen: Mohr, 1967).

[4] *Eleutheria*, 89ff.

[5] On its effects on Thucydides, cf. *Eleutheria*, 76ff., and (otherwise) on Epicurus, 112ff.

[6] *The Glory of the Lord* IV, 131–54, "Euripides".

[7] *Eleutheria*, 137.

man, only the community of the wise is the true *polis*. Even
under Roman domination, the Hellenistic *polis* maintains the
fiction of being politically free, whereas within the Roman
republic itself freedom is not seen as a privilege of the individual
citizen but in the "free play of the parties".[8]

In this earlier, non-Christian understanding, freedom is "never
a *vox theologica*"; the New Testament understanding is very
strongly influenced by the former—thus "freedom", even in
Paul, is "never made a central concept of his theology",[9] yet it is
proclaimed as a "word of salvation" (Gal 5:1, 13). The change
from the former to the latter view can only be assessed if we take
account of two new factors. First, the impersonal *nomos* (which
now appears in a more severe form in the Old Testament law) is
replaced by the living and personal Lord, whose service (which
is both personal and ecclesial, *polis*-like) is liberating, the service
of a free man. Second, this freedom is related to this same Lord's
love, in such a way that the person who has been set free can
only respond in kind: he can only render his service of love
according to the measure of love he has received.[10] The human
person's freedom is only fully illuminated when it is seen to be
bound up with a divine and personal freedom that is at pains to
promote man's freedom.

In Greek thought there is something like a premonition of this
interrelatedness and a proof of its necessity: namely, where the
mythos in which the divine *nomos* protected the *polis* is abandoned,
and the "divine" as such, loosed from all limitation, shines
forth, yet in such a way that its graciousness cannot be expressed
in any other than quasi-personal categories. Here the intermediate concept of the *daimōn*, the *daimonion* and *eudaimonia*
becomes important. Democritus says that anyone who chooses
the soul's goods chooses the more divine, whereas the one
who chooses the goods of the body chooses the "human"
(Fr. 37); by choosing these "more divine" goods, the soul
acquires *eudaimoniē* (Fr. 170), becomes "the dwelling place of

---

[8] *RAC* VIII, 277.

[9] *RAC* VIII, 281, cf. 284: "Freedom, therefore, while it is a word of salvation
in Paul, is not the final word. Each time the concept emerges, it is in the critical
situation where what is at stake is the winning or losing of one's being."

[10] Cf. D. Nestle's comments on 1 Corinthians 7 and 8: *RAC* 281–82.

the *daimōn*" (Fr. 171). The highest ethical knowledge of Socrates comes, not from the exercise of self-control (*autokrateia*) alone, but is ultimately given to him from above by the admonitory inspiration of his *daimonion*. Plato grasps the profound dialectic of finite freedom: on the one hand, it is something presupposed, if man is to be able to choose the better; and, on the other hand, it is a goal: he is to hold fast to the "better" he has chosen. In order to overcome this antinomy he adopts the hypothesis of an antenatal (intelligible) choice in which human freedom is associated with the *daimōn* given by the Parcae: the two are inseparably fused (*Rep.* 620de). The antenatal fusion corresponds to that which comes at the end, which is also portrayed in mythical terms:

> The necessity of a soul which (in choosing the best) has attained wisdom is by far the most powerful of all necessities, for such a soul governs itself according to its own law; and if such a soul has decided on the noblest course on the basis of the noblest insight, a perfect immutability, firmer and more immutable than steel, is imparted to this insightful will; the three Furies watch over it and make sure that everything each of the gods has determined (in his good pleasure) is carried out without alteration (*Epin.* 982bc).

For in its final state "the soul will be a friend to itself and a friend of the gods" (*Rep.* 621c). A substantial part of *eudaimonia* is the effort man makes to embrace whatever is best and most noble (and thereby to acquire a share in it) and the gift character of the divine, which communicates itself on its own initiative in the form of blessedness.

These pre-Christian intimations are completely brought out into the light in Christianity: both forms of freedom are always together on stage, even before anyone raises the question of how it is possible for them to coexist. There are dimensions implicit in human thought that can never be really explicitly formulated prior to the coming of Christ; in Christianity these dimensions are also opened up from the other side, from God's side.

b. The Advance in Christianity and the Incarnation

Within finite freedom there is an element of infinity that we may call "indifference" toward all finite goods, or the absolute longing for what is always beyond our grasp. If this element of infinity is not to become a Tantalus' torment (on account of the effort expended in trying to catch up with it) or be smothered by the confines of finitude; if its progress toward self-realization is also to be free and not caught in the chains of some dialectical law, it needs to have an infinite freedom in and above itself, empowering it to realize itself as finite freedom. This infinite freedom must be sufficiently free (according to its nature) to allow finite freedom to operate freely within it; or rather, as we are talking about infinite freedom, actually to *impart* finite freedom in the first place.

However, this cannot be done by a mere *idea* of infinite goodness: finite freedom might never cease aspiring toward it, but, by its very nature, it could never reach it. Nor can it be done by a *real* infinite good, which, if it is to be infinite, must be thought of as divorced from all finitude: such, for instance, is Aristotle's "thought thinking itself" or the absolutely simple One of Plotinus, whose freedom is absolute but operates entirely within itself: "It is turned entirely to itself and is interior to itself; it has no relation to the outside or to others but is totally concerned with itself" (*Enn*. VI, 8, 17). Thus, however it may be expressed, there comes about a reciprocal self-exclusion:

> In your search, therefore, . . . do not seek anything outside him
> but seek inside him for all the things that are subordinate to him;
> do not approach him, however, for he himself is the Outside, . . .
> he is also in the very depths, and the Other is outside him,
> touching him all round, as it were, and clinging to him . . . (*Enn*.
> VI, 8:18).

So this One is only "truly free" because it "lies above every-thing, not ministering to itself like a servant; it is only itself, truly itself, whereas every other thing is both itself and some-thing else" (*Enn*. VI, 8, 21). Such a God, bent on being free from everything, cannot *give* freedom, even if something like free-dom emanates from him and thus exists outside him (Aristotle too postulates this kind of finite and empirical freedom). Or if, presupposing such a "One", we were to accept finite freedom as real, we would have to relocate all the latter's dangers within infinite freedom itself (for example, Schelling), for (once again) the element of *giving* freedom would be lacking.

But if finite freedom, in order to fulfill itself, were able to cross the threshold to an infinite freedom that thus clings to its "being free", it would lose its finite shape and hence itself (as in Buddhism and in many forms of non-Christian mysticism). If such fulfillment is to come about (and in fact this can only be achieved in infinite freedom), not only must the Infinite take the finite into itself (and absorb it) but the finite must also be capable of taking the Infinite into itself. This confronts us with the problem which Old Testament theology cannot solve. Here genuine infinite freedom and genuine finite freedom are joined in a covenant, but, in the form in which it is made, this Covenant cannot attain fulfillment; it can only point toward it. True, God does grant some kind of participation in his sphere by making the Covenant and promulgating the Commandments that are intended to make Israel holy (in its place), *because* God (in his place) is holy (Lev 19:2). All the same, in granting this participation, God still holds on to himself, for that freedom in which the divine Commandments are to be perfectly fulfilled could only be realized within infinite freedom itself; in biblical terms, it was necessary for the Spirit of God to be implanted in the hearts of the Covenant partners (Jer 31:31), and this, for the present, remained but a promise. Therefore the Sinai Covenant itself must undergo mediation so that ultimate immediacy can be attained: and this takes place precisely through the christological paradox, according to which, without confusing the freedoms (*asunchutōs*, in the Chalcedonian expression), infinite freedom indwells finite freedom, and so the finite is perfected in the infinite, without the infinite losing itself in the finite or the finite in the infinite.

This was the point reached by the theology of Maximus the Confessor, guided by the ultimate consequences of patristic Christology as well as by the results of the christological heresies, finally driven into a corner: the entire theo-drama has its center in the two wills of Christ, the infinite, divine will and the finite, human will—and this goes far beyond the "Two souls dwell, alas, in my breast" of an inwardly torn stage-hero [Faust]. Rather, the encounter and reciprocal interpenetration that takes place here (Chalcedon, again, calls it *adiairetōs*, "inseparable") is the climax of the relationship between infinite and finite; hence it is also the climax of world history and of salvation history. It is only possible as a twofold movement: of the finite to the infinite and of the infinite to the finite, that is, it is a spiritualizing and a corporealizing process at the same time. So Maximus himself puts it in a memorable passage:

> God and man are patterns (*paradeigmata*) each to the other: God renders himself human out of love for man, just as far as man, empowered thereto by divine love, renders himself divine; and man is transported by God, in the Spirit, just as far into the region of unknowing as man, through right action, has succeeded in causing God, who is essentially invisible, to be seen.[11]

Looking ahead, therefore, it is clear that anthropology can only attain its full stature within Christology, and so it must adopt its standards from the latter. Its first consideration, in discussing man, will be the relationship between infinite and finite freedom in general; it will go on, secondly, to consider the concrete shape of finite freedom, that is, the spiritual-corporal being which recapitulates the cosmos in itself through a movement of transcendence toward the Infinite; and thirdly, it will reflect on the fact that, in concrete terms, this can be genuinely accomplished only "*en Christōi*".

This yields a further result: finite freedom—on the basis of its finitude and its corporality—manifests itself essentially as community; a single human freedom is inconceivable on its own.

[11] *Ambigua* 10 (PG 91, 1113BC). The significance of this assertion has been highlighted by Lars Thunberg, *Microcosm and Mediator, the Theological Anthropology of Maximus the Confessor*, Acta Sem. Neotest. Upsal. XXV (1965). One could set beside Maximus another great example from the history of Christian ideas, again showing the extreme swing of the pendulum between man's being transported to God and God's being incorporated in man: initially, German mysticism from Eckhart onward seems to be completely dominated by the idea of "un-forming" (moving toward an imageless God); but it no less sponsored the "embodying" of the divine; the German word *bilden, Bildung* has its roots in the mysticism of the fourteenth century. Cf. H. Schilling, *Bildung als Gottesbildlichkeit. Eine motivgeschichtliche Studie* (Freiburg, 1957), 25ff.

The social dimension cannot be bracketed out of this initiative
that establishes the interrelatedness of infinite and finite freedom. We cannot speak of freedom apart from the mediation
effected by the social dimension.

c. The Social Mediation and the Trinity

Again it is characteristic that, historically, the social dimension
of freedom—with its seeds in antiquity, as we have shown—
only asserted itself radically in the wake of Christianity. The
declaration of human rights, the entire current "freedom movement", only became possible when it was sufficiently realized
that this mediation was indispensable. And this also implies that
it will only be possible effectively to implement human rights,
and meaningfully to prosecute the ongoing "freedom movement", if this is done on a Christian basis.

Finite freedom only exists in the interrelationship of human
beings, particularly since each new human being comes about
through other human beings and only awakens to "being
human" through the encounter with others, with their freedom
and free response. The child arrives with its own freedom; and it
is given (by its mother) this other freedom that comes from
being in a society with others. Here we need not trace the
anthropological consequences of this fact but only ask how it
affects the encounter between infinite and finite freedom.

In pre-Christian times, for the most part, the divine is
imagined in an anthropomorphic way as a community of gods
united under a king, like the human *polis*. Philosophical reflection
was bound to banish this anthropomorphism: pure, absolute
Being can only be One. Finite man must relate to this One, both
as an individual and as a community; both forms of religion,
personal piety and social cult, developed in tandem. There are
two forms of human unity: "being-for-oneself" and "being-for-
another"; they are inseparable, yet they cannot be brought to
coincide completely; reflection's idea of the Absolute One,
however, has a hidden and divisive effect on this unity: finite
freedom enters into relationship with the divine either as the
unity of the *polis* (with the Stoics this is expanded to the
macropolis), or as the unity of the individual. In both cases,

therefore, the relationship is one-to-one, *"monos pros monon"* (*Enn*. 6, 8, 11). If, as in Aristotle, the *"bios theoretikos"* becomes the highest model of the human being, it follows that, however man's relation to the state is developed, it must fail to attain the ultimate relationship with the divine. And as for the community of contemplatives whom Aristotle takes with him into this divine relationship, in the end it remains a community of solitaries (*Nic. Eth.* 1177a, 26ff.). The same is true of Varro's solely normative form of religion, the "physical" religion of the philosophers, after he has criticized the other two forms, that is, the mythical form (of the poets, suitable for the theatre) and the civil form (of the priests who offer public sacrifice), which he regards as secondary.[12]

The question becomes a burning one in Israel's relationship with God (leaving Islam aside, because of its dependence on Judaism). It is the *people* that is chosen by Yahweh; the people swears to keep the Covenant, forsakes it and turns back to God. The *people* is the entity with which the One God primarily deals. Again it is a case of *"monos pros monon"*. The individual has value insofar as he is a member of the chosen people or represents it. Thus Moses acts as mediator; so too, at an even more profound level, does the Suffering Servant; so does Abraham, who, in his God-given fruitfulness, embodies (by way of prefiguration) the unity of the people and indeed of all the Elect. So too, however, does the lonely figure of Job, who is righteous but does not belong to the people—and at this point we begin to see the limits of the whole system of the Old Covenant: Job, solitary and rejected, stands face to face with the One God, against whom he vainly appeals to some other arbiter (16:19ff.; 19:22ff.).

In the long run this *"monos pros monon"* becomes untenable. It leads either to an escape from finitude into the unity of the divine or to the absolutizing of the intramundane unity—and the divine *polis* ("*Roma divina*") of late antiquity came too late to be credible; the world of the sage in his *"autarkia"* (Cynics) and *"autodespotia"* (Epicurus) was simply another kind of escape. And where, as in Israel, God is imagined to be a person, there is no possibility whatsoever of this kind of escape, except to

---

[12] Augustine, *City of God* VI, 3–8.

Manichaeism or atheism. The Old Testament notion of a personal, single God—even when it is softened by the idea of a heavenly host associated with him—is essentially transitional and hence transitory. It can be dissolved by a return to a pagan philosophical idea of a superpersonal One—in which case all that is of the world must be interpreted as a declension from it (this was the tendency of all Cabbalist Gnosticism, up to and including Hasidism)—or else it must go forward and be transcended into the idea of God found in the New Testament and the Church.

For

> a person is something unique, individual and, as such, unimaginable. By definition it develops and attains its value by opposition, cooperation and surrender, that is, through relationship with others, and such a relationship of dependence . . . cannot be reconciled with everything that must be said about being itself. Furthermore, given that we wanted to extrapolate what is specific to the person and raise it above all contingencies, as something incomparable, would not the ethical (and even the psychological) character of such an incomparable person conflict precisely with the noblest and most magnanimous aspects of personhood? Thus, to adopt a phrase of Leibniz', it cannot be understood and affirmed as a solipsism, as a metaphysical egoism. . . . That would be incomprehensible and self-contradictory.

Or are we obliged to let God develop his own self-consciousness through the entire course of the world process? "Did he have to produce other beings in order to come to self-consciousness?" But that too would conflict with all the attributes of the Absolute. "If God remains a single Person in remote isolation", he must ultimately refer everything else to himself and so would "lack all altruism". Thus Maurice Blondel guides us through philosophical reflection on the subject, toward the New Testament mystery itself, in which God manifests himself as personal self-surrender, self-giving and reciprocal love.[13]

This is the only way to banish the intolerable *"monos pros monon"*, which compels man to see himself either merely as an

---

[13] M. Blondel, *L'Etre et les êtres*, 2d ed. (P.U.F., 1963), 195–99. Similarly: M. Nédoncelle, *La Réciprocité des consciences* (Paris: Aubier, 1942), 99–100.

individual or merely as a community; the unity of both forms of
unity becomes intelligible as an "image and likeness" of God.
Apart from the New Testament mystery, which is only rendered
accessible to us through Jesus' conduct toward his divine Father
and through his promise of the divine Spirit, human together-
ness has no value in itself. Otherwise it is doomed to remain an
expression of the defectiveness of creaturely plurality over against
the divine unity, and in this case, as we have said, the latter's
image can only shine forth *either* in the individual who is a law
unto himself *or* in the self-sufficient *polis* and its communism.
Only on the basis of the Christian view of God does the
community's mediation of personal freedom acquire a value
that is intrinsic to and constitutive of freedom. Once again,
therefore, in the context of explicating the interrelationship of
infinite and finite freedom, Christian theology has shown itself
to be indispensable if this interrelationship, which lays the
foundation for all theodramatic action, is not to be obstructed
prematurely by a philosophical postulate.

Since we have no alternative but to start on the basis of the
interrelationship of the two freedoms, as the unfolding Christian
revelation shows us, it is a secondary matter whether we begin
with infinite or finite freedom. Starting with God, who, according to Thomas, is "the most evident in himself but not to
us", would give us the advantage of being able to present the
presuppositions of finite freedom before speaking of its reality.
Starting with man, whose structure of freedom is the only one
with which we are familiar, permits us to show why this
structure cannot get along without postulating an absolute
and—in Christian revelation—triune freedom. We shall take the
second path, but with explicit reference to our starting point,
that is, the interrelatedness of both: from the theodramatic point
of view, we cannot illuminate the structure of finite freedom
without the light that radiates from Christ and falls on the divine
freedom.

3. Finite Freedom

a. The Two Pillars

The concept of finite freedom seems self-contradictory, for how can something that is continually coming up against the limits of its nature (not only of its action) be free? How can it be anything but a prisoner? Nonetheless our direct experience of freedom cannot be expressed in any other way but in this apparent contradiction. For if, in the face of all objections, we still have an irrefutable awareness of our freedom, we are equally aware that our freedom is not unlimited, or more precisely that, while we are free, we are always only moving *toward* freedom.

Let us begin, with Augustine, Thomas (and to some extent with Descartes), with the fundamental *"cogito-sum"*—and here we must interpose a preliminary philosophical reflection. When I grasp some finite thing that is true or good, this act is accompanied by a self-awareness containing something inseparably twofold: the consciousness of being present to myself is not something I only learn by realizing that I am exercising some particular activity of my own; "even before the soul performs some abstraction, it has a habitual (self-possessing) knowledge whereby it can understand that it exists",[1] and this is because the soul's essence is present to itself,[2] so that it knows itself "in a

---

[1] Quantum ad cognitionem habitualem, sic dico, quod anima per essentiam suam se videt, . . . ex hoc ipso quod essentia sua est sibi praesens, est potens exire in actum. Thomas, *De Veritate* q 10, a 8 c.

[2] Intelligere dicit simplicem intuitum intellectus in id quod sibi est praesens intelligibile (I, d 3, q 4, a 5). Cum enim intelligimus animam, non confingimus nobis aliquod animae simulacrum, quod intueamur, . . . sed ipsam essentiam animae consideramus (*Ibid.*, q 10, a 8 ad 2 in contr.). But this must not obscure the profound difference between Thomas—who asserts that only angels do in fact have this actual, direct self-knowledge, whereas men do not (*De an.* lib 2, lect c, 7; lib 3, lect 8; *CG* 3, 45.46.47; *Qu. de an.* 16, *De Ver* q 10, 8; *S. Th.* I, q 87, 1) —and the whole Augustinian school. For Augustine, not only all theoretical certainty but also all religious knowledge is based on the soul's actually being present to itself: semetipsam per se ipsam novit, quoniam est incorporea (*De Trin.* IX, 3, 3). Thomas reduces actual knowledge to habitual, which is only actualized indirectly, through its powers, which are distinct from the soul's essence and are referred to objects (cf. Wilhelm Schneider, "Die Quaestiones

certain sense through its essence, as God knows himself".[3]
Present to myself in this way, I know not only that I exist but in
the same knowledge I am open to all being since, in this
consciousness that I *am*, I have touched the farthest possible
horizon, beyond which, evidently, there can be nothing more.
In fact, this presupposes an illumination of knowledge, a light
that discloses the first principles of all being and its transcendental
qualities as things that are both true and good; but this need not
detain us at present. We are concentrating on the fundamental
paradox that both things are unveiled in my own presence-to-
myself: namely, the absolute incommunicability of my own
being (as "I") and the unlimited communicability of being as
such (which is not "used up" by the fullness of all the worldly
existence in which it subsists). It would be a mistake to attempt
to clarify this duality by attributing unlimitedness one-sidedly
to being as such, while regarding limitation as a characteristic of

disp. de Veritate des Thomas von Aquin in ihrer philosophiegeschichtlichen
Beziehung zu Augustinus" in B.G.Ph.Th.M. 27, 3 [1930], 69–73). As far as
the entire Augustinian school is concerned, and Bonaventure in particular (for
a thorough presentation, cf. Bonifatius A. Luyckx, "Die Erkenntnislehre
Bonaventuras" in B.G.Ph.Th.M. 23, 3–4 [1923], 166–97), the reflex character
of all intellectual knowledge involves the knower possessing himself, especially
since Bonaventure makes no real distinction between the soul and its powers.
Thus "sibi praesens" (I, d 3, q 1, a 2 ad 3) has quite a different scope in
Bonaventure from that in Thomas (cf. Luyckx 175, n. 20). Matthew of
Aquasparta will produce a systematic treatment of the Augustinian teaching,
following Bonaventure's line and in a polemical attack on Thomas (*Quaestiones
disp. de fide et de cognitione*, 2d ed. [Florence, 1957], Quaestio V, 292ff.); but
Dominican mysticism will also contradict Thomas at this point. On this subject,
cf. Alois Haas, "Nim din selbes war, Studien zur Lehre von der Selbsterkenntnis
bei M. Eckhart, J. Tauler und H. Seuse" in *Dokimion* 3 (Fribourg, Switzerland,
1971), 41ff., 144. Ultimately the two opposing views meet: in the doctrine of
the *intellectus agens*, which is a participation in the divine light of knowing and
the very foundations of truth, and the *synderesis*, which is a sharing in the first
principles of the good, the doctrine of the intellect as proposed by Thomas
(continuing Aristotle), links up with what is of permanent value in the
Augustinian tradition. (Indeed, without this complement, the Augustinian
tradition is vulnerable.)

[3] Alio modo (i.e., not as in discursive knowledge) dicitur aliquid sicut in quo
cognoscitur, et sic non oportet ut id quo cognoscitur, alia cognitione cognoscatur
quam id quod cognoscitur eo. Unde sic nihil prohibet quin aliquid cognoscatur
seipso, sicut Deus seipso seipsum cognoscit; et sic anima seipsam quodammodo
cognoscit per essentiam suam. *Ibid.*, q 10, a 8 ad 9.

my "nature" (as one man among other men, as one individual of a species). For it is precisely in the experience of being "I" (and no one else) that I pass beyond all limiting knowledge of my nature and touch being (reality) in its uniqueness. The one, identical experience of being discloses two things simultaneously: the utter incommunicability (or uniqueness) and the equally total communicability of being. As an "I", as a person, I am not merely a part of a whole (the cosmos, for instance) but am ready to acknowledge that an unlimited number of others possess being (and the incommunicability that goes along with it). If this is true, then, for the moment, any mediation between the poles—that is, through the identity of the species and the genus in individuals—can be left to one side. It is enough for me to be able to say: I am unique, but only by making room for countless others to be unique. Not out of magnanimity, but because, in self-knowledge, the light of being expands me beyond limitation; indeed, without this expansion beyond limitation I would not even know myself (just as the animal lacks this expansion beyond itself and, accordingly, also lacks self-knowledge). In this primal experience, while I can distinguish between my "mode of being" (*modus subsistentiae, tropos tēs hyparxeōs*) and my grasp of (universal) being, I cannot separate them. Insofar as I hold fast to my experience of uniqueness and refuse to allow it to be watered down by subsequent reflection on my part (or on the part of others)—"I seem to be a unique person, but ultimately I am only one individual among millions"—I see that my being-a-person possesses a uniqueness that stands outside the "*arbor porphyriana*"; consequently it is an improper mode of speech when, in order to express the uniqueness of the purely spiritual creature (the angel), it is said that each of them represents a distinct "species". Certainly man, as a material being, is not only a person but also an individual of his species; but the question is whether, in his mind's presence-to-itself, as here described, he experiences this (endlessly multipliable) individuality—a nature that, in each case, is always(!) "mine"—or rather experiences something that is rooted, not in his essence and nature, but in existence as such, in the *tropos tēs hyparxeōs*. If, from this point, we wished to make an abrupt transition to the province of theology, the first result would be that *communicated being is not only in general an "image of God"*—in whom all beings participate in order to have any being at all and who, in his self-communication, is always richer than the sum of all who thus participate —*but it is actually an image of the three-personal God, in whom the incommunicability of the hypostases is one with the unity of "essence" in each of them.* However, this image is only visible to one who is assured of the uniqueness of his finite person, and ultimately he cannot have this assurance unless God's word has told him, thereby guaranteeing that he "shares in the divine nature".

In thus being a person, he also remains an individual of the human race, and so the second question arises: Am I "only really" an atom that is swallowed up in the mass, and is my ("supernatural") uniqueness something added on, as it were, something accidental? Or was I intended and chosen to be this particular, unique individual (for this, after all, is how I perceive myself), and has this individuality been given to me so that, through the medium of the nature I share with the species, I can communicate with those of like nature, those who have equally been chosen? The latter view would make it clear why Scripture speaks of creation through, for and in Christ (Col 1:16f.). But it would also encompass the former perspective: individuals are only created in Christ by their personal unity (mediated by their membership of the species) being adopted into his "hypostatic union"—which embraces the species and the persons who comprise it. We shall deal with this later in the context of Christology.

The foregoing was simply preliminary to an appraisal of the structure of finite freedom. Present to ourselves in the light of being, we possess an inalienable core of freedom that cannot be split open. Corresponding to the nature of being—which is both true and good—this "light", like everything else we shall have to say about freedom, is an indivisibly intellectual and volitive light; it is both an understanding and an affirming, and while it is true that only something that has been understood can be affirmed, the will provides the stimulus to such understanding.[4] Every one-sided attribution of freedom, whether to the area of rationality (Stoicism) or of the pure will (Scotus,

---

[4] Ipsum bonum, inquantum est quaedam forma apprehensibilis, continetur sub vero, . . . et ipsum verum, inquantum est finis intellectualis operationis, continetur sub bono. *De malo* q 6 c.

Descartes, Rousseau and others incline in this direction), leads back to the subhuman, instinctual level. However, this primal, secure self-possession is not a self-intuition or grasp of one's essence;[5] it articulates itself only *in and with* the universal opening to all being, leaving itself behind to embrace the knowledge and will of others and other things, particularly in shared being [*Mitsein*], whereby the original opening is always so great that no individual being (which is never the whole of being) can fill it. So there is a fundamental freedom (quite apart from all conscious or unconscious motives and compulsions) that enables us to affirm the value of things and reject their defects, to become involved with them or turn away from them. Certainly finite freedom, the openness to all being, can only strive for something it perceives as good (having a value)—even if in fact it is evil; but it is equally certain that the knowledge of the good *as good* (*bonum honestum*) removes the element of *interest* from such striving, so that the element of *indifference*—where the one who strives in the clear light of being has in principle superseded all finite "oppositions"—*turns out to be a new and deeper indifference in which he is able to let the Good "be", whether it be a finite or an infinite Good, simply for the sake of its goodness*, without trying to gain it for himself. Now the other pole of finite freedom comes into full view: if self-possession comes first, all that follows— the endeavor to acquire other good things, including God himself—could seem to be the egoistic attempt to remedy the originally imperfect self-possession by referring it back to oneself, totally, through absolute self-satisfaction. This could happen in the absence of that openness to Being in its totality that unveils this prime thing (myself) as only one being among others. We can put it this way (in the Thomist manner): the "part" (that is, myself, with my self-possession) loves the whole more than itself;[6] or, in the Augustinian, Anselmian and

---

[5] Secundum hoc scientia de anima est certissima, quod unusquisque in seipso experitur se animam habere et actus animae sibi inesse, sed cognoscere quid sit anima difficillimum est. *De Veritate* q 10, a 8 ad 8 in contr.

[6] On this whole question, cf. Richard Völkl, *Die Selbstliebe in der Heiligen Schift und bei Thomas von Aquin* (Münch. Theol. Studien II, 12 [1956]), 164ff., esp. 192ff.; "Gottesliebe aus Selbstliebe?": 246–64. "Even when [Thomas], following Augustine, defines eternal life and the eternal reward as the enjoyment

Franciscan manner, we can say that the right is desired for the
sake of its rightness, whatever "enjoyment" may or may not
be involved.[7] This insight is already at work in Clement of
Alexandria (which is why, later, Fénelon attempted to defend
his own extreme position in a book on Clement),[8] when he sees
man's love for God mediated by faith: thus it is not just a mere
striving, and the gracious quality of the goal that thus discloses
itself is brought out; only in this way is freedom fully realized.[9]
Kant, in his own way, will once again make a clear separation
between duty (doing good for its own sake) and happiness (a
boon that is graciously granted to us).

All this is simply to show that it is impossible to take the
second pole of finite freedom (which necessarily arises out of the
way our original self-possession is constituted and the conditions
that make it possible) and reduce it to the first. When giving us
ethical instructions for the attainment of such freedom, even
those who attempt to restrict finite freedom entirely to the pole
of self-possession (autarkia) must always urge us toward acquiring
indifference to everything else—both to what attracts and to
what repels. As for the converse attempts to persuade man that
his experience of self-subsistence is an illusion and to train him
to overcome this mere appearance (maya), they can only destroy
the outer, empirical layers of "I"-consciousness, not its inner
core.

The first pillar of freedom is unequivocally "given"; the
second is both "given" [gegeben] and "laid upon us" [aufgegeben].
We are given the necessity (this is our "thrown-ness", Geworfen-
heit) of going out from ourselves in order to make decisions and
prove ourselves in the environment of our fellow men and
fellow things. The manner and degree of our "self-realization"
remain open, and it is up to man himself to decide what,

---

of God (frui Deo), we must remember that 'enjoy' means being bound in love to
God for his own sake" (253). Like Augustine (De doctr. christ. I, 4), Thomas says:
"frui est amore inhaerere alicui propter seipsum" (II, II, q 27, a 3 sed contra et c.).

[7] Jean Rohmer, La Finalité morale chez les théologiens de saint Augustin à Duns
Scot (Paris: Vrin, 1939).

[8] P. Dudon, Le Gnostique de saint Clément d'Alexandrie. Opuscule inédit de
Fénelon (Paris: Beauchesne, 1930).

[9] Strom. 2, 8, 1ff.; 2, 11, 1ff.; VI, 73, 2ff.

ultimately, constitutes freedom and under what form it should be striven for. Thus a man may decide that, for the purposes of self-realization, the whole area must remain completely open (so that, if there were a preexistent and fully realized absolute freedom, the path of finite freedom would only be distorted and its course frustrated); conversely he may see that finite freedom, if it remains alone and is posited as absolute, is bound to become the hellish torment of a Tantalus if it is not permitted to attain full development in the self-warranting realm of absolute freedom. We shall see why we are bound to choose this second solution.

b. Freedom as Autonomous Motion

Insofar as it was possible in pre-Christian times, Greek thought explored the structure of finite freedom in all its dimensions; in doing so it left little for post-Christian philosophy to add.[10] And since Genesis and the Old Testament passages dependent on Genesis see human freedom as given, as something beyond question (including man's freedom vis-à-vis God), the Church Fathers and Scholastics did not find it hard to use the material produced by the Greeks in the service of a Christian doctrine of freedom that was theologically thought out.

The fruitful starting point will be found, not along the lines of the (political) *eleutheria*, but in man's experience of his self-possession (which is both a gift and a task), including his autonomous motion. Above and beyond all his somatic conditioning and emotional drives, man has the awareness of spiritually moving himself, of being the source of his particular willing and choosing. Thus Plato says, "The beginning of motion is that which moves itself", and "this is the very essence and concept of the soul."[11] For Aristotle, freedom is the foundation of all ethical conduct: "The ethically good has also been put into our power and likewise what is inferior. For at all points,

[10] Cf. the highly dense survey (with references) by W. Warnach, article "Freiheit" in Ritter, *Hist. Wörterbuch d. Phil.* II (1972).

[11] *Phaedr.* 245de. Plato is bound to deduce from this that the soul is not created, because this kind of beginning (*archē*) can only be conceived on the basis of biblical presuppositions. So Plato had to understand freedom as something outside time (prior to birth, intelligible).

whenever it is in our power to act, it is also in our power not to act." "Man is the moving principle (*archē*) or the generator (*gennetēs*) of his actions, just as he is the begetter of his off-spring."[12] This provides the material for Gregory of Nyssa's formulation of freedom—surely the most extreme formulation produced on Christian soil. And when Thomas Aquinas boldly formulates it thus: "*liberum est, quod sui causa est*",[13] while the immediate reference may be to a wrongly understood passage in Aristotle,[14] what Thomas actually says agrees with what we have cited from the philosopher. The Stoics are so insistent that we have power over our own acts (right up to the highest acts of knowledge, which still require our assent, *synkatathesis*) that they have to put up with the fact that this view contradicts their other view, that is, of a Logos which governs all things by necessity. Freedom is the power of acting from within oneself;[15] man's dignity is his *autexousion*, "being-from-within-himself", *autokratōs*, "governing himself"; according to Seneca, it is his royal prerogative: *in regno nati sumus*.[16] For Epictetus, *eleutheria* is the highest good,[17] even if this freedom only refers to things within ourselves; in his view, therefore, freedom is primarily the art of letting go. Although the Stoic paradox is never really solved,[18] it is brought very close to a solution when, in order to provide a foil to human autonomy (which "even Zeus cannot destroy"),[19] Epictetus turns eternal necessity into a fatherly, giving divinity: now man is free when he wills what God wills. At the end of the ancient world we have Plotinus' treatise on

---

[12] *Eth. Nic.* III, 7, 1113b, 6f. This formulation reminds us of the Diotima speech in Plato's *Symposium*, where the eliciting of virtue in the beloved is paralleled with the begetting of children (209a). On the limits of the freedom of the will in Aristotle, cf. Zeller, 4th ed., II, part 2 (1921), 589.

[13] *S. Th.* I, q 83, a 1.

[14] *Met.* A 2, 982b, 24–28, speaks of first philosophy as being the only philosophy to "be there for its own sake (*autēs heneken*)"; the Latin translation gave this as "*sui causā*", whereby the ablative could easily be understood as a nominative. Cf. J. De Finance, *Existence et liberté* (Paris-Lyons: Vitte, 1955), 7 n.

[15] *Stoic. Vet. Frag.* III, 355.

[16] *De beata vita* 15, 7.

[17] *Diss.* IV, 1, 52.

[18] Cf. *Theo-Drama* I, 495f.

[19] *Diss.* I, 1, 23.

divine freedom (*Enn.* IV, 8) to which we have already referred; here, but only on the periphery, the question arises whether an existent being which owes its existence to some other being (and so has its *archē* in that other) can simultaneously have its ground within itself.[20]

Only as the centuries passed did man come to realize clearly, at the level of reflection, how important finite freedom is as a presupposition for the whole biblical drama (and particularly for the Christian drama) that takes place between God and mankind. Christianity had continually to vindicate its authentic form by defending this point against the determinism and fatalism of the ancient world and in particular against the Gnostic view, which divided men into those who are naturally good (the spiritual), the mediocre (the psychics) and the bad (the hylics); and also against Manichaeism. The first pole of finite freedom, the "*autexousion*", is posited unrestrictedly as the prime datum; only in the second step is it demonstrated that freedom, thus given, must also realize itself, within the overall context of divine freedom, in a process that, on earth, is never-ending. Later, in a special excursus, we shall examine how the Fathers found this duality expressed in Genesis' two terms: "according to (God's) image and likeness".

It is quite natural, on the basis of their belief in the personality and freedom of God, that the Fathers regarded the creature's capacity for self-determination (both of angels and of men) as a power given and delegated by God. Thus Justin (*Dial.* 8, 5) emphasizes the rational aspect of freedom, which enables man "to choose the true and do the good" (*1 Apol.* 28; *2 Apol.* 6). Without freedom there is no responsibility, no ethics (*1 Apol.* 43, 44, 48); quoting Plato (*Rep.* X, 617e), he observes that "guilt falls on the one who chooses; God is guiltless". For Tatian, God alone is good by nature; angels and men are created free and have to choose between good and evil (VII, 2–4); if now we have become slaves and mortals, it is "by the freedom of our will" that we were brought down (XI, 6). In Irenaeus, Clement, Origen, Gregory of Nyssa, Nemesius, Ephrem, Maximus and

---

[20] *Enn.* VI, 8, 14.

finally Augustine, finite freedom is moved to center stage; the
same is true of Athanasius and Basil. But they never insist on
this pole for its own sake (as a modern philosopher, for instance,
might write a treatise on the freedom of the will) but in order to
establish one of the fundamental premises for theo-drama.

Particularly in Irenaeus, Origen and Gregory of Nyssa, the
nature and disposition of the encompassing divine freedom is
largely conceived and described by reference to the unrestricted
privileges of human self-determination.

For *Irenaeus*, man is described as being "created in autonomy
(*idian exousian*) from the beginning"—an anti-Gnostic thrust—
". . . so that he can follow God's counsel (*gnomē*) freely, without compulsion" (*Adv. Haer.* IV, 37, 1). Once he has been given
his freedom, he is not subject to superior force from infinite
freedom; for actually it is a mark of infinite freedom that it does
not use force: "There is no compulsion on God's side, but good
counsel is always available" (IV, 37, 1). Numerous scriptural
passages are adduced to illustrate both these points (IV, 37, 3–4).
Faith itself remains an *"eleutheron"* and *"autexousion"* on man's
part. Exposed in this way, however, is human freedom not
doomed to let man down? In other words: why, right at the
beginning, did God not create angels and men to be sinless (IV,
37, 6)? Irenaeus' lengthy answer reveals one of his favorite
themes: because finite freedom must experience its finitude
and poverty, must, as it were, explore the whole area of its
possibilities in order to learn by experience (*peira*) that it can
only fulfill itself by following the advice and counsel of God.
Here we may have the developed form of the primary experiential
concept of the New Testament, found in the parable of the
Prodigal Son: finite freedom's negative experience that, isolated
from infinite freedom, it must hunger and perish. "Those who
distanced themselves from the Father's light and overstepped
the commandment *of freedom* have strayed afar through their
own fault, since they were created free, capable of deciding
things for themselves" (IV, 39, 4). There is no attraction in
possessions that have not been fought for, as we see in the elder
son of the parable. At this point Irenaeus quotes all Paul's
martial images and concludes: "The harder we have fought for a

thing, the more valuable it appears to us; and the more valuable, the more beloved" (IV, 37, 7). If we ask why redemption came so late in history, the answer again is that man's experience needed time to ripen (IV, 38, 1–4). Now he turns his gaze to eternal freedom and—in a way that is both genuinely Greek and at the same time thoroughly Christian—establishes the fundamental quality of generosity and forbearance: in generosity God gave man his freedom; in forbearance he not only allows him to continue on his erring path but actually accompanies him, supporting him with his *Providence*, so that all man's error takes place within the realm of divine love.

This basic outline, that is, autonomous finite freedom operating within an encompassing Providence, which restrains the former at its limits, is followed through and varied in different ways in the two sketches by Origen and Gregory of Nyssa. Characteristically they hold fast unshakably to the first pole, the *autexousion*, although in Origen, more explicitly than in Irenaeus, it is seen in union with the second, that is, "mobility" (*kinēsis*), changeability[21] and hence freedom to choose. The emphasis on the *autexousion* in all the early Fathers must be understood as a specifically Christian position (in opposition to the united front of determinism and Gnosticism), as we can see from Clement of Alexandria, who, while he is most clearly aware that man can only attain his own fulfillment with God's help,[22] yet insists that "God does not compel us"[23] but rather "wishes us to be saved on the basis of our own decision. This, then, is the essence of the soul: it moves by its own power."[24] This, and the resultant concept of "synergism", has nothing to do with Pelagianism. When we ourselves realize the good, this is not "self-realization": ultimately, as in Irenaeus, it is obedience, only possible within God's foreknowledge, within his elective and perfecting *pronoia*.[25]

[21] Although this was prefigured in Gnosticism, particularly in Marcion.

[22] *Strom.* IV, 132, 1; VI, 151f.; VII, 48. W. Völker, *Der wahre Gnostiker nach Clemens von Alexandrien* (Berlin-Leipzig, 1952), 115–26: "Willensfreiheit und Synergismus".

[23] *Quis div. salv.* 10, 2.

[24] *Strom.* VI, 96, 2.

[25] We find the same emphasis on the autonomous motion of finite freedom in Tertullian (*De exhort. cast.* Oehler I, 739ff.: "cum solum sit in nobis velle . . .

In resisting Gnosticism and determinism, *Origen* takes up an extreme position that, formally, brings him close to modern views like those of Secrétan or Sartre: the creature is identical with freedom (that is, finite freedom, the freedom to choose), and so in preexistence all souls are essentially identical; they only attain their own particular nature on the basis of their decision. Quite apart from the myth of preexistence, Origen defines the autonomous motion of finite freedom by carefully distinguishing it from its antecedent stages: mere "dead" matter is only moved "from outside"; plants move "from within themselves" (*ex hautōn*); in animals there is a natural and psychic stimulus from within, "from themselves" (*aph'hautōn*); but only rational men move "by themselves" (*di'hautōn*). To deny that man has autonomous motion is to deny him rationality.[26] Here we have a clear statement of the inseparability of reason and freedom, on which Thomas will place such weight.

However, this insight must be embedded in the total context of Origen's doctrine of salvation, as the *locus classicus* in *Peri Archon* III, 1, 1–24 does. After defining freedom of the will as autonomous motion, endowed with reason, and hence as the

nobis est voluntas et arbitrium eligendi") and particularly in *Methodius'* treatise on the *autexousion*, where the attribute that Plotinus reserves for the Divine is also imparted to man (*De Aut*. 17, 1). The difference is that God, in his freedom, subsists in and from himself (*autosystatos* 16, 8), whereas man has received freedom as a gift, by way of a special dignity (12, 2; 16, 7).

[26] *Peri Euchēs* I, 6, 1–2. Also *Peri Arch*. III, 1, 1–3. Cf. *C. Cels*. IV, 3: Could not God have created man sinless from the beginning? But if we suspend the freewill exercise of virtue, we obliterate its very essence. The rational being makes judgments about his natural motions, by contrast with even the most intelligent animals: *Peri Arch*. III, 1, 3. Later (c. 400) *Nemesius of Emesa* will insist just as strongly on the inseparability of reason (reflection) and the freedom to choose; this is part of the Aristotelian tradition: "Freedom is common to both reason and conation" (*Eth. Nic*. 1113, a 11, cf. Nemesius PG 40, 733A–C). Thus (*De Hom. Nat*. 41): "the *logikon* implies the *autexousion*." One only has "control over one's own actions" (776A) if one possesses theoretical or practical reason. If we ask why God did not confirm finite freedom in the good, the answer is, as in Irenaeus and Origen (chap. 42): God's Providence and its infinite freedom encompasses finite freedom; without free choice the latter would possess no virtue, no merit (764C). Even the angels had to choose, and now they are unchangeable, although free (*autexousioi*), because they have chosen rationally (777A).

ability to embrace good or evil, he proceeds to an exhaustive
discussion of apparently contrary scriptural passages which
seem to imply predestination. The scarlet thread running
through these reflections is, as in Irenaeus, the idea of Providence.[27] When we read that God hardens Pharaoh's heart, we
must remember that God is essentially good and therefore can
only allow such things with a view to a good purpose (*prothesis
chrēstē*), a subsequent change of heart; furthermore, he accompanies the one who, for the time being, has strayed from the
good path (III, 1, 10). This idea of postponing conversion for
"therapeutic" considerations will crop up again (1, 17). Then
the—slightly modified—Irenaean motif is introduced:

> The man who has failed to grasp his own weakness and sickness
> and is oblivious of divine grace and, when he is healed, has not
> acquired some experience of himself (*heautou pepeiramenos*) and
> (hence) does not know himself, will imagine that what has been
> given to him by heavenly grace is his own achievement (1, 12).

The unwise must learn to entrust himself to a wise man, just as,
in the gospel, those who are sick go to the Lord (1, 15). There is
strong emphasis on the fact that "it is not enough for man to will
the goal if he is to reach it" (1, 19) and that he needs God's help
(1, 24); this counterbalances the idea presented elsewhere that
finite freedom, once it has arrived at the very bottom of (devilish)
wickedness, is able to turn again of its own power, just as,
originally, succumbing to weariness (*koros*) of the good, it
forfeited its angelic state and acquired a human, material nature.
The Irenaean motif of men's *koros*, their surfeit of evil, which
attaches them to the good, predominates: ". . . so that, through
acquaintance with evil and being permeated by the sin they
desire, they are sated and come to see the harm of it and so attain
(salvation, restored to them once more) all the more surely."[28]

---

[27] J. Daniélou (*Origène* [1948], 201–5) rightly emphasizes—in opposition to
Hal Koch (*Pronoia und Paideusis* [Berlin-Leipzig, 1932])—that, beside the
Hellenistic notion of providence there is a second pole that is decisive for
Origen, namely, created freedom; that, in other words, his world view is
essentially dramatic.

[28] *Peri Euchēs* II, 29, 13.

No doubt *Gregory of Nyssa* went farthest, in the Christian contest with the Stoics and Plotinus, in establishing the first pillar of finite freedom, though, as we shall see, he did so by incorporating the second into it (as Plotinus did). For the overall plan, he remains indebted to Irenaeus and Origen, just as his brother, Basil, had adopted Origen's idea of the *koros* and anticipated Gregory's idea of the finitude of evil: Adam, Basil says, was originally free and blessed, but "having become proud through a surfeit of the good, so to speak, he put what seemed attractive to the fleshly eye above the beauty of the spiritual world, . . . and so he deserved death by turning away from God". However, God "did not hinder our dissolution, lest the sickness itself should become immortal".[29] From his first work, *On Chastity*, via the *Dialogue Concerning the Soul and Immortality*, to the *Treatise on the Creation of Man*, Gregory multiplies expressions for the "royal dignity" (PG 44, 136C) of human freedom. To him it signifies "independence" (*to autokrates*), "self-control" (*to adespoton* 45, 24D): these qualities, which actually belong to God, make men "godlike" (*theoeides, isotheon to autexousion*; PG 46, 524A). Man governs himself by his own decisions (*autokratikōs*), he is free of any servant relationship (*adoulōton*) because he bases himself on his own insight (45, 77A). With regard to the exercise of freedom of choice, one can speak of man creating himself, for "in this case birth does not occur because of intervention from outside, as in bodily beings which are brought forth from outside. It is the pure product of one's own freedom of choice; thus, in a certain sense, we are our own fathers, since we beget ourselves as the people we want to be" (44, 328B). What is said here in the *Life of Moses* (following Aristotle, as we have seen) is highlighted once again in the *Catechetical Orations*; here the one choosing is warned to consider well what kind of father he wants to have as a result of his choice, "for, as we said, in this birth one chooses one's own parents" (45, 97D–100A). For this likeness to God brings a danger with it: it has the power to create something that even God cannot create: evil. Evil only attains reality (*ousiōthē*) in our

---

[29] Homily 7: "That God is not the Originator of evil" (PG 31, 344CD).

will (44, 725BC).[30] Only *one* contemporary of Gregory, Ephrem
the Syrian, dared to make equally extreme assertions, calling
Adam a "created god" in virtue of his freedom,[31] or praising
freedom since it can no more be hidden than the sun in the
firmament: "Who can deny its lordship, for its power is as
mighty as God?"[32] True, Gregory will immediately discern and
describe the mark of creatureliness in man's freedom of the will,
his ability to fall from God. But it is precisely man's freedom to
choose that makes him a genuine partner in dialogue with God;
it is precisely because he is *not* God that he can be an "image of
God" and "godlike".

Man's godlikeness, of course, can only be finite, like its
special product, evil. And, as in Irenaeus, this finitude is bound
to come to light in the experience of mankind; but Gregory is
more pessimistic than his predecessor; according to him, evil
must breed "to its highest extent" before coming up against its
own internal limits. He treats the theme in six different ways.[33]
The abscess must be ripe before the surgeon (Christ) can come
and lance it. No perversity must be missing, no evil must
remain hidden. "When the entire power of wickedness had
poured forth, . . . when all were 'consigned to disobedience'
(Rom 11:32), when the darkness of vice had reached its ultimate
intensity, then grace appeared, then the true light shone forth"
(46, 1132C). Since evil cannot continue to infinity (*aoriston*) but
is of necessity confined within a boundary, "it must be transformed, at the boundary, into good" (44, 201BC). Several
themes converge here in Gregory's (dangerous) description of
the boundary: the Irenaean idea that the sinner, having come to
his senses through the experience of evil, can now cling all the
more firmly to the good; Origen's theme of Providence, which
only intervenes with saving grace when the sickness has progressed
to ripeness; and finally a purely philosophical (Plotinian) idea

[30] Adam is the "inventor" of evil: *De virg.* 12, *Sources chrétiennes* 119, 402, 19,
"the creator and demiurge of evil" (*De hom. op.* 1, 24).

[31] First Oration on Faith, 2d ed., 37 (BKV I, 37, 32).

[32] Eleventh Hymn against Heretics, 2d ed., 4 (BKV II, 46).

[33] For an analysis, cf. J. Daniélou, *L'Etre et le temps chez Grégoire de Nysse*
(Leyden: Brill, 1970), the chapter entitled "Comble", 186–204, esp. 188–91.

that reflects on the finitude of evil but the infinity of man's longing for the good. We shall return to this.

Gregory closes a circle that will not open again in this way except, perhaps, in modern transpositions. Augustine and Maximus the Confessor make the next major contributions.

In his early period, *Augustine* likewise has to assert against the Manichees that the *liberum arbitrium* is the origin of evil; but even here he says that, in order to be free, it is subject to "the eternal law imprinted within it" (*Lib. arb.* I, 6, 15). This law, however, is simultaneously that eternal freedom which is to be the object of man's love: self-possession is the possession of God (I, 13, 29–31). Thus he arrives at the starting point for his anti-Pelagian concept of freedom in the writings of his old age, which will develop the second pole of finite freedom more than ever before.

Maximus reflects upon the problem of freedom from the standpoint of the Christology to be defended. Diadochus of Photike had already defined "self-determination" (*autexousiotēs*) as "the volition of the rational soul" (*Cap. gnost.* 5, quoted in PG 91, 277C); correspondingly, for Maximus, man in his essence is not only *logikos*, rational, but also *thelētikos*, volitional (91, 12D). While he knows just as well as Gregory of Nyssa and Augustine the havoc wrought by a will that chases after, and is enslaved (Augustine) by, the passions (*pathē, concupiscentia*), and which only grace can remedy, he envisages the structure of human free will on the basis of the requirements of Christology. First of all, therefore, he must identify a natural will (*thelēma physikon*, the *voluntas ut natura* of St. Thomas) that belongs to (Christ's) human nature and distinguish it from a will that has passed over into act (*thelēma gnōmikon*); the latter is situated in the tension between a philosophical understanding (*exercitium voluntatis*) and the de facto fallenness and lack of direction of the will in the "state of fallen nature". If, in Augustine, the reference point is the *gratia liberans liberum arbitrium*, for Maximus it is the cosmic centrality of Christ, which creates syntheses that man himself, particularly fallen man, cannot realize.[34]

[34] Cf. my *Kosmische Liturgie*, 2d ed. (Einsiedeln: Johannes Verlag, 1961), 274–359.

In what follows we need only identify a few of the great central points in the history of Christian ideas where freedom is emphasized as the autonomous motion of the finite.

In this context we can omit Anselm. His beautiful and significant definition of freedom is dominated by the Augustinian tradition, even where it drops one essential element of Augustine's (the "*desiderium*") in favor of another, the "*rectitudo* (the direction toward the absolute good) which is maintained for its own sake". What Anselm mentions on the periphery, that is, that even the fallen will per se, as will, has the (no longer realizable) possibility of doing right,[35] becomes a central affirmation in *Bernard*, where it assimilates the Augustinian and Anselmian element of "*rectitudo*" ("*ordinatio*" 6, 19).[36] Thus, in Bernard's treatise "On Grace and Free Will", the line of Origen and Gregory of Nyssa converges with that of Augustine. Just as Gregory designates finite freedom as *theion ti chrēma*, "a divine thing" (46, 148A), Bernard portrays this same freedom as *plane divinum quiddam praefulgens in anima* (*In Cant.* 81, 6); at the heart of this freedom he discerns an element of absoluteness that seems to break through the analogy between God and the creature and imply an essential identity: "*Libertas a necessitate aeque et indifferenter Deo universaeque . . . rationali*[37] *convenit creaturae*" (4, 9). Here the original and the image are eye to eye; for finite freedom, being "*liber sui*" (1, 2; 2, 3), having autonomous control over oneself, is actually the "image" of infinite freedom: "*aeternae et incommutabilis divinitatis substantive quaedam imago impressa*" (9, 28). Once given, freedom cannot be lost; if, in the damned, it wishes to hand itself over to evil and

[35] *De libertate arbitrii* 11: "semper enim naturaliter liber est (liberum arbitrium) ad servandam rectitudinem si (!) eam habet, etiam quando quam servet non habet", Schmitt I, 223. On the elements of his doctrine of the will for which Bernard is indebted to Anselm: E. Gilson, *The Mystical Theology of St. Bernard* (1940). On Anselm's dependence upon Augustine: J. Rivière in *Studi Agostiniani* (Rome, 1931), 837–51.

[36] Quoted in PL 182, 1002–30 according to chapter and number.

[37] For Bernard, as for all the Fathers (especially Origen and Maximus), following Aristotle, rationality is inseparable from freedom. Right from the start he discerns in the *liberum arbitrium* the element of spontaneity or autonomous motion (which, going from the plants to the animals to man, steadily increases), connected with the element of rational judgment; thus the "voluntas" is the "motus rationalis" (2, 2).

thus become a "captive"[38] freedom, this must be its own decision; no one can compel it, only itself (12, 39). True, this element of absoluteness is only conceivable in connection with a complementary relativity: if freedom is to desire what is right (and hence to desire itself), it has need of good counsel (*consilium*); and if it is to grasp and possess it, it needs a joyful and loving consent of the will (*complacentia*). Both of these can be lost by the decision to turn away from God; the first, the taste for the good, is restored (albeit imperfectly) to the just man through redemption, and the second is attained in heaven by the blessed, and on earth, in the manner of a foretaste, by the enraptured (5, 15); this brings in the Augustinian doctrine of grace. So freedom, as rational spontaneity, can indeed be described as the "nature" of the spiritual creature, provided it is linked with the second element, which is an integral part of finitude. Thus the "either-or" of autonomy and heteronomy that haunts the entire Christian tradition is overcome right at the outset. So, too, the extreme positions adopted by the moderns (Spinoza and Leibniz, on the one hand, Schopenhauer and Sartre on the other) are subsumed in the synthesis.

We can only mention in passing the doctrine of freedom in *Thomas Aquinas*.[39] It has its core in the indissoluble linking of the two poles of finite freedom in Thomas' central insight, namely, that *esse* grounds both self-being and communication with the Absolute. All the minute analyses of particular aspects, in the line of Aristotle and the early Scholastics, must never cause us to lose sight of this central vision of his. Since the tradition presents him with two strands of the problem, that is, the freedom of the will as such (in opposition to all kinds of determinism) and freedom of choice (in opposition to the confusion of finite with infinite freedom or with pure spontaneity), Thomas treats the two questions separately.[40] But when he says

[38] Thus Bernard translates Augustine's "*servum arbitrium*" (*C. Julian.* II, 8, 23; PL 44, 689), which Luther was to use as the title of his polemical work.

[39] For a synthesis of its widely branching aspects, all organized, however, from a single center, cf. G. Siewerth, *Thomas von Aquin, die menschliche Willensfreiheit* (Düsseldorf: Schwann 1954); G. Siewerth, *Die Freiheit und das Gute* (Freiburg: Herder, 1959).

[40] *De veritate* q 22 and q 24.

that every free will only seeks things under the aspect of the good, and to that extent seeks throughout the whole breadth of being ("which is the image—*similitudo*—of divine goodness": *Ver.* q 22, a 2 c, and ad 2) for the absolute Good, God; and that in this process it is determined by itself alone, and thus is undetermined in its choice of the path along which the good is to be sought—he is already on the threshold of the second question. For, as in the patristic tradition, the will's free, autonomous motion always involves positing the *"logikon"*, that is, it involves insight into being in its totality and the act of judging every existing thing and every value under the aspect of being and of the good per se; so much so that the two elements can only be grasped in a reciprocal priority.[41] By contrast with the animal, which also possesses a judgment as to what is to be done in the situation and so has "a kind of copy of the *liberum arbitrium*", "as it were, a conditional kind of freedom",[42] but cannot evaluate existing things under the aspect of being, only human reason is able to "judge its own judgment" and thus "be a cause of its own self not only in autonomous motion (that is, in spontaneity) but also in judging".[43] As we saw, Thomas can say *"causa sui motus"* or simply *"causa sui"*, but note that q 22 makes it clear that this does not imply the kind of self-positing in being such as God exercises. But because the *"motus"* of freedom is inseparable from the *"causa sui"*, because there is thus in the will a natural longing (*desiderium naturale*)[44] for complete, exhaustive self-possession, which would have to coincide with the "possession" of being as such, we arrive at the Thomist paradox (which Henri de Lubac has again brought to light): man strives to fulfill himself in an Absolute and yet, although he is *"causa sui"*, he is unable to achieve this by his own power or by

[41] Ratio autem et voluntas sunt . . . ad invicem ordinatae, et absolute considerando ratio prior est, quamvis per reflexionem efficiatur voluntas prior et superior, inquantum movet rationem. De veritate q 22, a 13 c. On the other hand, the will cannot choose anything unless the reason presents it as available for choice (*ibid.*).

[42] *De veritate* q 24, a 2 c.

[43] Homo vero per virtutem rationis judicans de agendis, potest de suo arbitrio judicare, inquantum cognoscit rationem finis et ejus quod est ad finem, et . . . ordinem unius ad alterum, et ideo non est solum causa sui ipsius in movendo, sed in judicando. De veritate q 24, a 1 c.

[44] *Contra Gentes* 3, 25; 3, 50.

attaining any finite thing or finite good. Precisely this, according
to Thomas, constitutes man's dignity.[45] It is no real criticism of
the Thomist position to pick up the "indifference" emphasized
by Anselm (that is, man is only free if he loves the good for its
own sake)[46] and play it off against the apparent unfreedom of
finite freedom regarding its formal object (the good in general).
The fact that finite freedom attains self-fulfillment in a dimension
beyond its own striving is only a further aspect of the paradox of
which we are speaking.[47]

Pico della Mirandola wrote an oration which, having originally
attracted little attention, eventually became famous: it was entitled "On the Dignity of Man". In fact it was never delivered as
an oration and was only published posthumously in 1494. On
the face of it he seems to proclaim a concept of freedom that is
new and that points forward to the modern age; but this view
has been thoroughly demolished by H. de Lubac.[48] Pico certainly emphasizes the freedom given to man by God as "the
greatest marvel in nature", enabling him to go beyond his
pristine indifference and determine his own nature: he can
become mortal or immortal, angelic or bestial.[49] "We have been
placed in a situation in which we are what we want to be",[50] and
thus we are brought close to God.[51] No "divinization" is

[45] *S. Th.* I–IIae, q 5, a 5 ad 2. Again we must stress that finite freedom cannot
be compelled in any way by infinite freedom, even if God (as *causa prima*) can
influence it from within, as befits its own nature (which is to strive for a good):
De veritate q 22, a 8. Furthermore, Thomas definitely accepted Bernard's
threefold division of freedom (and hence the entire Augustinian issue of a
"captive will"): *2 Sent* dist 25, q 1, a 5.

[46] Cf. nn. 6 and 7 above.

[47] H. de Lubac, *Le mystère du Surnaturel* (1946), 483–94; H. de Lubac, *Die
Freiheit der Gnade*, 2: Das Paradox des Menschen (Einsiedeln: Johannes, 1971).

[48] *Pic de la Mirandole, Etudes et discussions* (Paris: Aubier, 1974). Pico's oration
is quoted from the edition by Eugenio Garin (Edizioni naz. dei classici del
pensiero italiano 1 [Florence, 1942]).

[49] Definitis ceteris natura, . . . tu nullis angustiis coercitus, pro tuo arbitrio,
in cujus manu te posui, tibi illam praefinies. . . . Nec te caelestem neque
terrenum, neque mortalem neque immortalem fecimus, ut tui ipsius quasi
arbitrarius honorariusque plastes et fictor, in quam malueris tute formam
effingas, 104–6.

[50] 108–10.

[51] Man is not essentially an intramundane being but the *"mundi copula"* (102);

intended here, however.[52] For, on the one hand, man is still characterized by tension: he is the *complexio mundi* (microcosm), and at the same time he is (and must remain) transcendent beyond the world;[53] and, on the other hand, Pico stresses most strongly in his works that the perfection of man's freedom—which really brings him what, on the basis of his original indifference, he could be, should be and wants to be—can only be brought about by the mediating Spirit of God:

> The divine, moving Spirit constantly urges your spirit forward. . . .
> If you let him have his way, you will be brought to God. . . . This
> is real blessedness, being one spirit together with God and thus
> possessing God in God and not in us; it is knowing as we are
> known.[54]

These words show that the alleged Titan of human autonomy is thoroughly traditional; for him (as for Origen, Gregory of Nyssa and Bernard) there is no difficulty in incorporating a link with absolute freedom in human autonomous motion.

It is no surprise, therefore, to find that *Newman* occasionally designates man as the "first cause" (by which he means the Thomist "*causa sui*"), the "principle of creativity in the moral world".[55]

c. Freedom as Consent

Our describing of the first pole of finite freedom, the *autexousion*, continually brought the second pole into the discussion: freedom means that we have been set free in such a way that we occupy an

---

therefore he is not created according to an archetype, like the other finite beings (104). It follows that he does not have to content himself with any intramundane goal but can "withdraw into the center of his unity and become 'one spirit' with God" (106). Hence the challenge: "Let us despise what is earthly and aspire to what is heavenly; let us leave everything earthly behind us and hasten to that place (*curia*) that lies above the world in closest proximity to the Most High Divinity" (110).

[52] By contrast to the somewhat crude formulations of Ficino. Cf. de Lubac, *Pic de la Mirandole*, 74f.

[53] *Ibid.*, 82, 89.

[54] *Hexaplus*, expos. 7, Prooem. Garin (see n. 48 above), 336.

[55] *Oxford University Sermons*, 6.

elevated position of "indifference"; from this vantage point we can choose, and indeed we must choose, because we can only realize this elevated indifference by making choices, choices which affect everything with which we share existence. Going out of ourselves and into "the other" is a sign both of poverty and of wealth, and this twofold character precipitates a further choice: will finite freedom use the wealth of its being open to enrich itself further, or will it regard its being open as the opportunity to hand itself over to infinite free Being, to the Being who is the Giver of this free openness? According to the first alternative, everything—including God—would be a means (*uti*) enabling finite freedom to enjoy its own self (*frui*). The second alternative sounds less abstract if we remember our everyday experience, namely, that finite freedom comes up against other finite freedoms and cannot appropriate or incorporate them into itself (and hence should not do so in the realm of being either): the freedom of the "other" must disclose itself by opening up its own inner area. This social interchange in which the freedoms reciprocally enrich each other in "selflessness" gives us a crucial preliminary insight: ultimately, a relation between finite and infinite freedom must involve self-disclosure on the part of infinite freedom. The *autexousion* of finite freedom contains an element of absoluteness,[56] an "infinite finitude", which can neither get back to its own origin, insofar as finite freedom is present "as a given", nor (therefore) can it reach its goal by pursuing the totality of goods and values to be found in the world, be they personal or impersonal. On this boundary there arises the idea of a self-disclosure on the part of infinite freedom. The crucial question will be whether and how—if such self-disclosure takes place—finite freedom can fulfill itself in infinite freedom without casting doubt upon the initial datum, but also without making infinite freedom somehow finite, without relegating it to one existent entity among others.

It would be tedious to deal with this second aspect by once

---

[56] Cf. Siewerth's analysis of the "fourfold absoluteness in the free will" in *Thomas von Aquin, die menschliche Willensfreiheit* (1954), 88f. On the twelfth century: R. Javelet, *Psychologie des auteurs spirituels du XIIe siècle* (Strasbourg, 1959), chaps. 2 and 3: "Volonté et liberté" and "Liberté et personne".

again recapitulating the various systems of Christian *Welt-anschauung*; we can proceed rather more systematically, for the most part building on foundations we have already laid. First and foremost we must remember that—as theologians—our starting point is always the given relationship between God and man as set forth in biblical revelation but that, for the present, we resolved to abstract from the concrete dramatic modalities of this interrelationship (which is also a relationship of confrontation) in order to devote our attention solely to its fundamental articulations. Here, however, a difficulty arises. For the history of salvation as depicted in the movement from the Old to the New Testament, and within the latter, shows us a *"paidagogia"* (cf. Gal 4:2) that leads us from a condition of estrangement to one of *"parrhesia"* (that is, of free mutual openness) graciously granted to us by God. In principle we have access to this condition here and now, although we await its ultimate fulfillment; it is also that state in which God "will be all in all" (1 Cor 15:28). But since, on the basis of our presuppositions, this will not abolish finite freedom's self-determination, we must formally assume that this ultimate state is normative for the reciprocal relationship. In that case, however, in the preceding stages of estrangement, finite freedom will be of such a kind that God will not allow it to be "all in all"; rather, he sets it as one existing being beside others (albeit above them). We must admit that the Old Testament form of relationship between Yahweh and the people (or mankind as a whole) somehow implies the idea of an opposition between the Divine "being" (in heaven) and a multiplicity of human "being" (on earth);[57] in this context, the notion that the Divine being could be "all" occurs—as a baffling discovery (Sir 43:27)—only on the very periphery. Accordingly it is hard to avoid seeing an element of heteronomy in the old Law. Only in the preaching of Jesus and the post-Easter meditation upon it in the light of the Holy Spirit does the womb of the Father's divine freedom open so wide and so deep that we begin to suspect what "the fulfillment of finite freedom in infinite freedom" might mean. But man's tendency to fall back into sinful alienation remains strong: Christian preaching has to

[57] Cf. pp. 175ff. above.

combat the continual reemergence of the notion that God is one being among others, that his revelation is one factor among others and that the light radiating from him is one law among others.

In this situation, Christianity's confrontation with Hellenism appears in a new light. Both the Stoics and Plotinus in particular present Christians with a *formal* model of the relationship between the Absolute (the One) and the multiplicity that originates in it; as a rationally conceived model it corresponds to certain elementary requirements of thought, but as yet it lacks the living content of biblical revelation. When the Christian comes to proclaim this living content to pagans as something absolutely new, the latter (in their most refined thought) present a model that the Christian must not undervalue. We have already illustrated this claim by referring to Cusanus' dictum that God can only be the "Wholly Other" insofar as he is the "Non-Other";[58] it can also be expressed in Augustine's *"Deus interior intimo meo"*, which simultaneously holds fast and undergirds the autonomy of the subject. The Christian task, in the face of the Stoic and Plotinian enterprise, is to heighten the formal model into a relationship between freedoms according to which finite freedom can only arise out of, and persist within, primal freedom (just as in Plotinus the "other"—over against the "one"—can only be "other" because it itself is a "one" and thus participates in oneness); it is precisely because it has its origin in freedom that it is really free.

1. The Christian answer to the Neoplatonic paradox (which is already found in Plato's *Parmenides*) is the New Testament doctrine of the *Holy Spirit*, who, as the love of God poured into the hearts of believers, brings about two things at the same time: he liberates finite freedom so that it may embrace its own, ultimate freedom; and he does so by initiating it into a participation in infinite freedom. At this stage we can call this other pole of finite freedom "theonomy", but we must make sure that this does not obscure or interfere with the *autexousion*. There is no danger of this in all the New Testament passages that describe man's definitive and normative relationship with God

[58] Cf. p. 193 above.

in terms of liberation from "slavery" to be a "child of God" (and hence an "heir"), and as a "friendship" where perfect obedience and "submission" is at the same time a "being free", "*parrhesia*", straightforward access to infinite freedom, indeed, an inner participation in its specifically divine quality. On the one hand, since the governing reality is free self-disclosure, this participation is the experience of infinite grace: it is a sense of "being privileged" [*dürfen*] which swallows up all notion of obligation [*müssen*]. On the other hand, since infinite freedom is in full possession of itself and does not need to go looking for its perfection, like finite freedom, it is fulfillment and hence blessedness: *beatitudo*—we rediscover the Greek *eudaimonia* at the level of the freedoms—or, in Augustinian terms, *delectatio*—which coincides with the experience of new-found and fully liberated freedom. Bernard calls it "*complacitum*" (4, 11), mutual agreement and mutual liking, or "*consensus*" (12, 41; 13, 44; 14, 50),[59] harmony of dispositions. We find this at the confluence of the lines of thought that come from Gregory of Nyssa and Augustine; these two, above all, expressly on the basis of Plotinus, undertook to transpose the philosophical "One-and-many" model into the living relationship between infinite and finite freedom.

We shall take *Augustine* first. He wrestled with absolute freedom's immanence in finite freedom more than did the Greeks because, from his own experience of life, it had become the starting point for his existential thought. Here too, however, we must exclude the whole problem (so deeply pondered over by Augustine) of the historical stages of freedom (paradise—the Fall—redemption—heaven), since they form part of the drama's actual execution. According to Augustine, finite freedom as such is the rational,[60] autonomous motion of the soul,[61] in which the "I" possesses itself in freedom.[62] This presupposes a

---

[59] PL 182, 1019D, 1023BC, 1028BC.

[60] For Augustine, finite freedom is essentially oriented to truth: "quid enim fortius desiderat anima quam veritatem?" (*In Joh* 26, 5; PL 35, 1609). But this truth is one with the perfection of freedom; thus the path to truth can be designated the right path, the "*rectitudo*".

[61] "Ipse animi motus, cogente nullo, voluntas est. . . . Si ergo homo voluerit, de homine existit" (*C. Julian. op. imp.* 5, 60 (PL 45, 1495–96).

[62] "Non enim quidquam tam firme atque intime sentio quam me habere

free faculty of judgment (*liberum arbitrium*) in every freedom
(both finite and infinite); Augustine will not deny it to God,
angels and the blessed.[63] Thus his starting point is not the
definition of finite freedom as freedom to choose good or evil;
rather, his basic position is that finite freedom, which is necessarily equipped with this ability, can only fulfill itself within the
context of infinite freedom. Only in such a context can it
actually be freedom (*libertas*) at all.[64] On the one hand, finite
freedom cannot be compelled by anything but itself to leave the
path of infinite freedom and head for slavery,[65] and, on the
other hand, by definition, infinite freedom is free to impart itself
to others; it is not in the power of finite freedom; it remains
grace, that is, the freely given indwelling of infinite freedom in
finite freedom.

Augustine's (consistently) central position is more clearly
expressed when he has to take a stand against the Pelagians'
absolutizing of the first pole. The latter defined finite freedom as
an indifference lying above and between good and evil, that is,
as sovereign choice. According to them, God, respecting their
freedom, only has to present man with the laws of the good, and
he will decide to embrace them in virtue of his freedom to
choose. This is the starting point for Augustine's most beautiful
and balanced anti-Pelagian work, *De Spiritu et littera*[66] (412).
The core of his argument is that the apparent elevation of the

---

voluntatem" (*De lib. arb.* 3, 1, 3; 32, 1272). "Voluntas igitur nostra nec voluntas
esset nisi esset in nostra potestate; porro quia est in potestate, libera est nobis"
(*ibid.*, 8; 1275). "Quid enim tam in voluntate quam ipsa voluntas" (*ibid.*, I, 12,
26; 32, 1236).

[63] "Certe Deus ipse numquid quoniam peccare non potest, ideo liberum
arbitrium habere negandus est?" *De Civ. Dei* 22, 30, 3; 41, 802; cf. the whole
passage.

[64] Cf. M. Huftier, "Libre arbitre, liberté et péché chez s. Augustin" in *Rech.
de théol. anc. et méd.* 33 (1966), 187–281 (with refs.). The changes in Augustine's
terminology arise from a change of front. When opposing the Manichees he
must defend the first pole, freedom as the soul's own power of making
decisions; when combating the Pelagians he has to defend the second pole, the
necessary immanence of divine freedom in created freedom, so that the latter
can decide to embrace genuine freedom.

[65] *De Trin.* 4, 13, 16; PL 42, 896.

[66] PL 44, 201–46. In what follows, the numbers refer to the text's paragraphs
(not the chapters).

"Christian's freedom" beyond that of the New Testament by
Pelagius is in reality a falling back into the Old Testament (from
the "Spirit" to the "letter"). The relationship between the freedom given to man by God and the commandments addressed
by God to this freedom remains an external one; it is still a case
of the old law confronting a man who has not yet been liberated
to enjoy the genuine freedom of the children of God. This rigid
opposition, which locks finitude within itself, is only brought
into flux by "God's love which is poured into our hearts by the
Holy Spirit which has been given to us" (Rom 5:5)—a text
which is quoted fourteen times in this brief work. This Spirit is
essentially freedom (28),[67] but freedom as "gift" (26) or "grace".
Thus the Spirit is continually called *"spiritus gratiae"* (13, 15, 20)
and as such facilitates a living freedom, whereas the law, presented from the outside, remains the letter that "kills" (6, 7).
Furthermore such a law, like that of the Old Testament, can
only promise the reward of external goods (41), whereas freedom in the Holy Spirit is its own reward (36–37): *caritas* is
identical with "sweet delight in what is right" (*"per donum
Spiritus suavitate justitiae delectari"*: 16), with consent (*consensio*:
54, 60) to what the will really wills and now, genuinely free, is
given as a gift. And in all this no one is farther than Augustine
from a Stoic-Plotinian pantheism. Finite freedom is not absorbed
into infinite freedom (52) but stays eternally itself (59); yet it
does not remain as a mere counterpart to infinite freedom: it is a
freedom that is fulfilled in and through the infinite freedom,
which is freely self-giving love. Augustine always has both
aspects in view: we have become sons, and yet we do not cease
to be servants (56); there is both *"congruentia ibidemque distantia"*
(28); love overcomes law yet remains *"lex fidei"* (21) and *"lex
caritatis"* (29); God speaks through the Spirit to our spirit, from
within, in *"suasio vel vocatio"* (60), to which the latter can only
reply with "thankfulness" (11, 18, 22), "attachment" (*adhaerere*:
42), "shared joy" (*condelectari*: 26) and spontaneous consent (60).
Biblically speaking, finite freedom is lit up from within by the
glorious radiance that comes from infinite freedom (31), which

[67] This is substantiated by linking Romans 5:5 with 2 Corinthians 3:17:
"Where the Spirit of the Lord is, there is freedom."

DRAMATIS PERSONAE

"reveals itself to those who love it" (41); it is also the fulfillment of the creature's, man's, similarity with his Original (37). This all takes place in a sphere where command and gift mutually sublimate each other ("*da quod jubes*": 22—"give what you command"), a sphere of "*inspiratio*" (51) and ultimately a sphere of simple presence: "*Quid sunt ergo leges Dei ab ipso Deo scriptae in cordibus, nisi ipsa praesentia Spiritus sancti?*" (36). Again: as this consent takes place, finite freedom also attains its goal of infinite truth: to cleave to God is "*pietas, theosebeia*", and this is "wisdom" (18, 22).

The foregoing could be orchestrated many times over on the basis of Augustine's whole opus. What we have said suffices, however, to show Augustine's Christian answer to Plotinus. It is also clear that the later heretical misinterpretations (by Luther and Jansen) absolutized partial aspects and upset the balance of what Augustine said.[68]

2. The East pursues a different path in portraying the second pole of finite freedom. Whereas Clement of Alexandria, in his reply to Gnosticism, saw the freedom of the Christian gnostic as a stable ultimate condition, characterized by that inner freedom from passions (*Strom.* II, 142, 3; III, 41, 2f.) which is only brought about by the grace of Christ (III, 44, 4), Origen[69] went so far in his reaction that he equated finite freedom with the unshakable ability to choose between good and evil, whereby the (Platonic) "satiation" with the good can always lead to a turning away: freedom is pure mobility, and, vis-à-vis this mobility, even God himself appears as a good that does not necessarily have to be embraced. *Gregory of Nyssa* will attempt a genial synthesis, which, like Augustine's, is decisively inspired by Plotinus. In the latter, the *nous* (which in Gregory corresponds to created, finite freedom) was described as a spiritual, eternal

---

[68] The "*servum arbitrium*" is an historical manifestation of the *liberum arbitrium*, which has entangled itself and cannot free itself by its own power. (This will be discussed in the next volume.) Jansen sees the "*delectatio victrix*" as a quantitatively superior power, the "stronger motive" confronting the will from outside, whereas for Augustine it is one with *caritas* (and the joy that indwells it), which is given to us inwardly by the Holy Spirit.

[69] N.b., in the extreme position adopted in his youthful work, "*Peri Archon*".

movement toward the One, as a yearning (*Enn*. III, 8, 11), as a turning toward the One (V, II, 1), as a circle and a circular movement, governed by its center (II, 2, 3; III, 8, 8), as the motion of the idea that thinks itself (VI, 2, 8), whereby this motion coincides with the repose of self-possession (II, 2, 3): *hōste hen panta: kai kinēsis kai stasis* (VI, 2, 8). Since Gregory adopts word for word Plotinus' definition of infinite freedom: God's "will is identical with him; he will be what he is, and he is what he will be" (*Enn*. VI, 8, 13 = PG 45, 609B), plainly we should trace his definition of finite freedom back primarily to the same source, even if Stoic influences may have been strongly at work.[70] And as in Plotinus, the *nous* is the image that is the closest possible to the One, so too finite freedom in its purity— that is, as a pure motion coming from and proceeding toward infinite freedom—is the closest possible image of God. (Thus we see why Gregory, unlike the other Greek Fathers, cannot make a distinction between static "image" and dynamic "likeness".) So, by a rather different path from that taken by Augustine, he arrives at finite freedom's complete dependence on (*douleia*: 44, 701B) and indebtedness to infinite freedom. Certainly Gregory describes the loss of true freedom as a result of sin, and its restoration solely through grace, with no less pathos than Augustine[71] but from a different starting point. The starting point in Augustine is Adam in paradise, who is endowed with a somehow colorless "*posse non peccare*" and, through the experience of sin and the grace of redemption, will arrive at the state of "*non posse peccare*". In Gregory the starting point is dialectical: on the one side, there is the radiant picture of a finite freedom that is "infinitely" open to infinite freedom (a picture that will only be fulfilled, in real terms, eschatologically, in Christ), and, on the other side, this pure movement is mixed with a "pathic" element, introduced by God into man's original nature in anticipation of his coming estrangement from the good, so that human nature, when it falls, will come up against the limits inherent in temporality and evil; thence, coming to his

[70] Texts in J. Daniélou, *L'Etre et le temps chez Grégoire de Nysse*, chap. V: "Changement", 97–98.

[71] This whole section must be excluded here, since it belongs to the drama's actual execution (cf. *Theo-Drama* IV).

senses as a result of the harm he suffers (46, 524CD) and
liberated from the bonds of passionate craving (*pathos*, *epithymia*),
man will open up, in the end, to infinite freedom.[72]

But how does the movement toward the infinite enter into
finite freedom, which we have described as "autonomous motion"
and "autonomy"? Finite freedom is simply "there": it does not
create itself. Indeed, it is "there", anew, every moment: the
source from which it springs—which can only be infinite freedom
—is a "source that wells up eternally" (46, 105B). The result is
that, within this finite freedom that ceaselessly "receives itself",
an eternal movement is initiated: its aim is not to separate itself
from the source but to realize itself by assimilation to it. In this
framework, "freedom of choice" has a twofold aspect:

> It is a likeness to that which is without master (*adespotos*) and
> autonomous (*autokrates*), for this is the kind of freedom given to
> us by God from the beginning. Therefore, since, on the one hand,
> freedom is identity with its own nature and assimilation to it, it
> follows that everything that is free unites with its own kind. . . .
> On the other hand, if *arētē* (virtue, integrity, "*rectitudo*") is with-
> out a master (*adespotos*), all freedom must reside in it, for freedom
> *is* being without a master (*adespoton*). However, the divine nature
> is the source of all *arētē*, and thus all who have been purified of evil
> are united in that source, so that God may be all in all (46,
> 101D–104A).

Insofar as freedom is *autexousion* (and never ceases to be such)
and at the same time is an infinite movement toward its own
origin in God, finite freedom (*qua* finite) only fulfills itself
within infinite freedom. *Qua* finite: it springs forth from God at
every moment,[73] and this is a process of becoming, a movement

---

[72] To that extent, this craving ("thirst" [*Durst*], related to the Buddhist
trschna and the Augustinian *concupiscentia*) in Gregory is only a degenerate form
(although in fact an innate one) of the authentic eternal movement of finite
freedom; its own behavior shows it to be defective, for it goes round and round
in the void. Gregory employs the image of the Danaids trying to fill their
bottomless vessels (44, 344A), of the slave who, blindfolded, goes round and
round pulling the mill like an animal (46, 888) and of the futile attempt to climb
up a sand-dune (44, 628B), etc.

[73] "In a certain sense it [the soul] is constantly being created (*pantote ktizetai*)
in that it transforms itself, through growth in what is good, into what is better"
(44, 885D). On the ever-flowing stream: 44, 941D–944A, 977AD).

(*alloiōsis*, *kinēsis*) written into its very nature (44, 184CD); it is forever distinguished from God in that it comes from him and goes to him (for God is "without motion where all change is concerned": 45, 1253B). But insofar as freedom is a free gift of the Eternal and the Good, its motion, its "free flight" (*hormē proairetikē*: 46, 120B) is characterized by an inherent instinct for what is "always better". Here lies the answer to the question Gregory himself asked: "How can a changeable nature attain constancy and unchangeability in the good?" (*De perf.* ed. Jaeger, Opp VIII/1, 213). For a full answer we would have to unfold Gregory's whole theology of created freedom; the "necessity" of the experience (*peira*) of evil, its inner finitude and redemption from the slavery of sin.[74] We can include all this, for it is becoming clear from what we have said—contrary to Origen—that it is not "indifference" that constitutes freedom of choice: the latter's innermost nature is the movement toward self-realization within infinite freedom. This is how finite freedom can be the "image" of infinite freedom. Its innermost nature is revealed in an exemplary concrete manner in the humanity of Christ, which "employs the changeability (of created being) for the better" and thus sets off the movement of genuine freedom, namely, that which, "constantly moving forward toward the good, encounters no barrier of any kind" (45, 60A). In this way, given freedom to proceed from the good to the better, it can be "fixed" in the good (44, 201BC) in such a way that, in this genuine movement of freedom, *kinēsis* and *stasis* coincide,[75] and "repose itself serves as wings" (44, 405D). Since infinite freedom is ever-greater, it continually expands the finite freedom that moves within it, so that the (Platonic and Origenistic) "satiation" is no longer possible: "Virtue, once firmly possessed, can neither be measured by time nor limited

---

[74] "Instead of winning the freedom of self-possession" (*anti tēs autexousiou eleutherias*), the sinner who flees from God acquires "the slavery of sin" (44, 1181B): here we have the Augustinian, and even the Lutheran, concept. On this whole issue, cf. the impressive synthesis (though tending toward Hegel) of Jérôme Gaïth, *La Conception de la liberté chez Grégoire de Nysse* (Paris: Vrin, 1953) and also my own *Présence et pensée, Essai sur la philosophie religieuse de Grégoire de Nysse* (Paris: Beauchesne, 1942).

[75] Texts in *Présence et pensée*, 123ff.

by satiation. It furnishes the one who lives by it with an ever-fresh, new and vibrant experience of its benefits. Satiety and yearning mutually heighten each other" (44, 1244D–1245B). "It was Gregory's bold achievement to have realized that what Greek thought had hitherto regarded as essentially an expression of the poverty of human nature could actually ground its sublimity."[76] Before him, only Irenaeus had seen something similar, namely, that, by divine power, finite man can grow eternally into the eternally richer divine freedom.[77] Gregory's intuition embraces Origen's theology of freedom, but he supersedes the notion of "eternal recurrence"; he also embraces Plotinus' concept of spirit, even as far as the identity of *kinēsis* and *stasis*, but again he goes beyond the danger of latent despair at man's inability to catch up with the One: in Gregory, the element of infinity that indwells finite freedom comes from the free gift of infinite freedom: the latter not only "frees" finite freedom and gives it room to operate but actually opens itself to it as the context of its self-fulfillment. However, this only comes about in God's self-manifestation and self-disclosure in Jesus Christ, which is inaccessible to Plotinus.[78]

In *Thomas Aquinas*, the oriental and occidental streams converge, and in fact he responds to the challenge of ancient philosophy more directly on the philosophical plane (in *De Veritate*); only in his concluding *Summa* does it become totally transparent theo-

---

[76] Daniélou, *L'Etre et le temps*, 112.

[77] *Adv. Haer.* IV, 11, 2.

[78] Maximus the Confessor cannot follow this coincidence of motion and rest in the finite spiritual being. This is because he is engaged in a fierce controversy with Origenism (in a radical form promoted by Evagrius). The latter regarded "*kinēsis*" unequivocally as the sinful fall from the original, antenatal "*stasis*" of all spirits in God. (I say "unequivocally" because in Gregory of Nyssa *kinēsis* was ambivalent: it could signify the movement which naturally had its beginning, *archē*, in God, but it could also denote the "fall", *rhopē*, from the origin because of the pathic elements mixed in with nature.) Maximus must oppose this by holding rigidly fast to the Aristotelian structure of nature: *kinēsis* is (only) an intermediary phase between an originally grounded nature (*archē, ousia*) and the goal it has to attain (*telos*), and for a finite nature this moving course is necessarily finite. Cf. my book, *Kosmische Liturgie, Maximus der Bekenner*, 2d ed. (1961), "Kinēsis" (686), esp. 132–41, 600ff. (where he is distinguished from Evagrius, Dionysius and Gregory).

logically. In Thomas, therefore, the Augustinian yearning to possess and behold God appears primarily as the movement of finite freedom toward its formal object, the Good. This only reveals itself as the Divinely Free through a final decision on the part of freedom of choice (and to that extent Thomas is structurally closer to Gregory). As we have already said[79]—and here we are giving our own summary of Thomas' contribution —his distinctive thrust concerns the mediation of Being, which permeates and is at work in all finite being, the most unique as well as the most general. In answering the question of how infinite freedom can indwell finite, in order to allow it to be genuine, finite freedom, we must return once more to the primal act of self-knowledge (which is a knowledge of being) and recall that, in grasping our own being, we also grasp all being whatsoever, which goes beyond all particular beings. (This takes place in the soul's innermost—and self-evident— presence to itself.) In this grasp, what really *is* [*das Wirklich-Sein*] shows itself, directly, to be both *true* and a *good* to be affirmed. Thus, insofar as self-being [*Selbst-Sein*] in principle discloses all reality, it means that everything real that is encountered in the realm of being, insofar as it participates in being, is posited as worthy of recognition (as true) and worthy of approval (as good). This posits an irreducible bi-polarity in (individual) self-consciousness, indicating that this consciousness does not coincide with the totality of Being but only participates in it, that is, it is a contingent and factually existing consciousness. Thus the "I"-pole is open to all being in such a way that, according to the judgment and aspiration of this "I", every-thing appears as true and worthy of attainment to it; even though none of the existing things coincides with Being and its transcendental modes (of being true and good). If this pole were made absolute, the result would be that everything that shares in being (which is also finite and factually existent) would seem to be something for me to "use". But the "I"-pole always discloses being–in-its-totality as well, and within this horizon other beings are also seen to constitute poles of their own. Anyone who affirms being–in-its-totality must also allow the "other" to have

[79] Cf. above, pp. 174–91.

its own self-being: allowing being to be true and good in itself is of the same (fundamental) order as recognizing what is true and good for me. Now the soul is "for itself", and in the immediacy that this implies lies its freedom, which cannot be lost; however, it only possesses it in virtue of the luminous quality [*Gelichtetsein*] of the totality of being. Therefore it is an integral part of this imperishable freedom (which, in its necessity, excludes all arbitrariness) that the soul, precisely because it possesses itself in freedom, necessarily respects all other beings on account of their freedom (they are true and real) and *lets them be*; only on this basis does it seek to embrace them. An existent being is good for me because it is real, because it complements my particularity; but since it is real, I cannot absorb it into me: I must allow it to maintain its own independent reality, for only then can it be regarded as good.

At this stage two questions arise. The first asks about the origin of this self-possession, this self-luminosity on the part of the soul, which is shared, in principle, by all that has being. The answer can only be this: it comes from the very ground of Being, which we cannot "get behind" and which the questioning mind cannot approach, as it were, from the outside (because it is part of it). The spiritual soul's self-possession, its judging and striving, are the transcendental modes of all-pervasive Being; it *indwells* the soul, which knows and embraces itself in freedom. Spiritual being is one form, a highest form, of participation in Being. But since Being never presents itself to me except in finite beings, that is, never as self-subsisting, consciousness is faced with the second question: How can the nonsubsistent, nonfinite reality (the formal object under which I judge and affirm everything, letting it "be" and striving toward it) be realized in subsisting, finite centers? Particularly if these centers are spiritual and free—a peculiarity which can only come from a participation in Being?

This second question brings philosophy up against its limits. To be consistent, in the face of this self-propagation of nonfinite Being in finite subjects, philosophy would have to conclude that Being-in-its-totality has the quality of a "subject" [*Subjekthaftigkeit*], which would seem to conflict with its "formality" [*Formalität*] and its noncenteredness. In philosophy, therefore, while the question of origins must be asked—all the more since, in the realm of the finite, the meaning (of truth and goodness) of existing beings remains scattered and fragmented and so points to some primal meaning—it cannot be answered with any certainty. The only possibility is that, within Being, a nonparticipative subjectivity should disclose itself, coextensive with Being-in-its-totality, possessing infinite reason, infinite will and infinite freedom.

If we assume that such a self-revelation of infinite Being— infinitely (spiritually) existing being[80] has somehow already taken place (this is Paul's assumption in Romans 1:19ff.), the finite mind would also be faced (right from the start) with an ultimate decision: it would be challenged to see, in the necessary formal object, the manifestation (*phaneron*) of the absolute, creative and personal ground—that is, of God—and thus acknowledge (*doxazein*) that its own freedom is immanent not only in all-encompassing Being but in infinite freedom. Furthermore it would be summoned to see the immanence of divine freedom and infinite will in its own, finite free being and will as the ultimate ground of its own, given, de facto freedom. Alternatively it would withdraw from an immanence of this kind, aiming to be its own ground (for Being-in-its-totality, as such, is not a subject); but in doing so it would surrender itself to "idolatry" (Rom 1:21ff.) by fixing the necessity of the formal object, in each case, on contingent, finite beings. It would be seeking to nourish the spirit's infinite capacity for Being, for the True and the Good, with mere finite substance. It is of little consequence whether this finite substance consists of tangible "idols" or humanitarianism or the unique individual (the "man of genius", the "superman"). Buddha is right at this point: the insatiable "thirst" that characterizes finitude, and which arises from the constant finitizing of the formal object, must be quenched; and this can only be done, if Being is not Spirit, by attempting to dissolve the finite spiritual centers into nonfinite Being (that is, Being [*Sein*] that is not existing being [*nicht-seiend*]). Thus, in consequence, it becomes clear why finite freedom's

[80] ["Selbstoffenbarung des unendlichen Seins als des unendlich (geistig) Seienden" — Tr.]

realm of fulfillment cannot be simply the empty negation of its own limits; in other words, it cannot depend on the whim of its own decisions. It does not need to dream up this ideal empty space for its own development: the space is already given in its finite structure. It is the "unfillable realm that lies below freedom of choice" of which we have already spoken (pp. 25 and 227ff.). This realm, however, which is a coconstituent of finite freedom, is precisely *not* that within which it can fulfill itself, but, in Scholastic terminology, *desiderium naturale "visionis"*, a setting-out toward that which alone—*in* infinite freedom—can communicate itself *as* positive, infinite freedom. Buddha's "thirst", which only intensifies as man continues to take finite drink, is the "philosophical" dispelling of the illusion that man can fulfill himself within the interior realm of his own *"desiderium"*.

Once the residual philosophical problem has been overcome by the self-disclosure of infinite freedom, we begin to see that finite freedom, as *autexousion*, as consent to oneself in the freedom of self-possession, is by no means alienated but rather inwardly fulfilled by consenting to that Being-in-its-totality which has now unveiled itself as that which freely grounds all things, as that which, in infinite freedom, creates finite freedom. Just as Being-in-its-totality was entirely in the subject (so much so that the latter even asserted that its spiritual acts were rooted in its primal depths) and remained elevated by the subject, unconfined, above all finitude: so now, when philosophy is irradiated by theology, infinite freedom will be entirely in finite freedom (so much so that the latter will assert that its spiritual, free acts are rooted in the primal depths of infinite freedom: *Deus interior intimo meo*)—and hence will remain unconfined, sovereign above every finite freedom.

Now, however, we must go on to inquire about the possibility of this infinite freedom.

4. *Infinite Freedom*

a. The Dawn of Infinite Freedom

1. Infinite freedom, in the sense of personal command of oneself, dawns only in the New Testament. It is anticipated in many ways, both in philosophy and in the Old Testament, but the fragments of meaning do not form a whole.

In the extra-biblical world, two views struggle for dominance, unable to find common ground for understanding. On the one hand, there is a personal freedom that is ascribed to God but (even in the case of Zeus) remains anthropomorphic and limited, however much it may be refined. On the other hand, there is a superpersonal freedom, applied to the idea of the Good that is elevated above all finite being; lacking all envy, it can pour itself out and enable those who seek it to participate in its freedom from all entanglement. But it is not the latter that decides the ethical value of the individual life (like Plato's mythical judge of the dead). Where this highest norm remains superpersonal, as in Stoicism and Neoplatonism, it is always finite freedom (insofar as it exists) that judges itself through its own decisions. So it is in Plotinus, too, whose treatise on freedom, to which we have already referred (*Enn.* VI, 8), surely represents the most lofty utterance possible outside the Bible on the subject of infinite freedom. The One is free because it depends on nothing, because it does not "discover" itself as something that "happens to be", and so does not need subsequently to affirm itself, but "itself determines what it is"; nor is it "in form like the Good: it *is* the Good" (IV, 8, 9). Plotinus' basic formula is the utter, mutual interpenetration of being and will or being and act: the One is "almighty power, genuinely governing itself" (*dynamin pāsan hautēs ontōs kyrian*); "it is what it wills to be" (*ibid.*), or more precisely: "It is in harmony with itself, wills to be what it is and is what it wills to be; its will and itself are one and the same" (VI, 8, 13). But if this ultimate interpenetration of being and freedom remains the measure of all that, by participating in it, can be called "freedom", we cannot speak of the latter being created, defined or judged.

The missing component emerges most strongly in the Old

Testament. Right from the start Yahweh is a (politically) liberating God; first of all he demonstrates his personal power, which shows itself increasingly sovereign over all the powers that oppose him; thus it is absolute freedom. The fact is quite consciously acknowledged, even if its conceptual formulation is unsuccessful (for the present, being "free" remains a sociological relational concept) and even superfluous. For the very fact that God creates man and endows him with freedom, with his own "power", which as such is the image of God (Sir 17:3), shows clearly enough how free the Almighty is. It becomes more and more apparent that creation in no way sets limits to the divine freedom: on his own authority, God steps beyond his divine realm in order to permeate and rule every aspect of the worldly realm. All creatures live by the breath of God (Ps 104:30); his almighty wisdom penetrates all things: "unique, manifold, subtle, active, incisive, unsullied, lucid, invulnerable, . . . un-perturbed, almighty, all-surveying, penetrating all intelligent, pure and most subtle spirits" (Wis 7:22f.). And although a man can ask to participate in this wisdom (Wis 9), there still remains a limit (which only becomes fully visible in the New Testament): at the level of being, God's freedom somehow penetrates hu-man freedom (as it penetrates everything creaturely), but man's freedom is not granted any inner access to divine freedom. The "understanding" of the wise remains somehow intellectual, failing to take into account the concrete waywardness of finite freedom; it is unprepared for the paths God's freedom will take, in Jesus Christ, to redeem this waywardness from within.

This barrier, this lack of reciprocity, is broken down in Jesus Christ, who "penetrates all things" in quite a different way from the wisdom of "Solomon". In his being "made to be sin" and bearing the "curse", infinite freedom shows its ultimate, most extreme capability for the first time: it can be itself even in the finitude that "loses itself"—a capability which neither Jews nor Greeks could have imagined. For them it remains a stumbling block and foolishness. Yet only here, where "God's love is poured into our hearts by the Holy Spirit which has been given to us", is finite freedom driven out of its last refuge and set on the path toward infinite freedom; thus the abyss that has opened up in the Christian fact is clearly visible to post-Christian reflection. It is characteristic that Jewish speculation, where it forsakes its own nature, loses itself in a gnosis which claims to know all about God-in-himself and to deduce creation from him; Christian speculation, when it strays from the path, slides into a bottomless voluntarism.

In all Greek philosophy, the world, if it was not to be meaningless, had to be linked by a bond of necessity to the world of eternal, divine meaning, either by Plato's "idea", Aristotle's *eros* (for the "forms", too, are not created), the Stoic *logos* or the Neoplatonic *methexis*. All this collapses, essentially, if the world as a totality, its being and its existence, is dependent on the infinite freedom in which God desires to create in the first place and then actually does create. The world might just as well not exist. It does not even have that necessity that would result from a primal "fall" from the divine world. It depends solely on absolute freedom, humanly speaking on God's infinite "good pleasure". And if man still finds he needs to posit a world of "ideas", it is not in any way independent of God: it can only be he himself, an expression of his creative inventiveness. It stands to reason therefore that, after a period in which the ancient *logos*-philosophy exercises, as it were, a calming influence, a voluntarist radicalism bursts into philosophy and theology in the work of *Duns Scotus*. Avicenna and Thomas had seen knowledge of God as being mediated by the act of being as such; to Scotus this seems to be a theological a priori; in the face of a God who, if he is to be really known, can only disclose himself,[1] our cognitive ability is insufficient. Nor can we deduce any adequate norm for man's ethical conduct from the vague longing he feels for perfect happiness (*desiderium naturale*);[2] henceforth, therefore, the philosophical endeavor will have to content itself with empiricism, whereas theology will be the contingent recapitulation, mediated by free revelation, of that a priori absolute

---

[1] "Licet igitur anima habeat sufficiens activum et passivum intra se pro quanto actio respectu cognitionis convenit animae, tamen non habet sufficiens activum et passivum intra se pro quanto actio convenit objecto" (*Ord. Prol.* I, q un; no. 72). If the object is God, "solus Deus est sibi solis naturaliter cognitus" (*Prol.* 3, q 3; no. 151).

[2] "Homo non potest scire ex naturalibus finem suum distincte" (*Ord. Prol.* 1, q un; no. 13).

knowledge that God has of himself. We can leave to one side the strange anticipation of an extreme voluntarism in Peter Damian;[3] more important is its late medieval form, fully developed in Ockham. The way the latter alternates between intramundane empiricism and theological positivism (or a-priorism) represents the original form of all variations of "modern" thought. Here, divine freedom has absorbed all rationality into itself: the *potentia Dei ordinata* is his *potentia absoluta: Deus autem ad nullum actum potest obligari, ideo eo ipso quod Deus vult, hoc est justum fieri.*[4] This could be understood in a correct sense if external *"obligatio"* were excluded and the divine will were irradiated to its very foundations by the divine rationality;[5] but it is clear that Ockham means more than this when he says, for instance, that God could have destined us for hatred instead of for the love of God. The "nominalist" legacy survives in the two founders of modern times, diametrically opposed though they be: Descartes and Luther.

In *Descartes*, who sees God's essence, reason and will in an indivisible unity, everything in created being, including the laws of mathematics, which we regard as "eternally" valid, contains a dimension of contingency (things "could have been otherwise") behind the apparent necessity that operates as far as we are concerned. Here, as we shall show, the element of essence (that is, of Being) and its being irradiated by the divine

---

[3] On the true meaning and the limitations of Peter Damian's Letter on Divine Omnipotence, cf. the detailed introduction by André Catin: *Petrus Damiani, Lettre sur la toute-puissance divine*, critical ed., *Sources chrétiennes* 191 (1972), 13–381. Faced with the question: "Can God cause things that have happened not to have happened?", Peter Damian is clear, first of all, that God is above the necessities and impossibilities of created natures but also that God's free will is eternal and unchangeable; i.e., he could have determined that what now is should not be. Behind this there is the question that Peter Damian did not resolve, namely, "Can God will something he does not will?" He can, insofar as he has free choice. He cannot, insofar as he always wills what is better and more just (cf. Catin 107ff., 178ff.).

[4] *In Sent.* 4, q 9, E.

[5] Where Thomas conceptually distinguishes *potentia absoluta* and *ordinata*, such distinction, for him, only signifies that God could do very much more than he actually does, but this "much more" is always that *"in quo potest salvari ratio entis"* (*S. Th.* I, q 35, a 5).

self-possession ultimately takes second place to the primacy of the (electing) will; only in association with eternal reason can this will choose what corresponds to God's absolute being—which displays itself here and now, making itself present at every moment, analogously, in worldly being.[6] Ultimately, what is possible is not what can be put together out of non-contradictory elements (who could possibly judge, in such abstract terms, what is not self-contradictory?), but what can have its place within the totality of reality that "flows from" God. If we hold on to this, we can even admit, with Thomas, that "*ipsa quidditas creari dicitur*" (*De pot*. 93, a 5 ad 2), namely, by the divine "*creatrix essentia*" in which insight and will are comprised.[7]

Luther's voluntarism, which—whether meant seriously or in jest—is based on Ockham,[8] is of quite a different kind. Christologically centered, at an early stage he moves away from the Scotist-Ockhamist speculations;[9] the absoluteness of the divine will appears in the paradoxical justification of the sinner—which transcends all the philosophizing of human reason. But Luther so concentrates on this one, solely significant plane of action that created freedom is limited to purely intramundane opera-

[6] "[Deus] solum praesentialiter existit, unde ipse omnibus entibus praesens est, et omnia sibi, non solum secundum cognitionem, sed etiam secundum realem existentiam, praesentia." Dietrich von Freiberg, "De mensura durationis", ed. E. Krebs, B.G.Ph.M. V, 5–6 (1906), 100.

[7] On the opposition of the Thomist and the Cartesian doctrines, cf. E. Gilson, *La Doctrine cartésienne de la liberté et la théologie* (Paris: Alcan, 1913), and his later, more mature view in *Etudes sur le rôle de la pensée médiévale dans la formation du système cartésien* (Paris: Vrin, 1951), esp. 224–33. Whereas Thomas ascends the path of causality to an ultimate uncaused Cause, Descartes does not want to abandon the principle of causality where it reaches its goal: God is the self-causing Cause (i.e., he creates himself). Hence "it is quite evident that, a fortiori, he creates the truths that are grasped by our reason and are thus finite and, accordingly, must depend on him far more than he depends on himself." Augustine himself, who otherwise so insists on the direct infusion of eternal truth into our minds (cf. the doctrine of numbers in *De lib. arb.* II), said that God's "will is the necessity of things" (*De Gen. ad litt.* VI, 15, 26).

[8] *WA* VI, 600, 11; XXX 2, 3000, 9; *Tischreden* II, S16, 6; *Disput*. (Drews), 341 (= XXXIX, 1, 175ff.).

[9] Paul Vignaux, *Luther commentateur des Sentences* (Paris: Vrin, 1955).

tions; it operates downward, as it were, but not upward, toward God. Ultimately only God is free,[10] and as the Grace-giver he is such only if, in the face of his gift, all our gifts become as nothing.[11]

Most of all, however, it is the idea of God's self-positing, expressed and so carefully guarded by Descartes, that continues to exert an influence. First the voluntarist element disappears in Spinoza's definition of God as *causa sui*, but the element of self-positing reemerges in those Idealist systems that have subterranean connections with Spinoza, where the subject's perfect self-positing becomes a dialectical process, which cannot proceed in any other way but under the guidance of a will. This will steps forward naked in *Schopenhauer*, who, in part four of *The World as Will and Idea*, portrays it as free, blind and irrational. Here we see the manifestly post-Christian (and also un-Buddhist) character of Schopenhauer's thought—and also of his successors, such as Wagner and Thomas Mann, but also E. Hartmann and Scheler. We see the same thing in *Nietzsche*, who again describes the Absolute as will, in this case the will-to-power. Thus the pastor's son, Nietzsche, sets will (Dionysus) against idea (Apollo); the puritan D. H. Lawrence (in the line of Blake) exalts the pulsating instinctual life against the law which kills; and the Jews, Bergson, Freud and Scheler, see instinct in conflict with the intellect, and, finally, Klages opposes the cosmogonic *eros* to the a-cosmic "spirit": all these tragic dualisms presuppose an (admittedly perverted) Christian origin.

The same line is followed, however, by all the modern

[10] *WA* XVIII, 636, 27: "Sequitur nunc liberum arbitrium esse plane divinum nomen, nec ulli posse competere quam soli divinae majestati"; it would be sacrilegious to attribute it to man. *Ibid.*, 781, 8: "Scimus quod homo dominus est inferioribus se constitutus, in quae habet jus et liberum arbitrium, ut illa obediant et faciant, quae ipse vult et cogitat. Sed hoc quaerimus, an erga Deum habeat liberum arbitrium, ut ille obediat et faciat, quae homo voluerit. . . ." Similarly in the *Disputatio de homine* (1536), where Luther can actually describe human *ratio* as *"divinum quiddam"* and *"Numen quoddam"* (thesis 4f), but only *"ad has res administrandas in hac vita"*. As far as the relationship with God is concerned, which is shaped and created solely by God, all man's intramundane greatness amounts to *"paene nihil"* (thesis 11).

[11] *WA* IV, 278, 27: "Benefacere enim alteri divinum est. Sed non potest noster Deus et sua nobis dare, nisi primo doceat se nostra nolle et nostra nihil esse apud eum. . . . Vult quod nos tantum modo accipiamus, et ipse solus det, et ita sit vere Deus."

rationalisms that endeavor to systematize the "appearance" [*Schein*] in terms of functionalism, structuralism, and so forth, cutting the umbilical cord that links existent beings with Being [*Sein*]. They do this either by pointing out that ultimate reality cannot be brought within the systematization of the appearance, as Wittgenstein was most clearly aware, or else they have consciously (or even unconsciously) turned their backs on Being, reducing subjects and substances to their functions and relations and equating truth with feasibility. Such thought has forfeited all original sense of philosophy (either pre- or post-Socratic), and in this loss of the "innocence of being" it shows itself once again to be a typically post-Christian phenomenon: every causality that arises from the depths is replaced by a purely horizontal one.

The other strand links up directly with Descartes' definition of God. Its voluntarist implications are most boldly revealed in the Swiss philosopher *Charles Secrétan*: ascending the ladder of organic beings, he shows that the more perfect a being is, the freer it is in determining itself. Once the boundary to the Absolute is crossed, there must be perfectly free self-positing: "Evidently, being that is self-subsistent possesses freedom of itself: that is, positively, it gives itself freedom." In such a case, nothing is predetermined by a nature; God is "absolute freedom", and he can say, "I am what I will be."[12] This is to be taken literally (that is, with its covert anthropomorphism): God, who in absolute freedom—a freedom that is not illuminated exhaustively by the rational—defines himself as God, could (*per impossibile*) have determined himself as something else. O. Hamelin takes up this idea and says that we must be grateful to God for having made himself God. No doubt this follows from the absolute freedom of his Spirit. But how close we now are to the *angst*-ridden pessimism which fears that this freedom could equally well have turned into a blind monster![13] The final stage of such voluntarist thought is represented by Sartre: here, quite logically, freedom becomes the annihilating Void that defines its forms (natures) and dissolves them again.

A second, hardly less momentous consequence of the dawn

[12] *Philosophie de la liberté*, 3d ed. (Paris, 1879 [1st ed., 1849]), 363–65.

[13] *Essai sur les éléments principaux de la réprésentation*, 2d ed. (Paris: Alcan, 1925), 450.

of infinite freedom in the Christian event is the doctrine of (double) predestination, which casts its shadow over the west. It has come down to us certainly from the later Augustine on (although it started before him), in an almost unbroken sequence right up to the Reformation and Jansenism; and it also enters into the systems of the Counter-Reformation. Here an ultimate basis for the alternative outcomes of human existence—eternal salvation or eternal perdition—is sought in the unfathomable abyss of divine freedom; so much so that, in spite of all exhortation, man's efforts slacken and fail as he loses all courage in the face of the mystery. For it is not a question (as before) of how finite freedom can develop within an infinite freedom: this infinite freedom, which is necessarily the final arbiter, now threatens to swallow up finite freedom. It alone, according to the New Testament, is the final Judge: "I am not aware of anything against myself, but I am not thereby acquitted. It is the Lord who judges me" (1 Cor 4:4). This is not the place to enter the maze of speculations concerning (double) predestination. Our aim is simply to show, by reference to the latter's long-echoing influence on human ideas, how the self-disclosure of infinite freedom has lit up human history like a lightning flash.

The point at which this lightning struck, the New Testament, is unacquainted with the problems that arose later. It does not speak of predestination as some (as it were) neutral factor to be taken into account but as a form of proclamation of the Good News, with all the seriousness this implies. Nor, as yet, does the rising sun of infinite freedom outshine and so obliterate the landscape of finite freedom: it simply illuminates it, so that the "interrelationship" that was our starting point at the beginning of this chapter may come about. Now that infinite freedom has become accessible to finite freedom, the latter has the opportunity —for the first time—to fulfill itself. Who could "have treasure in heaven" while heaven was unattainable by the creature? In concrete terms, infinite freedom appears on stage in the form of Jesus Christ's "lowliness" and "obedience unto death". Thus he can call to himself the "weary and heavy-laden" and summon even the clumsy and hesitant to be his disciples. We need to keep ever before our eyes the way in which infinite freedom was pleased to appear in the midst of finitude, if we are not to be drawn aside into abstract (and hence falsely posed) speculative problems.

2. Thus, from the history of the phenomenon's continuing influence, we can estimate the impact of the originating event. Nothing in the world is more traceable back to an ultimate necessity; even if—in the Augustinian tradition—through the rules of mathematics and the insights of wisdom, a ray of infinite light shines upon finite reason, the fact that this happens in the wake of knowledge of contingent things and relationships is not itself necessary. The world as a whole now depends on God's free good pleasure. Is this arbitrary? That is what the philosopher will suspect, casting doubt on the innermost nexus between absolute freedom and (logical) necessity. This suspicion can be exactly documented in Descartes' remark that, although his ideas seem clear and distinct to him, he could be deceived by an "evil spirit", who, no less cunning than powerful, "applies all his diligence to lead me astray" (*Med.* 1). In fact, in the postbiblical age, this suspicion can never be laid to rest by purely logical deductions but only by what, in human thought, corresponds to and mirrors the unity of truth and truthfulness in God.

In the Old Testament, God's truth is identical with his faithfulness: *emeth* is the same word in both cases, and the unity of both aspects in one concept is not evidence of the deficiency of a primitive language but the expression of a real state of affairs— one which we cannot "get behind".[14] On the one hand, God's word is one with his act, with what he does in pursuance of man's salvation; on the other hand, this word is one with his being: he himself vouches for it with his whole self, he identifies himself with his word. But since all things are created by the word of God, there is an element of trust in God's dependability that cannot be excluded from our knowledge of these things. Ultimately this simply means that the ordinary human experience is vindicated in the realm of the Bible, that is, that it is only possible to have a reliable picture of the world, and to act on it,

---

[14] Cf. *Herrlichkeit* III/2, 1 (Alter Bund) (Einsiedeln: Johannes Verlag, 1967) 160ff. (*The Glory of the Lord* VI: *Theology: The Old Covenant*).

on the basis of an (inter-)personal dependability; that logical truth, in the end, cannot be abstracted from personal truthfulness. The wisdom of all languages, including the Indo-European, teaches us this.[15] Under the Old Covenant, God "demonstrates" the reliability of his word, which must be trusted, by the reliability of his deeds, although they can only be recognized as such by those who allow themselves to be personally involved in God's reliability. Every covenant is founded on reciprocal trust between the partners. The Sinai Covenant remains intact as long as Israel entrusts itself to the truth and faithfulness of the covenant God. In the New Covenant, the concept of "being proven and tested" [Bewährtseins] plays a decisive role; just as the truth of Jesus' message can and should be recognized not only by his words but also by his works and his whole attitude, so the truth of the gospel can and should be recognized by the transparent, existential "proven-ness" [Bewährtheit] of the apostolic preaching.[16]

Jesus Christ brings the Old Covenant to its completion; thus he is the realization of God's Yes, which was inherent in all his promises. "That is why we utter the Amen through him, to the glory of God" (2 Cor 1:19ff.): here Jesus is both God's Yes to the world and also, together with the world ("with us"), the world's

---

[15] Behind the German root war ("true"), there is the Old High German wara: covenant faithfulness. The Old Nordic goddess, Var, is the Goddess of oath-keeping; in Old Slavonic vera is "faith". Wahren is to "keep" or "ward" something [cf. "ware-house"]; we are "a-ware" of things. But there is also the sense of commitment: bewähren is to "guarantee" or "war-rant" something. Bewährt means "proven and tested". If we start with the German word Treue ("troth", "faithfulness"), it naturally includes the attitude of "trusting", "trusting oneself" and "entrusting", taking the risk of Trauung (marriage) for life. The same word lies behind the English "truth" and "truce" (cf. treuga Dei), that is, a cessation of hostilities on the basis of mutual trust. "Traun!"—one of Luther's favorite words—means "faith!", "upon my word!", "forsooth!". It is clear that the Hebrew is by no means alone in its equation of logical and ethical truth. In Greek too, besides alētheia, "truth", we have the adjective alēthinos, "truthful"; and in Latin, besides veritas, we have verax. In the Republic, after discussing God's truth (immutability), Plato goes on to speak of God's and man's truthfulness: 381A–83A.

[16] First and foremost, 2 Cor 4:1–6 as well as all the descriptions of the apostolic life: 1 Cor 4 and 9; 2 Cor 11–13, with the magnificent conclusion on the dialectic of the Christian's "being proven and tested": 13:3–10.

answering Yes (Amen) to God. He perfectly seals and implements the truth of the relationship between God and the world, in terms of a Covenant between infinite and finite freedom. God's infinite freedom in the Covenant rests upon his faithfulness to his own nature. This is expressed by God "swearing by himself"[17] (Gen 22:16 and its broad interpretation in Heb 6:13–17; 7:20ff.), that is, the highest form of witness to the truth, in which God's given Word—namely, Jesus Christ—becomes a "surety" (engyos: Heb 7:22) for the ultimate truth of the definitive, unsurpassable Covenant. Thus the creature, man, suspended in the medium of God's freedom, is anchored—objectively—solely in God's truthfulness and—subjectively—in his own attitude of trust. This attitude, however, cannot assure itself of the objective truth by reflecting upon itself: it must commit itself to this truth, which is freely offered to it. It is always God who is described as the "rock" on which a person can find a firm footing.[18]

Here we can see both the closeness and the distance between the biblical and the nonbiblical experience of the world. There is most definitely a relationship between them. Even outside the biblical world there remains (at least potentially) a sense of the nonabsoluteness of the finite, of the fragility, futility and insubstantiality of everything that belongs to the world and that is in process of becoming; by contrast, the Absolute is represented as repose, as that which supports all else, as the true. But in this experience of "natural religion" no light is shed, as yet, on the aspect of the world's createdness by infinite freedom. Consequently the evaluation of worldly reality alternates between two poles. On the one hand, the world is felt to be a quasi-necessary emanation and reflection of the Absolute, but, on the other hand, it seems to be a mere illusory appearance (maya): its veil must be rent if truth is to shine forth. The vanitas theme is also found in the Bible, from Qoheleth to Paul (Rom 8:20), and it can be traced through all the spiritual writings of Christianity, through the many treatises De contemptu mundi. But the meaning

---

[17] Gen 24:7; 26:3; 50:24; Ex 32:13; Dt 1:8; Is 45:23; Jer 22:5; 49:13; Ps 105:9; Lk 1:73.
[18] Often in the Psalms: 18:3; 95:1, etc. He is also the Rock in the desert from which water flows (Ex 18:1ff.) and the Rock on which the Temple is built. It is against this background that the promise of Jesus in Matthew 16:18 is to be read.

DRAMATIS PERSONAE

has changed. The world is not unreal as such. It is not negated *qua* world. It is not fundamentally transcended. It has been subjected to *vanitas* by God himself on account of man's sin, that is, because of man's failure to acknowledge the divine freedom in creation, and it can and should be liberated from this *vanitas*. It is not "vain" because it depends on divine freedom: its "vanity" (like the Law) has "interposed itself" (Rom 5:20) and has put the creation in a state of "slavery" (Rom 8:21) that is alien to its nature. On the contrary, in its finitude and distinctness from God, it was originally affirmed as "very good"; the final goal for which it "groans" is not to be dissolved back into God but to be fulfilled by him *in* its finitude and distinctness. Certainly, it needed to be thus affirmed by infinite freedom in order to feel sufficiently secure, thus suspended solely from God. Furthermore, what was necessary was an affirmation of the individual as such, who, in his unique distinctness, is a unique image of the free God and of Christ, the unique Son. No attention is paid to such an affirmation outside the realm of the Bible and outside Christianity. "I will give him a white stone, with a new name written on the stone which no one knows except him who receives it" (Rev 2:17). Thus the change from the natural feeling of finitude to the Christian sense of creatureliness involves a total revaluation: created reality discovers that it has no ground under its feet but "stands above itself" (Augustine) in the sole Will of infinite freedom, which is as such a Will of wisdom and salvation. But this infinite Will is also final: there can be no appeal to any other court. There is nothing that is not given by him, and that applies particularly to finite freedom itself. Insofar as the latter—like all created reality— originates in infinite freedom and receives its own freedom thence, it is willed and affirmed in its finitude down to the last detail. However unsure of itself it may become, it must hold fast to this Yes that has been pronounced upon it.

3. The influences unleashed upon world history as a result of the intervention of infinite freedom are irreversible. Since the making of the biblical Covenant, however, the truth of the world and of man is indissolubly bound up with the truthfulness of God (who looks for a similar response from man). It is now

impossible to produce a raison d'être for the world without going through this narrow gate. But can anything be said about *infinite freedom in itself*?

It is only through the Bible that we are aware of its existence; revelation presupposes a certain philosophical reflection on the implications of statements about God (Wis 13:1f.; Rom 1:19f.). Anyone who utters the word "God" is referring, on the one side, to infinite "reality", since the world's "entire being that has flowed from it",[19] which only subsists in finite entities,[20] can simply be deduced from an all-encompassing operating reality. On the other side, he means that this infinite reality knows and wills itself, grasps and affirms itself, to its uttermost recesses. It will always be idle speculation to try to discover a "primal ground" or "un-ground" in God, something that is prior to his knowledge and affirmation of himself or that he has first to master in some "process" or other. "God is light and in him is no darkness at all" (1 Jn 1:5). It is both superfluous and self-contradictory to look for a further reason behind that which grounds everything. The reason for the world's total reality (*totum esse*), which consists only of finite entities, can be neither the total reality of worldly being (since it does not subsist in itself) nor the sum of subsisting beings (since they are finite and caused): it can only be an infinite being, which, as such, is immediately subjective and equally infinitely self-illuminating and self-possessed and hence is absolutely free in itself, in no way restricted or rivaled. Nor is Being prior to this illuminating self-possession, as if the latter were subject to prescriptions coming from Being. Nor can the Absolute be mere "self-thinking" (Aristotle), mere "logic" (Hegel), for reality is not simply thought: thought itself is one mode of reality, and the world's reality could not spring from mere thought. Plotinus had already grasped this.

This coincidence of infinite being and infinite self-possession

[19] It is not only individual things that are to be regarded as issuing forth from God, "sed etiam emanationem totius entis a causa universali", Thomas Aquinas, *S. Th.* I, 45, a 1 c.

[20] "Prima rerum creatarum est esse. Sed esse rei creatae non est subsistens. . . . Nam ex eo dicitur aliquid creatum, quod est ens, non ex eo quod est hoc ens: cum creatio sit emanatio totius esse ab ente universali", *ibid.*, a 4 ad 1.

in knowledge and will gets us beyond the two concepts blocking our path: necessity and chance (contingence). God does not first have to transform the "need" of having-to-be [*die "Not" des Seinmüssens*] by seizing possession of himself, for the latter is his from the very first. Also, however, it is total and thus excludes chance (that is, the notion that God could primarily affirm something other than himself or could affirm himself otherwise or only partially). Thus his freedom is not some separate act resulting from his nature: it coincides with the act-quality of his nature.

This is as far as a philosophy that reflects on the Absolute, the ground of all being, can reach. The light which revelation sheds on God also shows us something else: God is not only by nature free in his self-possession, in his ability to do what he will with himself; for that very reason, he is also free to do what he will with his own nature. That is, he can surrender himself; as Father, he can share his Godhead with the Son, and, as Father and Son, he can share the same Godhead with the Spirit. Here, too, we are already placed beyond necessity and chance. The fact that the absolute freedom of self-possession can understand itself, according to its absolute nature, as limitless self-giving— this is not the result of anything external to itself; yet it *is* the result of its own nature, so much so that, apart from this self-giving, it would not be itself. In generating the Son, the Father does not "lose" himself to someone else in order thereby to "regain" himself; for he *is always* himself by giving himself. The Son, too, is always himself by allowing himself to be generated and by allowing the Father to do with him as he pleases. The Spirit is always himself by understanding his "I" as the "We" of Father and Son, by being "expropriated" for the sake of what is most proper to them. (Without grasping this there is no escape from the machinery of Hegelian dialectic.) From the point of view of finitude, one might suppose that the infinite self-possession of infinite reality would be bound to be the ultimate satisfaction and blessedness. But in God's self-proclamation in Jesus Christ the more blessed mystery is revealed, namely, that love—self-surrender—is part of this bliss of absolute freedom. Humanly speaking, (along with Ferdinand Ulrich), what we have here is the identity of "having" and "giving", of wealth and poverty. Nor does poverty come before wealth: it is not as if God must first go out, in the trinitarian procession, in order to gain himself (as Idealism imagines), nor does wealth come before poverty, as if the Father (the One) had always existed for himself before generating the Son (as Arianism, on a Platonic foundation, asserted).

If there is to be absolute freedom, it follows that, in what takes place between the divine "hypostases", there must be *areas of infinite freedom* that are *already there* and do not allow everything to be compressed into an airless unity and identity. The Father's act of surrender calls for its own area of freedom; the Son's act, whereby he receives himself from and acknowledges his indebtedness to the Father, requires its own area; and the act whereby the Spirit proceeds, illuminating the most intimate love of Father and Son, testifying to it and fanning it into flame, demands its area of freedom. However intimate the relationship, it implies that the distinction between the persons is maintained. Something like infinite "duration" and infinite "space" must be attributed to the acts of reciprocal love so that the life of the *communio*, of fellowship, can develop. While the Father from all eternity utters his eternal Word, the latter does not, as it were, keep interrupting him; similarly, the Spirit allows himself to proceed from Father and Son in order to show himself to be the Spirit common to both. True, all temporal notions of "before" and "after" must be kept at a distance; but absolute freedom must provide the acting area in which it is to develop—and develop in terms of love and blessedness. Above all we must fend off that "all-knowing" attitude that is fatal to man, that complacent notion of "being in the picture"; this eviscerates the joys of expectation, of hope and fulfillment, the joys of giving and receiving and the even deeper joys of finding oneself in the other and of being constantly over-fulfilled by him; and finally —since we are speaking of God—it destroys the possibility of mutual acknowledgment and adoration in the Godhead. "It is adoration because God is in the presence of God; it is fulfillment because God may expect everything from God."[21] And since each hypostasis in God possesses the same freedom and om-

[21] Adrienne von Speyr, *The World of Prayer* (San Francisco: Ignatius Press,

nipotence, we can speak of there being reciprocal petition. The paradigm of all Christian boldness (*parrhesia*) in prayer—which we shall shortly be discussing—is to be found in God himself. All this manifests "the absolutely positive aspect of differentiation" in absolute Being,[22] which implies that the hypostases do not possess the divine nature in common like an untouchable treasure; rather, the divine nature is defined through and through by the modes of divine being (*tropos tēs hyparxeos*). This nature is always both what is possessed and what is given away, and we cannot say that a particular hypostasis is rich in possessing and poor in giving away, for the fullness of blessedness lies in both giving and receiving both the gift and the giver. Since these acts are eternal, there is no end to their newness, no end to being surprised and overwhelmed by what is essentially immeasurable. The fundamental philosophical act, wonder, need not be banished from the realm of the Absolute.

The divine hypostases proceed from one another and thus (including the Father, the Primal Source) are perfectly open to one another—but, for all eternity, they are not interchangeable. As a result, this divine exchange or dialogue always contains two things: the partners are perfectly transparent one to another, and they possess a kind of impenetrable "personal" mystery. We have already discussed this coincidence in our early work, *Wahrheit* (1946). The hypostatic modes of being constitute the greatest imaginable opposition one to another (and thus no one of them can overtake any other), in order that they can mutually interpenetrate in the most intimate manner conceivable. Each of the divine Persons is just as sovereignly free as the others, although, in this freedom, each is codetermined by the *ordo processionis* and the trinitarian unity. No one can predict, for instance, how the Son will "use" the one and only divine freedom in order to invent ideas and acts of love; since the Son and the Spirit are consubstantial with the Father, it is equally their privilege, on the basis of the one divine freedom, to do surprising and astounding things, as it is the privilege of the

---

1985), 32. The magnificent chapter on "Prayer in the Trinity" should be read in its entirety: 28–74.

[22] G. Siewerth, *Der Thomismus als Identitätssystem*, 2d ed. (Frankfurt: Schulte-Bulmke, 1961), 104.

Father, as the original Source of all things. Only in the finite realm can the fulfillment of an expectation denote a conclusion, something that produces stagnation of life, boredom, satiety and surfeit (*koros*); in eternal life this is never possible—as Gregory of Nyssa showed most insistently. And this is not because God is always richer than finite freedom can expect (cf. Irenaeus, *Adv. Haer.* II, 28, 3), but because God himself is always greater than himself on the basis of his triune freedom. Only in this way can the creature endure being totally and utterly naked before God (Ps 139). The triune God is neither indiscreet nor—on the contrary—prudish. The divine hypostases know and interpenetrate each other to the very same degree that each of them opens up to the other in absolute freedom. None is overwhelmed by being known by the others, since each subsists by being *let*-be.

Thus, finally, it becomes clear why finite freedom can really fulfill itself in infinite freedom and in no other way. If *letting-be* belongs to the nature of infinite freedom—the Father *lets* the Son be consubstantial God, and so forth—there is no danger of finite freedom, which cannot fulfill itself on its own account (because it can neither go back and take possession of its origins nor can it attain its absolute goal by its own power), becoming alienated from itself in the realm of the Infinite. It can only be what it is, that is, an image of infinite freedom, imbued with a freedom of its own, by getting in tune with the (trinitarian) "law" of absolute freedom (of self-surrender): and this law is not foreign to it—for after all it is the "law" of absolute Being—but most authentically its own: "*Ecce unde liberi, unde condelectemur legi Dei: libertas enim delectat. Nam quamdiu servus facis, quod justum est, non Deus te delectat . . . : delectet te, et liber es.*"[23]

4. Everything that arises from one freedom remains a mystery for other freedoms because no adequate reason can be found for it but its own freedom. The archetype is seen in the way infinite freedom surrenders itself: it can allow us a glimpse of its own profound abysses, but, in doing so, the more it reveals itself as freedom, the more evident its mysterious nature becomes. That

---

[23] Augustine, *In Ioan. Evang.* 41, 8, 10 (PL 35, 1968).

is why it is possible to speak of "the mysteries of Christianity":
although it proclaims certain things in the most definite manner,
they remain, when disclosed, even more beyond our grasp. The
God of natural theology, distanced from all worldly being by
the *major dissimilitudo* of his act of being, is primarily negatively
incomprehensible; he slips through all the mind's instrumental
categories that try to pin him down with their "what?" and
"how?". However, when God, whom no man has ever seen, is
"interpreted" (Jn 1:18) by his Son in human words and deeds,
we find that the negative incomprehensibility turns into a positive
one. For it is far more incomprehensible that the Eternal God, in
his freedom, should set forth to come to us, caring for us by
means of his Incarnation, Cross and Eucharist and opening up
to us his own realm of freedom so that, in it, we can attain the
fulfillment of our own freedom. Now everything becomes
mystery. But that does not mean that we should fearfully back
away from the self-disclosing mystery or "shy away" as children
do. There is a kind of Christian familiarity with the mystery of
God on the part of the believer, equally at home with the most
profound adoration and a childlike closeness. For the realm of
infinite freedom, now opened up, is always both things at once:
it is both the realm of God's incomprehensible sovereignty—
beyond our grasp at all points—and the realm of unlimited
trinitarian communication of the inner-divine love. Thus everything can be both crystal-clear speech, a clarion summons to
responsibility, *and* a fairy-tale gift; and each pole heightens the
other and hence itself. Anyone who penetrates into the mysteries
of God recognizes more and more that the world as a whole is
created "for nothing", that is, out of a love that is free and has no
other reason behind it; that is precisely what gives it its only
plausible meaning. Recognizing or failing to recognize this
relationship will constitute the core of the action in theo-drama.

b. Facilitating Finite Freedom

On the basis of the foregoing, the question which philosophy
feels to be the most difficult of all, namely, *why* and *how* there is
relative, finite being beside Absolute being, should no longer
be distorted into hopelessness. Two modes of approach have

opened up: while the life of the Trinity must not under any circumstances be described as a "becoming" (since, despite the order of origin, Father, Son and Spirit are coeternal), the creaturely process of becoming can present an "image" of this primal life. Furthermore, as a result of the opposition of Persons in God, the "not" ("the Son is *not* the Father", and so forth) possesses an infinitely positive sense; thus, too, "*not* holding on" to the divine nature but giving it away is part of the absolute positivity of the divine life (for the Spirit too gives himself away to the love of Father and Son—which he is): this being the case, the transition from infinite freedom to the creation of finite freedoms (with all this implies) need not constitute the "absolute paradox" of thought. Neither is there a paradox in saying, as we naturally do, that God does not need the world to confirm him as God or to provide him with a series of stages to go through and so perfect himself; indeed, he does not even need the world to reveal to himself the possibilities of his omnipotence: "*Non quasi indigens Deus hominis*" (Irenaeus, *Adv. Haer.* IV, 14, 1).

Certainly we must put a caesura between the eternal Yes uttered by God's will to himself and his eternal life and the Yes which seals the decision to create. This is simply because the creation is not God and hence not necessary; not even in the sense in which Plato's or Plotinus' "Good" by nature overflows beyond itself or, in Leibniz, the idea of the best possible world "presses" to be brought into reality. The living God does not pour himself forth by nature; all the same, the freedom in which he determines that the world shall exist is, according to its nature, none other than the freedom by which he wills eternally to be what he is. The world, and finite freedom within it, will not have its ground in itself, like God, not even in an "idea": its ground is exclusively in God's freedom, which will always distinguish its nature from that of God, even at the highest level of union between divine and created freedom. But, being totally dependent on divine freedom, the world can receive its possibility and reality nowhere else but in the eternal Son, who eternally owes his divine being to the Father's generosity. If the Son is the Father's eternal Word, the world in its totality is created by this Word (Jn 1:3), not only instrumentally but in the sense that the Word is the world's pattern and hence its goal. "Through him" also means "in him" and "for him" (Col 1:16). We must add immediately that the world's location in the Son directly implies its location in the totality of the Godhead. The world can be thought of as the gift of the Father (who is both Begetter and Creator) to the Son, since the Father wishes to sum up all things in heaven and earth in the Son, as head (Eph 1:10); thus the Son takes this gift—just as he takes the gift of Godhead—as an opportunity to thank and glorify the Father. Having brought the world to its fulfillment, he will lay the entire kingdom at his feet, so that God (the Father) may be all in all (1 Cor 15:24, 28); as for the Spirit, he is given the world by both: he *is* eternally the reciprocal glorification of Father and Son, but now he can implement it in and through the creation (Jn 16:13–15).

If the world, according to its ability, is thus grounded in the Son,[24] light is shed on two questions: first, *where* can there be a place for the world if God is, after all, "the entire ocean of being" (John Damascene)? Then, *which* world did God decide to create?

1. The *where* question can be resolved by pointing to the realms of freedom within the Godhead. Naturally we can only speak of these in metaphors. Is the Father's womb not "empty" once he has generated the entire Son? And is the Son not "poor"—with all his riches—to the extent that he cannot take the Godhead for himself but can only receive it? And as for the Spirit, the mere "breath" of love between Father and Son, is he not somehow "insubstantial"? If this were not so, how could the creature, living in God (since outside of God there is nothing), fail to see him? The realms of freedom in God come about both through the self-giving of the hypostases and by each hypostasis in turn "letting" the other two "be". No one hypostasis wishes to be the other two. This is not a retreat or resignation: it is the positive form of infinite love. For that reason, God himself does not need to retreat either; he does not need to "close in on himself", he needs no "kenosis" when causing the world to exist within himself. The Jewish Cabbalists, particularly Isaak

contra Moltmann

↑ Bulgakov?

---

[24] As Bonaventure does, with particular care and profundity; cf. the relevant chapter in *The Glory of the Lord* II, 260ff.

Luria, felt it necessary to posit this kind of a contraction of God into himself (*tsimtsum*) in order to make room for creation.[25] Maurice Blondel makes several attempts to envisage a kind of creation-kenosis on the part of God. Starting from the impossibility of positing some realm outside God for "eternal entities or possibilities", he says that

> it would be better to assume that God, in order to bring into being creatures who are spiritual, capable of knowing and loving, has made room within himself, *Seipsum exinanivit*, as Paul says (Phil 2:7); this would permit such beings, as it were, to reconstitute and awaken within him his own life and thought.[26]

Elsewhere, however, Blondel corrects these "all too materialistic metaphors": they are used simply to restore balance by introducing a contrary image,

[25] Gershom Scholem, "Schöpfung aus Nichts und Selbstverschränkung Gottes" in *Eranos-Jahrbuch* XXV (1926), 87–119, esp. 115ff. This would threaten the notion of God's immutability. Scholem brings out the pantheistic thrust of this teaching: as creation emanates, there is a "constantly renewed and continuous contraction and withdrawal of the divine", intensifying with each higher level. God simultaneously descends into and transcends himself. Cf. the chapter on Isaak Luria in Gershom Scholem, *Die jüdische Mystik in ihren Hauptströmungen* (Zurich: Rheinverlag, 1957), 285–88. According to him, the earlier Cabbala followed a "one-track" method, asserting that the divine creative power operated outward, by degrees, in the divine *sephiroth*. By contrast, Luria spoke of God's contraction (*tsimtsum*): "*En sof* (the innermost divinity) descends into itself", which is regarded as God's "exile". This means that the world process becomes "two-tracked": God flows back in order to flow forth again. But the critical observation is apposite: "Basically Luria is pursuing an entirely rationalistic and one might say rather naturalistic line of thought: How can a world exist if God is everywhere?" (286). Without the *tsimtsum*, everything would immediately become pure divinity.

[26] *Exigences philosophiques de christianisme* (Paris: P.U.F., 1950), 101–2. Again: "It seems that in giving us our human nature, God has, as it were, retreated from one part of Being and, despite his omnipresence and omnipotence, consented to annihilate himself (ait consenti à s'annihiler) in order to leave the sovereign place to us. It is up to us, therefore, to restore him in us" (*ibid.*, 231). The same idea appears, in order to destroy the *possibilia* that flow forth necessarily from God's essence (Leibniz) or the notion of a "void" standing over against God: "Out of pure, unmotivated love, God has called into being, not possibilities that already existed, but nonexistent ones. . . . So we can dare to put it like this: in a certain sense God has withdrawn and emptied himself in order to create the Void, making room for possible being and endowing it with the means of awakening God" (*ibid.*, 258).

no less defective than the one used here; there is no vacuum outside God any more than inside him. But by calling to mind God's infinite condescension and humiliation vis-à-vis his creature, we perhaps do better justice to the significance of the plan of creation. Rather than envisaging a quasi-physical, preexistent Void that needs to be filled, we should think of the merciful Creator burying it [in himself]. But again: metaphors must not be taken literally.[27]

In fact, it is pure anthropomorphism to say that God had to create a void within himself in order to fashion the world from it. This void is precisely that: a nothing, and so it does not need to be created. The (essentially unrefined) formula "creation out of nothing" has been current since the first Christian centuries.[28] In order to express the same thing in a positive way, some of the

[27] L'Etre et les êtres, new ed. (Paris: P.U.F., 1963), 208. For the idea of kenosis, Blondel refers (207) to Ravaisson. Similar ideas were current in Orthodox theology. The lay theologian, Tareyev, says in his Grundlagen des Christentums (4 vols., 1908–1910): "We distinguish God's self-limitation, which is a presupposition for the creation, from the generation of the Son of God, which is a requirement for the temptation of the God-man and for self-limitation as a redemptive act in the mortal life of Jesus." It is similar with the sophiology of Sergei Bulgakov: he distinguishes three kenoses: the kenosis in creation mirrors the eternal kenosis in the Trinity, since the Father only exists by pouring himself into the Son, etc., and the third will be the Incarnation of the Son. Cf. Paul Henry, art. "Kénose" in Suppl. au Dict. de la Bible, 142f., 144f. In his Die christliche Lehre von Gott (Zurich, 1946), Emil Brunner puts it like this: "God desires and acknowledges the creature's independence and acts upon it by limiting himself accordingly. . . . God's attitude changes according to man's" (287).

[28] First of all in the Shepherd of Hermas, Mand. I, 1: "God who created all things . . . and brought everything into being out of nothingness." (Also 2 Macc 7:28.) Cf. also Vis. I, 1, 6. The so-called Second Letter of Clement applies the categories of creation to the work of redemption: "He [Christ] called us when we were not and desired us to step forth out of nothingness into being" (I, 8)—evidently based on Romans 4:17 and 1 Corinthians 1:28. Of the Apologists, only Justin speaks of the existence of matter having no beginning; the others think through "creation out of nothing" in a radical way: Tatian, Oratio 5, 7; Theophilus, Ad Autolycum I, 4 (PG 6, 1029B), II, 10 (1064B). Also Irenaeus, Adv. Haer. II, 10, 4 (PG 7, 736B); Origen, Peri Archon praef. 4 (Koetschau 9, 14); Augustine, In Ioan. tr 42, 10 (PL 35, 1703); Maximus the Confessor, Ambigua (PG 91, 1077C–80A); Thomas Aquinas, S. Th. I, q 45 c: "idem autem est 'nihil' quod nullum ens. Praepositio 'ex' non designat causam materialem, sed ordinem tantum" (ibid., ad 3).

Fathers tried to say that the divine act of will is the "substance out of which" created things were made. Thus Irenaeus: *"substantia omnium voluntas ejus"*.[29] And when Basil expounds the word of God in Genesis: "Let the earth bring forth", this does not mean, for him, that palms, oaks, cypresses lay hidden somewhere in the loins of the earth, "but the divine word is the substance of what has come to be".[30] Influenced by his brother, Gregory of Nyssa several times employs similar formulations: the entire universe is the result of a free "substantiation of the divine will";[31] this will is, "as it were, the matter, the form and the energy of the world and of everything in it and above it".[32] The most radical voice, under the influence of the Areopagite, is *Scotus Erigena*, for whom the nothingness out of which God created the world is his own supernothingness (or superbeing): he "condescends" to come forth from it and appear as worldly being. In this case, the "matter" from which he fashions things would be the *primordiales causae*, as yet formless in their generality; but while the wisdom of God descends lower into the various forms, *"ad seipsam veluti ad formationem suam respicit"*.[33] Both affirmations are equally valid: that God creates things out of his will, substantially—and here Erigena is explicitly quoting Basil[34] —and that therefore he gives form to himself in the world (*"a seipso creatur"*, *"seipsum in omnibus creare"*).[35] He expressly rejects the concept of nothingness as a "deprivation"—since there is nothing from which it could be subtracted—and the idea of

[29] *Adv. Haer.* II, 30, 9.

[30] All' ho theios Logos physis esti tōn ginomenōn: *In Hexaem.* h 8, 1, *Sources chrétiennes* 26, 450. On this issue: Ernst Benz, *Marius Victorinus und die Entwicklung der abendländischen Willensmetaphysik* (Stuttgart: Kohlhammer, 1932), 327.

[31] Autou tou telēmatos pros to dokoun ousiōthentos, *Or. cat.* 24 (PG 45, 64C).

[32] *De Vita S. Gregor. Thaumat.* (PG 46, 920A); cf. *In illud*, etc. (PG 44, 1312A): Things are not fashioned out of a preexisting matter, "but the divine will became the matter and substance of created things". G. Scholem is not aware of these passages; he endeavors to prove that the same statements in Persian texts represent the early stages of Cabbalism. He also misinterprets Scotus Erigena in the sense of "God destroying himself" (*Eranos-Jahrbuch*, 105, see n. 25 above).

[33] Noack translates: Because Wisdom, in descending, "refers back to its own original form".

[34] ". . . Sed divinum Verbum natura est eorum quae facta sunt" (cf. n. 30).

[35] *De div. nat.* III, c 19–20 (PL 122, 681A–86C).

nothingness arising from the absence of God (*tsimtsum*); hence the "nothingness" referred to can only be God himself.

Erigena and his interpretation doubtless went beyond what Irenaeus and the Cappadocians intended when he drew his pantheistic conclusions. But it is equally certain that the "nothing-out-of-which" the world came into being can only be sought in infinite freedom itself: that is, in the realms of creatable being opened up by divine omnipotence and, at a deeper level, by the trinitarian "letting-be" of the hypostatic acts.[36] The "not" which characterizes the creature—it is "not" God and cannot exist of itself—is by no means identical with the "not" found within the Godhead. However, the latter constitutes the deepest reason why the creaturely "not" does not cause the analogy of being between creature and God to break down.[37] The infinite distance between the world and God is grounded in the other, prototypical distance between God and God.

2. Having dealt with the first question regarding the world's "whence?", we have already partially answered the substance of the second question; here Scripture defines our path and renders it a safe one. The universe is created in the Son, who is the "reflection of God's glory" and bears "the stamp of his nature" (Heb 1:3). "We" (humanity, Jews and Gentiles) "have been chosen in him before the foundation of the world" and "destined in love to be his [God's] sons through Jesus Christ" (Eph 1:4f.); ultimately everything is to be recapitulated in him (*ibid.*, 1:10) so that he "may have the preeminence in all things"; he is "the image of the invisible God, the first-born of all creation; . . . He is before all things, and in him all things hold together" (Col 1:15ff.): consequently he can be designated as the one "idea" that embraces, facilitates and fulfills everything else. As we have

---

[36] Only in this context can we agree with G. Siewerth when he sees, in "nothingness", the "forgotten transcendental" that is grounded in God's intellect (*Grundfragen der Philosophie im Horizont der Seinsdifferenz* [Düsseldorf, 1963], 107; *Thomismus als Identitätssystem*, 2d ed. [1961], 40, n. 50). On this subject, cf. Manuel Cabada Castro, *Sein und Gott bei Gustav Siewerth* (Düsseldorf: Patmos, 1971), 92ff.

[37] As Karl Barth was inclined to assume, on the basis of their fundamentally opposed constitutions: "out of itself" and "not out of itself".

already shown, he is the exemplary and final cause, and as such, as the divine Son, he is the efficient cause of the world. But he is predestined to this "idea", not by this formal threefoldness that Christianity shares with Stoicism,[38] but by the Son's place in the mystery of the Trinity—given that there *is* a world and finite freedom. After all, he is the first to receive totally from the Father, just as, in breathing forth the Spirit together with the Father, he is the one who consents, responds and collaborates up to the last. Insofar as he is God, he is eternal, infinite freedom; insofar as he is the Son of the Father, he is this freedom in the mode ("*tropos*") of readiness, receptivity, obedience and hence of appropriate response: that is, he is the Father's Word, image and expression.

It cannot be denied that, at this point, there is a serious clash between the philosophical "*analogia entis*" (with its *major dissimilitudo* between God and world) and the theological "*analogia fidei*" (which extends right up to *participatio divinae naturae*). As we have said elsewhere,[39] the divine Son who becomes man is "the concrete analogia entis". The crux is that it is extremely hard to see how the Son, who "receives" Godhead, and hence eternal freedom, from the Father (and so seems to be closely related to the creature), can nonetheless possess this infinite freedom in the same sovereign manner (albeit in the mode of obedience) as the Father. John puts the paradox in all its abruptness, simply juxtaposing the two sentences: "For as the Father has life in himself, so he has granted the Son also to have life in himself (*en heautōi*)" (5:26). But "the Son can do nothing of his own accord (*aph'heautōi*), but only what he sees the Father doing; for whatever he does, that the Son does likewise. For the Father loves the Son and shows him all that he himself is doing" (5:19f.). Is this "having-life-in-himself" sufficient to distinguish the Son from the creature if, on the other hand, like the creature, he does not seem to possess this interior freedom "of himself"? Here we must recall, however, that in the first place what the Father "does" is nothing other than the Son himself. In receiving himself from the Father, therefore, the Son accepts the originless,

---

[38] H. Hommel, *Schöpfer und Erhalter. Studien zum Problem Christentum und Antike* (Berlin, 1956).

[39] *Theologie der Geschichte*, 4th ed. (1959), 59f.

self-possessing God, that is, that fullness of being that must always be included and reflected upon in any *theologia*. (That is why it will not do simply to replace the so-called "theo-ontological" categories of philosophy with "personological" categories, that is, to dissolve Being and its relationships.) It is only because the Son in very truth possesses the "form of God" (*morphē theou*, Phil 2:6), and hence the divine pole of the *analogia entis*, that he can "empty himself" and take "the form of a servant". The creature cannot do this, for it always comes into being *in* this state. Here we can see, incidentally, that when Marx and Nietzsche dream of true, positive humanity as the self-positing of finite freedom, their dream-illusion carries them outside the real *analogia entis* in which the Son's infinite freedom is realized solely in the eucharistic movement back and forth from and to the Father.

If a world is to come into being containing people endowed with finite freedom, requiring a drama to be played and a stage on which to play it, the Son alone can be its ground and goal; he alone can determine its entire course, irrespective, initially, of whether he himself will or will not appear in it as one of the main characters. Every worldly dramatic production must take its bearings from, and be judged by, the ideal nature of this coincidence of freedom and obedience or of self-being and consciously acknowledged dependence. So we can assume an infinite differentiation in God's plan for the world, since the one idea can split and radiate in myriads of mirrors without the "idea" itself being multiplied: its infinite content is always the same, in whatever prism its light is split.

Once this is granted, we shall have to proceed with caution, taking care to avoid two extremes in our thinking. The first would be to allow the abundant possibilities of mirroring the one idea to dissolve into an arbitrary selection, with the result that God would have to choose some world or other—for good or ill, so to speak—out of an infinite number of possible worlds. For it would be impossible to determine which was the best. What would seem to be the best in a particular world would obstruct the best in another. If we imagine God having chosen a world in which finite freedom had committed no transgression, such a world would have given the Son no opportunity to demonstrate the absolute quality of his obedient love by allowing himself to be "made to be sin" and nailed to the Cross, abandoned by God. This also brings the other extreme into view, namely, to conclude, on the basis of the accomplished "redemption through his blood" (Eph 1:7), that this world order which brought to light the most profound depths of God's love exercised some compulsion on his freedom—given that he wished to choose some world in the first place. Not only would this make sin the necessary precondition for love's epiphany; the Son's self-surrendering will—in his hypostatic distinction from the other members of the Trinity—would, as it were, compel the whole Trinity to adopt this choice. Once we have avoided these two extremes, there is nothing hindering us from extolling the world God actually chose as the best, *because* it has been chosen by God, in his absolute freedom, as the adequately clear embodiment of the "idea" of the freely obedient Son.[40]

---

[40] It is absurd to go on questioning any further, as a secular example will show. A consummate work of art, Mozart's *Magic Flute*, for example, stands before us as the product of an unimaginable creative freedom. Does it make any sense to ask this work whether it might not have been even more perfect? Obviously, the question can be put, in the abstract, but it is impossible to come up with any meaningful, concrete suggestion as to the direction in which this improvement might be made. On the other hand, the work of art radiates so much freedom that it would be just as mistaken to label it "best" once and for all, in such a way that, had Mozart lived longer, he would have been unable to write a more perfect opera. It is well known, furthermore, with what playful ease Mozart could insert new arias or delete existing ones (when a singer could not appear or was replaced by another one), without thereby endangering the harmony of his work—which forbids us to separate the "necessity" of a work from the freedom which lends wings to it. Moreover, it is clear that part of the "perfection" of the *Magic Flute* is the incredible variety of the characters, scenes and musical forms, the lofty and lowly, the tragic, heroic, burlesque and idyllic, pathos and the stolidly down-to-earth, profundity and absurdity: "Il faut de tout pour faire un monde." If a composer like God creates the opera of our world and puts the crucified and risen Son at its center, there must be no faultfinding and wondering if he could not have made it better. This is the standpoint from which to assess the value of what Leibniz, Malebranche and Rosmini have said about the world as the "best possible" as well as Thomas' objection to the concept in *S. Th.* I, q 25, a 6. The following, however, is worthy of note: "Deus plus amat quod est magis bonum, et ideo magis vult praesentiam magis boni quam absentiam minus mali, . . . ideo ad hoc quod aliqua bona majora eliciantur, permittit aliquos in mala culpae cadere . . ." (*De Ver.* 5, a 5 ad 3).

This means that we can and must abandon as fruitless all preoccupation with possible worlds other than the real world; revelation is exclusively concerned with the latter. The "possible" only has value insofar as it keeps open the realms of the real freedoms, divine and human, in their interrelatedness. It is in our real world that the eternal Son, the Word of God, has become flesh and has shown the world, in his Cross, the Father's perfect love for the world. Thus the exemplary "idea" of the world has been given a definitive concrete form, and there can be no other ideas independent of it and in competition with it. If we wish to ascribe a distinct, personal "idea" to each finite freedom (and we can and must do this), these ideas must only appear as facets of the one, total Idea. Later on, when we come to discuss the individual human characters as role-bearers in the world drama, they will all be definable as persons within the total Person, as supporting roles to the title role.

The personal "idea" of each individual finite freedom lies in the incarnate Son in such a way that each is given a unique participation in the Son's uniqueness. His divinity, with its infinite freedom, permits this inexhaustible multiplication of what is once-for-all and unique; thus it also permits each individual freedom to fulfill itself in an utterly distinct manner within the realm of infinite freedom. This is the very context for which the personal "*autexousion*" was designed in the first place; its arrival is expected; its prototype is already there, and this prototype is indispensable to finite freedom so long as it has not become alienated from itself. The Son's infinite hypostatic distinctness, since it is divine and unique, is what distinguishes each person founded thereon. And the more the person, in response to the Son's call, walks toward his prototype in the Son, the more unique he becomes. Here we can speak of "exemplary identity" (G. Siewerth), which is mediated, living and indestructible, by the analogy of Creator and creature.

However, the prototype is also the divine Being, *ipsum esse subsistens*, and anyone who participates in the latter is in touch with the all-embracing reality—even if, outside the divine Subject, *esse* only presents itself to all in a nonsubsistent mode. It follows, therefore, as we have already said, that the person's opening-up to the prototype must coincide with the abolition of all limitation vis-à-vis everything that shares in being: freedom is communion. Communion is the opening-up of ever-new and unimaginable realms of freedom and dramatic plot; but they are all kept together in the unifying prototype, which is only *universalissimum* because it is *concretissimum*.[41]

As we noted at the outset,[42] all this is true even if we prescind from the concrete historical modalities of the world's historical being. But what is important is that it holds good even in the worst of these modalities, namely, the *status naturae lapsae*. Here the obedience of the Son of God represents the concrete universal idea of the relationship between heaven and earth in the form of crucified love; thus, in the highest contingency of free, divine love-creativity, it also attains that maximal "necessity" (that is, omitting nothing) of a God-world relationship *qua major cogitari nequit*.

c. God Is Latent in Creation and Accompanies It

The creation of finite freedom by infinite freedom is the starting point of all theo-drama. Where finite freedom is seriously taken to be nondivine, there arises a kind of opposition to divine freedom and the appearance, at least, of a limitation of it. Renouvier expressly propounded this view.[43] And it seems to raise the demand (on the part of the creature this time) for a *tsimtsum* by God, so that human autonomy shall have enough room to expand. According to many, like Nicolai Hartmann, this *tsimtsum* must go as far as the complete disappearance of God.[44] The appearance of limitation is unavoidable, since the creature is given a nature that is not as such divine—*Deus "non intrat essentiam rerum creaturarum"*[45]—and hence too its own area of operation, which becomes all the more "autonomous" the nearer a being is to God—"*quanto aliqua natura Deo vicinior, tanto*

[41] All this simply confirms what was said above in "A single drama", pp. 77ff.

[42] See pp. 189ff. above.

[43] Laberthonnière severely criticizes this finitizing of God for the sake of human autonomy in his *Critique du Laicisme, ou comment se pose le problème de Dieu* (Paris: Vrin, 1948), 20ff., 70ff.

[44] "The Postulate of Atheism" in *Ethik* (1926), 735ff.

[45] Thomas, *De pot.* q 3, a 5 ad 1.

minus ab eo inclinatur et magis nata est seipsam inclinare".[46] Since God is the "idea" of all freedom and as such is infinite, as Creator he can only create finite freedoms, and they can only thrive by participating in infinite freedom. God sets the limit in order to remove it, so that there may be no barrier between finite freedom and himself. Nor can the limited party decide to throw off these limits of its own volition, because the realm in which such action could take place is itself free and must freely open up. On the other hand, it cannot "posit" itself as finite freedom through self-limitation (Fichte) either, because, in virtue of creation, it is already "posited" as such and cannot create itself. This brings out the paradox in the passage quoted from Thomas in its ambivalent and dangerous quality: "The nearer (*vicinior*) a free nature stands to God, the more it is able to move itself": this "nearer" can signify God's more generous gift of freedom, which includes the risk of drawing Lucifer's response —or it can signify the insight, on the part of limited freedom, that it can only cast off these limits and attain to complete freedom by progressively drawing nearer to God.

At this point one might be inclined to describe God, in the face of his world project, as the "tragic Creator": if he wants to have free creatures he is obliged to "expel them from him", to put an abyss separating himself from them.[47] But the main thing here is not the tragic aspect but the underlying paradox to which we have already referred: that finite freedom can only exist as participation in infinite freedom, as a result of the latter being immanent in it and transcendent beyond it; finite freedom can only realize itself in and with infinite freedom. If God's nature, theologically speaking, shows itself to be "absolute love" (*autocharis*)[48] by giving itself away and allowing others to

---

[46] Thomas, *De ver.* q 22, a 4 c.

[47] "God, besides being the Great Creator, is the Tragic Redeemer. Perhaps the Tragic Creator too. For I am not sure that the great canyon of anguish that lies across our lives is *solely* due to some prehistoric catastrophe. Something tragic may . . . be inherent in the very act of creation. So that one sometimes wonders why God thinks the game worth the candle." C. S. Lewis, *Letters to Malcolm*, 2d ed. (London: Fontana, Collins, 1974), letter 17, cf. 8. On the question of freedom's self-positing and self-limitation in Fichte, cf. W. Schulz, *J. G. Fichte, Vernunft und Freiheit* (Pfullingen, 1962).

[48] Gregory of Nyssa, *De beatit.* or 1 (PG 44, 1197A).

be, for no other reason than that this (motiveless) giving is good and full of meaning—and hence is, quite simply, beautiful and glorious—the same must apply to his "making room" for his free creatures.

They only gain room for freedom, however, if God, in allowing them freedom, withdraws to a certain extent and becomes latent. He who cannot be absent from any place thus adopts a kind of incognito, keeping many paths open for freedom, not only in appearance but in reality, for he is always at work and continually liberates his creation for freedom: *"voluntatem movet, non ut ex necessitate, sed ut indeterminate se habentem ad multa"*.[49] In thus opening up untrodden paths—"to new shores!" —he opens up, not simply the void, but the realm of infinite freedom and hence himself and, in himself, the exemplary idea that surrounds and governs all finite freedom. Instruction is given in the realm thus opened-up in connection with the exemplary idea. We have to consider both aspects: how God is latent in creation and how he accompanies it.

1. The parable of the talents which the merchant or king distributes to his servants before going abroad shows us how God is *latent*: he gives them an acting area in which they can creatively exercise their freedom and imagination; but what he gives them is *his* wealth, which they can use wisely or fritter away. First of all they are endowed with the talents; they possess something with which they can act and play—their finite freedom. But between the giving of this gift and the use and exercise of it lies a certain interval that belongs to the human *autexousion*.

God is latent in this way even in creation; he is evidently there but as in a picture-puzzle; if his presence were not evident, he could never be found, never deduced from purely finite reality. Yet, though evident, he is hidden, so that it is possible both to know him and fail to know him (Rom 1:21). Being, which is not exhausted by any existing being, is his present image, but, since it only exists in finite beings, his self-subsistence can be disputed; people can fail to see the "image of God" and can regard the finite, sense-mediated essences as the formal object of

[49] Thomas, *De malo* q 6, a un c.

human reason. Being cannot be exhausted by logic; this faces finite freedom with a decision: it can let this stimulate it to a ceaseless endeavor, to be a "pilgrim toward the Absolute", following the thread of the real: *"Ut (Deus) inventus quaeratur immensus est."*[50] Philo originated the saying which will constantly be repeated by the Church Fathers: "The highest good is to comprehend that God, according to his Being, is incomprehensible to all existing beings."[51] Thomas (in *C. Gent.* I, 8) will cite Hilary: "Anyone who reverently follows the Infinite will always keep walking and wandering, even if he never reaches the end" (*De Trin.* II, 10). We have already referred to Gregory's images of the Spirit's resting while on his infinite flight-path.[52] The other decision is resignation, burying the talent; the reinterpretation of the open path is a mere "condition for the possibility of finite, categorical knowledge". Thus the talent is no longer seen as the king's possession but as my own, and since what I possess is finite, a God who "is neither countable nor a 'thing' but universal and infinitely One, sublimely exalted above every single entity that can be uttered or thought",[53] has no face value for me.

The fact that, to finite freedom (which is given no fixed signposts but only hints at the direction to be taken), God is latent yields the possibility of *profound error in the realm of the finite*. Foreground goods are available, obscuring our view of goods that are greater but more distant and harder to acquire. Relative goods show us first one aspect and then another, and finite freedom, at will, can cause this or that aspect to glow and become an overpowering attraction. It can also simply turn away from an object of desire. It can be in doubt as to the goal to be pursued, be it a distant goal or one close to hand. It can withdraw from every decision because of the deceptive appearance of things; indeed, according to Thomas, it can at any

[50] Augustine, *In Ioan.* tr 63, 1 (PL 35, 1803).

[51] *Poster.* 15; cf. Justin, *Dial.* 127, 2; Irenaeus, *Adv. Haer.* IV, 20, 5; Clement, *Strom.* II, 2; Origen, *C. Cels.* VII, 42; Basil and Gregory of Nyssa countless times in their treatises against Eunomius; Chrysostom in his "On the Incomprehensibility of God" (*Sources chrétiennes* 28 bis, 1970).

[52] See pp. 234–35 above.

[53] Scotus Erigena, *Div. Nat.* III, 22 (PL 122, 687D).

time "refuse to think of its own happiness".[54] The gift of man's area of freedom, with God latent within it, implies and accepts the possibility of going astray, with all the consequences this may bring: *one* false step may lead in the wrong direction; the first mistake may lead right up to the last. We have already seen something of this argument and these implications in our discussion of the Greek Fathers.[55] Following their train of thought, we can ask whether, since God is latent in creation, finite freedom would have been able to find its way to God by following the path through all finite goods. Would finite freedom have been able to recognize in finite goods the hidden presence of the infinite Giver and make an appropriately grateful response—and do so without being explicitly enlightened as to the ultimate meaning and goal of finite existence?

In point of fact, man fell into error, and when he demanded his share of the inheritance, his Father did not attempt to hold him back but let him go. What happened then belongs to the action of the drama, and so we can only outline it here. The world and mankind are created in the Son; man's hopeless straying about in finitude brings to light the center of God's plan for the world, which up to now was hidden and latent: namely, the possibility that infinite freedom will follow wayward man into utter alienation. The Father's Word, the Son, becomes "flesh"; the divine precept, previously only hinted at, becomes unmistakably concrete—"whatever you do to the least of my brethren . . ."; a way, a manner of discipleship, comes into view, but, since it is still a question of facilitating man's freedom, it is even more deeply "latent" than before. Erring freedom is put back into its area of freedom, both outwardly (it is shown "the way, the truth and the life") and inwardly (the burden of its error is taken by Another); now it can choose, but the choice is confronted with a "*latens Deitas quae sub his figuris vere latitas*": the flesh of a Jewish individual, a crucified flesh and blood, shared out and made available as ordinary food, bread

[54] *De malo* q 6, a un. On this issue: G. Siewerth: "Die dreifache ontologische Indifferenz" in *Thomas von Aquin, Die menschliche Willensfreiheit* (1954), 28ff.; cf. also the section entitled "Das Böse aus Unwissenheit, Schwäche und Bosheit", 98ff.
[55] See p. 234ff. above.

and wine. The "enlightening" brought about by the revelation of infinite freedom's plan, which is also the peripeteia of human destiny, does not put an end to divine latency in favor of some universal knowledge attainable without a decision on freedom's part. God is now more profoundly latent, and thus he makes both a greater gift of love to finite freedom and a greater challenge to it. When God comes near, in the Son's Incarnation, this freedom receives a strengthening from within: God's Holy Spirit (*interior intimo meo*) inwardly expands man's faculty of seeing and choosing; but man has to accept that he must go through the narrow door of humiliation, of the Cross, encountering the infinite precisely in the most finite, in order to arrive at communion with infinite freedom.

Anselm's question to God: "*Domine, si hic non es, ubi te quaeram absentem? Si autem ubique es, cur non video te praesentem?*"[56] is put in the form of a prayer; its answer, likewise, can only come in prayer: God's "latency" is his loving respect for his creature's freedom; the creature must learn something of eternal love in order to discover how to "see" God, that is, in order to understand that this "latency" signifies, not that God withdraws from man, but that he actually accompanies him.

2. Finite freedom cannot be located in a void, for there is no such void.[57] It is "set loose" in the realm of infinite freedom and so finds itself, right from the start, in a realm of meaning, governed by the infinite "idea" of the Son, which, as the

---

[56] *Proslogion*, chap. 1. English translation in *The Prayers and Meditations of Saint Anselm* (Penguin, 1973). Cf. the profound study by Ferdinand Ulrich: "Cur non video praesentem? Zur Implikation der 'griechischen' und 'lateinischen' Denkform bei Anselm und Scotus Eriugena" in *Freiburger Zeitschrift für Philosophie und Theologie* 22 (1975), 70–170.

[57] However much a passage like the following may epitomize antiquity in point of style, it is completely valid in terms of the Christian understanding of existence: "Ipse continens cuncta, nihil extra se vacuum deserens, nulli deo superiori . . . locum reliquit. Quandoquidem ipse universa sinu perfectae magnitudinis et potestatis incluserit, intentus semper operi suo et vadens per omnia et movens cuncta et vivificans universa et conspiciens tota et in concordiam elementorum omnium discordantes materias sic connectens, ut ex disparibus elementis ita sit unus mundus ista coagmentata conspiratione solidatus, ut nulla vi dissolvi possit", Novatian, *De Trin*. 2, 9.

prototype of creation, uniformly permeates it and, insofar as the creation is in dramatic motion, *accompanies* it. We can approach this accompaniment from three sides. First, it is homogeneous and unchanging because it embraces everything; second, although we cannot get a complete view of it, it is definite; and third, it contains not only static elements but, as Providence, accompanies man in a dynamic way.

a. Statements about God's plan for the world (Rom 8:28–39; Eph 1:3–10) are *homogeneous* and universal. There is only one single plan, embracing everything—what precedes the age of the world, the age of the world itself and the end of time—just as God is eternally present to every possible and actual time. Thus this plan always includes God's "answer" to every word that may possibly be uttered by finite freedom: the Beloved Son in whom "we have been chosen from the foundation of the world" is always and right from the start the One in whom "we have redemption through his blood, the forgiveness of sins" (Eph 1:7). He is always the One in whose unstinting self-giving God has "given us all things" (Rom 8:32), so that he remains the unchangeably valid blueprint in every situation in the world and in history. Nor are only individuals and their destinies governed by this idea—as an atomistic doctrine of predestination would suggest—but also all social ("spiritual" and "secular") contexts, the destinies of groups, of the Church, of nations and states. In this regard Christian thought was able to adopt much (in terms of form) of the Stoic notion of the Logos permeating and ruling the cosmos, although (in terms of matter) it acquired a new content; for the world plan of the God who acts in sovereign freedom has a trinitarian and soteriological character. Since it is the plan of the free God, drawn up for free creatures, it is very far from being a predetermining fate: on the contrary, it makes room for free action in every respect. Every kind of self-transformation is freely available to the creature; yet all such transformations always take place within that all-embracing freedom that allows creatures to be free; depending on how the creature moves, it will encounter a different constellation of the same infinite idea. In this sense God is able to perform a new work in the face of a situation that, humanly speaking, is unforeseeable, without having to make a new decision.[58] For the primal Idea within which all worldly motion and change take place is not cosmic, like the Stoic Logos: it is the eternal Son of God himself, whose eternal freedom, in the hypostatic mode of readiness, is always the same, whether it is God's first Word "in the beginning", the "life and light" of men (Jn 1:1, 4), or God's final Word, shining forth in the darkness and uttering the cry of dereliction. God's all-embracing Idea is so comprehensive, and in this sense "catholic", that it integrates all particularity without interfering with the latter's freedom. Whatever paths the particular may follow, they will be within God's total Idea: for in the Son's Cross God has enfolded and undergirded the most extreme courses the creature can take.[59]

There is no reason, therefore, for polemics against the "immutability of God", as if this predicate were to foist on the living and personal God of the Bible an ontological attribute culled from the "subpersonal" and specifically "geometric" thought of the ancient world. For when God designates himself as *"yahweh ašher yahweh"* (Ex 3:14), this is not simply a promise that he will remain faithful to his people and go with them: the promise is also grounded in God's nature: "My nature is such that I am and will be the One who is present, actual and real, here and now, in every situation." As always, it is a mistake to strip the revealed word of the inchoate philosophical understanding it contains (inadequate in itself though it be, admittedly) on the pretext that it is simply based on ultimate intramundane categories (for example, the immutability of numbers and natural laws). It is true that we must go beyond the horizon of understanding available to ancient ontology if we are to see how the immutability of God's nature and his plan for the world (to which he has committed himself) can be upheld in the face of

---

[58] Cf. Augustine, *City of God* XII, 18: "Cujus sapientia simpliciter multiplex et uniformiter multiformis, tam incomprehensibili comprehensione omnia incomprehensibilia comprehendit, ut quaecumque nova et dissimilia consequentia praecedentibus si semper facere vellet, inordinata et improvisa habere non posset; nec ea praevideret ex proximo tempore, sed aeterna praescientia contineret."

[59] This general statement does not need to take account of so-called "double" predestination, for which, as is well known, there is no evidence in Scripture.

the Incarnation and the Cross—which, according to Scripture, were part of the redemptive plan for the world from all eternity (they were "predestined", "before the foundation of the world"). However, our central concern here is not the question of the immutability of God's nature[60] but the "unchangeable character of his purpose" (*ametatheton tēs boulēs autou*: Heb 6:18), although the latter, according to the explicit testimony of Scripture, resides in his essential self-affirmation, his eternal faithfulness and truth to himself: "If we are faithless, he remains faithful—for he cannot deny himself" (2 Tim 2:13). This purpose is, precisely, the revelation of the trinitarian life in God, starting with the modality of the Son, in which creation as a whole is grounded and which also reveals the *tropos* of the Father and that of the Spirit. Thus the content of God's purpose is maximal and therefore unchanging. But we can no more define this "maximum" in points or propositions than we can define the eternal life of God himself: eternal life is not the negation of time and space but the unimaginable superabundance of times and spaces in which freedom can operate, expressing the fullness of life that is eternally going on in God. An eternal plan on God's part, therefore, has "time" and "space" in it for all the created times and spaces in which this plan is able to realize itself in the context of the world.

Thus we can understand why, in many passages, the Bible of the Old Covenant gives the impression that God can change. The totality of the divine plan accompanies the Chosen People along the stages of its earthly development; and where a partial situation (partial, because Israel is journeying along its pilgrim path) is confronted with the totality of the plan, refractions occur: the totality can be referred to the fragmentary nature of the ongoing situation (where it only comes to light in the stage of the promised fulfillment, which is yet to be), or, by anticipation, it is referred to the ultimate situation. Where God, in being faithful to himself and holding fast to the warnings issued at the conclusion of the Mosaic covenant, should now proceed to punish and cast out the sinful people, he can look ahead to the

---

[60] On this subject, K. Rahner, "On the Theology of the Incarnation" in *Theological Investigations* (London: Darton, Longman and Todd, 1966).

coming Cross, where his ultimate faithfulness will be manifested, and have mercy on them. While twenty-four passages speak of God changing his mind, "repenting", there are eight passages in which it is said that God "does not repent". But the Cross itself has two sides: it is both strictest justice and the highest mercy. In its immutability, however, God's will can cause people to participate in both sides of the Cross in the most diverse ways and at different levels, including the ultimate, New Testament level, where the only category is that of the "disobedient" (Rom 11:30).[61] In the end the entire plan remains God's possession, the possession of the Final Judge; prior to the Last Judgment, the Cross' two-sidedness cannot be brought into a single conspectus by human insight.

In theology, therefore, we do well to avoid speaking of "God's immutability",[62] precisely because it is essential to keep before us his absolute freedom, manifested in his plan for the world as a freedom to pursue his (trinitarian) freedom. God stands by his own nature, namely, ever-greater love, which the Father reveals through the Holy Spirit in the Son's obedient self-surrender: this is the most permanent and, from the world's standpoint, the most moving reality there is. As such it is best suited to accompany man along his earthly course.

b. This suggests a second consideration. God's "idea" of the world, in its original integrity in the example seen in the Son, is

[61] This is shown by the whole historico-theological dialectic between Jews and Gentiles in Romans 9–11.

[62] Heribert Mühlen, *Die Veränderlichkeit Gottes als Horizont einer künftigen Christologie* (Münster: Aschendorff, 1969). The title of this book is misleading, since the author's concern is by no means to show that God is changeable but (as we have been doing, although in rather summary fashion) that he is *not* immutable in the sense of the Greek metaphysics largely influential in the patristic period. The whole range of problems is raised once again by Wilhelm Maas, *Unveränderlichkeit Gottes* (Paderborn: Schöning, 1974). Like his teacher, Mühlen, Maas takes shortcuts in the areas of patristics and philosophy (in dealing with God's economic "faithfulness", there is insufficient reflection on the manifestation of his nature). In the final section he adduces many well-balanced statements from modern theologians contributing to a more nuanced understanding of God's immutability. In sum, we cannot go back behind what Plato said about God's immutability, in opposition to the mythic poets, at the end of the second book of his *Republic*.

both infinite and *definite*. It is infinite because, in the Son, God reveals *himself*, and the model presented for man's participation and imitation is inexhaustibly richer than anything finite. He is the locus of absolute freedom, which operates through all the phases of the implemented plan. Not as if God, having freely promised his gift and given it, still had the freedom to withdraw it or to fail to fulfill it (for then he would contradict himself); but in the sense that, whatever—according to his plan—he gives, retains the character of a free gift, notwithstanding its being part of his plan. Even if God gives some grace as a "reward", it retains its character as a free gift (and perhaps even more so: "To him who has shall more be given"). But in the very midst of this free activity there is an ordered definiteness. We can see this from the answer the father gives to the brother of the returned prodigal son. The logic of grace, which, flowing from the Son, the prototype, exerts its influence through the entire *oikonomia*, cannot be represented in propositions referring to the world; but since it is the logic of the God who manifests himself, it is more rigorous than all intramundane necessity. In concentric rings around the nondeducible and sovereignly free fact of the Son's Incarnation–Cross–Resurrection, we can discern, according to the laws of theology, all the events of salvation history and world history, and of nature too, since ultimately everything exists for the sake of this center: "For . . . all things were created through him and for him" (Col 1:16). The first thing to be defined is the longitudinal axis, as it were, the vertical beam of the Cross: at its top is the Son's eternal readiness to obey the Father, at its lowest point is his obedience even in forsakenness. And this gives the horizontal beam its definiteness: his obedience is the internal norm of every human life and work. This two-in-one standard is applied to everything that exists, to all reality, not as an alien burden imposed from without, but as the infrastructure which makes the existence of worldly beings possible. The "weary and heavy-laden" are to be refreshed: "Take my yoke upon you and learn from me; for I am gentle (*prays*: mild, willing, offering no resistance, calm) and lowly (*tapeinos*: humble, low, submissive, pliant) in heart" (Mt 11:28f.).

This shows us that God's commandments—summed up in the chief commandment—can have both a binding and a liberating character for the believer in his finite situations. Each of these commandments is in itself infinite *and* definite. This is because the Son's self-surrender is the most definite reality possible, and every ethical norm governing man's concrete action (individually and socially) is only the proclaiming of this infinite will of God for a finite situation. The Letter of James is speaking with ultimate precision when it refers to "the perfect law of freedom" (James 1:25).

c. The third element is that infinite freedom *accompanies* man. This must be seen as intimately connected with the definiteness of which we have just spoken. It means that, in God's plan for the world, the possibilities are not simply static like places on a map, which the traveler can visit as he feels inclined: the paths themselves journey and wander, leading on those who walk along them. The word "providence" may come from a Greek context, but the reality itself, transposed into the realm of personal event, is well known to Scripture. In Romans 8:28–30, we find *"pro"* four times in connection with God's foreknowledge [*Vor-Kenntnis*] and predestination [*Vor-Bestimmung*] according to his pro-ject [*Vor-Satz*], which is to fashion the elect in the image of his Son, the first-born of many brethren, and to call, justify and glorify them. Here, explicitly, Providence circles around and accompanies man in this process of assimilation to the Son; this is what verse 28 refers to when it says: "In everything God works for good with those who love him": those who love God are those he has chosen; that is, they are loved in a particular way in the Son and with a view to the Son—which again confirms that Providence [*Vorsehung*] is christologically grounded, finalized and formalized: it is progressive assimilation to the Son. And even though, from the outset, it bears within it an orientation toward this assimilation (as *pro*-ject, *fore*-knowledge and *pre*-destination), it is also the case that the element of definiteness emerges all the more clearly, the more this assimilation progresses; and this in spite of the fact that the latter is performed on the "many brethren"—who would thus seem to be assimilated to one another.

But here again we see that the uniqueness of the sole, primal Idea has nothing to do with generic universality. Insofar as there can be participation in the divine One, viewed as undifferentiated (for example, in Plotinus), it can only be imitated in a twofold manner. First, by an individual (*individuum*) reflecting something of the absolute uniqueness and incommunicability of the One; and then—since there are many such individuals—in the universality of Being that unites all individuals in itself without them ever being able to absorb it or parcel it out. But the only Son of the Father (*Monogenēs*; Jn 1:14, 18; 3:16, 18; 1 Jn 4:9) is not only God but the primal Idea, the Word, who, generated by the Father, is addressed as the absolute "Thou"—"*Filius meus es tu, ego hodie genui te*" (Ps 2:7; Heb 1:5). Thus participation in him involves not only the aforementioned tension between the individual and the universal (nonsubsistent being): more than that, it involves the tension between the giving of a name that is unique in each case ("which no one knows except him who receives it", Rev 2:17) and a fellowship among these unique individuals. Since the Son is the Word, this fellowship is no longer simply the universality of being, overarching and enfolding all individuals, but something stamped by the uniqueness of the Word, something simultaneously universal and particular: it is the "body of many members", which, unique as they are, can only subsist in this body, whereas the Body signifies the form of the Son as participated-in by the "many brethren". Whereas philosophy can envisage a providence only within the dialectic between the individual and the community of being[63]—involving the dispute as to whether this providence is concerned solely with the universal plane or with the individual too—theology makes this dialectic concrete: it is a Providence that accompanies man toward the realm of the "Body of Christ", which unfolds in unique members, each of them "called" by name, "foreknown" and "predestined", with unique personalities which can only be realized in the form of ministries and charisms within the body-community. Just as, in the abstract, philosophical dimension, nonsubsistent Being

---

[63] It is characteristic, therefore, that in Plato the individual soul as such is eternal and intransitory, an indestructible monad, and that the perfect community is represented in the *Republic* only in the form of a communism. However, this is not to ignore the valid things Plato has to say about the organization of the state and the analogy between personal and social organism.

embraces all finite entities in itself, realizing itself in them without being dissolved into them, so, in the concrete realm of theology, the Word which is shared out eucharistically (but is self-subsistent) is the medium in which such persons, called and chosen, can subsist as unique individuals within the body-community that enfolds them. Naturally they are "predestined to be conformed to the image of his Son" (Rom 8:29): like him, they are uniquely free-in-themselves, precisely because, with him, they are expropriated for the sake of the Whole.

Thus, anticipating the perspectives of the Incarnation of the Word, we have formally outlined the plan, the definite character and the thrust of Providence according to God's unique idea of the world. Once again we can see how unnecessary it is to speak of a "change" in God when reflecting on the universality of the divine Idea: the One is inexhaustible and can present itself within the world in a new form at any period of world history, without undergoing change. The only thing to change is our perspective on the One. We can also discern the infinite range of the term "definite" as used here: it embraces the most personal counsel [Weisung] of the divine will, addressed to me in my unique situation, while including (at the same time) our "banishment" [Verweisung] to the "trackless" [weiselos] realm of the Son's attitude in carrying out the Father's commission, an attitude that is both a primal image [urbildlich] and more than an image [überbildlich]. Both modes of "definiteness" belong together (including everything that lies between these two extremes, all concrete and universal ethical norms); they are only aspects of one and the same guiding, accompanying Providence.

5. The Acceptance of Freedom

As we have seen, finite freedom can only be made possible by infinite freedom; consequently it can only fulfill itself, as finite freedom, within infinite freedom. In its finitude it has a "whence" and a "whither"; by its very nature it is set [ge-setzt] on a path and pointed in a direction [ge-wiesen]. Infinite freedom provides it with law [*Gesetz*] and instruction [*Weisung*], not imposed externally but inscribed internally. While its genuine given-ness conditions the "latency" of the Giver, this latency cannot be complete: the Giver's gift is recognizable in the inner light that comes from man's "having been set on a path" and equipped with "instruction". This light will shine most brightly where the one so endowed is enabled to see himself in the primal radiance of the absolute gift: in the God whose nature, from all eternity, is to give himself to the eternal Son, the prototype of creation. It will not be totally obscured, however, in the case of a possessor of finite freedom who finds himself, to his own bewilderment, in a "given" world and who subsequently discovers that there is nothing and no one in this world who has not had the same experience of the world's baffling "givenness".[1] There are witnesses enough in the extra-biblical world testifying to this fundamental experience; its three dimensions will be unfolded in what follows. As far as possible we shall do this in the same abstract and ideal sphere as before, prescinding from man's concrete, bodily constitution (with which we will deal later) and from the dramatic situations that arise where freedoms encounter one another.

In the anteroom where we find ourselves for the present, we can distinguish three aspects of the situation of finite freedom. The first is where it is aware that its own self is a "given"; the second is where it is illuminated by the insight that this is something that can only occur within infinite freedom (and that, willingly or unwillingly, it is profoundly involved with the latter); and the third aspect emerges where it realizes that—in the context of infinite freedom—it must come to a decision about itself: it must choose its own "idea".

a. Self as Gift

The man endowed with consciousness and freedom, if the light of being is not totally obscured in him, will experience the very fact that he exists as a good, as something that is given to him

---

[1] Cf. *Herrlichkeit* III/1, part 2, 2d ed. (Einsiedeln: Johannes Verlag, 1975), 943–57 (*The Glory of the Lord*, V: *The Realm of Metaphysics in the Modern Age*).

without any merit or contribution on his part. From time to time other values can seem higher, for example, a value of the community to which he belongs or the value of the Absolute to which he accords precedence or the value of nonbeing, when his own existence no longer seems worth living. But in awakening to its own being and freedom, consciousness utters an involuntary, limitless Yes to the reality it has been given. The man who utters this Yes knows that he himself has been affirmed from some quarter: someone has bestowed on him the Yes of being. To be, really to *be*, is precious.

We have to feel our way back; we have to overcome a certain blindness to the primal value of being. This sick blindness is called Positivism, and it arises from regarding reality as raising no questions, being "just there"—for the phrase "the given" already says too much, since there is no one who "gives". In fact the only question that arises is: "What can we do with this material?" When men are blind to the further question, it signifies the death of philosophy and even more the death of theology. For philosophy begins with the astonished realization that I am this particular individual in being and goes on to see all other existent entities together with me in being; that is, it begins with the sense of wonder that, astonishingly, I am "gifted", the recipient of gifts. As for theology, born of the knowledge that eternal freedom eternally gives itself away and thus generates the Son, it begins when, addressed as "thou", I hearken to the One who thus addresses me.

"This day I have begotten you", says the Father to the Son. This day I have created you, says eternal freedom to finite freedom. The fact that no human "I" can awaken to itself unless it is called "thou" by some other "I"[2] is only the prelude, within the parameters of the world, to what is meant here. For in and through the human "I" there is manifested an Absolute "I", who has from eternity generated an equally Absolute "Thou" and, in the Holy Spirit, is One God with him. It is precisely this process of generation, this giving and receiving of self, and this oneness of both in the Holy Spirit that causes the absolute

[2] Cf. "Bewegung zu Gott" in *Spiritus Creator*, *Skizzen zur Theologie* III (1967), 13–50.

preciousness—we call it *holiness*—of Absolute Being to shine
forth in its limitless self-affirmation and freedom. To himself,
God is never "just there" in the Positivist sense: rather, he is
always the most "improbable" miracle in that the utter self-
surrender of the Father-Origin truly generates the coeternal Son
and that the encounter and union of both truly cause the one
Spirit, the hypostasis of all that is meant by "gift", to proceed
from both.

Only on the basis of this miracle can finite freedom, endowed
with the gift of self, know itself to be addressed as a "thou" and
so designate itself an "I" vis-à-vis the Giver. Indeed, it must
draw the appropriate conclusion from being thus addressed and
go on to call infinite freedom "Thou". This is an astounding
word to use here, for God in himself is no one else's "other": he
is the All-embracing One (*Non-aliud*). Left to itself, in the face of
the Ground that calls into being and upholds all things, the finite
could at most *worship* this overall reality and *extol* it as the
Ultimately Precious in its unconditioned self-affirmation. It can
only dare to call it "Thou" if, in doing so, it is answering to a
"thou" that comes addressed to itself from the inner nature of
the Absolute—from the divine Trinity.[3] The two things affect
each other: I only appreciate fully that God is my "highest
good" when I learn (in the Son) that I am a "good" to him,
affirmed by him; this is what guarantees my being and my
freedom. And it is only when I learn that I represent a "good"
and a "thou" to God that I can fully trust in the imparted gift of
being and freedom and so, affirmed from and by eternity, really
affirm myself too.

In this way worship is no longer threatened with dissolution
as a result of the finite being swallowed up in the infinite;
furthermore, the hymn of praise that celebrates our participation in Being does not need to shrink to a mere awareness of
distance between the finite and the infinite. The trinitarian

---

[3] In the extra-biblical world, nations can only address their gods as "thou" on
the basis of a mythical assumption, namely, that these gods are limited (by one
another or by the world). Where mythical religion passes over into philosophy,
either the divinity is no longer addressed as "thou" at all (Plato) or this manner
of address becomes an essentially extrinsic form borrowed from mythical
religion, e.g., as in Cleanthes' hymn to Zeus.

initiative in creation preserves us from both (pantheistic) mysticism and (formalistic) ritualism. The creature's metaphysical and theological locus is the diastasis of the divine "Persons" in the unity of the divine nature. Here the real difference between the creature and God no longer needs to occasion any anxiety in the former, because ultimately it is grounded in the real difference between the divine hypostases, in virtue of which God can be the Most Worthy and Most Holy One. Only the mystery of the Trinity keeps the world from two misinterpretations: namely, either assuming its existence to be a brute fact devoid of value, only yielding material for men to manipulate; or regarding its existence as an equally valueless nonfact since, it is alleged, outside the Absolute nothing can really be given, imparted and entrusted to man. In the mystery of the Trinity, the creature can affirm itself as an act of thanksgiving to God. Receiving itself, freely identifying with itself—and here the gift of God separates itself from God as the fruit separates itself from the tree—it really performs the perfect act of thanksgiving, accepting precisely what God wishes to give.

"How couldst Thou have given Thyself to me", prays Nicholas Cusanus,

> if Thou hadst not given me to myself before? When I am at peace in the stillness of contemplation, Thou, O Lord, repliest in my innermost heart: Be thou thine, then I am thine. O Lord, Thou Fragrance of all sweetness, Thou hast given me the gift of freedom so that, according to my own volition, I may belong to myself. Otherwise Thou wouldst have overpowered my freedom, since Thou canst not be mine unless I too am mine. And since Thou hast entrusted this to my freedom, Thou dost not compel me, but waitest for me to choose to belong to myself.

Cusanus is well aware that God's self-giving remains entirely free: "No one has access to Thee, for Thou art unapproachable; no one will be able to grasp Thee unless Thou first give Thyself to me."[4]

Bérulle puts it no differently: "If God gives us life, his gift includes all other natural gifts: he gives us the world and our

---

[4] *De Vis. Dei* c 7 (quoted in H. de Lubac, *Pic de la Mirandole* [Paris: Aubier, 1974], 335).

own selves." Our deepest life, however, God gives us in his Son,

so that we are doubly indebted to God: for life, on the basis of which we owe the world and ourselves to him, and for Jesus, who is a second world and a second "we". . . . For just as God, in giving us life, gives us the world and our selves, so, in giving us Jesus as the Life, he once again gives us as a gift to ourselves, for without this Life we would have been lost.[5]

Fénelon, too, puts it very clearly:

There was nothing in me prior to his gift that could have served as a vessel for it. The first of his gifts, laying the foundation for all the others, was what I call my "I". God gave me this "I"; I owe him not only all I possess but all that I am. O unspeakable gift, so quickly expressed in our poor languages but which the human spirit can never understand in all its depth! The God who created me has given me to myself; the "I" which I so love is nothing but a gift of his goodness. . . . Without it I would not be myself; without God I would have neither the "I" to love nor love with which to love it nor the will to love it nor the thinking by which I know myself. All is gift; the one who receives these gifts is in the first place himself a gift, given and received.[6]

Or Laberthonnière: "God gives us to ourselves, so much so that we really *are*, albeit only through him; and we really *act*, even if only through him."[7] Or Gabriel Marcel: "All is gift. He who receives the gift is the first gift."[8]

It is also clear that in the Thomist understanding of the ontological difference, according to which the finite entity is given a participation in the nonfinite (nonsubsistent) act of

[5] *Oeuvres de piété* 31, no. 2–3, ed. princeps (1644) II, 799–800.

[6] *Lettres sur divers sujets de métaphysique et de religion* I, c. 4, no. 1 (*Oeuvres spirituelles* I [1810], 274).

[7] Letter to Enrico Castelli, October 23, 1930, in E. *Castelli, In morte di Laberthonnière*, Archivio di filosofia (Padua, 1932), 78. Cf. Laberthonnière, *Critique du laïcisme* (1948), 169: ". . . en nous prenant pour des êtres vraiment distincts, réellement existant en soi, (en reconnaissant) que pour exister ainsi nous avons été donnés nous-mêmes à nous-mêmes par ce que j'appelle un don véritable." Cf. also *Le Réalisme chrétien et l'idéalisme grec* (1904), 101.

[8] *Le Mystère de l'être* II (1951), 174. Quoted by Henri de Lubac, *Le Mystère du surnaturel* (Aubier, 1965), 108.

being, there is no question of the entity having some kind of preexistence in which this participation is granted. The entity is just as much a gift as its reality; this particular "I" with its distinctive qualities receives its entire self from the hands of infinite freedom, and the hallmark by which it can recognize that it is a gift is the ontological difference that operates in it. But the "I" cannot regard its nature [Wesen] as inferior to its being [Sein], for the latter permeates the nature, right down to its most unremarkable attributes. Thus the core of the difference remains the simple fact of its "being there" [Vorfindlichkeit], its being admitted to reality; or, in theological terms, the gift-character of existence, ontologically implying gratitude and calling for it as a free act.

What is given to me is not just any subjectivity, inter-changeable with any other, but a subjectivity which, in order that it can communicate itself, is itself incommunicable. This implies—provided that I accept the fact that I am addressed as a particular "thou", not to be confused with any other—that my act of gratitude will not be addressed to an anonymous "Ab-solute Good": that is, it is more than the mere worship of some-thing all-embracing and the praise of something universally real. Since I have been chosen to be a unique person, it follows inevitably that I must address infinite freedom as "Thou", however excessive such language may seem. It becomes more intelligible when we learn that God has always expressed himself (Heb 1:3) in his eternal Word. The "word" (in whatever form) does not remain an inadequate tool at a level inferior to ineffable Being, as all non-Christian mysticism thinks. True, there is an abiding tension between the "word" as a mere reassurance and the fully realized "incarnate" Word; and our gratitude for the gift of ourselves must tend toward fashioning our whole existence into a word of thanksgiving. It will remain a lifelong task; but that does not mean that it should be abandoned as impossible.

At this profound ontological level, gratitude for the gift of self means "owing oneself". Finite freedom, genuinely set free and equipped with its own sphere of freedom, cannot set off in just any direction but must pursue the path of self-realization, that is, toward absolute freedom. Its coming forth (egressus) from its origin is the beginning of its return (regressus) there.

And, as we have seen, this is not heteronomy but the only possible way in which finite freedom can imitate the perfect identity between divine freedom and divine being. This identity —the absolute affirmation of the absolutely Good or Holy—is its watermark, in virtue of which it *is* freedom. The watermark starts to become visible when finite freedom affirms itself, as a result of being addressed as "thou"; it can only be perfected when it has become "thou" in God's sight in its fully divine, absolute manner, when it has become identical with the "idea" reserved for the finite "thou" within the infinite "Thou", within the eternal Word and Son. When Paul says that God's elect are "predestined to be conformed to the image of his Son" (Rom 8:29), this is also mankind's being fashioned "after the image of its creator" (Col 3:10), just as Adam was formed in the image and likeness of God. But in New Testament terms, this "image of the Creator" is, in fact, the Son (Col 1:15), the "reflection of his glory" (Heb 1:3), into whose "image" we are to be "changed" by his Spirit (2 Cor 3:18). The exemplary prototype of finite freedom "in Christ" is that "place" where we participate in his eternal Sonship (Eph 1:5; Rom 8:17) as "sons": there each of us is a unique "thou" in the eternal "Thou". Moreover we can add, by way of anticipation, that this ultimate identity at the end of time cannot entail any alienation of man from himself, because in the Incarnation the eternal Word himself becomes earthly and because his "Mystical Body", the Church, comes into being in that exemplary identity which bridges the cosmic distinction between heaven and earth.

We render thanks for our selves, therefore, by responding, giving an answering word [*Ant-Wort*], to the fact that we have been called "thou". We do this by progressively incarnating the word of thanks in our lives. This in turn is the progressive self-realization of finite freedom within the context of infinite freedom. More precisely, it is the realization, by the finite "copy" [*Abbild*] of the definitive model [*Vorbild*] exhibited by the infinite prototype [*Urbild*]; in this way finite freedom can truly participate in infinite freedom.

b. Answered Prayer

Finite freedom can only fulfill itself within the realm of infinite freedom. If this realm is free, it follows that finite freedom has no claim on it. If and when this realm is open to finite freedom, it is pure grace. Furthermore, when we journey in this realm, we do not do so according to laws laid down once and for all: we are freely accompanied on our journeying—and this again is an aspect of grace. Thus it is that prayer, which up to now was worship, praise and thanksgiving, necessarily acquires the character of intercession. God's antecedent, fundamental pledge of faithfulness, his pledge to accompany us, renders this more (not less) necessary. For God's pledge is also a mode of free, personal commitment to the finite "thou"; it cannot be recast as some kind of impersonally valid natural law.

Once again we are excluding all the implications for petitionary prayer that arise in the concrete modes of (fallen and redeemed) existence. We are keeping to the most universal laws that operate between the Infinite and the finite. In concrete reality the most basic prayer will be that I may be accompanied out of my alienation, helped out of the masks of the empirical "I" behind which my true "I"—unknown even to me myself—remains hidden. "No human thought can fathom our inner self. This human being—it is not I—is something alien to me, something I must newly take upon myself each day, like a cross. It is a role I must play until the performance is ended. . . ."9 We need to be stripped of the illusions that fascinate us so that we can see the path and proceed along it: this path is called the accompanying will of God. Each of us is called to walk along a specially designed personal path toward identity with the exemplary prototype; we do this in freedom, simply asking for the liberating freedom (*gratia liberatrix*) that we cannot attain by our own efforts.

For the moment, however, let us leave to one side the situation in which finite freedom has become entrapped; let us take it in its pure state, in its own realm, created and endowed with freedom. Even in this state it is dependent on God; even in its nondivine,

9 Karl Heim, "Das Gebet als philosophisches Problem" (1925) in *Glaube und Leben* (Berlin: Furche, 1928), 510–38. This quotation: 513, 512.

material reality it has certain "claims" on him. And insofar as every individual endowed with freedom has his own, personal path disclosed to him, this path will look different in God, depending on whether a man walks along it or refuses to, pursues it eagerly or lethargically, directly or by a roundabout route. Through prayer—expressly formulated or inarticulate—a man can request that he or others may be accompanied along life's path. The man who does not pray will not be thus accompanied.

Once again we touch on the question of God's mutability, which seems to follow if God takes seriously finite freedom's relationship with him. This can be countered by observing that the eternal Creator, since all time is present to him and since he is the First Cause, has antecedent knowledge of all the possibilities and decisions of his creature and so guides Providence that all secondary causes are always taken account of.[10] We should add, as we did above, that God's infinite freedom, in itself, has infinite ways at its disposal; God has many ways of causing all things to work for good for those who love him. He does not do this by redesigning his world order in the wake of the decisions of finite freedom[11] but by being able to enfold all the errant wanderings of the finite in his ever-richer infinity: "Our striving, all our toilsome day / In God the Lord is rest for aye."

---

[10] Origen was the first to produce a philosophical reconciliation of eternal and temporal freedom. It has been repeated countless times ever since: "If we regard free will as established, continually inclining to virtue or vice, to what conflicts with duty, the future constitution of free will, like everything else, is necessarily known by God even before it comes into being—'ever since the creation and foundation of the world'. And God, in his prior counsel, according to his foreknowledge of each (future) free-will act, has assessed the merit of every motion on its part and determined what Providence will accord to it; furthermore he has determined what will happen to it according to the interplay of future things. Note, however, that God's foreknowledge is not the cause of all the things which, in the future, will result from free will. . . . If every man's free will is recognized by God, it follows that God has already taken care that Providence shall reward every one according to what he deserves and that it has already been ascertained what, in faith, this or that man could pray for. . . ." *De Oratione* 6, 3–4. Cf. Thomas, *S. Th.* I, 23, a 8; I, 115, a 6; II, IIae, 83, a 2; Meister Eckhart, "Von abgescheidenheit", ed. Quint, *Deutsche Werke* V, 416.

[11] Cf. *Theo-Drama* I, 181f.

We are endeavoring to think within the context of a biblical theology that both contains and launches the philosophical dimension, encountering extra-biblical philosophy and its antecedent mythical imagery, acknowledging and preserving what is valid in it. This becomes particularly relevant in the case of petitionary prayer. At the level of mythical imagery, thought has no difficulty in addressing prayers of intercession, in an "earthy naïveté" (as Friedrich Heiler says), to the divinity; according to its anthropomorphic ideas of God, it is beyond question that the divinity, like a king, can listen to and grant the requests of subjects. As yet, the philosophical problem of God's immutability has not blighted this straightforward boldness with its mildew. When philosophy begins to reflect, this naïveté slowly and gradually retreats in the face of a critique which, logically, can only end in two attitudes: either prayer becomes a way of subjectively attuning oneself to what is, after all, good —that is, beneath its outward dialogue form it is actually a monologue on the part of the ethical subject; or it disappears entirely because the "exemplary identity" between man and his "idea" has become, in God, a pure identity in which there is no longer any other subject to be addressed but man. On the way to this conclusion there can be transitional forms; whereas in the mythical period (to say nothing of magic) the divinity can be entreated for anything, gradually restrictions are introduced: only what is good may be asked for, that is, that which the divinity is already prepared to grant, and with which, in fact, it is exclusively concerned.[12] But if God gives what is good in any case, it seems superfluous to ask him for it; instead one can do

[12] Socrates (in Xenophon's *Memorabilia* I, 3, 2) and Xenophon himself (*Frag. Diels* I, 15f.); Pythagoras (who warned against presenting concrete wishes: *Diod. Sicul.* X, 9, 8). Thus Maximus of Tyros wrote in his *"Ei dei euchestai"* ("Whether one should pray"); he lists the proper matters for prayer: "Virtue for the soul, tranquility of life, blameless conduct, a hopeful death, and the wondrous gifts given by the gods" (*Diss.* XI, 8). Apollonius of Tyana sums it up in this formula: "O gods, give me what is fitting", what is good (Philostratus, *Vita Ap. Tyan.* IV, 13). Many other references are given in Henricus Schmidt, *Veteres philosophi quomodo iudicaverint de precibus* (Rel. gesch. Vers. u. Vorarb. 4 [Giessen, 1907], 1–74), which documents philosophy's gradual distancing from the naïve prayer of the people and from the public cult. An important witness to this transition is the pseudo-Platonic dialogue *Alcibiades* II (Schmidt 15ff.).

one of two things: either allow the request to pass over into a contemplation of God's goodness[13] or replace it with ethical action.[14] The aspect of petition itself dissolves in the Stoic attitude of resignation to the "will" of fate or of "providence",[15] in the Spinozist conviction that "the laws and rules of nature are God's genuine decrees"[16] and in Kant's pedagogical recommendation that children should be taught that, in petitionary prayer, it is "simply a case of stimulating the mind to a manner of life that is well-pleasing to God; the mode of speech employed is only a vehicle for the imagination."[17] "It is not God who changes," says Rousseau, "but we change by lifting ourselves up to him. Everything we ask from him, as we ought, we ourselves give; . . . we enhance our strength by acknowledging our weakness";[18] "the most perfect prayer is total resignation to what God's will may appoint. 'Not what I will, but what Thou wilt.' 'Thy will be done.' Every other prayer is superfluous and contradicts the latter."[19]

Here we have the philosophical prayer quoting Christ's words in order to counter his explicit exhortation to petitionary prayer. This constitutes a provocation to theology. Again, Friedrich Heiler is right when he joins the primitive, prephilosophical prayer of petition together with Christian prayer in opposition to the philosophical view. But he is hardly correct to regard both of them as a homogeneous, "irrational" phenomenon over against the rationality of reason and to set them, as "life", against "abstract thought".[20] The Christian doctrine of prayer

[13] As, essentially, in the Stoics. In part this contemplation still appears in the garb of petitionary prayer (Cleanthes, *Vet. St. Frag.*, 527) or expressions of admiration (Epictetus I, 16, III, 5, 10).

[14] The various gradations of "philosophical prayer" are well described and illustrated in Friedrich Heiler, *Das Gebet*, 4th ed. (1921) [*Prayer* (Oxford, 1932)].

[15] Seneca: "Cease hoping that the gods' arrangement of destiny can be changed by prayer" (*Nat. quaest.* II, 35ff.).

[16] Spinoza, *Tractatus theologico-politicus*, chap. 6 (Gebhardt III, 83).

[17] *Religion innerhalb*, part 4, Weischedel IV, 874. On Kant's ambivalent stance, cf. Fernand Ménégoz, *Le Problème de la prière*, 2d ed. (Paris: Alcan, 1932), 25ff.

[18] *La Nouvelle Héloïse* VI, 7.

[19] *Lettres de la montagne* I, 3.

[20] *Das Gebet* (see n. 14 above), 15.

cannot be split into two contradictory parts, where the first, "philosophical" part is as convinced of God's immutability as are Spinoza, Kant and Rousseau, and the second, "popular" part (also the part of the "religious genius") takes no account of this insight and holds converse with a changeable God. The "God of the philosophers", in his absoluteness, tends to ossify into a concept; his immutability (which we must maintain) can only be combined with eternal, inner vitality if, with Christianity, we dare to take the step forward toward the mystery of the Trinity.

The trinitarian God, and he alone, never changes into mere "fate" but accompanies his creature in such a vital manner that, in doing so, he can also attract and call him to a more intimate fellowship, encourage him to bolder action, entice him to play a unique role. Again, diverse possibilities can lead to the same goal; different aspects of the divine justice–mercy can correspond to the same divine truth, and finite freedom can be permitted, in asking for the one, to exclude the other. Anselm's prayers are magnificent examples of this boldness in praying to God: at the crossroads of various possibilities, he insistently beseeches God for a specific answer to prayer summoning God, as it were, to be consistent, secure in the knowledge that, whatever happens, it will be God's will, and it will be for the best.[21]

Our task now is to elucidate this on the basis of the Trinity's self-disclosure to us, that is, on the basis of Jesus' prayer of petition in the Gospels. Initially, displaying his absolute certainty that his prayer will be answered, he stands before us as someone utterly unique and inimitable; but then, unexpectedly, he opens himself to us and enfolds us in an analogous certainty that our prayer will be answered. At this point, therefore, we are equally elevated above the primitive, mythical understanding of prayer as well as the merely philosophical.

Where Jesus is concerned, there is an interplay of apparently irreconcilable aspects. On the one hand, he is unlimitedly available to the Father's will, "the will of him who sent me"

---

[21] *The Prayers and Meditations of Saint Anselm* (London: Penguin, 1973).

(Jn 6:38), even to preferring the Father's will to his own, which, in extreme fear and anguish, struggles to resist the former. On the other hand, there is Jesus' absolute certainty that the Father "hears him always", for which he publicly expresses his gratitude (Jn 11:41). And particularly in his last hour, as he goes obediently to his death, he is able to utter his unmistakable "Father, I desire" (Jn 17:24). This announcement of the Son's desire seems to conflict with the perfect fulfilling of the Father's will, although (in the "economic" Trinity) the former is decidedly dependent on the latter. In order to resolve the apparent contradiction, we must remember that the Son's obedience is in each instance the a priori of his human existence and that emptying himself of "the form of God" is the expression both of his eternal filial obedience to the Father and of his own eternal will. This eternal will of his—the same as the Father's will—displays its particular filial content in the midst of the "economic" fulfillment of the Father's will, at the point where the implications of the Son's obedience for believers are brought out (as in Jn 17:24) or where a sign is to be given, sealing Jesus' being delivered up to death as his glorification (Jn 11:4, 40). It clearly shows itself, however, to be the filial will: it keeps to the plan of salvation drawn up by the Trinity. Thus, at his arrest, (the Synoptic) Jesus says: "Do you think that I cannot appeal to my Father, and he will at once send me more than twelve legions of angels? But how then should the scriptures be fulfilled?" (Mt 26:53f.). But, in Jesus' mind, this "can" is just as unreal as that he "could" have consented to Satan's temptations in the wilderness. What could be the case *"de potentia absoluta" filii* is impossible *"de potentia trinitaria"*: that the Son should overstep the bounds of his mission. But whereas, in his public life, the field of Jesus' mission is totally clear and radiant, in his suffering its edges are necessarily unclear. Thus in Mark 14:36 he can pray: "Father, all things are possible to thee; remove this cup from me; yet not what I will, but what thou wilt." His vision is darkened and his fear gains the upper hand (because he is loading upon himself the blindness and horror of sin), yet, for him, the realm of the Father's freedom remains wide open. Beyond his entreaty lies the certainty that the Father's will must be fulfilled.

DRAMATIS PERSONAE

Thus Matthew puts the second and third prayers on the Mount
of Olives in a negative form: "My Father, if this *cannot* pass
unless I drink it, thy will be done" (26:42).

However, what is crucial in all this is that, in spite of his
abiding certainty that his prayers are answered, Jesus never
dispenses with petitionary prayer. His life is not governed by
some divine Fate, working itself out impersonally and necessarily
through his own destiny, but by the infinite tenderness of his
"Daddy" ("Abba"); in yearning and love the Son stretches out
his hands to embrace the latter's wishes, "in childlike receptivity
to his will and his gifts".[22] The Son's trinitarian relationship
becomes transparent in his creaturely attitude: this prevents the
attitude of living prayer from becoming petrified by philosophical
reflection. Even when Jesus is certain in advance of being heard
(for example, in the case of miracles or in the prayer for Peter in
Luke 22:32), he does not omit the upward glance to his Father
or thanksgiving (Mk 7:34; 8:6 par). In John, he explicitly states
that he is certain of being heard (11:41f.; cf. 12:30); but it
emerges just as clearly in the Synoptics. Now, however, it
comes triumphantly out into the open: "I will pray the Father"
(14:16), and what he asks for, namely, the Spirit, will infallibly
be given to his disciples. Even when Jesus is "troubled" in the
Temple (which parallels his anguish on the Mount of Olives)
and wonders whether he should pray the Father to be delivered
"from this hour", his prayer immediately expands to its full
scope: "Father, glorify thy name" (12:28).

This establishes the pattern—which explodes all our pre-
conceptions—according to which the Christian can appear before God with his petition: this pattern is the Son and the Son's
mind (as John explicitly says), the attitude of the perfectly

[22] Armin Dietzel, *Die Gründe der Erhörungsgewissheit nach den Schriften des
Neuen Testaments* (Diss., Mainz, 1955): this predominantly Protestant study
includes a very full bibliography. On the answering of prayer in John, cf. the
commentary by R. Schnackenburg (III, 82 [London, Burns and Oates]). Liselotte
Ruppoldt, *Die theologische Grundlage des Bittgebetes im Neuen Testament in religions-
geschichtlicher Beleuchtung* (Diss., Leipzig, 1953), is too ready to find magical
elements in the NT. But she does see clearly that God can only answer prayer
within the context of his saving will (68); that prayer imposes an ethical
obligation on the person praying (72); and that all answering of prayer takes
place within the grace of Sonship mediated by Christ (76).

obedient One. And precisely in this obedience he feels inspired
to ask the Father for what lies in the depths of his will, for the
extension (as yet, perhaps, invisible) of his will. Prayer to the
Father "in the name of Jesus" will infallibly be heard (Jn 15:16;
16:23, 24), and if Jesus' attitude, his "words", are perfectly
"in" the person praying, his mediation will have done its work
(Jn 15:7; 16:26). And insofar as the Son, at the end of his journey
of obedience from the Father, will be equipped with the fullness
of divine power that has been "laid up" in the "economic"
Trinity, he will hear the prayer made "in his name" just as
infallibly as the Father (Jn 14:13, 14). As we have seen, in the
prayer on the Mount of Olives—in terms of the economy of the
Trinity—Jesus' human will could encounter a restriction in the
Father's will; he acknowledges this restriction in the hypothetical
formulation "if it be possible", submitting to it in advance. As
far as his will of absolute obedience is concerned, in which he
transcends his own human will, no restriction exists. The person who has a lively faith may experience something analogous:
he may have permission to penetrate the depths of the will of
God and "wrest from him" things which a less committed
person would not receive; but he may also come up against a
limit (of which man cannot have prior knowledge) where, for
the sake of a more all-embracing good, some particular good
cannot be granted. For the person who prays in faith, however,
this limit no more implies rejection or a refusal to answer than it
does in the Son's case. In fact, in a way that is as yet hidden from
him, the believer's most basic will *is* being heard, namely, that
God's will shall be done on earth as in heaven: that saving will
which, in the Passion, is carried out precisely through the
severity of the Son's apparent abandonment.

It is on the basis of the Johannine prayer "in the name", that
is, in the spirit and obedience of Jesus, a prayer which is
infallibly answered, that the (in part) paradoxical utterances of
the Synoptics are to be interpreted. God expects man to ask him;
this is an integral part of God's respect for the freedom and
responsibility of his spiritual creature. And it belongs to his
covenant faithfulness to hear and answer the prayers made to
him insofar as they are presented in the spirit of the Son, who
embodies the Covenant between God and man. The constancy,

even "importunity", in petitionary prayer expected of man (Lk 11:5–8; 18:2–7) can be interpreted as a way of testing his faith—a feature characteristic of the Covenant. The "good gifts" for which, in the spirit of the Covenant, man asks and which he infallibly receives (Mt 7:7–11) are (in Luke) nothing other than the "Holy Spirit" of God, and this the heavenly Father cannot refuse his beseeching children (Lk 11:10–13). If they are really his children, that is, belonging to his Covenant, they are already supported in prayer by the Holy Spirit who prays within them (Rom 8:15, 26f.); this fact, that they do not appear before God simply on their own merits but as people who are already accepted and loved, because they belong to the Covenant, is an essential constituent of faith. Thus, in Mark, Jesus says: "I tell you therefore: everything you ask and pray for, believe that you have it already, and it will be yours" (Mk 11:24 JB). (Even a sinner who lacks sanctifying grace and who addresses a genuine prayer to God for reconciliation cannot do so without the help and grace of the Holy Spirit.) In this sense it is always God who prays to God, along with finite freedom. And the faith that (as is promised) can move mountains, provided it does not doubt (Mk 11:23), is "faith in God" (*pistis theou*), which means man's unconditional covenant trust in God's truthfulness—and the eliciting of this trust in man's heart by the gracious faithfulness of God himself. The same apparent circle, which is nothing but the closed circle of the Covenant relationship, shows itself again in the Lord's Prayer: "Forgive us our debts, as we also have forgiven our debtors"—and Matthew spells it out for us: "For if you forgive men their trespasses, your heavenly Father also will forgive you; but if you do not forgive men their trespasses, neither will your Father forgive your trespasses" (Mt 7:12, 14f.; cf. 5:23f.). In the Lord's Prayer, petition seems to come first, and forgiving others seems to come second, inherent in the former; in Matthew's commentary, however, forgiving others is presented as a precondition for God's forgiveness. Again, everything is seen within the context of the Covenant: man can forgive because he lives in an attitude communicated to him by the God who forgives; this by no means dispenses him from the obligation continually to ask God for the essential gift of covenant grace. In New Testament terms, the one who asks for forgiveness is Christ's brother; as such, he is a person who sees Christ in his brothers and forgives them "as God in Christ forgave you" (Eph 4:32); he can only be heard by the Father if he appears before him bearing the mark of Christ. So the first, fundamental petitions of the Lord's Prayer—for the Name to be glorified, for the coming of the kingdom, the implementing of God's will—can only be presented by those who ask in the name of Jesus and who endeavor to follow him (cf. Lk 11:1ff.). Jesus himself initiates his disciples into the proper attitude of prayer and living: it must not be hypocritical and self-righteous (Lk 18:9–14), pagan and unbelieving (cf. 1 Kings 18): it must be vigilant (Lk 21:36) and, above all, full of confidence in faith. Prayer and bearing fruit are complementary (Jn 15:16). The circle of petitionary prayer and life—according to the teaching of the First Letter of John (3:21; 5:14ff.)—or the circle of request and thanksgiving—as often in Paul (1 Th 1:2ff.; 3:9ff.; Rom 1:10; Phil 1:4–9; Philemon 4–6; Eph 1:16ff.)—is characterized by a trinitarian certainty that prayer is answered. Paul is just as much aware of the trinitarian form of Christian prayer as John.[23] The presupposed unity of prayer and life is once more expressed in Jesus' twofold promise: "If two of you agree on earth about anything you ask, it will be done for you by my Father in heaven. For where two or three are gathered in my name, there am I in the midst of them" (Mt 18:19f.). The phrase "in my name" brings us back to what we said about John: here, too, the (Church's) unity—which is fundamentally *communio* in the Holy Spirit—is pronounced to be the realization of the mind of Christ in the assembly; this is what guarantees that its prayer will be answered.[24] The themes of answered prayer in the Old Covenant, arising out of the covenant relationship (leading to a conditional certainty that prayer is answered), are developed in the New Covenant on the basis of the Covenant perfected

[23] Cf. Rom 8:15; Gal 4:6. Hermann Kuhaupt, *"Abba, Vater", Christliche Lehre vom Gebet* (Freiburg, 1948), 169; G. Ebeling, *Vom Gebet* (Siebenstern Taschenbuch), 89.

[24] On this whole issue, cf. José Caba, "La oración de petición" in *Analecta biblica* (Rome, 1974). Hans Schaller, "Das Bittgebet—ein Testfall des Glaubens" in *Geist und Leben* (1976), 191–202. Cf. Wilhelm Gessel, *Die Theologie des Gebetes nach "De Oratione" von Origenes* (Paderborn, 1975).

in Christ; all this participates expressly in the trinitarian *circum-incessio*.

There is no way that finite freedom can realistically be understood to "influence" infinite freedom except in the context of the realization of the historical Covenant relationship, where ultimately God's trinitarian mystery is revealed. Otherwise we are stuck in the cul-de-sac of an either/or: either the Absolute is rigidly immutable—in which case finite freedom can pray for nothing but conformity with the infinite Will, and prayer merely has the psychological effect of promoting such conformity—or else God is "changeable" and thus, from our vantage point, finite and mythological.

c. The Form of Life: Being Born of God

Once the decision to create a world has been made in eternity, the infinite Will no longer has that sublime indifference to the finite which philosophy is bound to propose wherever the idea of a free creation cannot come to fruition. In the latter case, the finite will's ideal can only be to cast off its finitude, that is, its particularity, in order, by renouncing all will, to become assimilated to this infinite indifference. But if God wills the finite as such, it follows that he also has a particular will for each finite subject. Not as if God's will could be parcelled out among the plurality of creatures; not only does his act as such, since it is divine, remain indivisible: his goal, too, embraces in unity the plurality of the world (which is created for the sake of this very unity). Once again we recall that the "first-born of all creation" in whom "all things were created" (Col 1:15) is the "principle" (*archē* 1:18) of all things, in whom "all things hold together" (*ta panta en autōi synestēken*).

If we call the incarnate Son God's primal Idea [*Uridee*] in creating the universe, since all things were created "for him", and hence "in him" and "through him" (Col 1:16), this all-embracing primal Idea contains the (primal) ideas of the individual creatures. In God's view, these individual creatures are and should be as they are envisaged and contained in the primal Idea. In the one, exemplary, primal Idea, the incarnate Son, raised from the dead (1:18), all creatures, especially those endowed with freedom, have their own exemplary idea: for "he chose us *in* him before the foundation of the world, that we should be holy and blameless before him. He destined us *in* love to be his sons *through* Jesus Christ, according to the purpose of his will, *to* the praise of his glorious grace" (Eph 1:4ff.). This announces a finality and a corresponding movement toward it: in a threefold "*eis*" (for, to, toward) that has its abiding basis in a twofold "in" and a "through". God wants to accompany the individual along a path that leads through Christ, the "Way", to an indwelling in him, the "Beloved" (Eph 1:6)—which is why Christ is the principle and "head of the Church" (Col 1:18) with her "many members".

Later, in the context of Christology, we shall have to consider what this means for the incarnate Son: not only his Incarnation but also his representative suffering and his Eucharist. For the present we are only concerned with the creature's proper relationship with God, which now appears mediated through the exemplary idea, upheld and kept safe in Christ, of each individual, finite freedom. The question is how finite freedom can succeed in recognizing this, its own "idea", and in taking it as its goal. It is assumed, on the basis of what we have already said, that it is its very own "idea", not an alien one: finite freedom can only fulfill itself in the realm of infinite freedom, and not by using infinite freedom for its own finite aims, but by opening itself up to the self-disclosure of infinite freedom. In Christian terms, it must allow the love of God to work upon it, loving it in return for its own sake. So when infinite love presents the creature with a way (in Christ) of responding to infinite love, it is not up to the creature simply to strive for the prototype of finite freedom thus set forth as its own ideal—for in this way it would never escape from the prison of its own finitude. First and foremost it is infinite love that freely condescends to address the creature and invites it to embrace its own fulfillment.

All the same, the abstract, universal relationship, which does nothing more than situate finite freedom in the context of infinite freedom (which is necessarily nondefinite as far as the former is concerned), is not false: it is only incomplete. Finite freedom, however, is not able of itself to concretize a relationship of this kind: it must accept it as offered and try to fashion it.

Here, too, the philosophical relationship with the Absolute is and remains internal to the theological; here, too, grace perfects and elevates nature. Thus, primarily and radically, finite freedom must succeed in relativizing its finite goals and aspirations insofar as they arise from the center of a finite, empirical "I" or "we". It must allow everything it regards as good to be measured against an ultimate standard that lies on the yonder side of its finitude. It must slip out of its masks, roles and costumes, quit the world's stage on which it is accustomed to act and appear before the sole Master of the world play.[25] He is, in the first place, simply infinite Freedom; what he will decide and do is a priori unknown to us, nor can it be deduced or even guessed from anything in the finite world. Finite freedom must become unmade, must come to have no path of its own, must attain calm composure or indifference: this is the categorical pre-condition if it is to receive a vocation and destiny (going beyond the philosophical relation to the Absolute) from the hands of infinite Will. Man must "first let go of himself, then he will have let go of everything. . . . Then, whatever he still has, wealth or honor or anything at all, he has let everything go".[26] The "idea" presented, as his very own, to the man who has attained this calm composure lies *in* infinite Will, that is, it is nothing created but an aspect of God himself: it was precisely so that it might live according to this idea, without departing from it in any

---

[25] C. S. Lewis describes this unclothing of finitude: "For what I call 'myself' (for all practical, everyday purposes) is also a dramatic construction; memories, glimpses in the shaving-glass, and snatches of the very fallible activity called 'introspection', are the principal ingredients. Normally I call this construction 'me', and the stage set 'the real world'.

"Now the moment of prayer is for me . . . the awareness that this 'real world' and 'real self' are very far from being rock-bottom realities. I cannot, in the flesh, leave the stage, either to go behind the scenes or to take my seat in the pit; but I can remember that these regions exist. And I also remember that my apparent self—this clown or hero or supernumerary—under his grease-paint is a real person with an off-stage life. The dramatic person could not tread the stage unless he concealed a real person. . . . And in prayer this real I struggles to speak, for once, from his real being, and to address, for once, not the other actors, but—what shall I call Him? The Author, for He invented us all? The Producer, for He controls all? Or the Audience, for He watches, and will judge, the performance?" *Letters to Malcolm* (1964, Fontana, 1966), 82–83.

[26] Eckhart, "Reden der Unterweisung" 3, *Dt. Werke* (ed. Quint) V, 194, 507.

way, that the creature was given existence in God.[27] On the other hand, God's "idea", which, with a view to the creation, is the incarnate Son, is a unity in itself; but it works toward a goal, referring the individual created beings to Christ. Indeed, he is the blueprint for their design, even in their pluriformity,[28] yet in such a way that the individual's "idea" has its truth *from* the unity and *for* the unity; thus the individual is called to pursue this unity and also remains defined, in his particularity, through his relationship with it.

The doctrine of the mystical Body of Christ, to which every creature is oriented, in which every creature is incorporated and to which it is attuned—to a greater or lesser extent—presents the solution to the question raised here. If the individual is unmade, indifferent, calmly receptive to the whole of God's will, he does not sink into the "pathless" abyss of Godhead: the Father's infinite will fashions him in and according to his Son; thus he is given a path, which, as "being in Christ" or "Christ's being in him", is totally specific. The *Spiritual Exercises* of Ignatius of Loyola are designed to help us accept this "path": "We shall thus see how we ought to be preparing ourselves to achieve perfection in whatever state of life our Lord God shall grant us to choose" (no. 135). This presupposes that the form of life offered us by God is only a mode of life in Christ, of discipleship of Christ, personal in each case; that is, that it has the same definitive character—embracing man's whole existence—which we see in the call of the disciples in the Gospels. With the disciples, too, in the first place, there is the "philosophical" aspect of leaving everything (including oneself, one's own controlling "I"), then the second, "theological" aspect: each one is incorporated in a special way in the ministry of Christ. First of all, finite freedom is required to commit itself unconditionally to infinite freedom; then the latter inserts it into God's infinite initiative on the world's behalf. And just as, in his Son, God's initiative is final and unconditional, Christian discipleship will be lifelong. As Augustine puts it: *Totum exigit te qui fecit te*, because grace, freely

[27] Maximus the Confessor, *Ambig.* 7 (PG 91, 1080BC).

[28] "Singula igitur propriis sunt creata rationibus . . . (quae) in divina mente continentur", Augustine, *De div. quaest.* 83, q 46 (PL 40, 30). This is already outlined in Plotinus: *Enn.* IV, 7, 1 and 10.

given, can do no other but summon finite freedom to enter into infinite freedom. [29]

In the order characterized by sin and original sin, the opening-up of finite to infinite freedom presupposes that the many forms of ego-entanglement have been broken through; this can only be done as a result of deliberate and perhaps wearying effort. This is the point of the first week of the Exercises of St. Ignatius: its whole aim is to liberate this freedom. It is also the point of Tauler's insistence on self-knowledge, which—equally radically—aims to bring to the light of day the "profound collapse of the subject", man's nothingness, which is not only ontological (man is *natürlich nicht*, "nothing by reason of his nature") but also inimical to God (man is *gebrestlich nicht*, "nothing by reason of his weakness"). [30] The danger, inherent in German mysticism, of taking the creature's ontological nonbeing and emphatically attributing it to the universal Being of God—and Eckhart does not entirely avoid this danger—is lessened in Tauler as a result of

[29] "Non exigo participationem sapientiae meae ab eis quae non feci ad imaginem meam, sed ubi feci, inde exigo, et usum ejus rei postulo, quam donavi." *In Ps 103* s 4, n 2 (PL 37, 1379). In his *Pragmatismus der Geistesgaben* (1835), F. A. Staudenmaier gives a thorough discussion of the eternal "idea" of every personal spirit and man's falling-away from this idea; he can only be reunited with it through the charisma of the Holy Spirit, which refashions him into the eternal Son (175ff.). This charisma is not something imposed on him from outside but something that liberates him so that he may take charge of himself, understand his own "immediately guiding genius", his own "geniality". In order to lay hold of what is eternal in man through things that are temporal, there must be "vows and covenants", without which "nothing great takes place in life". But this does not mean that a man "forfeits freedom" (228). In fact, only thus does he become free, and "the freer, the more you hold fast in unshakable faith" to this vow "and its eternal fulfillment. Where the Spirit of the Lord is, there is freedom; but where this living Spirit dwells, he also unfolds a necessity from within Himself, the highest necessity, because it is a divine necessity; and its ultimate fulfillment consists precisely in the unity of freedom and necessity" (229). This fundamental idea will be developed speculatively in the *Dogmatics* III, sections 10ff.

[30] Alois Haas, *Nim dîn selbes war, Studien zur Lehre von der Selbsterkenntnis bei Meister Eckhart, Johannes Tauler und Heinrich Seuse*, Dokimon 3 (Fribourg, Switzerland, 1971), 94ff.; 121–23. Just as Ignatius encourages the sinner to come to know himself before Christ's Cross, Tauler desires the sinner to perfect his self-annihilation by entering into the kenosis of God in the passion of Christ: *loc. cit.*, 123 and 79—a topic that goes beyond the context under consideration here.

his shift of emphasis. In Ignatius it entirely disappears. All the same, even prescinding from man's sinful state, we must uphold the ontological distinction between the possible models that finite freedom may come up with and the "idea" proposed by infinite freedom. For the definite profile, the life-"idea" which the man who has attained peace receives from God, if he really decides to allow God to make all the decisions where he is concerned, is a divine and hence an infinite profile. Eckhart puts this most clearly, anticipating the goal of the Ignatian Exercises:

> If a man wishes to start a new life or work, he should go to his God and, with great earnestness and complete devotion, beseech him to bring about whatever is best, whatever is most well-pleasing and most worthy of him. Let him not desire and strive for his own will but solely for God's blessed will and nothing else. Then, whatever God sends him, let him accept it directly from God's hand, let him take as what is best for him. . . . Even if, later on, he is attracted to some other path, he should say to himself, "This is the path God has set before you", and he should regard it as the best path for him. He should trust God in this matter and draw all good paths into this one path. . . . For the good which God has imparted to any *one* path can be found in *all* good paths. Thus, in embracing one path we should embrace all good paths, not the particularity of this one path. For a man can only do one thing at a time: he cannot do everything. It must be one thing at a time, and in this one thing he must embrace all things. For if a man wanted to do everything, this and that; if he were to abandon his path and take up another one that seemed much better at the moment, this would indeed produce great instability. So it is that the man who leaves the world and enters an order once and for all can become perfect, more so than the man who goes from one order to another ever can, however holy he might be. . . . Let a man embrace *one* good path and only make sure that it comes from God.[31]

What Eckhart calls a "path" [*Weise*] and Ignatius calls a "life" or "form of life" can be described, in gospel terms, as a charisma or vocation. It is at the heart of Paul's "inner" and "new" man; it is not accidental to the empirical human being but the substantial nature of the person in his earthly manifestation. For its sake a

---

[31] Eckhart, "Reden der Unterweisung" 23 (see n. 26 above), 284–86, 532.

man must "leave everything"; it is the "treasure in heaven" which he must gain; he must "lose his life" for Christ's sake in order to "save it" (Mk 8:35). According to the Gospels, this act, in which man chooses the "idea" offered him by God, is once-for-all; like God's own initiative, it should be undivided (Mt 8:21f.; 10:37); there should be no looking back (Lk 9:62).

However, the "idea" that God offers him and man is to make his own can only be one aspect of the total Idea, which, in the Son (who is to become man), is infinite. Thus it can only come into being at the point at which the Father declares himself in generating the Son. From the point of view of finite freedom, we see an act of total self-surrender to God's eternal, loving will, which chooses us in Christ. From God's point of view, this is the mystery of being "born of God" (Jn 1:13): the creature is adopted into the process whereby the Son comes forth from the Father; thus, in the Holy Spirit, we become "sons and heirs of God, fellow heirs with Christ, provided we suffer with him in order that we may also be glorified with him" (Rom 8:17). This "being born of God" becomes operative, for the individual believer, in that the Son is begotten in man: in the womb of the Virgin Mary, which bears him and brings him into the world, and thence in the womb of the Church, which is both his Body (and his bodily presence in mankind) and his "Bride" (the goal of this bodily presence). Thus it acquires concrete form in baptism-confirmation: Christ (the Church) draws believers into the mystery of being born of God; this represents the first utterance of the Word (and the first breathing of the Spirit), where the world order—freely decided upon—is prefigured in the infinite Idea. Here, even "before the foundation of the world" (Eph 1:4), a particular place is reserved *for me* "in Christ", in whom "the whole fullness of deity dwells bodily" (Col 2:9).

The Fathers of the Church tried to grasp all these aspects in a single view in their teaching on "being born of God".[32] Their concept is essentially theocentric: the eternal Father's heart gives

---

[32] On this topic, cf. the excellently documented study by Hugo Rahner, "Die Gottgeburt. Die Lehre der Kirchenväter von der Geburt Christi in den

birth to the Word and implants this same Word in the hearts of believers through the Church's mediation, so that, as in Mary's heart, it may take shape and come into the world. This process moves in two opposite directions, as it were. On the one hand, we have the Church (with the Virgin Mary as her prototype), the totality of the Logos' coming-to-be in the world, which precedes the "idea" of her individual members and incorporates them (both ideally and really, sacramentally) into herself and into Christ. And, on the other hand, we have the individual, who, born of God (or conceived by Christ) in the gift of baptism, must give evidence of this birth and conception in a life lived according to Christ's pattern, so that he himself may become a fruitful "mother of Christ". Thus the doctrine of the Trinity, Christology and ecclesiology, the teaching on grace and the sacraments and instruction on the Christian life—all are united in a single view, which effortlessly comprehends such apparently diverse acts as baptism and the Ignatian "*electio*".[33] From man's perspective, we seem to have man allowing himself to be refashioned and assimilated to Christ (Rom 8:29; Phil 3:21); from the perspective of the Word of God, what we see is the Word allowing himself to take shape in the totality of his Body (the Church) and in her individual member (the believer). Under the influence of Irenaeus, who sees the Word of God as allowing himself to be "carried" by man and man as "making room" for the Word, Hippolytus arrives at a position where the Logos is being constantly born out of the heart of the Church[34] and—through her—*in* and *out of* the hearts of believers: "Constantly giving birth to the saints, he (the Logos) is constantly

---

Herzen der Gläubigen" in Z.f.kath.Theol. 59 (1935), 333–418, reprinted with slight changes in *Symbole der Kirche, die Ekklesiologie der Väter* (Salzburg: Otto Müller, 1964), 11–87.

[33] Naturally, the individual aspects can also be considered in relative isolation from each other. Thus Maximus the Confessor: "We are born of God in a twofold way: according to the first, those who are thus born are potentially (*dynamei*) given the entire grace of being children of God; according to the second, they are given this grace actually (*kat'energeian*): the person's entire will is refashioned and directed to God." Maximus goes on to show how the Holy Spirit effects this transformation in the believer, since he cannot refashion any will in the likeness of God "against its will" *Quaest. ad Thal.* 6 (PG 90, 280CD).

[34] *Antichr.* 61 (Achelis 41, l. 18ff.; 42, l. 1).

being born by the saints."[35] While this twofold event is ontically rooted in baptism, Origen displays an almost inexhaustible variety of ways of describing the ethical consequences for the Christian life, how the Logos takes shape in the hearts of believers: the Logos-child grows and is brought into the world by integrity, prayer, asceticism, preaching, and so forth. But the unity of this birth "from God" is always kept in mind:

> Blessed is whoever is born of God. The just man is born not simply once; he is born of God in every good work, for in this work God gives birth to the just man. . . . If the Redeemer is continually being born of the Father, in him God also gives birth to you, whenever you manifest the Spirit of sonship.[36]

Thus, at the same time, the soul becomes "the woman who is with child", who "has received the seed of the Word of God".[37] Methodius discourses on the ecclesial and sacramental aspects as well as the personal and ethical:

> It is inadequate to proclaim the Incarnation of the Son of God from the holy Virgin without at the same time confessing that he comes into the Church as into his flesh; for every one of us must acknowledge not only his advent in that holy flesh which grew of the pure Virgin but also his advent in the spirit of each of us.[38]

The formation of the Son in the soul by the Holy Spirit is seen together with the Son's coming forth from the Father,[39] but it is also regarded as the result of the Church as a whole being "with child", producing the mystical Body of Christ in the multiplicity of her members.[40] As the idea of "being born of God" progresses, its various aspects are unfolded, finally arriving at the three great syntheses of Maximus the Confessor, Scotus Erigena and Meister Eckhart, who owes much to the Scot and, through him, to the Byzantine and to Origen.

Certainly, this whole idea, which is originally profoundly

---

[35] *Commentary on Daniel* I, 10, 8 (Bonwetsch 17, l. 16ff.). Further texts in H. Rahner, 350.

[36] *In Jerem.* h 9, 4 (Klostermann 70, l. 11ff.).

[37] *In Ex.* h 10, 3 (Baehrens 248, l. 9). Further texts in H. Rahner, 351–58.

[38] *De Sanguisuga* 8, 2–3 (GCS Bonwetsch 486, l. 19ff.).

[39] *Ibid.*, I, 4–6 (478, l. 6ff.).

[40] *Sympos.* 8, 8 (Bonwetsch 90, l. 6–14), cf. 8, 11 (93, l. 9ff.).

biblical, could be drawn into a Neoplatonic undertow; then the Son would appear as God's single, primal Idea, and thus the entirety of creaturely being would be nothing more than a variety of participations in this sole Idea. The natural "self-being" [*In-sich-Sein*] of beings at the natural level would threaten to merge with their participation in Christ through grace; being created and being born of God would become one single process.[41] All the same, as long as the idea was alive and people spoke uninhibitedly of the Logos being conceived and born in the Church and the believer, there was never any suggestion that God, the Infinite and Immutable, thereby acquired some additional "growth" or "becoming" in the world. When God "takes shape" in the realm of "becoming", it simply means that the realm of "becoming" is made to correspond more and more to his Being, that it is increasingly drawn into this first and all-embracing Idea and becomes the expression of it. The plurality of created things and beings stands in a relation of potentiality to the pluriform unity of Christ, for whose sake they are all created; they are meant to participate in his uniqueness in ways that are ever-new, in order to manifest his fullness. Colossians 1:15–17 makes a clear distinction between this aspect of the "first-born of all creation", in whom, through whom and for whom all things are created according to their natures, and the following: "He is the head of the body, the church" (1:18). The Church does not belong on the side of created beings; she belongs in a different way to the "First-born", the "Image of the invisible God"; she is the organism in whom he imprints himself upon the universe, fashioning it after his own pattern, as "the fullness" of him who, as Ephesians 1:23 says, "fills all in all". The Church, the fullness filled by the fullness of Christ, Christ's "Body", stands in clear contrast to the created universe, which has been "put under his feet" (1:22). We shall return to these relationships in the next volume.

---

[41] A certain inclination toward this monism can be detected in Scotus Erigena and Eckhart, at least in their formulations, although both of them are aware of the distinction between the orders (cf. the former's distinction between *"datum"* and *"donum"*, *The Glory of the Lord* IV, 352).

6. Grace

There is a further topic that has a bearing on the living relationship between infinite and finite freedom, but we can make only brief mention of it here, since it will have to be discussed in connection with the unfolding of the drama. Some reference *must* be made to it, however, because it is indispensable to the full realization of the relationship between the two freedoms; and in fact we have already mentioned it on several occasions. There may even be advantages in not pursuing the topic in too much detail, for it concerns the most delicate and most mysterious of aspects; our words and concepts are better employed in protecting it against misuse rather than in subjecting it to the microscope of worldly reason.

There can be no doubt that the existence of finite freedom presupposes a genuine creation, the gift of freedom on the part of infinite freedom. At this birth, in a certain sense, an umbilical cord is cut; finite freedom now exists "in itself" (it has an "essence", a "nature") and may not be defined simply in terms of relation to infinite freedom. On the other side, the "gift of freedom" remains a gift; as we have seen, the more seriously finite freedom appreciates that it is a gift to itself, that it has been handed over to itself, the more it will be full of thanksgiving as it takes control of itself. Nor will it be so occupied with giving thanks as to forget or neglect fully to realize itself, continuing to act as if the umbilical cord is not severed: it will exercise its own "autonomous" freedom in the Holy Spirit of absolute freedom. Precisely insofar as it does this is it justified in calling itself "autonomous".[1]

The choice with which it is inescapably faced and of which we have already spoken is between two ways in which finite freedom can envisage its autonomy. Either, on the basis of its center of freedom, it annexes an area in which no one may interfere (and

---

[1] Here, of course, we are speaking of the concrete world order with which we are familiar, in which God created all things "in Christ", that is, in his gracious plan of salvation. We know nothing of any other world, a world of "pure nature". In the real world, therefore, finite being will always be able to experience its own gift-character, and in a particular and verbal form too. Whether this comes about through external or purely internal revelation (cf. Thomas, *De Ver*. 18, 3 c) is immaterial here.

this can be understood in individual or social terms; the latter as the "golden rule" or the "categorical imperative"), or else it comes to understand that autonomy cannot be seen in isolation from the infinity of freedom and that, in trying thus to isolate itself, it must either deny the existence of infinite freedom or endure it as an external law outside and above itself. There are two things to be said here, by way of escaping from these deadends. On the one hand, the gift of freedom, from the perspective of infinite freedom, is not a final (and hence finite) act. It is not as if, once the gift has been made, the issue is settled and so from now on infinite freedom can devote its attention to something else, or to itself (the view of Deism). Rather, the giving of freedom remains a constant and continuing act (creation proceeds by preservation, *conservatio in esse*), which not only produces the gift but—and this is the gift's characteristic —also proffers itself, the Giver. This is not only because the creature comes from God but equally because its goal is in him. God thus offers to provide a home in the realm of the infinite (that is, of God) for finite freedom's essential self-transcendence; he offers it the right of citizenship there. This is something to which finite freedom cannot itself lay claim, on the basis of its own transcendental structure, for instance; any such "claim" would conflict inwardly with the act of thanksgiving for the gift of self.

This brings us to the "other side", that is, reflecting on the relationship from the perspective of finite freedom. The fact that it "must" give thanks for its very existence—and not for mere existence either, since the latter has been endowed with the ineffable gift of self-determination—does not render it unfree or servile vis-à-vis infinite freedom; rather, it is the appropriate expression of its genuine given freedom. However, this imperative (it "must" give thanks) is a constant reminder that it owes its autonomy to infinite, freedom-bestowing freedom (whether or not it actually performs the act of thanksgiving), and that it can only fulfill its own freedom in and through the divine freedom which thus—in bestowing freedom—manifests its presence. This becomes even clearer when the aspect of man's coming-from-God is complemented by his going-to-God. Finite freedom must transcend itself, but it cannot annex to itself the realm of the infinite. Calling to mind the ultimate goal of its self-realization, it will continually encounter the gift-character of the divine realm in a new and heightened way.

It can only genuinely realize and express its indebtedness if it acknowledges the presence of the Giver in the gift of freedom and, furthermore, if it acknowledges that the realm it penetrates —as a finite entity, through self-transcendence—is not its own property but a realm given to it (and not only lent) by the Giver. Even if it regards its faculty of self-transcendence as inherent in its nature, every act it performs in the direction of transcendence can only be performed because the realm of infinite freedom has disclosed itself. Moreover, since finite freedom, in stepping over into this realm, is taken beyond itself, its very act will be essentially codetermined by the act-quality of infinite freedom.

Here we see emerging before our eyes the essence and the concept of *grace*. The creature is "in" grace when it follows through its indebtedness for itself in both directions: to its origin and to its goal. The creature is not "in" grace, grace is in fact withdrawn, when it refuses this fundamental act, when it endeavors to rest content with the freedom it has received and even to regard this freedom as originating in itself, imagining that, in virtue of its transcendent structure, it can open up the realm of self-transcendence through its own efforts. Ultimately the creature is held in being (and in the acts which constitute its existence) by God, even contrary to its wishes; even if, in its self-transcendence, it is steering toward certain finite goods rather than toward God as its final goal, it is still upheld by God, albeit unconsciously. This lies in the nature of creatureliness; at a deeper level it arises from God's faithfulness to his purpose as Creator. But the creature's refusal to acknowledge the presence of the Giver *in him* erects an internal barrier within him in virtue of his finite freedom, a barrier that positively excludes God's self-giving as his origin and goal.

Little need be added by way of qualification. We should recall that, in speaking of God, we are not restricted to personal categories, particularly if they are played off against ontic categories; the dimension of the personal is itself ontic. And according to Plotinus' dictum (which is and remains irreducible), God is what he will be, and he will be what he is. That is, the presence of the Giver in the gift [Gabe] (and in its implied task [Aufgabe]), that is, the grace of God offered to us, can and must be expressed equally as an offer of *love* and an offer of *being* on God's part. And "being" must not, of course, be confused with some "thing".

This becomes more and more clear, the deeper we immerse ourselves in God's self-revelation in Christ, which opens up to us the realm of infinite freedom—which is not isolated from finite freedom. For here the very being of God coincides with his "being gift" and his "being love". It raises a new question, however: How are events within the Trinity related to God's offer of himself, of grace, to the creature? This question has many layers and touches on the most profoundly mysterious; all we can do here is outline its context. In the previous section we saw a convergence between the creature's complete surrender to the divine will (or to the eternal Idea of the creature in Christ, as a member of his Mystical Body) and the same creature's being born, together with the Son, from the generative primal womb of the Father. Such a creature, therefore, would have been fully endowed with God's perfect gift-character (that is, the Holy Spirit: Rom 5:5). Finite freedom's absolute nonresistance to infinite freedom would set off everything at once: it would allow itself to be created from the Father together with the Word, the Son ("Let it be done to me according to your word"); it would let the Holy Spirit enter in, the absolute divine gift, and allow this encounter to result in fruitfulness, enabling the creature perfectly to transcend itself toward God. This movement would also signify the making-present (the embodying) of God in the world, the overcoming of the distance between heaven and earth. From the vantage point of this "preeminent" instance, the perfected Idea, we could go backward, in stages, and reconstruct the various defective instances:

— the man who, in principle, does not wish to offer any resistance to God but cannot carry this principle out totally: such a man shares in being "born of God" (that is, he shares in *gratia sanctificans*)[2] even where the fruitfulness of his life within

---

[2] We need not hesitate to describe the result of God's (eternal) act of generation as a constant abiding (and hence a *habitus*) in grace. Even the term "infusion" can be substantiated biblically; in fact it arose solely from Romans 5:5 and 1 Corinthians 12:13. Protestant polemics against these terms are only justified where the latter are misused (suggesting that grace can become a possession of man's nature). To reject them would be like rejecting a genuine,

the divine freedom remains limited by his weaknesses;

— the man who offers no actual resistance to God because he has not yet attained the age of reason; he shares in being "born of God" in virtue of his solidarity with the Church (in baptism); his subsequent life will decide whether he wishes to persevere along this path;

— the man who (in very varying degrees) rejects the presence of infinite grace within him and so lives in a contradiction: at a personal level he fails to acknowledge what, objectively, he owes to God (his being and his freedom); thus he cannot share in being "born of the Father" but nonetheless has living within him God's antecedent offer of love (*gratia praeveniens, gratia actualis*); grace makes it possible for him to embrace it, but he can harden himself to the point of hurling a resounding No in the face of love (the "sin against the Holy Spirit").

Infinite freedom, because it is by nature infinite, simply cannot fail to be present wherever finite freedom is. It operates through the latter yet in a latent manner which allows finite freedom to realize itself as genuine decision (for or against its being-in-God). If it decides correctly, it simultaneously chooses both itself (which can only be realized in God) and God; it grasps that God's immanence in it, in grace, is nothing alien (*alienum*), no more than God himself can ever be a stranger to it (*aliud*); everything that is relative and created comes to itself in the Absolute. It both attains participation in the Absolute (being begotten together with the Son, "as in heaven") and fully exercises its gift of creaturely freedom (ultimately in being coincarnated with the Son: "on earth").

Third Excursus: "The Image and Likeness of God"

This topic is a little premature here, since biblically the phrase refers to man, whom we have not yet discussed. So far we have merely been concerned with the relation of infinite to finite freedom as the most formal presupposition of any theodramatic theory; this even included the finite freedom of angels. All the same, the topic can be included

---

inner sanctification of the justified person—something for which Karl Barth fought very early on. After all we have said, therefore, there can be no question of an ontic "increase" of grace in a man without a corresponding increase of faith-knowledge and love. "Everyone who loves is born of God and knows God. He who does not love does not know God; for God is love" (1 Jn 4:7f.).

here, since it concerns the pure dialogue-relationship between man and his Creator. These two mysterious concepts characterize this relationship prior to all action whatsoever.

This pair of concepts—and their implications for biblical studies, the history of theology and systematics—has been the subject of a vast array of monographs.[1] It must be said, however, that this topic, which was central in the patristic period and still received adequate attention in Scholasticism, scarcely plays any part in works of the more modern dogmatic theologians, although many of them insist on its central position.[2] Staudenmaier,[3] E. Brunner[4] and Karl Barth[5] are exceptions.

Several elements of tension transform the discussion of these two terms into a kind of battlefield. *First*, there is the fact that, while the phrase in Genesis 1:26f. is in a very important position, it does not seem to have had much influence on the Old Testament (at most on Psalm

[1] For a useful collection, containing twenty-one important articles on this subject, with a learned introduction, cf. Leo Scheffczyk, *Der Mensch als Bild Gottes*, Wege der Forschung 124 (1969); it has a very comprehensive bibliography. (Quoted here as Sch.) For the twelfth century in particular (with generous treatment of the preceding history), cf. the work by Robert Javelet, almost too generously documented: *Image et ressemblance au 12ᵉ siècle. De s. Anselm à Alain de Lille*. 2 vols. (Letouzey et Ané, 1967) (= J), unfortunately missed by Scheffczyk. Also R. Javelet, *Psychologie des auteurs spirituels du XIIᵉ siècle* (Strasbourg, 1959), chap. 4: "Image et ressemblance". On High Scholasticism: Richard Bruch, *Die Gottebenbildlichkeit des Menschen nach den bedeutendsten Scholastikern des 13. Jahrhunderts* (Diss., Freiburg, 1946). On the New Testament: C. Spicq, "L'Homme image de Dieu" in *Dieu et l'homme selon le Nouveau Testament*, Lectio Divina 29 (Cerf, 1961), 179–213.

[2] E. Brunner's dictum, "The doctrine of the *imago Dei* determines the destiny of every theology" (*Zwischen den Zeiten* [1929], 264) is often quoted. For on the basis of this doctrine, "from the very beginning, the relationship between reason and revelation, church and culture, faith and humanity, was decided; and it is still decided on this basis" (E. Brunner, *Der Mensch im Widerspruch* [1937], 83). Wigbert Hess, O.S.B., says: "Man is *imago Dei*. This, surely, is the greatest statement about man that has ever been and can ever be made" (Sch 405). Carl Stange: "Now, as at all times, the creation of man in the image of God is the key to an understanding of human life" (Sch 463). Görres referred to the doctrine of the "image" as "the firmament of all philosophy and all knowledge" (*Ges. Schriften*, ed. von Schellberg/Just [1926], 300).

[3] On Staudenmaier's constantly new approaches to the doctrine of the *imago*: Anton Burkhart, *Der Mensch-Gottes Ebenbild und Gleichnis. Ein Beitrag zur dogmatischen Anthropologie F. A. Staudenmaiers*, Freiburger theol. Stud. 79 (Herder 1962).

[4] Cf. the works mentioned in n. 2 above, and his *Dogmatik* 2 (1950), 64ff., 90ff.

[5] *Church Dogmatics* III/2 (Edinburgh, T. & T. Clark), 218–324.

8)—particularly if we exclude the explicit expansion of the Genesis text in Sirach 17:1–14 and Wisdom 2:23, which the Protestant Bible regards as apocryphal; and that, in the New Testament, the phrase is only used in passing, in connection with the new christological concept of "image" (Col 3:10; 1 Cor 11:7; James 3:9). On this basis certain exegetes have tried to play down the importance of this element and stigmatize the central position it acquired in the Fathers as an erroneous theological byway.[6] In reply it must be said that the express formulation in Genesis 1:26f. is only the summary of a fundamental truth that is always presupposed in the whole biblical drama involving God and man. Theology has explicitly to devote attention to this truth, and it can do this most simply by expounding the Genesis formula.

Second, there is an element of tension within exegesis itself. It concerns the actual meaning of the Hebrew words *selem* ("image") and *demut* ("likeness"). For a long time people proceeded in a more a priori manner and sought man's image-character in what raises him above the animals: self-consciousness, reason, free will, personality, responsibility and then in his dominant position in the cosmos, which is explicitly highlighted (Gen 1:28). From the fact that, apparently in one breath, Scripture says that "God created man in his own image; male and female he created them" (1:27), Karl Barth tried to conclude that the core of the image was the man/woman relationship and human relationships in general, pointing to a (trinitarian) community in God himself. Premature interpretation such as this was opposed by the exegetes, starting with H. Gunkel, then, more energetically, P. Humbert,[7] seconded by L. Köhler,[8] to some extent by von Rad and Zimmerli and also J. J. Stamm.[9] According to the basic etymological meaning of *selem* (carving, statue), they saw it as referring to man's distinctive bodily form, particularly his upright posture. For the most part they also insisted that the living soul, which causes the body to stand erect, should not be excluded.[10] Reference was made to Hebrew thought,

---

[6] Primarily K. L. Schmidt, "Homo imago Dei im Alten und Neuen Testament", *Eranos-Jahrbuch* (1947) = Sch 10–48.

[7] "Etudes sur le récit du Paradis et de la chute dans la Genèse", *Mémoires de l'Université de Neuchâtel* 14 (Neuchâtel, 1940).

[8] "Die Grundstelle der Imago-Dei-Lehre, Genesis 1, 26" in *Theol. Zft.* 4 (1948), 16–22.

[9] "Die Imago-Lehre von Karl Barth und die alttestamentliche Wissenschaft" in *Antwort. Festschrift für Karl Barth* (Zurich, 1956), 84–98 (= Sch 49–68).

[10] "The bodily and the spiritual should not, as far as possible, be torn apart: it is the whole man who is created in God's image." G. von Rad, "Die Gottebenbildlichkeit im Alten Testament" in *Das erste Buch Moses* (1949), 45.

which always sees man as a body-soul unity, and also to early anthropomorphic ideas of God, which attribute a bodily form to him; or, by contrast, to the late ideas of the Book of Wisdom (for the first account of creation in the Priestly Codex is a late document), which envisaged an embodied wisdom in God as a possible prototype for man.[11] As far as the meaning "bodily form" is concerned, scholars looked for parallels and precedents in the ancient Orient, partly in the notion that the god is rendered present in his statue,[12] partly in the ideology of kingship.[13] However, as we can see today, these various emphases on the body lead away from the straightforward and none-too-precise fundamental assertion; particularly as scholars agree that the second term, *"demut"*, is more probably a more generalized and diluted form of the first[14] and that the compiler of the Priestly Codex cannot be credited with crude anthropomorphisms.[15] "Image of God" remains, therefore, an attribute

[11] Wigbert Hess, "Imago Dei" in *Benediktinische Monatsschrift* 29 (1953), 371–400 (= Sch 405–45). "This view would have been possible in the period of the Wisdom literature. The prototype would thus be the Wisdom of God, conceived as a Person": 412.

[12] J. Hehn: "Zum Terminus 'Bild Gottes' " in *Sachau-Festschrift* (Berlin, 1915), 36–52. In Babylonian mythology there was a god Salmu, who "is nothing more than an idol elevated into a god". Further points are made by J. J. Stamm (see n. 9 above), 66.

[13] H. Wildberger, "Das Abbild Gottes Gen 1, 26–30" in *Theol. Zft.* 21 (1965), 245–59; 481–501.

[14] L. Köhler (see n. 8 above), 8. In Scholasticism the translation of *demut*, *similitudo*, was often regarded as the weaker of the pair insofar as it expresses only a general similarity. The *Summa* of Alexander offers both interpretations: *similitudo* can signify a mere general similarity, but it can also refer to the highest perfection of similitude (II, no. 339; the editors refer to Peter of Poitiers). Thomas, too, often uses *similitudo* as a technical term (*S. Th.* I, q 4, a 3); it can refer to three things: complete coincidence (*aequalitas*) or similarity by virtue of origin or analogous similarity between the cause and its (inferior) effect. With regard to the latter, he stresses that it is only the creature which is similar to God: God is not similar to the creature (*1 Sent.* d 19, 1, 2, etc.). Thomas likes to underline the abiding distance between God and the creature; thus, for instance, he takes over the patristic translation *"ad imaginem"* (i.e., "toward the likeness": [Augustine, *De Trin.* VII, 6, 12] *S. Th.* q 91, 1); thus he expounds Hilary's definition of the "image" (imago ejus ad quem imaginatur, species indifferens est, PL 10, 490B), interpreting *"species"* in terms of the most general analogy of being: *S. Th.* I, q 92, 2 ad 3.

[15] On the other hand, we cannot (with K. L. Schmidt) dilute the "corporality" of *selem* to such an extent that we equate it with that other *selem* (from a different Semitic root) that means "shadow" (and hence, in Genesis 1, God's "shadowy image, shadow outline", as in Psalm 39:7; 73:20)—even if Schmidt cites the

of man: he is created different from the other beings and is placed in a particular "relation" to God,[16] just as he is, that is, as a whole, living, body-soul being. Psalm 8 speaks of the entire human being, saying that God has "made him a little less than the divine beings and crowned him with glory and honor"—where *kabod*, "glory", is a distinctive divine predicate and *hadar*, "honor", at least includes the physical—"thou hast put all things under his feet. . . ." "Thus man is characterized as a creature whose being does not come from below; because of his origin, his being points toward the upper region."[17] The fact that God has laid his hand on him is shown by the commandment forbidding him to shed human blood; Genesis 9:6 traces this back to the fact that God has created man in his own image. "Human life, of all other life, is closest to the divine; it mirrors the latter, and so no one may presume to interfere with it, let alone extinguish it."[18] This is an indication of man's mysterious nobility.[19] Does this not imply that, just as the original, God, cannot be defined, neither can the copy, the "image", whose distinctiveness comes precisely from the fact that it represents, in worldly and created terms, this nondefinable divine reality? Epiphanius (*Haer*. 70) felt obliged to draw the conclusion that no one should attempt a closer definition of what constitutes the divine image in man, since it is known only to God.

On the other hand, the two are essentially ordered to each other; this can be expressed by the word *analogia* (which also implies a mysterious, irreducible "similarity in dissimilarity"). Since Genesis 1:26ff. is concerned with man's distinctive *essence*, all exegetes today (and, following them, the theologians, both Protestant and Catholic) agree that man's "image"-quality—even after he has fallen from God—cannot be lost.[20]

(oral) authority of Martin Buber: cf. "Homo imago Dei" (n. 6 above), 28. Wigbert Hess opposes Schmidt in "Imago Dei" (see n. 11 above), 412.

[16] J. J. Stamm (n. 9 above), 68.

[17] G. von Rad, "Die Gottebenbildlichkeit in Alten Testament" in *Th. W.* II, 389.

[18] Oswald Loretz, "Der Mensch als Ebenbild Gottes" in *Anima* 19 (1964), 109–20 (= Sch 114–30); this ref., 124.

[19] J. Wendland, "Die Lehre vom Ebenbilde Gottes und von der religiösen Anlage in der neueren Theologie" in *Zft. f. Theol. u. Kirche* N.F. 17 (1936), 67–82 (= Sch 331–47); this ref., 334. In his first publication on this topic (*Theol. Quart. schrift* [1830], 212f.), Staudenmaier emphasizes that the Church never dared to define the content of the "image".

[20] In Catholic theology this has been an unshakable proposition ever since Irenaeus, who said that the "image" remained even in sin, while the "likeness" was lost. In Protestant theology, even in Luther and Calvin, the radical thesis that the image of God was totally lost proved untenable; there had to be the

Since it is a case of uncreated and created reality, it is hard to see how the expression *analogia entis* could be avoided here. In order to circumvent it, Karl Barth understands it as an analogy of (abiding) relationship: just as man, in order to be man, must necessarily relate to his fellow men, God, in order to be God, must relate to himself in a trinitarian way (*analogia proportionalitatis*). But, even according to this relational definition, it is still a case of reality, *ens*. Similarly, though not so much on the defensive as Barth, Gordon D. Kaufmann sees the analogy as an *analogia historicitatis* (or *dramatica*) insofar as man's essence (both socially and as an individual) consists in determining and being determined by history, whereas God's essence consists in determining himself in his *aseity* (that is, in the Trinity); in other words, his origin is in himself.[21] H. Thielicke would like to acknowledge the ontological aspect of the analogy, but at the same time he wants to prohibit man from devoting any "attention" to this God-given similarity to God that might divert his gaze away from God and toward himself: "We can only speak in *chiffres*, as it were, about what is proper to man."[22] Against this, we must insist that a sober self-knowledge on man's part, recognizing that he is an "image", clearly indicates that he owes his existence to God, his origin; it is not *as such* and of necessity a "pious *incurvitas*".[23]

The discovery that, philosophically speaking, the affirmation of Genesis—that is, created man's likeness to the uncreated God—implies the *analogia entis* brings out a *third* element of tension in the doctrine of the "image". In spite of what we have already said about the mysterious nature of this relationship of "likeness", we cannot avoid the question:

---

theory of a "residue" guaranteeing man's abiding dignity. (On this, see the essay by J. Wendland, 335ff.) Exegetes also agree that Scripture never speaks of man forfeiting the image imparted to him in Genesis 1:26ff. Most dogmatic theologians are of the same opinion (including Karl Barth). But we must keep in mind that the New Testament bids us take off the old man and put on the new, "which is being renewed in knowledge after the image of its creator" (Col 3:9–11), which implies that something connected with the "image" *must* have been lost. Emil Brunner distinguishes the formal image, which remains, from the material image, which is lost. We shall return to this question.

[21] "Imago Dei als Geschichtlichkeit des Menschen" in Sch 466–90; original title: "The Imago Dei as Man's Historicity" in *The Journal of Religion* 36 (1956), 157–68.

[22] "Die Subjekthaftigkeit des Menschen. Studie zu einem Hauptproblem der Imago-Dei-Lehre" in *Theol. Lit. ztg* 75 (1950), 449–58 (= Sch 348–63); this ref., 357. *Ibid.*: "It would be totally mistaken, in protesting against the ontological mode of thought, to allow oneself to be drawn into denying the ontic facts themselves."

[23] *Ibid.*, 355.

In what does this "likeness" consist, which, by contrast with the animals and other beings in the world, man possesses? In the first place, obviously, we think of man's nature as spirit and person; we can emphasize man's reason or man's freedom (which are two aspects of the same thing), resulting in man's dominant position over the rest of creation, as we find stressed in Genesis. We have listened to the objections of the exegetes: *selem* is thought to refer primarily to the (bodily) form; and we can take note of the objections of the Protestant dogmatic theologians who fear that, under the guise of "spirit", Greek thought is being insinuated into the Bible. But, as we have seen, exegesis has moved away from a one-sided emphasis on the physical; the issue is the living man seen as a totality. In fact, the Church Fathers often ask the explicit question: Cannot the human body—particularly in view of the Incarnation of the Son and the resurrection of the flesh—also be part of the image of God?[24] Indeed, here we stand at the frontier between (Greek) philosophy, which establishes what is proper to man, his spiritual nature, but then is compelled to treat it as absolute; and (biblical) theology which, on the basis of a revelation that reason cannot fathom, is able to affirm that the mortal body is part of that totality which God wishes to enfold in his salvation and cause to share in his immortality. Once again *analogia entis* leads logically to an integration of philosophical reflection (insofar as it sees correctly) into

---

[24] Naturally, those Fathers who distinguish the spirit from the body (which man shares with the animals) will deny that the latter participates in the "image". Clement of Alexandria can speak thus from time to time (*Strom.* II, 102, 6; VI, 136, 3; 98, 4), but elsewhere he does regard the body as part of the "image": *Paid.* III, 64, 3; 66, 2. Justin, Irenaeus, Tertullian pursue an anti-Gnostic line when they expressly speak of the body as belonging to the "image". For texts, cf. W. Hess (n. 11 above), 418f. and A. Hoffmann, O.P., in the Latin/German edition of St. Thomas 7:226f. G. Söhngen proposes the following thesis: "Since, for the new man, likeness to God is likeness to Christ, it embraces the whole man, including his body." ("Die biblische Lehre von der Gottebenbildlichkeit des Menschen", *Münch. theol. Zft.* 2 [1951], 52–76 = Sch 364–404, this ref., 383. Occasionally we find Thomas saying that the soul conjoined with the body is more like God than the soul on its own (*De pot.* 5, 10 ad 5). Here, and in his interpretation of the significance of man's upright posture (*S. Th.* I, q 93, 6 ad 3), he proceeds along the lines of the detailed twelfth-century discussions on the body's participation in the "image". For the most part it is denied, but occasionally, in view of the Incarnation, the resurrection of the dead, and also in virtue of the fact that the body is animated by the soul, it is affirmed in a nuanced manner. Cf. Javelet, "Nature et corps, vestige de Dieu" (see n. 1 above) I, 224–36; II, 196–207.

theological anthropology. Christian thought is mistaken when it tries to deduce the whole of anthropology from a Bible that is cleansed of its Hellenistic and philosophical portions instead of keeping open to the discoveries of rational wisdom. With regard to the problem of the "image", G. Söhngen has given us the most convincing integration of this kind; any one who really thinks about revelation is already philosophizing, in solidarity with others who think and philosophize. Irenaeus begins his anthropology in company with the Gnostics but eventually develops it in opposition to them;[25] Clement of Alexandria starts off with the Gnostics and Pythagoreans.[26] Something similar could be said of Origen and the Cappadocians. The distinction first made by John Damascene between an image "*kata physin*" (Son-Father) and "*kata thesin*" (artefact-artist) can be traced back to Platonic and Aristotelian roots[27] but is ideally suited for maintaining orthodoxy: "Christ is the natural image of the Father, and man is God's image by means of imitation."[28] Ladner says, "Likeness to God or to Christ, as a theme of patristic thought, thus arises from a combination of biblical and Hellenistic ideas in which the Christian element was naturally predominant."[29] But this also applies to statements within the Bible itself, for example, chapter 17 of Sirach[30] and Wisdom 2:23, where the image resides in the "imperishability" (or "eternity") of man (not of the "soul") and death "entered the world through the devil's envy": here we have Platonic-Stoic ideas mediating between the "image"-

[25] Cf. in the first place A. Struker, *Die Gottebenbildlichkeit des Menschen in der christlichen Literatur der ersten zwei Jahrhunderte. Ein Beitrag zur Geschichte der Exegese von Genesis 1, 26* (Münster, 1913).

[26] Gerhart B. Ladner, "Der Bildbegriff bei den griechischen Vätern und der byzantinische Bilderstreit" in Sch 144–92. This ref., 170.

[27] *Ibid.*, 146, 175; on prior developments in the Fathers: 179ff.

[28] John Damascene, *De imaginibus*, or 3, 18 (PG 94, 1337D–40B).

[29] Ladner (see n. 26 above), 168.

[30] On this, cf. the disapproving verdict of E. Schlink ("Die biblische Lehre vom Ebenbilde Gottes" [1963] in Sch 88–113, this ref., 94f.): if the image of God is here seen "in domination over the animals, in intelligence and the ability to think and speak, it already signifies a shift in Old Testament views under the influence of Greek thought". "We must reject the Greek remolding of the doctrine of God's decisions regarding man(!) into a doctrine of man's qualities and faculties" (112). We are bound to ask: Is it not the case that the Bible accompanies mankind as it moves from a predominantly pictorial ("mythological") age into a predominantly conceptual one? And as for the "philosophy" of the Wisdom literature, does it not constitute an indispensable foundation for the Pauline, Johannine and even the Synoptic utterances of the New Testament?

doctrine of the Old Covenant and that of the New. This legacy of ideas is automatically transformed once it is drawn into the relationship between infinite and finite freedom, but it remains indispensable if there is to be a reflection on revelation that is appropriate to man's dignity—that is, not clinging to the letter. It will not do, therefore, to dismiss as a false trail the tremendous efforts of patristic and Scholastic speculation concerning the "image", particularly since it proceeded in a highly nuanced manner.

In fact, however, it is precisely this nuanced approach that arouses hostility, producing a *fourth* element of tension. In part, the Fathers took up the two terms found in Genesis, "image" (*selem*) and "likeness" (*demut*), and reflected upon the Bible's implicit distinction between man's imperishable nature and his turning away from God; this turning away brought about God's sentence of punishment, namely, the partial withdrawal of his dominant position in nature, death (Wis 2:23, cf. 6:19) and a universal estrangement from God. Accordingly, they introduced a theological distinction between two elements or phases of the image which, while it undoubtedly cannot be read from the literal text, was in itself both justified and unavoidable.

From the outset, however, this distinction, which can crudely be described as that between the ontic and ethical aspects of the image, appears in company with a further, even more important distinction in the history of theology, fusing this fourth with a *fifth* element of tension. This is the distinction between the Old Testament "image", which applies to man in general, and the New Testament "image", which—and this is something totally new—is Christ alone. For he is the express "likeness of God" (2 Cor 4:4), "the image of the invisible God" (Col 1:15). So we must be "conformed" to his image (Rom 8:29; 2 Cor 3:18); "Just as we have borne the image of the man of dust (Adam), we shall also bear the image of the man of heaven" (1 Cor 15:49). If the two tensions are combined ("image-likeness" and "earthly and heavenly image"), complex fugues result; the two can be treated in relative isolation, but they can also be fused in such a way that the first motif is rooted in the second right from the start.

This is immediately visible in *Irenaeus*. For in Christ, man

is perfected according to the image and likeness of God. The truth of this was manifest when the Word of God became man, assimilating himself to man and mankind so that man, becoming like the Son, should become precious in the Father's eyes. In earlier times it was said that man was created in the image of God, but it was not a manifest truth, for the Word according to whose image man was created was invisible, and so the likeness was easily lost. But the Word, becoming flesh, firmly established both: it demonstrated the truth of the image by becoming precisely what its image was and restored the likeness by assimilating man to the invisible Father through the mediation of the now visible Word (*Adv. Haer.* V, 16, 2).

Irenaeus can also express this clear, fundamental idea in a different way without distinguishing the terms;[31] he can also make it more precise, saying that, through sin, man, who consists of body, soul and (Holy) Spirit, loses the Spirit and hence his "likeness" to God; he has only managed to hold on to the "image".[32]

Irenaeus' distinctions provide the basis for a more nuanced theology of the "image"; its elements cannot be dispensed with, despite Protestant polemics. Thus there is the distinction between an essential constituent of man's nature, which cannot be lost even in the sinner (Irenaeus defines it as "body-soul" and as the initially hidden image of the Logos), and the gift of the Pneuma (grace), which gives man a true likeness to God and which *can* be lost. Of course, the Fathers do not make the distinction between nature and supernature that is made in modern technical theology; yet it is not at all clear why, from the vantage point of the latter, people should engage in polemics against analyzing the "image" into a "natural" and a "supernatural" element.[33] Next there is the distinction between an (as it were) inchoate image in

---

[31] Thus *Adv. Haer.* III, 18, 1: What we lost in Adam, i.e., being in God's image and likeness, we have won back in Christ. The concluding sentence of the entire work (V, 36, 3) stresses that man, through ongoing assimilation to the incarnate Son, is transformed into the image and likeness of God.

[32] *Adv. Haer.* V, 6, 1; V, 8, 1.

[33] Thus, for example, Stephan Otto, "Der Mensch als Bild Gottes bei Tertullian" in *Münch. theol. Zft.* 10 (1959), 276–82 = Sch 133–43. Otto adopts a polemical stance against d'Alès and J. Ratzinger and attempts to play off the "salvation-historical" development (from paradise to man's final state) against the "categorical-analytical distinction made between a 'natural' and a 'super-natural' element in man". In the Fathers, in fact, the two coinhere. E. Brunner, too, engages in similar polemics in his doctrine of the formal *imago* (which cannot be lost) and the material (lost) *imago*. On the one hand, he sees this prefigured in the distinction made by the Fathers, and rightly so, in that the "likeness" is referred to man's ultimate destination—divine sonship—which has become visible in Christ. Here he is one with Irenaeus. But, on the other hand, he maintains that this teaching has been falsely overlaid by a second distinction, that between the "natural" and the "supernatural". Brunner has misunderstood here: he thinks that, in the "image", the patristic distinction posits a "self-subsistent rational nature", unrelated to God (*Dogmatik* II, 92). The afore-mentioned essay by G. Söhngen (n. 24 above) clears up these misunderstandings; he plainly acknowledges the (unavoidable) overlap of biblical and philosophical terminology: "The terms 'nature' and 'natural' are thus no longer taken in a

the first Adam, involving a totally appropriate difference between his essential being and its active fulfillment through choices in accordance with God's will, and an image that is fully unveiled only in Christ, the Second Adam. This second image not only restores the first but causes it to transcend itself and attain a totally unexpected likeness to God. Third, this makes it possible to express the same basic structure (depending on the perspective) in the most varied ways. This often happens in the same writer; the context is seen to justify the use of a particular turn of phrase.

Here the possibility emerges, most importantly, of defining the

---

biblical, salvation-historical sense but in an abstract metaphysical sense. The expression is no longer that of Paul but that of Aristotle and the Stoics." Here Söhngen sets the *"physei"* of Ephesians 2:3 against the *"physei"* of Romans 2:14. "But the manner of expression is one thing, and the thing expressed is another" (389). At this point the relation of the image to its original, as the simple expression of the *analogia entis*, becomes a *datum of human consciousness*. Augustine saw the awareness of God's presence lighting up in the soul's "trans-psychological memory" (Gilson, *Augustin*, 3d ed. [1949], 139 n. [*The Christian Philosophy of Saint Augustine* (London, 1961)]), in the "abstrusior profunditas nostrae memoriae" (*De Trin*. XV, 21, 40); in this illumination it recognizes both that it comes from God and that it is not God; Augustine's doctrine of the soul distinctly experiences the fundamental relationship between God and the creature as that of original and copy—and it does so without any "pious *incurvitas*". William of St. Thierry expresses this experiential element of the doctrine of the "image": "The soul is aware that it is somehow a copy of its Creator. It understands that it is the image of God, seeing in him the light by which it sees and in itself the light that can be lit up" (PL 180, 721AB). And with reference to the *imago Trinitatis in anima*, he addresses the soul thus: "Draw closer to the form that fashions you so that you may more faithfully express its features. . . . The greater the weight of love that presses you to it, the more it will stamp its seal upon your substance. Thus the image that illuminated and guided your initial coming-into-being will be perfectly established in you" (*ibid*., CD). The more the ontic "image" acquires depth and a clear outline in existential "likeness", the more the *analogia entis* it expresses becomes an *analogia cognitionis*. The latter does not imply, any more than the former, a capability for, or transition toward, identity. Augustine's *"inardesco et inhorresco"* remains the fundamental form of any intercourse with God on the part of the creature. But when Richard of St. Victor explodes the individualistic image of the Trinity in the soul and expands it into the interpersonal perspective (in his *De Trinitate*, SC 63, 1958), he presents us with a new opportunity, in the selfless encounter with fellow human beings—an encounter of which he makes the greatest demands—of also experiencing the *analogia imaginis* in terms of consciousness. This line of thought is pursued, no doubt without being aware of the connection, by Aegid Van Broeckhoven, *Freundschaft mit Gott, Ein Tagebuch* (Einsiedeln: Johannes Verlag, 1972).

"image" of God in man as finite freedom (which is naturally only conceivable in a rational nature) and locating it in the essence of this freedom; it must act as such, that is, it must decide to move toward God—and thus realize the "likeness" it already possesses—or away from God, so losing this likeness. This is how *Tertullian* defines the image, although with some borrowing from Irenaeus.[34] God alone, he says, is good according to his essence, because he has no beginning. (His being is from himself.) Man exists by being instituted (*institutione*); since he has a beginning, he also has a form of being that is good as such, because his Creator is wholly good.

> But man is to possess as his very own the good which God has put at his disposal; it is to become man's property and "nature", so to speak; accordingly, from his very beginning (*institutione*), he has been given freedom and the ability to make decisions, which tips the scales in favor of the good which God has given him, so that henceforth man should produce the good in all freedom.[35]

Here freedom is conceived in the Stoic manner: the good, natural disposition (*physis*, what Tertullian calls *forma* and *dispositio ad bonum* = the ontic *imago*), if it is to be ethically good, must exercise itself in free decisions; the only difference is that, for the Christian, Tertullian, this disposition has been instituted (*instituta*) by God, and the ability to act freely has been "granted" (*emancipatum*). In fact, this image of man in his body-soul reality has been created after the image and likeness of Christ, the "truer and more dependable man";[36] the first Adam has his freedom with a view to the Second. This strong emphasis on freedom as the core of the image of God—but a freedom which, fundamentally, must choose in order to possess itself—is continued in *Origen*,[37] who can use both ways of speaking: like Irenaeus he can distinguish image

---

[34] ". . . Exempto scilicet reatu eximitur et poena. Ita restituitur homo deo ad similitudinem ejus, qui retro ad imaginem dei fuerat—imago in effigie, similitudo in aeternitate censentur", *De baptismo* 5, 6–7. Cf. Stephan Otto (see previous note) 134–35.

[35] *Adv. Marc.* II, 6, 4–5.

[36] *Adv. Prax.* 12, 4. Other places where freedom appears as the image and likeness of God: *Adv. Marc.* II, 6, 3; 5, 5; 9, 4. Scotus Erigena (*De praedest*. IV, 5 and V, 5) will likewise insist that man must be free if he is to bear God's image.

[37] We can pass over Clement of Alexandria here. He uses various models, and Christology is at the center of his thought. Occasionally he even thinks in ecclesiological terms (pagans have the "image", baptized Christians the "likeness", *Paid*. I, 98, 1–4; the baptized Christian is the image of God because he is in Christ, *Paid*. I, 49, 3; *Strom*. III, 42, 5f.). Accordingly, he takes over from Philo the formula "image of the Image": in Philo, the (primal) Image is the Logos, in

(as "nature") from likeness (as "assimilation")—a distinction which will recur, for instance, in Basil[38] and Maximus the Confessor;[39] and, like Tertullian and the later Latin Fathers (Tyconius, Ambrose, Augustine and also Gregory of Nyssa and Cyril of Alexandria), he can see "image and likeness" as a unity. On the near side of this parting of the ways we find the two fundamental ideas: Christ is the authentic image of the invisible God;[40] and man, at his best and most spiritual, is "according to the image".[41] This spiritual dimension, of course, is what relates man to the Logos; thus it is also the dimension of freedom. For Origen, the latter is not (as is often said) a sublime indifference in choosing; that aspect is only emphasized for polemical, anti-Gnostic purposes. Rather, it is a clinging to God, such as, preeminently, what the soul of Jesus does.[42] From this standpoint, Origen can from time to time make a clear distinction between "image" and "likeness"; the philosophical distinctions (the disposition and its development) are traced back to features in Genesis. Here, initially, he speaks of two aspects, whereas later he only speaks of the image, by which he means the disposition and its capacity for fulfillment, which is only attained through ethical conduct.[43] Elsewhere the fully realized image is the final concept.[44]

In *Gregory of Nyssa* the christocentric idea is predominant. Christ

---

Clement, it is Christ; this is also adopted by Origen (*Joh. Comm.* 2, 3) and others. Clement is consistent in borrowing from Philo (*Leg. alleg.* 1, 31ff.; *Op. mund.* 139) the distinction between "as image" and "according to the image" (both possible translations of "ad imaginem"): the first is applied to Christ, the second to man (*Paid.* 12, 98, 3; frequently in Gregory of Nyssa: *Hom. op.* 16, *Vita Moysis* [PG 44, 429A], *Prof. christ.* [PG 46 244C]).

On Clement in general: Aug. Mayer, "Das Gottesbild im Menschen nach Clemens von Alexandrien" in *Stud. Anselm.* XV, (1942).

On Origen: Henri Crouzel, *Théologie de l'Image de Dieu chez Origène*, series Théologie 34 (Aubier, 1956).

[38] *Hom. 10 in Hex* ("Sur l'origine de l'homme" in *Sources chrétiennes* 160).

[39] *Ambig.* 42 (PG 91, 1345D), *Qu. ad Thal* 6 (PG 90, 281AB), *ibid.*, 53 (505A), I, 16f. (207-13).

[40] After Colossians 1: *Peri Arch.* I, 1, 8; the humanity of the Logos is a kind of shadow of an image; the Logos adopts our image in order to restore us to his image and thus effect the likeness: *Joh. Comm.* 20, 22. Crouzel (see n. 37), 139, 141.

[41] This corresponds to the distinction drawn by Philo, who, like Origen, presupposed a twofold creation, one for the inner, spiritual man, and one for the external, sense-oriented man: *In Gen. hom.* 1, 13. Texts in Crouzel 148-53.

[42] Crouzel 173.

[43] *Peri Arch.* III, 6, 1; *Joh. Comm.* 20, 22; *C. Cels.* IV, 30; further texts in Crouzel 218ff.

[44] *Peri Arch.* II, 11, 4, conclusion.

(and the Christian who is fashioned after him) is *the* Image, so much so that the first creation "in image and likeness" remains a purely ideal one, whereas the second, concrete creation already contains an admixture of dissimilarity (anticipating the Fall). Finite freedom, in its yearning, penetrates ever more deeply into infinite freedom: this is the progressive unveiling of the image; or, more precisely, the original Image [*Urbild*] is increasingly reflected and rendered present in the copy [*Abbild*].[45] But at this very point, where it is a case of penetrating through the ever-greater transparency of the image to its source, the two terminologies coalesce. Again we see Platonic thought married to Christian; just as, in Plotinus, the *nous* and the soul find their real center, not in themselves, but in that mid-point in which all mid-points coincide, in Christianity finite freedom finds its fulfillment, its ultimate liberation, in that freedom which is absolute and infinite. In the Middle Ages, Bernard, William of St. Thierry and Richard of St. Victor will so describe it.

Now in Plotinus, but also in Christianity if we keep in mind God's unity, infinite freedom is imageless. If we look from finite freedom to infinite, that is, in an "ascending" manner, the actual "image" in finite freedom persists as it transcends itself toward infinite freedom, in what Gregory of Nyssa calls "*epektasis*" and the medieval theologians call "*excessus*". Here the image is assumed into the likeness; we find the seeds of this even in *Augustine*[46] (as an echo of Plotinus), and the consequence is that a certain forgetfulness of God, a slackening of the movement toward God, which obscures the image, covers it over and attacks it. On the other hand, Augustine, together with Gregory of Nyssa, tirelessly recommends the inward path as the prime way of seeking God in our own soul-spirit and beholding him as in a mirror; not so that we should come to a full stop with ourselves ("*transcende te ipsum!*") but should rather throw ourselves entirely into the movement toward God. *Bernard* takes up this line of thought (in the 81st *Sermo in Cant.*), characteristically highlighting the aspect of freedom, which he regards as man's chief likeness to the divine Word.[47] Because of its

---

[45] Cf. my book *Présence et pensée. Essai sur la philosophie religieuse de Grégoire de Nysse* (Paris: Beauchesne, 1942), esp. 81ff.: "La Philosophie de l'image". Roger Leys, *L'Image de Dieu chez s. Grégoire de Nysse* (Brussels-Paris, 1951). Hubert Merki, *Omoiosis Theoi. Von der platonischen Angleichung an Gott zur Gottähnlichkeit bei Gregor von Nyssa* (Fribourg, Switzerland, 1952).

[46] Augustine, *De Trin.* 14, 13, 17 (PL 42, 1049); 14, 14, 19 (1050–51); 14, 17, 23 (1053).

[47] "Arbitrii libertas . . . plane divinum quiddam praefulgens in anima, tamquam gemma in auro." *Sermo in Cant.* 81, 6 (PL 182, 1173CD).

Neoplatonic origins, however, this ascending movement of self-immersion in the primal divine Ground (which attains its full form in Eckhart) has difficulty preserving the distance between the creature and the Creator. In some of Origen's more extreme formulations, the souls all flow into the one sun of the divine *henad* at the end of time; it is the same in Scotus Erigena; and, in the school of Chartres, the divine world of ideas is existentialized. "Paul," says Herbert of Boseham,

> he who learned the nuptial mysteries while transported to the third heaven, seems to teach that the uncreated Spirit and the created spirits, which nonetheless were eternal in God's eternal Spirit for all eternity, together constitute a kind of perfectly fulfilled unity. Thus all the spirits of the blessed will be as if transsubstantiated.[48]

This predominantly Platonic, ascending tendency, which tends to dissolve the "image" into the "likeness", is balanced by the twofold Christian thought that infinite freedom itself produces an Image, the eternal Son, within the Godhead, thus laying the foundation in him for the images of finite creatures. Accordingly, the assimilation of finite freedom to infinite has an infinite prototype [*Urbild*] as its ideal and goal, but all the same it *is* an image [*Bild*], and an incarnate one at that. The encounter between the (ascending) image and the (descending) prototype leads, not to identity, but to a nuptial union, as Bernard emphatically insists.[49] It may be possible to speak of a certain "*liquefactio formarum*" when the elect enter the eternal Jerusalem, the Bride of the Word,[50] since the Son, the Prototype [*Urbild*], encompasses and reworks all the copies [*Abbilder*] in himself; yet it is not a question of absorbing and extinguishing the finite images but of setting them within the embracing Idea; for it is within this Idea, from all eternity, that they were conceived and created as individuals. True, both the eternal Image and the created image—to use one of Bonaventure's favorite categories—are *expressio* of God's generative-creative primal Ground, but even where the created image is adopted into the mystery of generation—to be "born of God"—the fundamental distinction remains: "*Fatemur similitudinem, aequalitatem renuimus*" (Bernard).[51]

[48] *Liber malorum* III (PL 190D–51A, quoted in J I, 118). Ultimately there will be only one will: that of the Creator, and of man, made in his image and likeness: Anselm of Canterbury, *Med.* 18 (PL 158, 807A–8A), cf. Bernard, *In Cant.* 71.

[49] *S. in Cant.* 81, 1 (PL 182, 1171B).

[50] Thus Gerhoh von Reichersberg, *In Ps* 7, 73 (PL 194, 349D–50A).

[51] In line with our topic, we have deliberately kept to the fundamental relationship between infinite and finite freedom. Thus we have left to one side Augustine's teaching on the *imago Trinitatis in anima* and its continuing influence in theology, although it would be essential to a complete grasp of the issue. If the

The theme of the correspondence between divine idea and created reality becomes a central concern once more in *F. A. Staudenmaier*. First of all, the two things, the eternal design of the world in God's knowing and willing and the concretely created world, are clearly distinguished (contrary to Hegel) and yet seen as inseparable. Just as the idea outlines in advance the entire history of the Son's Incarnation and of his Church, it also contains the individual ideas of each qualitatively unique personality, which is "a distinctive thought on the part of the Divinity", for which each individual must strive as he is inspired by the Holy Spirit.[52] But all this takes place within the encompassing totality of the Idea; the point at which a man is inserted (his particular charisma) is determined by the Holy Spirit. In Drey's view, nature and supernatural vocation are seen in complete unity on the basis of the total Idea, so that (as in Gregory of Nyssa, for instance) the process of "likening" strives, through the operation of the Spirit, toward the originally perfect image—the "supernatural" image that resides in the fullness of Christ.[53] Even if the image is not lost, because God has continued to

"natural" image primarily consisted in the copying of a mystery internal to the Godhead, which can only be recognized through revelation, the *analogia entis* would threaten to elude our grasp (cf. Bonaventure in R. Bruch, *Die Gottebenbildlichkeit* . . . [n. 1 above], 24; Thomas, *De Ver.* 10, 7; *De pot.* 9, 9). In fact, High Scholasticism avoids this danger, whether through stressing the universal analogy in man's spiritual nature (*mens* as the seat of the *imago*) or through an a priori relationship between the created subject and the prototypical Idea in God. This is a prominent theme in Alexander and Albert (cf. Bruch 52–62); it is less so in Thomas (Bruch 62ff.). On this issue: M. Schmaus, *Die psychologische Trinitätslehre des Hl. Augustinus* (Münster, 1927); M. Schmaus, "Das Fortwirken des Augustinischen Trinitätspsychologie bis zur Karolingischen Zeit" in *Vitae et Veritati, Festschrift für Karl Adam* (Düsseldorf: Patmos, 1956), 44–56; Ludwig Hödl, *Frühscholastische Lehre von der Gottebenbildlichkeit des Menschen* (1960), quoted in Sch 193–205.

[52] Thus in *Pragmatismus der Geistesgaben* (1835) and *Geist der göttlichen Offenbarung* (1837). He clearly manifests the influence of Leibniz, and most of all of Schleiermacher, Jacobi, Fichte and Möhler's *Einheit*.

[53] First systematic outline: "Die Lehre vom göttlichen Ebenbilde im Menschen" in *Theol. Quart. schrift* (1830), 199–284; 403–524. (The second part, containing Staudenmaier's personal view of the question, remained unpublished.) The historical survey of the period of the Fathers and early Scholasticism is very remarkable for its time, although A. Struker regards it as cursory. For an evaluation: A. Burkhart, *Der Mensch* . . . (see n. 3 above), 81–112. In addition to Burkhart's work, cf. P. Hünermann, "Trinitarische Anthropologie bei Franz Anton Staudenmaier" in *Symposion* 10 (Freiburg: Alber, 1962). Here we can follow the stages of Staudenmaier's development: from his pneumatocentric starting point (8ff.) to his study of the Fathers' teaching on the image and

accompany the sinner, the sinner in himself is still a "worthless", "purely finite" person.[54] He acquires authentic personhood, along with his eternal destiny, solely from God, who also apportions him the strength to reach it. Staudenmaier is well aware that man's freedom is involved in God's free ordering of the world.[55] Since he always reflects on the basis of the concrete idea of a creation in Christ,[56] it is quite inappropriate to suggest that he has not devoted sufficient attention to the possibility(?) of a natural final destination for man.[57] For Staudenmaier, however, the concrete idea is that living medium within which finite freedom is able to pursue its destiny, which certainly requires "man's free self-determination, which coincides with his ability to make decisions regarding himself".

---

likeness (25ff.) to his more christocentric (and ecclesiological) essays (62ff.; 117ff.) right up to the new systematic outline of 1840, in which natural (negative) knowledge is more clearly distinguished from historical and revelation-based knowledge, but only in order "to attain a richer synthesis in a speculative unity of the counterposed (not contradictory) elements" (121ff.).

[54] Texts in P. Hünermann 55ff.

[55] "Das göttliche Prinzip in der Geschichte und seine Bedeutung für Philosophie und Theologie" in *Jahrbücher für Theologie und christliche Philosophie* (1835) IV, 3–48. On the freedom of the Spirit: *Dogmatik* III (1848), section 56.

[56] And consequently does not interpret *imago* and *similitudo* in terms of "nature" and "supernature" (in the modern understanding of these concepts), as many of the Fathers have wrongly been accused of doing. Cf. L. Scheffczyk, "Gottesebenbildlichkeit in der modernen Theologie" in Sch XXXIVf.

[57] As Burkhart several times asserts: 152, 160f., 231–35 (man's destiny of supernatural union in God is inscribed in his nature, but his natural powers are inadequate for its attainment), 243–44. He does admit that Staudenmaier "always includes the supranatural element in his thought": 272. Also 305ff. (distinguishing him from Baius). The lengthy concluding critique of Staudenmaier's doctrine of the *imago* (417–43) culminates in the statement that he lacks "the at least theoretical possibility of a *natura pura*" (436). But he grants that Staudenmaier emphasizes and preserves the unmerited quality of the one, ultimate, supernatural destiny. P. Hünermann (n. 53 above), 90ff., 113, has a similar view of Staudenmaier's limitations: "Certainly he never speaks of a 'natural goal' on man's part but of a 'purely natural activity'. The concept of a 'natural goal' is of no significance in his doctrine of the concrete, real ideas." Thus his teaching is in precise accord with that of the great Scholastics, as de Lubac and H. Rondet have exhaustively shown. Why then does Hünermann find it necessary to say: "Staudenmaier is well aware that he takes a different view from the medieval(?) Scholastics on an essential point" (113)? The double concept of nature suggested by Burkhart (433) corresponds to the distinction I have developed in my book *Karl Barth*. But the postulate of "the possibility of an ultimate natural goal" in no way follows from it.

But the subjective perfecting of man can add nothing to the objective divine perfection; it cannot complement it by expanding its scope; it cannot heighten its value in virtue of its content; all it can do is enter into it, comprehend it, will it and fulfill it by freely applying it to itself. Thus the Divinity has left man as he is—in virtue of nature and grace—to himself; and so, since grace is utterly free, it has left the work of freedom to freedom itself.[58]

If we include this tremendous risk on God's part in handing over his Idea, at least in part, to man's freedom, we may describe the divine Idea as a living thought that fulfills itself.[59] The doctrine of redemption must show that the misuse of the finite power to choose is "inevitable" and "cannot be rendered impossible"[60] and how it can be overcome within God's encompassing Idea.

Staudenmaier's concept of the "image" is practically identical with that of Gregory of Nyssa: it is protological and ideal, on the one hand, and eschatological and christological on the other. And as for the "likeness"—man's assimilation to this image through the grace of the Spirit and through human moral effort—it is a dynamic element, part of the image. There is no other way of understanding the statement that the creature's ultimate union with God, that is, perfect "likeness to God", goes farther than man's "imaging" of God.[61] Staudenmaier revitalized the theological and anthropological concern of the Fathers and of High Scholasticism in his own time (the time of Hegel, Schelling, Günther and the Tübingen school); today the identical concern needs to be presented, expressed perhaps in a slightly modified form, that is, in terms of finite freedom's nonheteronomy within the absolute character of infinite freedom.

The core of Staudenmaier's argument is again formulated in M. *Deutinger's* "Denklehre"; let the latter's words conclude our remarks on finite and infinite freedom:

In man, nature and freedom confront each other as opposites. This opposition can only be resolved by the revelation of a higher, divine Will, in such a way that man, in attaching himself to this Will, touches both the ground of being and the ground of freedom. On the other hand, if man negates the divine Will, he also negates the ground of freedom, and hence the ground of being too, setting himself in contradiction to both. If free choice is to be genuinely free, therefore, it must acknowledge a being— namely, freedom—superior to both existence and relation. If there were a

[58] *Dogmatik* III, 807–8.
[59] *Ibid.*, 86.
[60] *Ibid.*, 212.
[61] *Ibid.*, 775.

necessary being superior to freedom, it would dissolve all relative freedom and all choice. We must assume an absolute Will if we wish to comprehend the law found in the relative will. This Will, this higher personality, is absolute because it is not bound up with existence but is one with being. . . . Being is freedom, and freedom is being.[62]

Grundlinien der positiven Philosophie III: "Die Denklehre" (1844), 393–94.

C. MAN

1. *Man the Undefinable*

The entire section on "infinite and finite freedom" was a kind of "Prologue in Heaven";[1] it was cast in an abstract and ideal form that allowed us to postpone the question, "What kind of being is man, who is thus endowed with finite freedom?" In most cases, at least, he could just as well have been an angel. The ancient theological-philosophical cosmologies (Augustine) often begin with a description of the world of spirits. While in biblical revelation these spirits do have a part to play which cannot be explained away—we shall come to them in due course—it is man, God's "partner", who is the focus of interest. The relationship between infinite and finite freedom may constitute the basic formal datum of every theodramatic theory, but once man appears in all his concreteness, this drama becomes suddenly, abruptly real. So real that we cannot even attain an external vantage point from which to contemplate and evaluate it; we are caught up in the drama, we cannot remove ourselves from it or even conceive ourselves apart from it.

This means that, if we want to ask about man's "essence", we can do so only in the midst of his dramatic performance of existence. There is no other anthropology but the dramatic. This is why the topic could not even emerge within the framework of the theological aesthetics. Only within the ongoing drama can we ask whether there is something essential and (relatively) unchanging in all man's acts and states, and what this might be. Theologically speaking, we can ask what the implications are, on the basis of this "third act" that mankind is currently playing, for the first act, the *status naturae integrae*, the second, the *status naturae lapsae*, and the last act, the *status naturae glorificatae*. If we continue in this theological mode, however, we cannot imagine these "acts" of nature as a purely temporal succession of different, mutually exclusive states, for the *natura reparata* that roughly designates our place in the drama coincides

---

[1] [The opening section of Goethe's *Faust* — Tr.]

to a large extent with the *natura lapsa* yet is able to participate proleptically (*spe, non re*) in the ultimate state. More difficult is the question of whether and how far a child, for example—or, more precisely, a baptized child or even a saint—can share in the *status naturae integrae* or the supralapsarian state.

Here and now man knows that he is in a condition of alienation, having fallen away from his origin; this theorem is by no means exclusive to the Bible: it is the property of mankind as a whole. Indian religious metaphysics is based on it as is Plato's doctrine of the soul's fall from the contemplation of the realm of the Ideas. In other philosophies, those which envisage things in terms of macrocosm and microcosm, the theorem moves into the background and even disappears entirely: in this case, man's task would be simply to assimilate himself to the healthy model of being, that is, nature writ large. There are many gradations between these views, and they are also reflected within Christian theology itself; at one extreme we have the mere *spoliatio in gratuitis* (where "nature" keeps its identity), and at the other extreme we have a total *corruptio naturae* as a result of the original Fall. In Christian anthropology, too, therefore, it remains an open question how much of man's original "essence" has been retained in the "scene" currently being enacted.

We have already discussed finite freedom without describing it in concrete detail. If we now proceed on the basis of man's realistic existence, as we know it, this finitude will manifest the most striking and diverse features. According to our experience, our personal freedom operates only within a universal spiritual nature that has its own rules of thought and necessarily sets goals and embraces values; we all share in this, although personally we do not participate in the freedom of others. Moreover, we learn that our freedom rests on a highly subtle organic and mechanical system, which is itself dependent on a given external world, and that it cannot separate itself, even for an instant, from this system. Finally we come to see that this freedom is "bound" in a way it finds utterly disconcerting, not by instincts or drives as such, but by their overwhelming power: "For I do not do what I want, but I do the very thing I hate" (Rom 7:15). The Apostle goes on to discern a kind of contradiction in man: "I see in my members another law at war with the law of my mind and making me captive to the law of sin which dwells in my members" (Rom 7:23). Here, all too clearly, we see that the condition in which man finds himself can only be one "scene" within a dramatic action; it points back to his origins and forward to a destination, however hidden these may be and however impossible to reconstruct.

However, we do not even need to have recourse to theological categories to demonstrate this contradiction, this hiatus in man. His strangely exposed situation in the realm of the cosmos is explanation enough: he is rooted in it with all his physical and sensory nature and at the same time reaches above it with his intellectual and spiritual faculties, which are not only theoretical but also practical and ethical. But this dimension that rises above the material is not simply a heightened continuation of the sensory and instinctual level (as Nietzsche, for instance, wanted to say): it is also actually contrary to it. And at times, whether in philosophical images of the world (Klages) or as a result of simple observation of life, this contrariety can reach the level of mutual destruction. Let a poet speak of this:

There is a strange duality in the human which makes for an ethical paradox. We have definitions of good qualities and of bad; not changing things, but generally considered good and bad throughout the ages and throughout the species. Of the good, we think always of wisdom, tolerance, kindliness, generosity, humility; and the qualities of cruelty, greed, self-interest, graspingness, and rapacity are universally considered undesirable. And yet in our structure of society, the so-called and considered good qualities are invariable concomitants of failure, while the bad ones are the cornerstones of success. A man—a viewing-point man—while he will love the abstract good qualities and detest the abstract bad, will nevertheless envy and admire the person who through possessing the bad qualities has succeeded economically and socially, and will hold in contempt that person whose good qualities have caused failure. When such a viewing-point man thinks of Jesus or St. Augustine or Socrates he regards them with love because they are the symbols of the good he admires, and he hates the symbols of the bad. But actually he would rather be successful than good. In an animal other than man we would replace the term "good" with "weak survival quotient" and the term "bad" with "strong survival quotient." Thus, man in his thinking or reverie status admires the progression toward extinction, but in the unthinking stimulus which really activates him he tends toward survival. Perhaps no other animal is so torn between alternatives. Man might be described fairly adequately, if simply, as a two-legged paradox. He has never become accustomed to the tragic miracle of consciousness. Perhaps, as has been suggested, his species is not set, has not jelled, but is still in a state of becoming, bound by his physical memories to a past of struggle and survival, limited in his futures by the uneasiness of thought and consciousness.[2]

This passage is taken at random from a vast number of similar ones. This hiatus or fundamental structural "fault" can also be described in other categories and under other aspects, as for instance in the opposition of Socrates and Callicles in Plato's *Gorgias*. Callicles only acknowledges the standpoint of power and success; he finds Socrates' philosophical arguments unreal and remote from life. Can he understand them at all, let alone do justice to them? He quits the scene prematurely and leaves the philosopher alone to settle accounts, in his sublime manner, with Athenian power politics; in doing so he has a premonition of his own violent removal. In the same way, in the grim dialogue between the Athenians and the Melians (in Thucydides V, 85–112), the standpoint of the stronger party is opposed to that of fairness and sincerity. The Athenians say:

> Do not imagine that we are ignorant that, among men, there can only be justice where powers are equal; the powerful man does what suits him, and the weak man must put up with it. . . . In our view the right of the stronger applies to the whole world and to the divinity in which we believe, and this accords with man's experience. . . . Nor should you clutch at the notion of honor, which has so often brought imperilled men to ruin; many a one has been incited, by the seductive sound of the word "honor", freely to plunge forever to his own destruction. . . .

(Hesiod took the right of the stronger to be a natural law in the animal kingdom—and it remained an open question how far *nomos* coincided with *physis*. . . .) After the battle the men of Melos were all slaughtered.

[2] John Steinbeck, *The Log from the Sea of Cortez* (New York: Viking Press, 1951).

There is little hope of man undergoing a substantial change in empirical historical time, if we heed the arguments of the biologists and those anthropologists who adopt a biological standpoint. They emphasize that, from birth, man has a relationship with the world that is essentially different from that of the animals: man's spiritual nature is bought at a price, namely, he finds that he is "the eternal protestant", opposing the laws of self-preservation (Max Scheler),[3] albeit the spirit has to draw all its power of negation, of initiating its own action, from these same instincts. The price of spiritual being is that, unlike the animals, whose existence may be termed "centric", man's existence is "ex-centric" (Helmut Plessner): man's own center maintains "a certain distance from itself, so that, by means of this distance, it facilitates the total reflexivity of the life-system". "Man's life possesses itself . . . , and so there is the 'I', the vanishing point of personal inwardness that lies 'behind itself'; withdrawn from all possible life-events, in virtue of its own center, it constitutes the spectator of this inner scenario."[4] This results in "a real hiatus in man's nature. He lives on both sides of this hiatus."[5] "This ex-centricity presents the person involved in it with an insoluble contradiction", indeed, it "remains an absurdity even if and when it is embodied in reality"; it remains "an understood unintelligibility".[6] Man is homeless, and this compels him, "displaced, needy and naked" as he is, to build a house of culture, an artificial naturalness; but ultimately he cannot thus create a home for himself. According to Plessner, even the concept of God, the absolute Ground of the world, remains oriented to the circle of nature, whereas man's sign is "the straight line of endless infinity".[7] Thus, according to Arnold Gehlen,[8] man is the being who is compelled to come to some view of himself, who constitutes "a task to be performed".[9] This is the case not only with regard to the "top story" of his

[3] *Die Stellung des Menschen im Kosmos* (Darmstadt: Reichl, 1928), 65.

[4] *Die Stufen des Organischen und der Mensch. Einleitung in die philosophische Anthropologie* (Berlin: W. de Gruyter, 1928), 290.

[5] *Ibid.*, 292.

[6] *Ibid.*, 342–43.

[7] *Ibid.*, 346.

[8] *Der Mensch. Seine Natur und seine Stellung in der Welt*, 2d ed. (Berlin: Junker und Dünnhaupt, 1941).

[9] *Ibid.*, 20–21.

constitution, which sets him apart from the animal kingdom,
namely, his ability to reflect and inhabit an open rather than a
closed environment (J. von Uexküll); for the "top story"
determines the structure of the whole, right down to the
foundations of body and sense. Man is "a prototype of the
whole of nature. He is unique, nothing like him has ever been
attempted before";[10] since man is his own task, nature "has
deigned to create a new principle of organization for him".[11]
There is no gradual approach to it in the animal kingdom; there
are no transitions between a closed environment and the open
world, between nature and civilization, between instinct that is
here-and-now and reason that plans for the future in a way that
is Promethean, that is, pro-methean ("taking account of, pro-
viding for, the future").[12] Gehlen analyzes particular aspects:
for example, the way we are obliged to act in order to relieve the
pressure on us of the clamoring world; the manifold roots
leading to the development of language; the kind of stimuli—
not instincts!—that are necessary to maintain such a being in
existence; but we can bypass them. It is scarcely possible to
criticize the fundamental intuition:[13] that is, the biologically
negative aspect of man, his ill-adaptation and helplessness, is a
necessary expression of something positive: man must "take
upon himself the perilous nature of his own being".[14]

We can express the same paradox in the axiom that man has a
given "compulsion toward freedom";[15] this is "not a freedom
with a view to possibility, that is, freedom to do this or that, but
a freedom to embrace necessity".[16] But it is precisely this kind

[10] *Ibid.*, 7.

[11] *Ibid.*, 9.

[12] *Ibid.*, 20, 39.

[13] Cf. A. Mahn, "Über die philosophische Anthropologie von Arnold
Gehlen" in *Zeitschrift für philosophische Forschung* VI, 1 (1951). H. E. Hengstenberg, "Der Mensch ist kein Mängelwesen" in *Philosophische Anthropologie*, 3d
ed. (Stuttgart: Kohlhammer, 1957), 93–100. Gehlen does not say that man is
given a task to perform on himself because he is biologically inadequately
equipped; rather he assumes that the biological situation and the fundamental
metabiological fact are necessarily mutually correlative.

[14] Gehlen 411.

[15] Hengstenberg 41f.

[16] Nicolai Hartmann, *Ethik* (1926), 204.

of freedom, confronted, not with a closed world, but with an
open one, which ultimately only offers "material" and refrains
from prescribing any norms, that is faced with the difficult
question: From where is it to draw its norms for human self-
realization? All it can do, ultimately, is to hold fast to the
twofold fact: on the one hand, this "material" world, of which,
along with its biological infrastructure, it remains a part, is the
stage on which it is to realize itself; and, on the other hand, its
factual existence, its simply being there, in the form of freedom
points to its finitude and, at a deeper level, to the fact that it has
been given to itself as both gift and task; thus it also exhibits a
relation to infinite freedom, assuming that its factual existence is
not to remain an insoluble and tormenting riddle forever. Can
we not say, however, that this twofold relation automatically
makes man aware of a perspectival vanishing point so that,
where the lines (of the world and of God) intersect, we are
presented with the fully implemented program of human self-
realization? But do the lines actually intersect? Insofar as finite
freedom is related to a freedom that is infinite, it is already
superior to all the finitude of the world (not only of the environment); but, in this situation, it cannot understand and use
infinite freedom as a means of self-perfection within the terms of
the world; for this would conflict with the concept of freedom
itself. On the other hand, the "material" aspect of the world
does not even hint at the direction man ought to take if he is to
realize himself; the biological data are insufficient for this purpose, as Scheler, Plessner and Gehlen have increasingly urged.

Man, therefore, cannot be defined by anything outside of
him; he can and must define *himself*. Yet, as we have seen, he
cannot step out of the dramatic action in which he finds himself
in order to reflect on which part he will play. He is part of the
play without having been asked, and he in fact plays a role. But
which role? As far as he is concerned, as Nietzsche said, man is
"the animal not yet defined"; it is up to him to define himself.
At the same time it remains an open question whether this
definition—insofar as it can be drawn up at all—is to be
vindicated only by him and in his presence (in man's success or
failure) or in the presence of another judicial authority.

We must add this: man, involved as he is in the "play", lives in a dramatic movement that proceeds from a "first act" and leads to a "final act". If the play is to be meaningful, the brokenness of the present situation must be overcome, in principle, at least in the last act; indeed, this process begins even in the first act, whether in the ideal or in the real dimension. We cannot get a direct idea of the original totality or of the ultimate one; religious and mythical images of an original unspoiled, paradisal state and a final golden age are nothing more than the formal announcement of a postulate. To say that such things are anchored in an original memory-deposit of the human race, or in an ultimate state for which mankind unequivocally strives, remains an indemonstrable assertion. All the more since people's experience of the present brokenness is very diverse, and certain *Weltanschauungen* regard man as capable of relative wholeness, even in the present situation. Normally, nonetheless, the attempt to embrace both the beginning and the end will also highlight the direction already taken (and to be followed in the future); thus it will contain an outline of the unbroken totality.

As we have said, this totality cannot be synthesized by any combination of the elements that lie to hand. It is only possible to construct it on the basis of the "now" by rejecting elements that do not seem to fit or by substantially restricting their scope. Thus, for instance, the fact that man is bound up with and dependent on the world, and has a "world mission", can be played down in an eschatology of individual souls; conversely, the significance of the individual living here and now can be minimized in a communist apocalyptic. Such attempts at harmonization suddenly bring to light a hitherto concealed, paradoxical feature of the human being: the tensions inherent in man (for example, between the individual and the community) cannot easily be brought into equilibrium, as it were, at a purely worldly and natural level; they tend, in fact, to polarize even more, in such a way that the most urgent and central thing seems to be now the individual's salvation, now the salvation of all mankind, which can only come about where there is a reciprocal integration of the salvation of all individuals. We discern something similar—and even harder to reconcile—in the case of the tension between man's worldliness and his "other-worldliness". As we have shown, in man's worldliness

[*Weltlichkeit*], by contrast with the animal's dependence on the environment [*Umweltlichkeit*], there lies an element of infinite revelation, of distance vis-à-vis all that is particular within the world; in other words, in spite of the fact that man is bound up with the world, there is something a-cosmic about him. This will come into greater prominence the more man's relation to the divine is distinguished from his relation to the world. For now it becomes impossible to treat the element of world-transcendence in man as a mere condition that enables him to think and act within the parameters of the world: for the divine, insofar as it is seen and acknowledged as such, is the highest value; it is its own value and as such claims the allegiance of self-transcending man. Yet, by being "a-cosmic" in this sense, does man not commit treason against the world?

In a Christian theodramatic theory we have the right to assert that no other, mythical or religio-philosophical anthropology can attain a satisfactory idea of man, an idea that integrates all the elements, but the Christian one. It alone can release man from the impossible task of trying, on the basis of his brokenness, to envisage himself as not broken, without forfeiting some essential aspect of himself in the process. It releases him from this burden by inserting him, right from the start, into the dramatic dialogue with God, so that God himself may cause him to experience *his* ultimate definition of man. This does not mean that man is dispensed from the effort of planning and fashioning himself, but he is shown the way to do it and the ultimate destination he should have in mind.

This calls for the simultaneous development of two elements of revelation and dogmatics: that God is the Creator of the world and of man (who is *in* it and rules *over* it); and that God bestows his favor on man (and on the world that is bound up with him): he wants man (and hence the world) to make his home in him, freely, so that, in God, man can become and be what, left to himself, he would never succeed in becoming and being. Here a loud protest is heard: Surely, if this is the case, man does not shape himself but is fashioned by something extrinsic to himself! Instead of replying at this point, we simply affirm the contrary: only in this way can man fully become and fully be the *dramatis persona* he is meant to be from the outset. A partial refutation of this protest has already been given in the section on infinite and finite freedom; further arguments will emerge as our dramatic theory unfolds. In theological terms, these two principles, taken together, that is, creation and God's freely bestowed favor, constitute the principle of Jesus Christ. (Anthropology can only attain its fully rounded form on this basis.) For he is both "the firstborn of all creation", in whom, by whom and for whom all creation came into being (Col 1:15f.), and the "only begotten Son" (Jn 1:18), in whom we have (eternal) sonship and become "coheirs of God with Christ" (Rom 8:17), together with the whole creation (Rom 8:18–23). This twofold system of coordinates found in Christian revelation and dogmatics, which speaks of God as the free Creator of the world and also as the One who freely bestows his favor, granting created man a space within himself where he can attain fulfillment—this is enough, in itself, fundamentally to distinguish Christianity from all other approaches. Of course, the third coordinate—human sin, and the Cross and Resurrection of Christ —is also necessary if Christianity is to reach its full stature and render the human-Christian milieu livable in three dimensions.

For the present, however, in order formally to identify the possible anthropologies, we can content ourselves with the first two coordinates; they will enable us to separate out the various interpretations of the meaning of human life. These interpretations are either (1) pre-Christian,[17] (2) Christian or (3) post-Christian. A "pre-Christian" interpretation may well show elements (*logoi spermatikoi*) of the reality that is only fully manifested in Christianity: God does not extend his favor to man only at the time of Jesus; he gives his favor, hiddenly but effectively, ever since "the foundation of the world" (Eph 1:4). "Pre-Christian" means, rather, that the "mystery of Christ . . . was not made known to the sons of men in other generations as it has now been revealed" (Eph 3:4f.); that is, previously it was hidden in myths and speculations concerning the beginning, the end and the meaning of life. By "post-Christian", on the other

---

[17] Or, more precisely, prebiblical; but here we understand the Old Testament anthropology as a path leading to that of the New, which enables it to reach its fulfillment.

hand, we mean that modern philosophies and ideologies concerning man are profoundly and inevitably marked by the Christian system of coordinates. They may consist in a Gnostic distortion or a passionate negation of the latter, they may even be indifferent to it and ignore it and often seem to fall back into pre-Christian views; but the Christian watershed cannot be reversed, nor can it be repeated, and it puts its stamp on succeeding ages. And as for the fact that man cannot be defined from outside his dramatic performance, this is not contradicted when he is drawn into the Christian mystery; in fact, it is confirmed and substantiated. It is substantiated, negatively, in that man's essential relatedness to the mystery of Christ (although it cannot be read from his "essence") shows that, without this relation, man *must* remain an insoluble riddle; not only has a solution not been found: as a matter of fact it *could not* be found. It is confirmed in that, through this relationship, man sees himself face to face with the mystery of God himself; thus, positively, it becomes clear that, since man is the "image and likeness" of him who is essentially unknown and cannot be objectified, man himself *must* show some traits of this mystery. In a "negative anthropology"[18] that takes its bearings purely from man, negativity is a critique that radically attacks every objectified picture of man;[19] in Sartre it is the absolutizing of finite freedom, which eventually undermines every definition of being. In Christianity, however, negativity is oriented to the positive, to the God who is ever-greater, in such a way that we can never catch up with him. Accordingly, we who are his "image and likeness" do not despair because of our inability to arrive at a definition; instead, we are aware of a comparative dimension: man is *more* than what can be included in a conceptually clear definition. It is not simply mistaken and pointless to attempt such definitions. (Statements about God's essence, too, have an abiding validity.) While we can never come to the end of our attempt at integration, there *are* valid building stones

[18] Ulrich Sonnemann, *Negative Anthropologie. Vorstudien zur Sabotage des Schicksals* (Rowohlt, 1969).

[19] "Anthropology cannot be a science except insofar as it criticizes its object. Paradoxically it must infuse itself back into the latter's immanence in the form of praxis and explode it by its destructive power." *Ibid.*, 138. Cf. 227ff.

to be used in the process. In the perspective of theo-drama, integration is God's act, not man's.

2. Man and Nature ("Pre-Christian")

a. Rooted in the Cosmos

While it is true that man has always reflected upon himself and the riddle he is (Oedipus and the Sphinx), the distinct science of "anthropology" only arises in modern times. In pre-Christian times the question of man is only posed in connection with the question of the whole of being. This totality embraces both the visible cosmos, which enfolds man and of which he is also essentially a part, and the divine (*theion*), which is not directly visible as a whole. Indeed, it is hard to make out how far the latter is immanent in the cosmos—as its highest sphere, for instance, glimpsed from afar in the wondrous, unchanging order of the constellations—and how far it is transcendent. But even in its transcendence it remains in contact with the cosmos.

However, this immanence-transcendence—which cannot be defined any more precisely—on the part of the divine in relation to the world does not mean that man is not aware, in an elementary and prereflex mode, of the qualitative difference between the cosmic and the *theion*. No Greek would have dreamed of confusing himself with a god; the Delphic inscriptions, "Know thyself" (that is, "Overreach not thyself, O mortal") and "Nothing above its proper measure", put those who were not divine quite definitely in their places. Even if he makes no sharp distinction between the cosmos and the *theion*, pre-Christian man, the "naturally" religious man, lives in the awareness of a primal *analogia entis*. (In all cultures, speculations tending toward mystical identity are late in emerging.) Pre-Christian man has a natural awe of the divine world, whether it is conceived as plural or monistic, personal or impersonal. This awe can express itself in contrary forms: confidence or distrust; it can be based on eudaimonism or it can be selfless: in any case it is a fundamental attitude that embraces every approach to the totality. At a natural level (*physikōs*), the order discerned in the world is the given; it also governs man's being and his life with others. By contrast, the order imposed by man is secondary (Antiphonos the Sophist). But this all-embracing context—and this applies most definitely to the so-called Ionic natural philosophers as well—is by no means (subhuman) "nature" in the modern sense: it is existent being (*das Seiende*) as a whole, which always includes the *theion*. Thus, in the *dikē*, which is the governing norm of worldly nature (as in the Egyptian *maat* and as in the *tao*), operative law is fundamentally inseparable from justice. This helps us to understand how, in pre-Christian thought, the *dikē* of the *polis* can be projected into the cosmos (cf. Anaximandros), and the *dike* of Being can appear as the *dikē* of the *polis* (Solon). Only at a relatively late stage do people ask what is the law that governs man, which results in him being defined as the "measure of things" (Protagoras); but this normative function on man's part is immediately relativized within the reciprocal relationship of man and (*theios*) *kosmos*, where the *polis*, with its structure and order, mediates between the individual and the cosmos. When, in Plato's *Republic*, it is asked what is the proper order within the *polis*, the individual's inner order and the right political order can be shown as reflecting each other: insofar as particular conditions are maintained (in the end summed up as justice), the state exists in this order as an "immense man", just as the individual human being exists in it as a "little state". Ultimately, however, the concept of order is read from the enfolding cosmos (*Timaeus*), in which the gods stand in their appointed places. In Plato's *Laws*, in fact, it is God, explicitly, who measures man, the state and the cosmos, emphatically contradicting Protagoras: "In our view it is God who is preeminently the 'measure of all things', much more so than any 'man', as they say" (*Laws* 716C).[1]

The gods essentially retain their position within the cosmos as "representations of the divinity" and "helpers of men". This is evident from the fact that even dualistic views of man, such as those of Plato and Aristotle, do not slip out of this framework. In Plato, man's immortal soul, falling from the realm of Ideas "above the heavens", can join itself to a mortal body: this

[1] On this whole topic: W. Jaeger, *Paideia* III, 2d ed. (Berlin, 1955), 317ff.

dualism is held together by a unity of being that embraces the cosmos and the divine world, as is shown in the *Phaedrus*, the *Symposium* and most strongly in the *Timaeus*. When Aristotle discusses man's composition, he says that the spirit is added to the biological composite "*thyrathen*", from outside and from above; and this "outside and above" is nothing alien to the world's being, for the latter's transcendent apex is the Divine, which thinks itself and moves everything else. As for the objection that, of all living beings in the cosmos, man has the greatest dignity, Aristotle says that it carries "no weight. For there are beings whose nature, as to divine status, far exceeds man's: those (the constellations)—to name only the most visible —from which the universe is constructed" (*Eth. Nic.* VI, 1141ab). The certainty that divine beings exist proves that man is not absolute.

We would be doing an injustice to pre-Christian thought if we were to take this fluid *analogia entis*, exhibiting as it does the gleam of an original religiosity that has not yet been the subject of reflection, and either force it into a dualism (as is often done in the case of Plato) or simplify it to a pantheistic monism (as often happens to the Stoic and Neoplatonic model of the world). It cannot be thus reduced to a single pole. Such an over-simplification would also lead to a misconception of the attempts made in later, Christian times to put forward a model of the world by reviving and drawing on antiquity's view of it.

However, it was possible to allow pre-Christian cosmologies and (hence) anthropologies to persist in the Christian period— where, as many people think, they ought properly speaking to have been repudiated—because the relationship between the cosmos and the *theion* survived, in a Christian transposition, right into modern times, in spite of the fact that now there was a far more abrupt distinction between the divine, absolute world and the contingent world freely created by God. In order to understand this, we only need to recall the reciprocal relationship of heaven and earth that we described at the outset, which, within the framework of an ancient view of the world, could be interpreted in an unabashedly cosmological manner (which is no longer possible today). The heaven of the Bible can belong to the created world, while nonetheless it is the "locus" of God in creation; an analogy to this (cf. Dante) would be the way the Platonic world of Ideas and the "Chaldaean" *empyreum*, in spite of their transcendence, belong to the world's totality. Ever since Aristotle, the stars, seen as moving causes of world events, have been regarded as endowed with soul, as divine;[2] according to late Platonism, the Ideas are understood to be intelligences, and they remain thus in Arabic philosophy, whereas in the Christian Fathers and the Scholastics, they become angelic heavenly beings; but in Christian anthropology, as in Plato and Aristotle, man can once again consist of an inner-cosmic (biological) and a hyper-cosmic (spiritual) element, without ceasing to mirror the whole cosmos and its normative organization. With no detriment to the specifically Christian elements, to which we shall turn subsequently, the ancient world's way of rooting man in the cosmos—and the *civitas* that mediated between them, cf. the medieval empire, Thomas, Dante[3]—could persist unchallenged for a long time.

This also provides us with a standard by which to evaluate correctly the correspondence between *microcosmos* (man) and *macrocosmos* (the universe) and the to-and-fro of their relationship.[4] We must always keep in mind the original reciprocity of the two poles, which, before it emerged in Greece, was doubtless a part of much more primitive civilizations,[5] wherever the political cosmos acted as mediator between them. Thus medicine

[2] *Met.* XII, 8; 1074bff.; *Phys.* VIII; *De gen et corr.* II, 10.

[3] W. von den Steinen, *Homo Caelestis* I (Berne: Francke, 1965), 141ff., 172ff.

[4] We are excluding from this discussion the ideas associated with Adam Kadmon's "Grossmensch" and the notion that mankind is descended from a god or giant. Here we are solely concerned with man as he is, as God's dramatic "partner". The most important texts on the theme of the "microcosm" are collated in the article of the same name by Rudolf Allers in *Traditio* II (New York, 1944), 319–407, although they are organized there in a way that renders them difficult to digest. Also G. P. Conger, *Theories of Macrocosmus and Microcosmus in the History of Philosophy* (New York, 1922); H. Hommel, "Mikrokosmos" in *Rhein. Mus. f. Philol.* 92 (1943–1944), 56f.; Arnold A. T. Ehrhardt, *Politische Metaphysik von Solon bis Augustin*, I: Die Gottesstadt der Griechen und Römer (Tübingen: Mohr, 1959), 150ff. A. Meyer, *Wesen und Geschichte der Theorie von Mikro- und Makrokosmus* (Diss., Berne, 1901) is unsatisfactory.

[5] This is a vast topic; here we refer only to the brief account in Cyrill von Korvin-Krasinski's *Mikrokosmos und Makrokosmos* (Düsseldorf: Patmos, 1960).

thinks cosmically: the "con-spiration" (*sympnoia*) of the elements in the human organism (Hippocrates, Galen)[6] corresponds, in Poseidonios, to the cosmic organism. It is on the basis of Poseidonios—not Philo—that the Church Fathers, especially Gregory of Nyssa, teach that there is the same *sympnoia* in the human and the cosmic organisms.[7] According to Galen the term *microkosmos*, applied to man (probably influenced by Pythagoras), first occurs in Democritus;[8] it crops up again in Aristotle (in relation to man and animals)[9] and settles down in Stoicism (Poseidonios).[10] He in turn influences Philo and the Cappadocians. For Philo, the human being is a concentration —an abbreviation—of all cosmic forces, the high and the lowly[11] —which does not prevent him from seeing in man, at the same time, the reflected glory of the Supercosmic.[12] We find the same combination in Gregory of Nyssa: "If the whole cosmos", he says, "is a musical harmony, composed and created by God, and if, on the other hand, man is a microcosm since he is also the image of him who built the cosmos; then what the Spirit shows us in the macrocosm is also found in the microcosm."[13]

Utterances such as these, even from writers inspired by the Bible, show that this elastic relationship between man and cosmos remained unproblematical, indeed taken for granted.[14] Thus we see how man was rooted and secured by a relationship not subject to his own reflection, even though we must not

[6] Galen, *De usu part*. III, 10, when describing the human being as a "tiny world", quotes "ancient authorities in matters of nature (*physis*)".

[7] Quotations from Gregory of Nyssa in J. Daniélou, *L'Etre et le temps chez Grégoire de Nysse* (Leiden: Brill, 1970), 51ff. The same terminology is found in Methodius, *De Res*. II, 10, 2, and Gregory Nazianzen, *Or*. 27 (PG 36, 57A).

[8] Diels 68 B 34.

[9] *Phys*. VIII, 252b, 26.

[10] K. Reinhardt, *Poseidonios* (Munich: Beck, 1921), 343ff.

[11] *Leg. alleg*. II, 22.

[12] J. Giblet, *L'Homme image de Dieu dans les commentaires littéraux de Philon d'Alexandrie* (Louvain, 1949).

[13] *Inscript. Psalm*. I, 3 (PG 44, 441C).

[14] "What today we call a 'cosmic' view of man was an utterly natural presupposition in Greek metaphysics; so natural, indeed, that it is often not expressed at all but only emerges once we have understood the way the ideas are interrelated." J. Stenzel, "Metaphysik des Altertums" in *Handbuch d. Philos*. I (Munich, 1931), 29.

interpret this correlation one-sidedly, as if the human world were totally enveloped by the cosmos. For in the first place, as we have already emphasized, the cosmos is in part (as "hyper-cosmos") the *theion*; and secondly, the concrete representation and concentration of the cosmos is the *polis*, fashioned and guided by men, radically reflected on and adumbrated by Plato. The *polis* is the meeting place of the divine *nomos* of justice, which governs the cosmos, and that wisdom which "ought" to govern man, which alone can guarantee justice in a particular state. If the supreme divine norm operates both in the cosmos and in the *polis*, Plato is well aware how much, in the latter case, it depends on the ethical "ought", which in turn requires wisdom on the part of the state's ruler. Thus "the cosmos of the *polis*" is always vulnerable,[15] and so, perhaps, is the macrocosm behind the *polis*: order in the macrocosm cannot be guaranteed in sheer independence of man. For "the cosmos is only a small part of the universe; all else is as yet unformed matter" (Empedocles).[16]

In this period man was secure within a certain fluidity; prior to Christianity, in fact, his security was greatest in this fluid environment. It was inevitable that man would attempt to overcome the fluidity by moving toward a more fixed system, either by universalizing the *polis* so that ultimately it coincided with the cosmos (in the Hellenistic cosmopolitism of the in-dividual) or by the contrary movement, whereby the cosmos is drawn into the *polis*, resulting in the identification of the divine *nomos* with that of the ruler (Alexander, the divinity of the Roman emperors). Both tendencies burst the bounds of the human, per-sonally and socially. Both of them lead to the borders of Christ-ianity: the cosmopolis will be superseded by the "hexaemeron" and the "Civitas Dei", the divine Emperor by Christus Panto-krator. But even the latest pagan syntheses, despite all attempts to systematize them, retain a certain fluid character, and it is this that justifies them: the various expressions of Stoicism rest on the fluid interplay of "world logos" and personal logos in the individual, and the successive forms of Neoplatonism rest on

[15] Cf. the quotation from the first speech of the Pseudo-Demosthenes against Aristogeiton (I, 19) in Ehrhardt (see n. 4 above), 153.

[16] Diels 31 A 47.

the "golden chain" of ascending and descending stages of being, where each one supports and interprets the following; in the system of "emanations", the idea of a fall from the Most High and the idea of the latter's superabundant self-presentation (*bonum diffusivum sui*) cancel each other out ontologically and ethically.

In pre-Christian times this fluidity, that is, the fact that the man/cosmos relationship cannot be pinned down, can retain a certain uncanny quality; outside the "order" chaos threatens, as our quotation from Empedocles shows. In the most ancient times the threat lurking in the background was called *moira* or *apeiron* (whereas Plato endeavored to restrict it within his concept of the divine); in the late period it returns in the form of *heimarmenē*. The fundamental Aristotelian concept of the *meson*, the moderate middle between the immoderate extremes of too much and too little, reveals something of that primitive Greek moderation which opposed Titanism, withdrawing to the narrow area that is appropriate for man. Classical tragedy shows how, even in this narrow realm, it is beset, from without and within, by violent forces to whom all moderation is alien.

As for what is concentrated at moderation's center, the order of the world and human order, while it is clearly distinguished from immoderate excess, *hubris*, the ethics of pure power and pure pleasure, it itself hovers between the natural and the ethical. Central concepts of human perfection such as *kalogathia*, *eugenia*, *aristie*, *aretē*, *eudaimonie*, and many others used by Plato and Aristotle (to say nothing of the Stoics), hover, undefinable, between felicitous natural endowment and ethical perfection. Even where the latter comes unequivocally to the fore—as in the trial of Socrates—it can only be expressed in the concepts that have come down to us, many-hued, changeable and confusing. Aristotle makes a clear distinction between physical and ethical *aretē*; the animal and the child may have good natural endowments, but they must be complemented: the spirit must be guided in accord with the correct plan (*orthos logos*), and there must be voluntary action if there is to be "real *aretē*" (*Eth. Nic.* VI, 1144b). But what goal (*telos*, *skopos*) will guide the action, if not an ideal of "nature"? For us to have an "eye" (1143b) for what is right, we need to be well-born; such noble birth will assert itself provided we freely cooperate in bringing it to

fulfillment—which now must be an ethical fulfillment as well. [17]
On the other hand, Plato and Aristotle are able to say much
about man's ethical struggle and, accordingly, about the inner
confusion of his nature, the "uncontrolled" aspect of the sub-
spiritual (the myth of *Phaedrus*, Book VII of the *Nicomachean
Ethics*). [18] This can serve as a prelude to the Christian reflections
on concupiscence, and initially it lays bare the element of dramatic
struggle in the Greek ethos itself. In his old age, Plato sees the
world as an "immortal struggle" between the good that governs
it and the superior strength of that which is not good; this
struggle "calls for an extraordinary vigilance". [19] Thus man,
rooted in nature, is involved, together with the entire universe,
in a battle that is all around him.

Somehow, however, since man is the microcosm that not
only "images" the macrocosm or presents it in a concentrated
form but penetrates it by virtue of his spirit—"the spirit is, as it
were, everything" [20]—he is superior to the universe and has an
affinity with the distinctively divine. There is nothing Titanic in
the famous Aristotelian formula nor in Plato's assertion that
God has

> invented the power of vision for us (so giving us the highest good,
> philosophy) so that we can observe the way reason permeates the
> world's edifice and apply it to the circling of our own thought.
> For our thought is related to the reason that is in the world, to
> the extent that the profoundly shaken *can* be related to the
> Unshakable. [21]

Thus, even in pre-Christian times, there is something in the
cosmos that is "free of all error", which we can see with the eyes
of the spirit and, even in the midst of our erring path, imitate.

[17] Cf. the commentary on Aristotle's *Nicomachean Ethics* by Franz Dirlmeier,
WW 6 (1956), 471f., passim. Olof Gigon, *Einleitung zur Nik. Ethik*, Bibl. der
Alten Welt (Zürich: Artemis, 1951), 33ff.

[18] M. Pohlenz, *Griechische Freiheit, Wesen und Werden eines Lebensideals*
(Heidelberg, 1955), esp. 87–109 ("Self-Control and the Freedom of the Spirit").

[19] *Laws* 906B.

[20] Aristotle, *On the Soul* III, 431b, 21. Thomas comments on this summary
sentence in *De Anima* III, bk. 13, Pirotta 787ff.; he quotes it frequently: *S. Th.* I,
14, 1 c; 16, 3 c; 80, 1 c; 84, 2 arg 2, ad 2; *C. G.* I, 44; II, 47, etc.

[21] *Timaeus* 47bc.

This brings us back to the double meaning of the "microcosm" image, which will persist even in the Christian period: on the one hand, man is the epitome of the cosmic tensions and oppositions; so, following Aristotle, the "ancients" saw him, and so he will be described by Scotus Erigena,[22] later Hildegard[23] and, in a new way, the Florentine Renaissance. The other line corresponds to Aristotle's view that the soul intends the comprehensive unity of the world; thus Thomas, who takes up the *quodammodo omnia* as being distinctive of the human soul, will describe man as microcosm only in a limited sense: man has an affinity with the universe, but "*quantum ad aliquid*", not in every respect.[24] The effects of this distinction will be seen in modern times, when man, in virtue of his own spirit, will finally lift himself above the protective and encompassing universe. For the present—in the ancient world and the Middle Ages—the encompassing relationship remains intact in both approaches; nowhere more so, perhaps, than in Hildegard, where the cosmos as a whole is created "hominiform", with a view to man. Man is physically and spiritually borne up and permeated by the energies of the cosmos, while the totality remains secure in the Creator's love and in his first and original plan, namely, to unite history and cosmos in himself by becoming incarnate. Here we even have the return of the Greek equivalence of the physical and the ethical, although on the Christian plane, purified and clarified: again, the world's energies and the virtues are one; man, who is body and soul, cannot allow himself to be determined by his physical powers without at the same time acting responsibly and ethically: he must contribute to shaping the meaning of his existence. And once again it is the "*polis*" that mediates between physis and ethos, now in the form of the Ecclesia, towering over all salvation history in world events.

[22] "[Homo] officina omnium jure appellatur, in ea siquidem omnia conferunt quae a Deo condita sunt, unamque harmoniam ex diversis naturis veluti quibusdam distantibus sonis composuit" *Div. Nat.* II, 4 (PL 122, 530D).

[23] In the tremendous Fourth Vision of the book *Liber divinum Operum* (or *De Operatione Dei*, PL 197, 713ff.) translated by H. Schipperges under the title *Welt und Mensch* (Salzburg: Müller, 1965), 79–184. Hans Liebeschütz, "Das allegorische Weltbild der hl. Hildegard von Bingen", *Stud. d. Bibl. Warburg* 16 (Leipzig, 1939), 59ff.

[24] *Quodl.* 4 a 3; *S. Th.* I, 91, a 1 c; 96, a 2 c; I–II, 17, a 8 c and ad 2; *De pot.* 5 a 10.

We can discern the end of this rootedness and a transition to something new in the world view of Cusanus. True, man is still seen in terms of the microcosm,[25] but behind both man and world there appears—more strongly than in Hildegard—the Divinity who "explicates" himself in both. This means that man, the "*deus humanatus*", acquires a preeminence—with an ultimately christological significance—so that he is related much more directly to God than to the world; he steps out beyond the cosmos into a realm where he is unprotected.

b. Spirit and Body

When man thus eventually steps forth and becomes a question to himself, however, he takes himself along, together with all his constant attributes. For he is spirit and body, man and woman, individual and community.[26] These constants are part of his nature, his essence, which does not mean that they solve his riddle; in fact, they render it more profound and more pressing. In all three dimensions, man seems to be built according to a polarity, obliged to engage in reciprocity, always seeking complementarity and peace in the other pole. And for that very reason he is pointed beyond his whole polar structure. He is always found crossing the boundary, and thus he is defined most exactly by that boundary with which death brutally confronts him, in all three areas, without taking account of his threefold transcendence.

The tension between body and spirit is manifested in the

[25] On the transitional nature of these texts, cf. Allers (n. 4 above), 379–83.

[26] Erich Przywara developed these three dimensions in his anthropological studies. First, briefly, in *Deus semper Major, Theologie der Exerzitien*, 2d ed. (Vienna-Munich: Herold, 1964), 1:49–68; then in *Humanitas. Der Mensch gestern und morgen* (Nuremberg: Glock und Lutz, 1952), passim, with a vast array of material; and finally in *Mensch, typologische Anthropologie* I (Nuremberg: Glock und Lutz, 1958), a titanic and ambitious attempt at a synthesis, unparalleled in its aim to bring together a vast subject matter. The attempt clarifies the shapeless material amassed under the heading "Humanitas" but, at the same time, deliberately—in the sense of the late form of the *analogia entis*—explodes every *Gestalt* that claims to be comprehensible within a single view (cf. *All-Rhythmus* in "Analogia Entis", *Schriften* III, 2d ed. [Einsiedeln: Johannes Verlag, 1962], 215–522).

contrary pull of the two poles. Initially each seems to embrace the other only in a unity. Man is spirit only as the crown of a series of forms that ascend from the energies of matter; he recapitulates these forms in himself. *Qui autem intelligit, eum et esse et vivere certissimum est*, says Augustine (*Lib. arb.* II, 3, 7), only putting into words the evident truth uttered before him and after him. Such recapitulation of the prior stages—mechanically motile plant and animal life—presupposes that spirit has genetic origins in matter. In Aristotelian terms, the developmental process presses forward from *dynamis* to *energeia*; in Augustinian language, everything that comes into being in the cosmos lies originally in the *rationes seminales*; as Thomas puts it, the human embryo recapitulates the ascending cosmic substantial forms; finally, in the modern evolutionist world model, the human form represents the end product of a process whereby life forms diverge and differentiate as a result of mysterious leaps and mutations that are never really explained.

On the other side, the faculty of reflection—as Scheler, Plessner and Gehlen have shown us—implies such a distance from the realm of the vital and immediate that it fundamentally modifies the infrastructure necessary for its operation (cf. especially Gehlen); indeed, it reduces it to the level of a tool. What (ascending from below) seems to be the goal (*telos*) of the development is seen, from the vantage point of the attained end, to be its meaning. (Similarly, according to Thomas, the *causa finalis* is the first cause, setting all operations in motion.) The Idealist simplification, therefore, will say that the spirit itself assumes the cosmic development as a condition for its realization; but this remains hard to achieve unless, in this process, reality is attributed to the spirit. Nor can a spirit that is still searching for itself (for example, the "World Soul"), struggling to attain self-consciousness, suffice to explain the teleology of evolution: not fully, at least. The formative spirit in nature, as yet unconscious, presupposes an absolute and real Spirit that communicates to it the Idea to be aimed at, namely, man, so that this Idea is always approaching, always realizing itself. Edgar Dacqué has striven to explicate this in numerous books. In his view (which reflects Aristotle's) the potentiality for the higher must also be present in the lowly natural form; in this case "the

entelechy, man, . . . is the pervading metaphysical meaning of
the entire tree of life". All the same,

> all the animal forms that have ever lived show themselves to be
> . . . either much more one-sidedly specialized than man or else
> they have taken a one-sided path leading away from the hypo-
> thetical genealogical tree that . . . might lead to man. . . . In other
> words, the central trunk of the tree of life does not exist at all, at
> the level of natural history, in physical animal forms. It is only
> there in the idea.[27]

This "in the idea" contains an ambiguity, but it is cleared up
when we learn that, for Dacqué, the "primal Idea" of Adam is
the result of a prototype of creation and that this primitive
man, endowed with freedom, turned from his Creator and so
(and not until then) became entangled in "denser matter", in
a "nature that is demonic through and through"; thence—
according to the scientific and palaeontological view—he
emerges as an "empirical natural being", a "partial expression"
of that primal Idea. No doubt it is true, at the secondary level,
that all animal forms are partial representations of the human,
but this is only because the primitive, original man fundamentally
turned away from God and set off the whole natural process.
Here, quite clearly, we are close to the myth of the "soul's" fall
into matter, as found in Plato, the Gnostics and Origen.[28]

---

[27] *Natur und Erlösung* (Munich: Oldenbourg, 1933), 130. In more detail in
Leben als Symbol (Munich: Oldenbourg, 1928). Next to Dacqué, today, we must
mention Ernest Wilder-Smith, who, on a purely biological basis, raises objections
against the Darwinian dogma. Cf. *Grundlage zu einer neuen Biologie* (1974).
Herkunft und Zukunft des Menschen, 2d ed. (1975), *Erschaffung des Lebens, Evolution
aus kybernetischer Sicht* (1972), all published by Hänsler, Stuttgart.

[28] At this point there is no need for us to enter into Dacqué's further
speculations on God, the spirit world, the origin of evil and the secondary
character of man's bi-sexuality—traits which bring him to the position held by
Jakob Böhme (cf. *Das Bildnis Gottes* [Leipzig: Insel, 1939]; *Die Urgestalt* [1940]).
Nor do we need to discuss his doctrine of redemption, which alternates between
Schopenhauer and Christian dogmatics. There is a brief characterization in
A. Dempf, "Edgar Dacqué und Josef Görres" in *Philos. Jahrb. d. Görresgesell-
schaft* (1951/3), 304–13. On the other hand, this is the place to introduce a word
on *Anton Günther's* basic outline of anthropology. For him, man is the "synthesis"
of the two realms of creation which are otherwise irreconcilable: nature and
spirit (in subjective terms: the concept and the idea). In opposition to every

We have mentioned Dacqué's outline here only because he does not see the priority of "spirit" (the Primal Idea, in his terms) over the body ("nature") in the context of a mere fall of "form" into the amorphous but is able to interpret this descent as the a priori of that evolution that ascends to a peak in the human being. Thus man can be the ultimate blossom of nature, the epitome of the world, while at the same time, despite his bodily being, he remains profoundly alien to the time-space world of nature and strives to regain the lost original world.

Right from this first aspect, that of the three fundamental human tensions, anthropology must accept the idea that there is an ambiguity to be taken into account here: what seems like a natural polarity is also an unnatural dichotomy. To see this, we need only compare the myth of the Fall in the *Phaedrus* or the *Symposium* or the *Republic* with the myth of creation in the *Timaeus*. Or we can detect, even in such a poised, monistic view of the world as Stoicism, the tension between "life according to nature" and the implacable renunciation of the "passions", which evidently contain some element that is anti-natural and harmful to reason. Initially it may be possible to see no problem and to describe the dualism in man as a mark of his dignity: man ascends, leaving behind and transcending what is below him: he is the crown of creation and ruler of the world, and this transcendence of his—the pre-Christian model holds good for the Christian period too—coincides with a direct relationship to the divine: man comes from the divine and has been instituted

---

evolutionism that sees nature unilaterally ascending to spirit (which he regards as Idealist or biological pantheism or materialism), he insists, like Dacqué later, that the spirit cannot be reduced to a product of nature. "Man is not a simple being but twofold; he is a composite of the great contraries in the universe. In him spirit and nature meet, so that he may constitute the final stone in the edifice of creation"—Günther also calls him a "compendium of the world", the "measure of all things", the "world sphinx"—"so that spirit may become the light, the eye of nature, freely communicating with her, while nature in turn communes with spirit and is thus raised to personality and freedom" ("Die doppelte Souveränität des Menschen" in *Aufwärts* [Vienna, 1848], 56). But there remains a difficulty in this approach: the two principles, since each is self-subsistent, cannot really interpenetrate. Just as nature cannot ascend to spirit, so spirit cannot descend and become embodied in nature; in spite of Günther's attempts to mediate between them, they simply collide with each other in man, from below and from above.

by it. This fundamental plan, which is found everywhere in the ancient world, is articulated in the Jewish and Christian commentaries on the second account of creation, where man is both formed out of existing clay by the hand of God *and* directly endowed with the breath of divinity. So it is in Philo[29] and, following him, Origen[30] and Basil.[31] In this perspective, man's "grandeur" becomes plain. Realistically speaking, however, this greatness cannot deny its inner torn-ness, its "misère", where "spirit" and "flesh" are "at war" with one another, resulting in man being made "captive" (Rom 7:23). Aristotle, who says that the ethical ideal is not the denial of the passions but their control, is obliged to admit the fact of man's profoundly "wicked, uncontrolled and animal nature".[32] Of the Fathers, Maximus the Confessor grappled most deeply with the paradox that the *pathē*, which are in themselves "natural", cannot ultimately be brought into harmony with the spirit.[33] However much one is bound to hold fast to the unity of man, who originates from below and from above and extends both upward and downward, a great temptation is exerted all the same by the dualistic theorems, such as those of Gnosticism-Manichaeism in the ancient world and those of Klages and Scheler in modern times. However, they are continually blocked from being carried through by the fact that dualism cannot be posited as a dualism between body (that is, matter) and spirit but, to be precise, must pass right through spirit's center; and, as we said at the beginning, the spirit needs the physical-spiritual infrastructure (although, nonetheless, it transcends it) in order to perform its specific operation, reflection.

The paradox is expressed in the age-old description of man as a "boundary", a "boundary phenomenon": *methorion*. Positively, this says that he is the mediator between the lower and the upper world; he participates in both and can cause spirit to permeate nature and lift nature up into the realm of spirit. Seen "statically",

---

[29] *Leg. alleg.* I, 31; *De op.* 45, 135.

[30] *In Jer.* h 1, 10 (Klostermann 3, 8).

[31] *In Hex.* h 10, 3 (Smets SC 230f.).

[32] *Eth. Nic.* VII, 1145 a 16f.

[33] Texts in *Kosmische Liturgie*, 2d ed. (Einsiedeln: Johannes Verlag, 1961), 161ff. ("The dialectic of passion").

he can be said to be a "mixture" of the two "inimical" worlds;[34] "dynamically", he can mediate between them, ascending and descending. But there is also something negative, or at least something problematical, in this description, for in Plato *methorion* can denote a "frontier zone" (*metaxy*) between two regions, a "hybrid": a no-man's-land.[35] If, positively, man is the "perfecter of the cosmos" by virtue of his position as mediator,[36] because (according to Gregory of Nyssa) he "stands on the boundary (*methorios*) between the divine, nonphysical nature and irrational, animal life",[37] for Plotinus this has a negative meaning: because of its middle position (*mesē taxis*) between the intelligible and the sensible, the soul is incapable of attaining a precise knowledge of either of these natures.[38]

The twofold character of these aspects arises thus: either it is possible to link both worlds mediated by man by means of a regular series of crossing points,[39] or else they must be presumed to be utterly contrary to each other. In the first case, man can be (and can seek to create) a kind of natural synthesis of these worlds; in the second case, the most he can do, after making a free choice, is to relate to one of them.[40]

The first aspect appears in its purest form in Thomas Aquinas,

[34] *Mīxis te kai anakrasis . . . tōn enantiōn*: Gregory of Nyssa, *Or. Cat.* 6 (PG 45, 25C).

[35] *Laws* IX, 878 B. Immediately afterward, Plato applies this to "an act done in anger"—which shows the anthropological scope of the image.

[36] Cf. R. Guillet, "L'Homme divinisateur cosmique dans la pensée de S. Grégoire de Nysse" in *Stud. Patr.* (1962), VI: IV, 62, 83.

[37] *De hom. op.* 16 (PG 44, 181BC). Cf. Theodore of Mopsuestia: man "is the world in sum, the hyphen between the visible and the invisible creation, the bond and node of all things, the central point toward which everything runs". *Quaest. in Genesim* 2.

[38] *Enn.* IV, 8, 7; cf. IV, 4, 3.

[39] Examples in Daniélou, *L'Etre et le temps*: Aristotle (*Animal.* VIII, 1, 2), Aetius, Philo (*Mos.* II, 62), Sextus Empiricus, Origen (*Joh. Comm.* IX, 71).

[40] Here we can exclude those texts which designate man, in the very broadest sense, as the "middle" between God (or angels) and the world, as Augustine likes to do: the soul is above the body, and God is above the soul. (Cf. "medium quoddam, sed inter pecora et angelos . . . , infra angelis et supra pecoribus . . . , cum pecoribus mortalitatem, rationem cum angelis [participans]": *Civ. Dei* X, 13 (PL 44, 267); *De Trin.* XII, 4, 4; 7, 12 (PL 42, 1000, 1005, 1007); he is followed by Hugh of St. Victor, *De Sacr.* I, 4, 26 (PL 176, 246): "homo quasi in medio collocatus, habet supra se Deum, sub se mundum". Peter Lombard, *II Sent.* 1, 7.

following a natural philosophy cultivated in the ancient world that posited intermediary elements as mediators between contrary elements. In this sense, in Aquinas, each level of being has a certain participation in the next highest and next lowest;[41] to that extent the human soul is *quasi quidam horizon et confinium corporeorum et incorporeorum*.[42] Cusanus gives us the most extreme description of this notion:

> *inter genera unum universum contrahentia talis est inferioris et superioris connexio, ut in medio coincidunt, ac inter species diversas talis combinationis ordo consistit, ut suprema species generis unius concidat [!] cum infimo immediate superioris, ut sit unum continuum universum.*[43]

Here the world model of antiquity and the Middle Ages, with its ascending and descending forms of being, has already been left behind in favor of the Leibnizian infinitesimal continuum; thus any discontinuity or breach—which emerged as a possibility in the second aspect—is rendered impossible. Man becomes a kind of sliding center, able to move upward or downward without forfeiting his synthesis-character. Ficino expresses this view in sharp opposition to the second aspect: "If man is associated with the higher and the lower nature, as their *vinculum, appetit utraque. Quapropter naturali quodam instinctu ascendit ad supera, descendit ad infera. Et dum ascendit, inferiora non deserit, et cum descendit, sublimia non relinquit.*"[44]

The other aspect questions this very assertion. The borderline on which man is placed compels him to make a free decision between "up" and "down", and the no-man's-land he occupies is his open, undefined freedom.

---

[41] *C. G.* II, 68: "Semper enim invenitur infimum supremi generis contingere supremum inferioris generis": the lowest animals are scarcely superior to plant life, and the lowest form of soul—the human—touches the highest form of animated body—again the human.

[42] *Ibid*. The term "horizon" evidently comes from the *Liber de Causis*, section 2, already used by Alain of Lille: "anima est in orizonte aeternitatis inferius et supra tempus". Cf. Baumgartner, in B.G.Ph.M.A. II, 4 (1896), 100, n. 2. On *confinium* in Thomas, cf. also *De anima* 1 c: "in confinio corporalium et separatarum substantiarum".

[43] *Docta ignor.* III, 1 (Hoffm.-Klib., 1931), I, 120.

[44] *Theol. platon.* III, 2 (Opp 1576, I, 1, 119).

The soul is the boundary between two realities: the one is intelligible, incorporeal, incorruptible, and the other is physical, material and irrational. Once it has purified itself of its attachment to the present material life, it turns, through the practice of virtue, to the Divine to which it is related.

Thus Gregory of Nyssa[45] and, following him, Nemesius,[46] who cites Philo ("the Hebrews"). According to the latter, man is "on the boundary (*methorios*) of mortal and immortal nature, sharing in both".[47] Nemesius clarifies this by saying that man, if he inclines to the changeable earthly passions, accordingly becomes subject to changeability; if he prefers the goods of the soul, he attains immortality. Augustine recognizes the same alternatives in paradisal man; together with Origen, however, Gregory of Nyssa sees man as constantly "able" to choose either. Of course, the perspective has changed here: it is no longer primarily a question of the spirit/body dimension but, more profoundly, of the freedom to embrace good or evil—a freedom which is attained at the boundary, at the point of indifference. However, as Gregory is well aware, the soul which has to choose is unthinkable apart from its physiological infrastructure.[48] Together with the latter—not against it—it has to choose the higher value. The spirit/body dimension, the dimension of immediacy and mediacy in relation to God, becomes transparent and allows us to discern the absolute/relative dimension, whereby either God is preferred to the world or the world to God.[49]

[45] *In Cant.* II (PG 44, 1009AB).

[46] *De nat. hom.* I (PG 40, 513B).

[47] *De Op.* 46, 135. For Origen, too, the soul occupies a middle position (*meson ti*) between spirit and matter (*Joh. Comm.* 32, 18; IV, 455); it strives toward either one or the other (*Peri Archon* 2, 11, 1; V, 183).

[48] *De an. et resurr.* (PG 46, 60–61).

[49] This would be the place to refer to the last writer who continually spoke of the concept of the *confinium*, namely, Kierkegaard. In his case it means both the essentially exposed character of existence, the borderline situation, and also the necessity of having to choose. So he can say: "I live on the *confinium* of existence, like a night watchman, close to the powder keg, a loaded weapon in my hand, in the midst of the storm." And again: "I am a *confinium* between poet and witness to the truth." Once he seriously chose, he would be solely a *confinium* in the sense of a witness to the truth.

Looking back to the two aspects of the borderline situation of body/soul, a question opens up like a gaping wound: Is it possible for human existence to be a single whole and to have an ultimate meaning? The fundamental decision called for in the second aspect casts doubt on the possibility presented in the first aspect (Ficino) of an aesthetic balance between the spirit and the senses, that is, on the possibility of a "beautiful form" of existence, at peace with itself. Kant, and Schiller even more, knew how aesthetic "gracefulness" (*Anmut*) broke down into that "dignity" (*Würde*) which has to be attained dramatically.

However, the fundamental decision does not absolve man from the task of fashioning himself, by means of his freedom, into a responsible spiritual-physical being. It is precisely the radical nature of his decision in favor of the Absolute that forbids him to absolutize either of his poles; he is redirected to the Aristotelian "middle", the *meson*. Pure spiritualization (in the wake of Neoplatonism) must appear as hubris, as wanting to be like God. And yet the fundamental demand *must* be for an upward movement, involving control of the physical and emotional, the natural and mediate. Thus it is impossible to proceed in the opposite direction, that is, the purely sensory and sensual claiming the primacy (partly evident in Epicureanism and returning in Feuerbach), although the downward pull, whereby the idea is implanted in flesh and affective nature is permeated by the energies of the spirit, is only the complementary side of the control of the senses. For any external control of the body and its powers, any control from "above", must remain imperfect; if the spirit is to be genuinely "above", it must come "down" into flesh: only thus can it bring the flesh with it, up into a true spiritualization. A one-sidedly "Platonic" view, which sees man as a soul "ruling"[50] a body, "using"[51] a body, must—if it follows its logic through—turn into the complementary "Aristotelian" view: the world of the emotions must be "ethicized" from within.

[50] Compare the definitions of the soul in the young Augustine: "(animus) mihi videtur esse substantia quaedam, rationis particeps, *regendo* corpori accomodata." *De quant. animae* 13, 22 (PL 32, 1048).

[51] "Homo . . . anima rationalis est mortali atque terreno *utens* corpore." *De mor. Eccl. cath.* lib 1, 27, 52 (PL 32, 1332).

While we have thus opened up a perspective on an ideal and a synthesis, it is clear, after what we have said, that the unity of the contrary movements can only arise out of a dramatic engagement. This is not the place to portray such an engagement; all we are concerned with here is the outline of the dramatic person. All the same, we may allow ourselves a preview of the theological conclusion. If man is not to resign himself to a narrow Aristotelian "middle"—in view of the destructiveness of extreme spiritualization and sensualization—he must be given *Lebensraum* in the form of a concrete blueprint that will liberate him from this straitening "middle". Such a blueprint would have to execute fully both movements without hubris and without degeneration: it would have to come down into flesh "from above", as the pure breath of God, plumbing the dimensions of "world" and "flesh" to the very bottom. And this descent must not imply a (Buddhist, Platonic or Gnostic) "fall" from God: rather, it must undergird and embrace every possible declension from God. And from below, on the basis of a perfected fleshly being, it must go beyond the realm of the "world" so as to bring both world and flesh with it, in its transcendence, up to God, "transfiguring" it, not "spiritualizing" it in some incorporeal manner.

However, a theological blueprint of this kind would also have to demolish the last barrier that lies athwart all our reflection on the spirit/body tension: *death*. In every one of the anthropological tensions, death will keep rearing its head as the ultimate riddle that torments us. For the demand set before us, in its present form, is that we should realize spirit in body, and body in spirit, and this contains a contradiction. Philo, Gregory and Augustine saw the first man in a kind of indifference with regard to mortality or immortality. But somewhere, in fact, the decision has been made in favor of mortality. How, then, is man in the concrete to opt for immortality? Or what would be the point of endeavoring to fashion something "immortal" out of mortal matter? But this *is* man's situation, and so, as we began by saying, he remains an open question that has no answer but that of Christ.

c. Man and Woman

1. The tensions we have just discussed recur, and in a deeper form, when we go on to examine human nature's sexual differentiation into man and woman. Right from the start, this differentiation also brings the third tension into play: that between individual and community. For the man/woman relationship can stand as a paradigm of that community dimension which characterizes man's entire nature. Following the "very good" of the first account of creation, we hear the "not good" of the second: "It is not good for man to be alone", which is why God gave him woman as a "helpmate", a "counter-image".[52] The special quality of this complementary relationship becomes clear from the context: God forms the existing animals (in pairs) and leads them to Adam; he can name them and rule over them, but none of them is a fit partner for him. Such a partner would have to be both cosmic (sexual) and, to match Adam, metacosmic, in touch with the *theion*.

The animals are named and ruled, even if Adam cannot have any inner experience of their feelings. But as for the "counter-image" whom God introduces to him, although she is fashioned from one of his ribs, although she is "at last his flesh and blood", he will never be able to govern her. The male body is male throughout, right down to each cell of which it consists, and the female body is utterly female; and this is also true of their whole empirical experience and ego-consciousness. At the same time both share an identical human nature, but at no point does it protrude, neutrally, beyond the sexual difference, as if to provide neutral ground for mutual understanding. Here there is no *universale ante rem*, as all theories of a nonsexual or bisexual (androgynous) primitive human being would like to think. The human being, in the completed creation, is a "dual unity", "two distinct but inseparable realities, each fulfilling the other

---

[52] Scheeben, *Dogmatik* II, no. 423. Cf. Karl Barth, *Church Dogmatics* (Edinburgh, T. & T. Clark), III/1, 289. L. Köhler, *Theol. des AT* (1936), 241: "Literally the partner (*Gegenüber*), the counterimage (*Gegenbild*)"; sim. H. Gunkel ("his counterpart"), E. A. Speiser: "corresponding to him". Quoted in C. Westermann, *Genesis* (1974), 309 [English trans. SPCK, 3 vols.], where he enunciates the principle that "all human community has its core and center in the community of man and woman."

and both ordained to an ultimate unity that we cannot as yet envisage";

> it is dual, without multiplying the unity by two; it is simply two poles of a single reality, two diverse presences of a single being, two *entia* in a single *esse*, one existence in two lives; but by no means two different fragments of a whole, to be fitted together like a puzzle. . . .[53]

Tentative formulations such as these are attempting to describe a mystery: as a human being, man is always in communion with his counterimage, woman, and yet never reaches her. The converse is true of woman. If we take this man/woman relationship as a paradigm, it also means that the human "I" is always searching for the "thou", and actually finds it ("This at last . . ."), without ever being able to take possession of it in its otherness. Not only because the freedom of the "thou" cannot be mastered by the "I" using any superior transcendental grasp—since, in its proper context, all human freedom only opens up to absolute, divine freedom—but also because this impossibility is "enfleshed" in the diverse and complementary constitution of the sexes.

If this difference is linked with the body/spirit tension that first revealed the cosmic and metacosmic character of the human being, one might be tempted to assign the sexual difference to man's cosmic side; in such a case, insofar as man is spirit, he would rise above the sexual difference. But then we would only see the ascending movement (from body to spirit) and not the complementary, descending movement (spirit embodied). When the Adam of Genesis fails to find a partner among the animals, it is not because he lacks communication from spirit to spirit: what he misses is the relationship in which bodily things are communicated spiritually and spiritual things bodily. This becomes even clearer when we take into account the theme of the creation of woman from the man's rib.

In the natural realm, the sexually differentiated human being appears as an epitome of the cosmos, a microcosm. And the metaphysics of all cultures have endeavored to explain the

---

[53] A. Frank-Duquesne, *Création et procréation* (Paris: Ed. de Minuit, 1951), 42–46. This also corresponds to Scheler's demand, cf. "Mensch und Geschlecht" in *Zur Idee des Menschen, Vom Umsturz der Werte*. 4th ed. (1955), 195.

male/female difference as a fundamental rhythm of existence in the world. In its most visible form, it seemed possible to read this difference from the relationship between the heavens (the sky) and the earth: the sky fructifying and animating by means of its rain and sun, the earth responding on the basis of its own potential (*materia-mater*); of course there was the omnipresent danger of equating the male, the heavenly, with the "spirit", and the female, earthly, with "matter", or at least with "nature" in the modern sense, that is, the danger of depreciating the latter. So it is from Plato (*Tim.* 90e, 91a; *Laws* 5, 739c) to Aristotle (woman as "material" and hence something to be "used", *Poet.* 15, 1454a 20, as the *aischron* in contrast to the *kalon*, *Phys.* I, 9, 192 A 13–14) and on to the well-known misogynistic utterances of the Fathers and Scholastics.[54] In fact, the danger grew to the extent that, in early Christian theology, the "image of God" represented by man was increasingly seen as man's purely spiritual side. Accordingly, it was associated with the male principle in the cosmic rhythm. The recurrent myth, in countless variations, of the "sacred marriage" (*hieros gamos*) between heaven and earth escaped this devaluation of the feminine to some degree. Characteristic of this theme is the reciprocal alternation between anthropology and a cosmology that attains its fully rounded form in a divine context, which we described at the beginning of this chapter: the human and sexual is projected into the world of the gods and of Nature writ large, and man copies and reenacts the divine-cosmic marriage (in the person of the King, for example, whose action is seen to guarantee the fruitfulness of the earth and the continued thriving of the people, and so forth).[55] Even before the Tao, the world principles of Yang and Yin imply every all-embracing form of polarity, including (among many others) that of the sexes; the equality of the sexes is presupposed, but no primary significance is attached to them. Thus, in the *I Ching*, the first two signs are the masculine-creative (heaven) and the feminine-receptive

[54] For Thomas, the man/woman opposition is reduced to that between *forma* and *materia*: 2, d 20, q 1, a 2: "agens quod inducit formam, et patiens quod offert materiam."
[55] For a short summary of the various forms of the *hieros gamos*, with references: J. Schmid, in *RAC* II (1954), 528–64 ("Brautschaft, heilige").

(earth); they form the basis for all subsequent variations. The fundamental theme here is that of "transition" ("The Book of Changes"); the opposite principles are, as it were, only the presupposition for their mixing.

It must be said that no metaphysical polarity can be adduced to explain the difference of the sexes in mankind. It will either explain it one-sidedly and misleadingly on the basis of such polarities, or else the entire attempt will not get beyond the vague assertion that each pole sheds a certain light on the other, without itself coming clearly into view. As we have shown, however, this vagueness rests on the fact that the relationship between the cosmic and the *theion* is itself unavoidably fluid. For if, one-sidedly, we make the *theion* the prototype of the sexual dimension, the latter becomes a copy of an explicit sexuality in the divine world—whether in the form of the marriage of gods or their intermarrying with earthly beings or the Gnostic *syzygia* or the importing of sexuality into the Christian God (Sophiology), all of which leads, theologically, to the realm of the fantastic. On the other hand, if, equally one-sidedly, the cosmic is made the prototype of the sexual, man is locked into the cosmos: he is then one "instance" (perhaps even the "highest instance"); his transcendence is no longer visible.

This shows us what a difficult task "pre-Christian" anthropology must have had in finding the correct locus of sexuality within a total interpretation of being. The problems associated with it remain more acute than those relating to the other two tensions, and it will remain a highly sensitive area even when given a Christian interpretation. Again—but in a more dramatic way—human sexuality's cosmic and hypercosmic situation will exhibit not only a tension but also a hiatus, a breach.

In order to gain an unprejudiced approach to the phenomenon, one can cite the two accounts of creation in Genesis. These accounts embody much legendary wisdom on the part of mankind, purified of mythical bias, while, on the other hand, the transition to the Christian interpretation still lies a long way off. The beginning of the Bible devotes space to a phenomenology of the sexual; initially it is viewed in the sober framework of man's *creatureliness*.[56] Nowhere is man more aware of his con-

---

[56] A beautiful example of this is Karl Barth's chapter on man and woman in

tingence than where each sex has to realize its dependence on the other: neither can be the whole human being on its own; there is always the "other" mode of being human, a way that is not open to its counterpart. And—as will become even clearer—there can be no question of saying that sexual intercourse suspends this contingence and renders the union absolute, makes it something at rest in itself (as Feuerbach thought and as Aristophanes gently suggests in the *Symposium*): for the normal issue is a child, causing the objective finality of the union to go beyond the subjective experience and continuing the process of contingence. This shows us the other side of creatureliness: every human being who comes into being owes his existence to a sexual process; he has been begotten and born.

The first account puts the creation of the first human couple at the end of an ascending process of creation. There already exists the fruitfulness of plants and animals, in response to the command to multiply and fill the earth and the sea. Then comes God's resolve to create man in his own image and likeness so that he may rule over all created things: "So God created man in his own image, in the image of God he created him; male and female he created them", in order to give them dominion over the world (Gen 1:26f.). The assertion concerning the "image of God" is interposed between the subhuman and the human fruitfulness, separating them. The statement "male and female he created them" is at all events under the shadow of the "image of God", although it puts man (existing in two sexes and explicitly a creature) back in the framework of the cosmic and sexual. So we cannot (with Karl Barth) identify the content of the "image and likeness" with the "reciprocity of man and woman", particularly as such human reciprocity would not actually require sexual differentiation;[57] rather, with Erich

---

his *Church Dogmatics* III/2, 285–324. It is true that here (as in his treatment of the theologoumenon "image and likeness") Barth succumbs to the temptation to pass over rapidly to the New Testament fulfillment (Eph 5). While the New Testament very definitely refers back to Genesis (in Jesus and in Paul), it does not follow that Genesis points forward with equal definiteness to the New Testament. The theology of the sexes found in Genesis is initially a general theological anthropology, freed from mythical overpainting, and in that sense it is "pre-Christian".

[57] *CD* III/1, 288–329; *CD* III/2, 285.

Przywara, we must say that the relationship between the image of God and sexuality is one of "in-and-above": on the one hand, there is a similarity with the God who, in the Bible, will reveal himself in symbolic words of fatherhood and motherhood, and indeed in terms of a nuptial relationship with Israel (albeit very strictly distinguished from the mythical sexual cults of the surrounding peoples), and, on the other hand, there is a dissimilarity in that human sexuality is part of the sexuality of all created things.

> On the one hand, we cannot regard sexuality as a closed circle, as if man cannot be human except within the sexual relationship between man and woman. On the other hand, however, the spiritual side of the "image of God" is not isolated from the creature's internal cosmic sexuality, as if man cannot be human except in the spiritual and personal "interiority of the image of God".[58]

Contrary to the plain words of the text, people have continually tried to separate the first account of creation from the second. It has been suggested that the first account speaks of the creation of an ideal humanity, of humanity as a whole (insofar as the word "Adam" is in fact a collective noun), or—in a more extreme view—of an "idea" of an as yet sexually undifferentiated (or androgynous) man, whereas in the second account the very "real" Eve is formed from one of Adam's ribs. This is doubtless the view of Origen, when, as so often, he begins with a "perhaps": "Perhaps the blessing with which he blessed them —'grow and multiply and fill the earth'—looks forward (*praeveniens*) to the future creation of woman, . . . since the *homo* (man? human being?) could not multiply except through association with woman."[59] At this point Origen is within the

---

[58] *Mensch* I (1959), 134.

[59] *In Gen. hom.* 1, 14 (Baehrens VI, 18). In the first Adam ("in his loins . . . or in some other ineffable manner", *In Rom. Comm.* 5, PG 14, 1029D), the entire human race is contained. He was one of the spirit princes who fell from God and entered a denser material medium; for, according to Origen, everything created, including the world of spirits, always has a material side. On this whole issue, cf. the penetrating study by Georg Bürke, "Des Origenes Lehre vom Urstand" in Z.f.kath.Theol. 72 (1950), 1–39. It should be mentioned that Origen does not say whether the first Adam was sexless or not.

great tradition that assumes a double creation: first, that of an (ideal) first man—we have already encountered him when speaking of E. Dacqué—and then that of a sexually differentiated (real) man.[60] In fact, there is no trace of a merely ideal man in the first account of creation, and the explicit reference to creation in two sexes forbids us to think along the lines of a (sexless or androgynous) myth of original man. Moreover, there is no sign of any problem associated with man's existence in two sexes. Any such problem would have to be sought in the second account (they recognized that they were naked in the wake of sin and engaged in sexual intercourse after being banished from paradise).

Over and above these problems, however, a weighty question does arise from the first account. Man and woman, created by God according to his image, are to be fruitful. But will they bring forth "images of God"? Will they bring forth beings who (according to the second account) are in such a close relation to God that he himself will breathe life into them? Here, once again, human fruitfulness is separated from exclusively worldly fruitfulness by a deep abyss. Purely worldly beings reproduce their entire nature in new members of the species. What does man reproduce? It would be naïve to say that human parents care for the child's body while God looks after the "soul"; indeed, it would suggest that the human generative power were far below that of animals. Nor is it enough to say, with Fichte, that the "union of two freedoms" is required in order to bring forth one new human freedom;[61] every case of rape contradicts this. Rather, we should speak of human generative power, in its

---

[60] Cf. the references given in Carten Colpe, *Die religionsgeschichtliche Schule. Darstellung und Kritik ihres Bildes vom gnostischen Erlösermythus* (Göttingen: Vandenhoeck und Ruprecht, 1961), and Hans-Martin Schenke, *Der Gott "Mensch" in der Gnosis* (Göttingen, 1962). For the more modern period: Ernst Benz, *Adam. Der Mythus vom Urmenschen* (Munich-Planegg: Barth, 1955), refs. on 295.

[61] *Angewendete Philosophie* (*Vorlesungen*, 1813), Medicus VI, 521. Cf. 520: "For a human being to be produced, freedom must intervene, the united and consenting freedom of two persons." 521: "As a result of this supernatural and ethical law within nature, a unity of will is required between at least two free individuals if the highest human right is to be exercised, namely, the creation of humanity from itself."

natural operation, extending into the divine creative power, which opens up and makes itself available in the creation of man. From God's point of view, this constitutes a "humiliation" of God that is inherent in the most fundamental act of creation; thus he hands over his creatorship, making it dependent on events initiated at the will of creatures.[62] The real depth of this mystery only emerges when the child is seen no longer as *res patris*" but as a personality in direct relationship with God: in Christianity.

Adam can beget offspring "in his own likeness, after his image" (Gen 5:3), but when Eve holds her first-born son in her arms, she cries: "I have gotten a man with the help of the Lord" (Gen 4:1). She understands that the human child is not a mere gift of nature but a personal gift of God. "Thus we see with what necessity the self is grounded in its Creator: it is not within our own power to know ourselves. If we are to measure the whole scope of the self, we must penetrate into the very womb of the Godhead, which alone can define and solve the entire mystery of our being" (Hamann).[63]

The second account (Gen 2:18–24) relates the creation of the "human being" (Adam) from the dust of the ground; God breathes his own breath into the nostrils of the man thus made. Then follows the observation that it is not good for the man (Adam) to be alone; the animals are created and brought before Adam, but they fail to relieve his loneliness. Finally a deep sleep is brought upon Adam, Eve is formed out of his rib and introduced to Adam: "This at last is bone of my bones and flesh of my flesh." He grasps that she "was taken out of Man" and calls her "Wo-man". This implies three things: first, a primacy

[62] Cf. the lengthy discussion in Scheeben, *Dogmatik* II, section 151. The impossible assumption that the parents can only care for the child's "body" does not, as such, vitiate the conclusion (no. 482) that, in every fruitful act of conception, God performs an act of quasi-creation (not an absolute act of creation, since it is not creation out of nothing): "His creation is only perfecting a product already initiated by the begetter; it is only putting the finishing touches to an image for which the begetter has already served as a pattern. . . ." Thus God operates "by implementing a system he has already established and instituted in the creature itself".

[63] *Brocken* 1 (*Werke*, Nadler, I, 1949), 301.

of the man, for in this original situation he is alone before God and with God; although potentially and unconsciously he bears the woman within him, he cannot give her to himself. Second, this loneliness is "not good". Again this banishes the idea of a primal, androgynous human being, supposedly originally at peace with himself and only subject to unsatisfied longing after being split into two sexes. But it also refutes the notion that the lonely human being (or man) can attain fulfillment by knowing and naming the world (*transiit classificando*: Valéry). Third and finally, it affirms that the woman comes from man. It is through being overpowered in a "deep sleep" and robbed of part of himself, near to his heart, that man is given fulfillment. In sum: the man retains a primacy while at the same time, at God's instigation, he steps down from it in a *kenosis*; this results in the God-given fulfillment whereby he recognizes himself in the gift of the "other".

In the relationship between the two, where each is created by God and dependent on the other, even though one is "taken" out of the other, the man's (persisting) priority is located within an equality of man and woman. Paul will formulate this in terms of woman being "from man" (1 Cor 11:8) and "for man" (11:9); all the same, "man is for woman" (11:12), in such a way that neither of the two can do what he likes with his own body; in each case it is the other who has control (7:4).

> It is true, on the one hand, that the man is the "head" of the woman, the "body"; but it is also true, on the other hand, that the woman, the "body", is the man's "fullness" and "glory". Thus she fulfills her origin: for she was created in man's "ecstasy", as his "dream"; she is the "fullness" and "glory" (1 Cor 11:7; Eph 1:23) into which he is "incorporated" as into his "house and household" (Gen 2:22; *ōikodomēsen*).[64]

The second account links up with the first, without cancelling itself out. Both accounts give common witness to the dual existence of the human being. This dual existence is difficult to live out in its full implications; the archetypal image of Christ/ Church must first radiate the fullness of light onto the creaturely copy. For, theologically speaking, the first Adam is created for

---

[64] E. Przywara, *Mensch* I, 140–41.

the sake of, and with a view to, the Second, even if he appears first in chronological time (1 Cor 15:45).

2. Everything we have said so far concerned the cosmic-hypercosmic tension between the sexes, in the context of the overall tension found in the human being. Now, however, we come to a more radical complex of problems in the sexual area, attested by the great tradition of Christian theology but today trivialized under the pretext that such problems are only the remnants of Manichaeism. Some developments in the sexual field can and must be regarded as healthy, but others are destructive. If we take seriously the problems identified by the tradition, the picture of human life as we know it looks once again like a still photograph taken when the dramatic action has already begun. Accepting, therefore, that on the basis of the present state of human nature—which is *"vulnerata in naturalibus"*[65] —man's supralapsarian constitution cannot be reconstructed, what picture of man can we take as our guide in our attempt to define his "essence"?

Ambivalence raises its head immediately when we consider the *reciprocity of generation and death*. The Bible asserts that it is through sin that death came into the world (Rom 5:2; cf. Wis 2:24); the same must apply to generation. Fichte says,

> When mankind received the ability to regenerate itself, its old members were put under the obligation to remove themselves from the stage; anyone who produces another human being in his place is also obliged to hand this place over to him at the proper time. Thus death and birth presuppose each other. Only a world that has no birth can have no death either.[66]

This echoes an ancient teaching, as we can see from Augustine: "Were sons born to you to live with you on earth? Will they not rather eject you and be your successors? . . . It is as if children were to say to their parents: Isn't it about time for you to be

[65] "It is a fundamental misunderstanding of man to proceed by subtraction, so to speak, and imagine that 'nature' is what fallen man has in common with original, unfallen man and to contrast that with 'supernature', understood as what has been lost." E. Brunner, *Der Mensch im Widerspruch* (Berlin: Furche, 1937), 102 [*Man in revolt* (London, 1939)].

[66] *Angewendete Philosophie* (see n. 61 above), 521–22.

going? It's our turn to take the stage!"[67] And Chrysostom: "Where death is, there is marriage; and where there is no marriage, there is no death either."[68] Hegel added depth to Fichte's assertion by thoroughly evaluating the relationship between the individual and the species, and it is not clear why the first human beings, provided we take their sexuality literally (as we have done), were not bound to have fallen under the concept of the species in this regard. Hegel sees death implicated in the process of generation in three ways: first, reproduction looks toward the dying of the individual; second, the division of the species into mutually alien types acts as a stimulus to violent death; and finally and generally, the self-preservation of the species requires the disappearance of the individual in natural death.[69] What interests us is the first point, which is related to the third. The individual's disproportion vis-à-vis the species (since it can never be the latter in its totality) drives it "to seek and find its sense of self in some other member of the species, integrating itself through union with the other"; the individual becomes "an absolute species, . . . but this signifies the death of this individual. So it is that animals lower down the scale die immediately after mating; for they have dissolved their individuality in the species."[70] Schopenhauer will take the idea to its extreme by saying that individuality is illusory and that the life of the species is only maintained by the incessant coming and going of individuals, just as the rainbow stands still in the midst of the waterfall.[71] "Birth and death belong equally to life; they keep the balance by conditioning each other . . . as poles of the

[67] *En. in Ps.* 127, n. 15. Sherwood Anderson says to his father: "Move out of the footlights a bit, old man. Let your son try his hand." *A Storyteller's Story* (1924), chap. 8.

[68] *De virginitate* 14, 6 (SC 125, 142). *In Gen. hom.* 15, 4 (PG 53, 123); 18, 4 (PG 53, 153); 20, 1 (PG 53, 167); *Propter fornic.* 1, 3 (PG 51, 213).

[69] *Naturphilosophie*, section 367 (*Werke* 7/1, 642).

[70] *Naturphilosophie*, section 358 (645–48). True, Hegel is here talking about animals, but the same principle applies to man insofar as he is a member of a species. Cf. Hegel's remarks on marriage in his *Philosophie des Rechts*, section 161ff., and even in the *Phänomenologie* (*Werke* 2, 274f.), where he puts forward the very general principle that "the absolute brittleness of individuality is pulverized, . . . smashed to pieces against the equally hard but continuous reality".

[71] *Die Welt als Wille und Vorstellung*, vol. 1, IV, section 54; vol. 2, IV, chap. 41 (Grisebach I, 372, II, 1260).

entire phenomenon of life." They are "essential correlates, neutralizing and cancelling each other out".[72] Hegel's reference to those animals that die immediately after mating recurs in Schopenhauer; he adds the observation—to be taken up later by Simmel and Scheler—that the higher and more complicated the individual, the more threatened and mortal it is.[73]

The classical objection against applying this simple law to man's existence in paradise is that, in the state of innocence, the *foecunditas carnis* does not necessarily presuppose mortality. In the first place, human reproduction (at least until the coming of Christ) has the purpose not only *ut successores quaerantur morituris* but *ut multo rectius socii quaerantur victuris*[74]—and here Augustine is obviously not concerned with the problem of overpopulation. Second, man in paradise, possessing an *animale corpus*, was not faced with the prospect of death: he looked forward to the transformation of his body into an *angelica forma* and a *caelestis qualitas*.[75] Given the realism of man's primary sexuality, this theory must have seemed like an irruption of Platonism, introducing division into the solidarity that man enjoyed with the cosmos. Here, right at the heart of human existence, gapes the dualism which Steinbeck so eloquently described for us. We can also recognize it in the portrayal of Adam's situation by that great realist, Thomas Aquinas (and in the background we should be able to hear the words of Hegel):

> Man, by his nature, is established, as it were, midway between corruptible and incorruptible creatures, his soul being naturally incorruptible, while his body is naturally corruptible. We must also observe that nature's purpose appears to be different with regard to corruptible and incorruptible things. For that seems to be the direct purpose of nature, which is invariable and perpetual, while what is only for a time is seemingly not the chief purpose of

[72] *Ibid.*, I, 368–69.

[73] *Ibid.*, II, 1255.

[74] Augustine, *De Gen. ad litt.* lib 9, c 9, n 14.

[75] *Ibid.*, n 17. With regard to man in the concrete, Augustine can say without any inhibition: "To be born in this mortal body is the beginning of sickness" and hence of dying. *In Ps. 102*, 6 (PL 37, 1320): "Quid enim aliud, non dicam nati, sed omnino concepti, nis aegritudinem quamdam inchoavimus, qua sumus necessario morituri", *De Gen. ad litt.* lib 9, c 18, n 17 (PL 34, 399).

nature but, as it were, subordinate to something else; otherwise, when it ceased to exist, nature's purpose would become void. Therefore, since in things corruptible none is everlasting and permanent except the species, it follows that the chief purpose of nature is the good of the species, for the preservation of which natural generation is ordained. On the other hand, incorruptible substances survive not only in the species but also in the individual; and so even the individuals are included in the chief purpose of nature. Hence it pertains to man to beget offspring, on the part of the naturally corruptible body. But on the part of the soul, which is incorruptible, it is fitting that the multitude of individuals should be the direct purpose of nature, or rather of the Author of nature, who alone is the Creator of the human soul. Therefore, to provide for the multiplication of the human race, he established the begetting of offspring even in the state of innocence. [76]

What is interesting in this passage is that, in an Aristotelian manner, [77] Thomas speaks explicitly of *corruptibilitas* of what is bodily, that is, what the individual shares with the species, even in the case of the human being. Nor does this hinder him from assuming a (hypothetical) *translatio in statum gloriae* in the case of Adam, which would thus (at the end of his life) lift him out of the cosmic law of the species. [78] Ultimately, faced with the question "Did sexual intercourse in paradise involve a *defloratio* of the woman?", it was only logical for Thomas to say yes first of all (with Aristotle), [79] whereas later, having listened to Augustine, he will say no. [80]

But where is the dividing line in the sexual field, as far as it concerns the supralapsarian and the infralapsarian state? Augustine, who has speculated on it in the greatest detail, suggested four possibilities for the former state:

Either the first human beings had intercourse as often as they felt the urge to do so; or they suppressed the urge when intercourse

[76] *S. Th.* I, q 98, a 1 c (trans. Dominican Fathers, London: Burns, Oates and Washbourne); cf. *De Ver.* q 5, a 3 c.

[77] He refers to two passages of Aristotle in the parallel place: 2, d 20, q 1, a 1 c.

[78] *Ibid.*, in accord with the text of the Master of the Sentences: "de hoc autem statu transferendus erat. . . ."

[79] *Ibid.*, 2, d 20, q 1, a 2, a 1: "in omni concubitu solvitur virginitas quantum ad integritatem carnis, etiam in primo statu."

[80] *S. Th.* I, q 98, a 2 ad 4.

was not necessary (that is, for the procreation of children); or the libido was aroused at the command of the will, when reason considered intercourse to be necessary; or there was no libido at all, and man used his sexual organs as he wished, just as he uses hands and feet.[81]

Augustine rejects the first two possibilities as inappropriate to man's first state. This leaves only the operation of the sexual organs without arousal, or with an arousal that remained subject to the will.[82] Where do these speculations lead us, representing the essential concomitants of the natural process of procreation as alien to paradisal man? First we have the denial of death, then the denial of defloration and ultimately the denial of normal sexual arousal; while at the same time (in accordance with the first account of creation—but also the second), the original differentiation of the sexes is insisted upon. It all amounts to a problem that remains simply insoluble from our postlapsarian standpoint.

The solution as suggested by Augustine in his middle and late periods (a solution which has had a great influence on the entire classical theology of the West) remains a hybrid: it both subjects man to the natural law of species-and-individual and lifts him out of it. A second solution lies at a *lower* level: it takes sexuality's situation in the wake of the Fall and elevates it to the original state, binding man and the subhuman cosmos to each other in such a way that the transcendence of the human personality— which comes out clearly in both Genesis accounts—is compromised. A third solution lies at a *higher* level: this is the solution of the Greek Fathers, initiated by Gregory of Nyssa, extended by Maximus the Confessor, John Damascene, Scotus Erigena (and explicitly rejected by Thomas).[83] Paradoxically, however, this "higher-level" solution combines with the "lower-level" one to form a unity that can take over from Augustine's less credible construction.

---

[81] M. Müller, *Die Lehre des hl. Augustinus von der Paradiesehe* . . . (Regensburg: Pustet, 1954), 25. *Contra duas ep. Pelag.* 1, 17 (PL 44, 566).

[82] *Op imperf. c. Julian.* lib 6, n 22 (PL 45, 1553). Hugh of St. Victor rightly opposed this hypothesis and stressed that it is not the "will" which prepares the body for intercourse but only married love (quoted in M. Müller, 78–83).

[83] *S. Th.* I, q 98, a 2 c.

The Gnostic, Philonic[84] theory, developed further by Origen, was of a twofold creation of man: the first was spiritual, androgynous or sexless, and the second, as a result of an original sinful Fall, was concretely physical and sexual. Gregory endeavored to preserve this theory by transposing it into the terms of orthodox theology. In the first account of creation, man stands in God's sight and is said to be created according to God's image and likeness; in Gregory's view, "man" includes not only the entire collective of mankind (in its time-space limitations) but also Christ, the prototype of this mankind, who will appear at the end of time. Mankind as a whole is created in and for Christ, and in Christ there is "neither male nor female" (Gal 3:28). What stands thus before the eyes of God is the encompassing reality of "mankind", which, seen in the internal, temporal perspective of the world, at the beginning of human history, is as yet ideally, that is, potentially, present in the first man. Gregory explicitly puts forward the latter as an hypothesis: since man, the creature, was to decide freely in favor of God, but God foresaw that he would turn away and embrace sensual values instead of spiritual ones, he created him with sexual characteristics (Gen 1:27). Now, instead of a process *unknown* to us (perhaps an angelic manner of multiplication, that could have come into effect in man's original state), animal reproduction will take care of the total "idea" of mankind, and it will be a sign of sin but not (as in Origen) a consequence of it. All the same it must be said that this theory involves a kind of reciprocal causality between the deliberate turning to the world of sense, on the one hand, and sexuality on the other.[85] Maximus the

---

[84] Philo can be regarded as a direct influence on Gregory; he too distinguishes between two creations: the first, the creation of man "according to the image", and the second, that of animal man (*De Op.* 181); no doubt, however, in the first case he means intellectual knowledge and in the second case knowledge through the senses. Cf. the observation of J. Daniélou in the edition of *De hominis opificio* (SC 6, 1944) on chap. 16, p. 155, and the introduction, p. 47).

[85] Cf. *Présence et pensée. Essai sur la philosophie religieuse de Grégoire de Nysse* (1942), 51ff. Gregory's theory is developed in chaps. 16 and 17 of his work "On the creation of man" (PG 44, 177–92). N.b. if we remember that, for Gregory, "Adam" signifies the common human substance rather than an individual (cf. *C. Eunom.* III, PG 45, 592D: in begetting his son, Adam begets "not so much another as himself, another 'himself' "), his use of the species/individual frame-

Confessor, whose starting point is the inner link between "pathos" (sense-orientation) and death, clearly distances himself from the Origenist solution and associates himself with that of Gregory: "I repeat what the great Gregory of Nyssa taught me: the first thing to happen when man fell from perfection was that the *pathē* were introduced, growing up in the irrational part of man's nature;[86] only then did that manner of procreation enter into human existence that is connected with fleshly pleasure, on the one hand, and death on the other.[87] Maximus radicalizes this "only then" by asserting that man's turning away from God coincides (temporally, not logically) with his coming-to-be in the concrete.[88] John Damascene will echo Gregory's view more in passing (in his discussion of virginity). Replying to the objection that in Genesis God commanded the first couple to "multiply", he says,

> The command to "grow and multiply" surely does not mean multiplication by means of marital intercourse. God could multiply the race in some other way, if men kept the commandment to the end. But God, who knows everything before it happens, foreknew that they would commit trespass and be condemned to death. So, by way of anticipation, he created man and woman and commanded them to grow and multiply.[89]

Scotus Erigena adopts the ideas of Gregory, combining them with elements of the teaching of Philo, Origen and Maximus: the first creation in the primal depths, in the "idea", spiritual and angelic, is not purely ideal,[90] but it does not manifest the opposition of the sexes.[91] If man had adhered to his "idea", he

work for the doctrine of the Trinity (*Ad Adlabium*, PG 45, 117; *Adv. Graec.*, *ibid.*, 180) will seem far less strange.

[86] *Quaest. ad Thal.* 1 (PG 90, 296A).

[87] *Ibid.*, 61 (PG 90, 632B).

[88] *Quaest. ad Thal.* 59 (PG 90, 613C); *ibid.*, 61 (PG 90, 628A). On this whole subject: *Kosmische Liturgie*, 2d ed. (1961), 182–85.

[89] *De Fide Orthodoxa*, bk. IV, chap. 24, 2d ed., BKV, 252f.

[90] *Div. nat.* IV, 9.

[91] *Ibid.*, II, 6: Human beings multiplied like angels. The idea that God originally did not command marriage but only allowed it, and that he could ultimately have caused mankind to multiply in some other way, also recurs in the Middle Ages, e.g., in William of Champeaux (cf. M. Müller, 49, 290).

would have been omnipotent in God (and in the will of God).[92] Yet Erigena wants to maintain that there was no lapse of time between creation and Fall.[93]

What conclusion can be drawn from the Greek doctrine? The "reciprocity" referred to can be seen as pointing to a middle position—that cannot be recreated—between the "higher-level" and "lower-level" solutions. It would not be enough, for instance, to say that death belongs to "nature"; after all, death is connected with a fallenness, a futility, *vanitas*, which indicates that mankind has declined to a low level. We cannot lift the fact of sexuality out of that context, as the Church Fathers observed long before the philosophers of Idealism. If we reflect on the Fathers' assertions in the light of Idealism, we do not need to reject them out of hand as hostile to sex. In reality they are aiming to draw a dividing line, today beyond our grasp, which cuts right through the sexual field and would forbid any synthesis: on the one side, the fruitful encounter between man and woman in personal mutual self-giving—and, on the other side, their sexual union.[94] Karl Barth has insisted that Genesis 2 "speaks of man and wife in their relationship *as such*, that is, not of "human fatherhood" and "motherhood", not of the founding of the family,[95] which is a central concern in the rest of the Old Testament. But "here the Bible thinks in more seriously 'erotic' terms than the entire Greek world." This is important for Barth

[92] *Ibid.*, IV, 9.

[93] *Ibid.*, IV, 20.

[94] It is impossible to allocate sex to the inner-cosmic side of human nature and eros to the hyper-cosmic; accordingly, it is impossible to separate the sexual from the erotic (as the two "main purposes" of marriage) in the act of intercourse and assign priority to the latter. That is why technical regulation proves so hopeless today. "However unique (as opposed to the animal kingdom) the marital union may be, its high point borrows its language and its delights from that act which is the direct cause of procreation. Even if the act does not always need to be fruitful, it cannot be detached from sexual fruitfulness. Failure to recognize this results in splitting the human being in the very act in which it manifests its deepest unity." Gustave Martelet, *Amour conjugal et renouveau conciliaire*, 2d ed. (Lyons: Mappus, 1969), 33.

[95] *CD* III/1, 312. Barth links this argument with the Song of Songs, where what is celebrated is a purely man/woman eros without consideration of offspring.

as a pointer to the fulfilling relationship between Christ and the Church, a relationship that has all fruitfulness *within* it, not *in addition to* it. But in Gregory of Nyssa, too, the sexual is only a secondary echo of the higher "idea" of total humanity, and this humanity is nothing other than the fulfilled and fulfilling Body of Christ.

The question is bound to arise: What kind of "erotic" relationship is this supposed to be, in the paradise story, between man and woman, if it is not sexual? Are we to think of the boundary concept such as, among others, Soloviev has described and celebrated?[96] Or rather, should we cross this boundary and move toward another form of fruitfulness, as Gregory of Nyssa, Maximus, John Damascene have done? We must leave the question open, even if it gapes like a wound. The center of what is human cannot be constructed out of itself. Man acts out his role between earth and heaven, and in heaven there is no marriage (Mt 22:30): there the Marriage of the Lamb is celebrated.

Let us sum up thus: in *pre-Christian* times, what we mean by "natural" is something (ultimately indefinable) "between" two poles: on the one hand, human sexuality is embedded in the cosmic-*divine* which (in the form of the *hieros gamos*, the Dionysian ecstasy, and so forth) is the projection and affirmation of it, right up to the highest level; and, on the other hand, the spiritual dimension—regarded as the authentic *theion*—is distilled out of the inner-cosmic realm of the sexual, which means that the latter is in danger of being suppressed ascetically in favor of the spiritual or depreciated as inferior or demonic. Not infrequently the two extremes turn into their opposites—as in Gnosticism, for example.

d. Individual and Community

Of the three anthropological tensions, this last one, in the pre-Christian period, is the most subdued. This is because it is rooted in the total context without any difficulty. And when it is

---

[96] "The Meaning of Sexual Love", German trans. in *Werke* (Verlag Erich Wewel, 1957–) VII, 201–72. Cf. *The Glory of the Lord* III (San Francisco: Ignatius Press, 1986), 279ff.

taken beyond itself in the Christian framework, it is not made into a problem but only rendered more intense. The two poles acquire dimensions hitherto undreamed-of: the individual is seen to be an eternal person, and the community is revealed as a reflection, in the "Mystical Body" of Christ, of the life of God.

1. Now, even within the anthropological tension, the community is something that surrounds and protects the individual (as a *zōon politikon*). However questionable the concrete condition of an empire or a *polis* may be, we cannot "get behind" its framework-function as such; as a framework it fits directly into the overall cosmic-divine framework. Thus, in primitive cultures and in all ancient high civilizations, as Mircea Eliade has shown in many examples, the center of the empire or *polis* coincides with the center of the cosmos; the heaven/hell axis goes vertically through this center.[97] And in this connection we immediately discern the reciprocity: if the founding of a *polis* implies the insertion of a new community into the community of the cosmic macropolis that exists from time immemorial, at the same time it always involves an entering into, and a participation in, this cosmic act of foundation by the gods themselves. "Settling somewhere—building a village or merely a house—represents a serious decision, for the very existence of man is involved; he must, in short, create his own world and assume the responsibility of maintaining and renewing it."[98] What we mean by "world", however, is an ordered multiplicity, a community; the individual is unthinkable outside it. So the individual grasps himself primarily and unquestioningly as a member of a tribe, a clan, a *polis*, an empire, all of which are central to the cosmos. The tribe, the *polis*, the empire to which I belong is not one (relative) community among others: it is the only one, the real one, and all the others around it are peripheral, preferably to be subjugated to it. Each empire is an "empire of the center".

As we have already shown, this coincidence of world order and the order of the *polis* is precarious and difficult to maintain.

[97] *Le Mythe de l'Eternel retour* (Gallimard, 1949), 30–43, with refs.; *The Sacred and the Profane* (Harcourt Brace Jovanovich), 37.
[98] *The Sacred and the Profane*, 56–57. *Le Mythe . . . ,* 38ff.

This is demonstrated by the history of all civilizations. They constantly oscillate between the attempt to bring the established law of the community into harmony with the order of the universe and the realization that the tension between *physis* (where "might is right") and *nomos*, where right is "apportioned" equally to all members of the community is inevitable. (*Nomos* comes from *"nem"*: "distribute".) Or should we adopt the view (with Heraclitus) that, in the cosmos too, there is one *nomos* that is paramount, superior to all the individual laws? "All human laws are upheld and nourished by the one *nomos* of the *theion*; it rules wherever it wills, is equal to all situations and extends, indeed, far beyond them."[99] This would give us a common point of reference for the various communities, and it would relativize the assumption each makes, that is, that it alone is "central". This is the starting point for Plato's great vision of a contemplative, kingly ruler-philosopher who discerns the world law and hands it down, so that it can be turned into political legislation and human praxis. But the vision knows that it is under threat from the utilitarian perspectives and power-hungry desires of the communities and their "tyrants". The cosmic and hypercosmic (divine) point of reference for the processes of legislation was ambivalent in itself and remained so. Purely within the cosmos there is a notable absence of justice: animals devour one another; in the hypercosmic realm there is the *dikē* set before men by Zeus.[100] Even assuming that a political order would correctly copy and apply the hypercosmic justice, how long would it last, seeing that human conditions are continually changing, and in any case the various areas of justice—the rights of the individual, the family, the *polis* as a whole—exist in tension with one another? Cannot man, in the face of new laws, have recourse to ancient justice, a justice that is directly in harmony with the law of the world?—so asks Sophocles' Antigone.

This is where the essential uncertainties lie in pre-Christian thought concerning the individual and community: both poles are taken together as a whole and extrapolated to the all-

[99] Diels 22 B 114.
[100] Hesiod, *Erga*, 276f.

embracing law of the world. On the other hand, the inner tension between the poles does not, as yet, grow so far as to cause a rupture. This tension is tangible in borderline cases, where, for instance, an individual fails to remain in his community or is expelled from it. In such a case, the individual forfeits his place in the universe; only the precarious law of the fugitive seeking sanctuary, which links all the communities, can protect him—under certain circumstances.[101] For the individual stripped of his community is in a pitiful situation, contrary to nature; some community or other should cast its cloak about his nakedness, to enable him to continue to exist. At the periphery of the community, but wholly related to it, are those who are imperfectly integrated into it, the slaves without rights, the *metoikoi*, those who are somehow tolerated because they are exploited. What is meant by "person" only emerges in Christianity.

In the organic relationship between individual and community, the individual tends toward the community in two contrary movements. First of all, the individual grows into the community; in primitive peoples he is adopted into it by special initiatory rites, stepping forth out of the "physical" unity of the family into the encompassing unity of the *polis*, the state, in order to participate in its law and freedom and so grow beyond the limitations of individuality. The good of moving from limitation to freedom is bought at the cost of obedience to the laws, indeed, by preferring the common good (*bonum commune*) to the individual's own good (for instance, where the individual patriotically sacrifices his own life for the common good). By inserting himself into the world of the community, constituted by laws, the individual becomes a carrier of community values; insofar as the community—according to Heraclitus' dictum— lives and is nourished within and by the transcendent *theios nomos*, the individual also acquires a share in the latter.

What is the origin, however, of rights within the community?

---

[101] Cf. *The Glory of the Lord* IV, 106–13. It is the insight into the universal character of *nomos* that gives the Greek his superiority over the barbarian. In Euripides' *Medea*, Jason tells the heroine: "First of all you live in Hellas, not in grim barbarian lands; here you learned right and custom and to obey the law, not brute force" 236–38.

Who mediates between the divine and the human law? In the pre-Christian world it is the outstanding individual: he is endowed with knowledge of the *theios nomos* and so has authority to promulgate the law of the *polis*, to mold the community and to represent the existing order in the presence of the gods. (If he is a founder, this authority is also explicitly attributed to him.) Thus the founder, the hero, the king becomes a mediator between the human and divine worlds. In him, and in him alone, individuality is present in its fullness, that is, in its power to sustain community. This "macro-ego" is neither an abstraction from the idea of all particular individuals nor the mere exponent of a state organism that is conceptually distinct from it: it is the essential incarnation of the latter; all particular individuals are subsumed into it. In this "macro-ego", the human *nomos* is transcended in the direction of the cosmic, divine law; the ontological transcendence can express itself in the form of the genealogical (born of or married to a goddess, adopted by a god, and so forth), the prophetic (inspired by God) or in terms of simple representation [that is, where the outstanding individual acts as a figurehead]. But it can also become subject to question: if the human *nomos* no longer seems to echo the divine; or if different laws, proposed by and embodied in different persons, come into conflict with one another; or if the "great man" turns out to be an isolated individual, no longer in harmony with his allotted role—whether through his own conscious or unconscious "guilt" or because of a divinely appointed destiny that could not be accounted for by human legislation. These are the subjects of classical Greek tragedy, where an assembly of individuals contemplates the "macro-ego" of the hero, the demi-god, the king, in its superhuman and problematical nature. At bottom, Western drama is born of a situation of ultimate indiscretion: faith in the mythical and representational role of heroes and kings is still strong enough for them to be portrayed as objects of special and universal interest but not strong enough to leave them (as in Mesopotamia and Egypt) unchallenged in their role as originators of the law (as, for instance, in the Babylonian New Year festival). Plato's *Republic* and *Laws* are not the first to demythologize the "macro-ego" idea of the ancient world; even the tragedies do it, as the comedies that succeed them make very clear.

In his design for the state, Plato elevates what once was concrete reality into the realm of the ideal. In spite of Marcus Aurelius, the realm of politics has never seen a contemplative ruler in Plato's sense, taking over from the earlier king (because the divine no longer "speaks" but is now only "contemplated") and communicating the fruits of his contemplation to men of action. Even those forms with mythological aspects, like the "Roman Empire of the German Nation" and certain expressions of later Absolutism, no longer match up to the earlier reality. They still share in the idea of "representation"—representing society to God and God to society—but political interest takes pride of place over imagery. In the meantime, pre-Christian individuals have developed into Christian persons.

2. Perhaps the light shed by Christianity was necessary not only to illuminate what is meant by "person" in terms of supernatural vocation and dignity but also to show us those elements of pre-Christian individuality that had already prepared the way for the meaning of "person". At that time there was no reflection upon this issue, or at least no adequate reflection; here, however, when we are speaking of man as a whole, in tension between individual and community, we seem to be required briefly to reflect on it. In doing so we shall be illuminating what we have already said from a new angle.

In ancient philosophy, the *in-dividuum* (*a-tomon*) signified something that was ultimate (*eschaton*) because it could not be divided further, such as the species and genera, which are sublated upward into the "principles"—at the very highest point into Being and the One. Now, however, we find ourselves at a dead-end (*aporia*): what is most universal, that is, Being, the One, "embraces (*periechein*) everything that is; its collapse will also bring everything else to an end, since everything is one Being, everything is a single One". Thus the question arises, What is actually meant by "principle"? Is it what is most universal (Being, the One), without which there can be no individual thing, or "the last of the entities to be abstracted from the species, since it cannot be divided (*atoma gar*)"?[102] We do not

---

[102] Aristotle, *Metaphysics* XI, 1, 1059b 24–1060a 2.

need to examine in detail the way Aristotle answers his own question; what interests us is its implications for anthropology.

Every human being is a perfect member of the human species, whether male or female,[103] embodying the whole concept of what it is to be human. Part of this concept is that everyone who thus embodies it does so as an individual, excluding all others. Furthermore it belongs to the concept of man that each human being has self-awareness and is free; and that in turn means that each one, in himself, is something that excludes all participation by others. Thus the concept embraces an aspect that is common to all men and *simultaneously* exclusive to all men. This holds good in spite of the fact that the more spiritual these mutually exclusive centers of self-awareness and freedom become, the greater capacity for the world they possess, the more profound their knowledge of one another grows and the more their communication with one another develops. Low forms of self-awareness possess a world-around-them (*Umwelt*), but they do not have a "world" (*Welt*): they are only in peripheral contact with one another; they share in a life that flows through them all but fills none of them as individuals. Man, too, still experiences this kind of external contact through his physical body; he is a part side by side with other parts, which only touch externally and in no way integrate the whole into themselves; whereas in free self-awareness, the whole, the community, is mirrored, albeit indirectly. Again, this very incommunicability is the precondition or reverse side of all spiritual communication. Not only does it require the reciprocal knowledge and recognition of the other as "other" but also the freedom to detach oneself from the totality of the world (and hence from the community) and encounter the latter creatively, out of the uniqueness of one's own self.

In this way, beings existing for themselves simultaneously exist for one another. Nor do they do so in a timeless realm: each free, human self-awareness enters the dance at a particular time. But it cannot enter by its own volition: it cannot waken itself to free self-awareness (otherwise it would have eternally to precede itself); it can only be wakened to free self-awareness by some

---

[103] *Ibid.*, X, 9, 1058a 29ff.

other free self-awareness: for example, the child by its mother. By way of explanation let us refer back to the earlier analysis of consciousness (pp. 207ff.); then we were concerned primarily with openness to being-in-its-totality, now our main concern is to establish the element of shared humanity. At the moment of awakening, different elements form an inseparable unity:[104] first (in the *cogito/sum*), the radiance of reality as such (as being true and good), which discloses itself and liberates man to journey toward it. In the *cogito/sum*, we experience the identity of being-for-me and being-in-itself, but it is an awakened, gift-identity, which has to respond in gratitude to an absolute identity of spirit and being. Second, we experience the call to shared humanity: free self-awareness experiences itself as an "I" only when it knows that it is addressed and treated as a "thou"— through word, gesture, smile, protection, and so forth—that is, when it realizes that it is admitted into the appropriate community. The fact that neither the "I" that does the calling and awakening nor the "I" that is thus called and awakened can constitute the absolute identity of spirit and being does not have to be realized immediately; it is already implicit in the initial experience. Thus, third, it emerges that, a priori, the *cogito/sum* includes shared humanity; this clarifies the above paradox, namely, that the exclusivity of what is "for-itself" simultaneously *includes* what is excluded, not only logically, in the "concept of species", but in the individual subject. Precisely because being-in-its-totality has disclosed itself to him, and he has experienced

[104] "Nine Propositions on Christian Ethics" in J. Ratzinger, H. Schürmann and H. U. von Balthasar, *Principles of Christian Morality* (San Francisco: Ignatius, 1986), 96–97, and the book referred to there: Hans Jürgen Verweyen, *Ontologische Voraussetzungen des Glaubensaktes* (Düsseldorf: Patmos, 1969). Formally speaking, this is precisely the starting point adopted by Anton Günther: "In self-awareness there lies a knowledge of self and of other things. This 'other' is, in part, conditioned, like the ego itself (singular and plural), and in part unconditional insofar as it concerns the egos and individuals of nature, the realm of the spirits and the natural world." *Die Juste-Milieus in der deutschen Philosophie gegenwärtiger Zeit* (Vienna, 1838), 126. The problem is that Günther insists too one-sidedly on the "*Kontraposition*" of the "other" as the basis of creatureliness (inferred from the limitation of the ego) and devotes too little attention to the gift-character of being as a whole, right up to the fact that consciousness is given to itself in its "relative absoluteness", as Günther says (*Vorschule zur spekulativen Theologie* II, 2d ed. [Vienna, 1848], 142).

the gift-quality of his own nature and hence his relativity, his "response-character" (E. Brunner) and so the limitation of his nature, the individual subject realizes that he is "for-himself-with-others".

On the basis of his definition of the "spirit" as that which is eccentric (ex-centric) to the subject's own experience of himself (in Scholastic terms, *reflexio completa*), Helmuth Plessner, citing Fichte, can express the same thing by distinguishing an "individual I" and a "universal I" in the spiritual person: the "universal I" appears in being together with other persons "by means of the first, second and third persons concrete".

> The human being refers to himself and others as "you" ("thou"), "he", "we"—not as if he first had to infer the existence of persons on the basis of analogies or empathy between himself and beings which seem most like himself, but in virtue of the structure of his own mode of existing. . . . The fact that the individual human being, so to speak, comes up with the idea—indeed is permeated from the very beginning with the idea—that he is not alone and has the companionship not only of things but also of sentient beings like himself: this realization does not rest on a particular act whereby he projects his own life-form outward but is one of the preconditions of the sphere of human existence. Indeed, it requires constant effort and the careful sifting of experience if we are to find our bearings in this world. For, despite being structurally the same in essence as me, as a person the "other" is an individual reality (just as I am) whose inner world is basically more or less totally hidden from me; first of all this inner world needs to be opened up by very diverse modes of interpretation.[105]

Plessner calls this a priori form of ego-experience "the experience of a shared world" (*Mitwelt*).

> The "shared world" is that form of his *own* position which man grasps as the sphere of *other* human beings. Consequently we must say that it is by man adopting a position that is "ex-centric" to himself that the "shared world" is fashioned and its reality is guaranteed. . . . The existence of a "shared world" is necessary if a living being[106] is to grasp itself in its position, namely, as a

[105] Helmuth Plessner, *Die Struktur des Organischen und der Mensch* (Berlin: W. de Gruyter, 1928), 300–301.

[106] This means the human being. The animal has awareness and "self-

member of this shared world. . . . The shared world carries the person and is at the same time carried and fashioned by the latter. . . . Thus the spiritual character of the person lies in the "we"-form of his own "I".[107]

The only thing missing in this analysis is the preliminary structure erected above (p. 389): at the most fundamental level, the dawn of self-awareness in freedom (*autexousion*) is not the realization that we are simply "there": it is rooted in the fact that we are "gift" and "gifted", which presupposes a "giving" reality. In this sense "all knowers know God implicitly in every mental act", insofar as "being itself (which, as a given reality, manifests its unity with spirit and hence its truth) is a likeness of the divine goodness"; thus "all men naturally tend toward God" (Thomas).[108] It is by embracing and keeping the gift of being, by exercising the privilege of being, that I am freely myself: initially I owe myself to no one but nonfinite Being itself. For the latter gives itself to each being (as I know from experience), revealing itself and making itself available as a whole; and in all this it is inexhaustible. As for me, in my *cogito/sum*, therefore, I never cease recalling these things and giving thanks. Now, however, I become aware of being's awakening summons, coming to me from a man endowed with the strength to waken me in the power and in the name of being, someone who himself lives under the sign of gift and thanksgiving. Mediation mediates the nonmediate, and into the nonmediate: shared humanity [*Mitmenschlichkeit*] and nonmediate presence before God [*Gottunmittelbarkeit*] are inseparable in every individual. And what is nonmediate can only be mediated through the medium of shared humanity; accordingly, the relationship with God cannot be described as exclusively a priori and the relationship with one's fellow men as exclusively a posteriori.[109]

---

presentation" and possesses an outer and inner environment (*Umwelt*: "world-around-it"), but it does not have a "shared world", *Mitwelt*.

[107] *Ibid.*, 302–3.

[108] *De Ver.* q 22, a 2 ad 1 and ad 2 and c.

[109] Properly speaking, this discussion ought to be complemented by an analysis of *language*, which manifests both the dichotomy and the relatedness between individual and community and also lays the foundation for the whole

Once the "spirit" is seen in terms of the "shared world" or the "we" (not only "I-thou"), the individual's relationship with the state, seen as the organized society that imposes obligations on all, is clarified. In this context the state no longer appears as a "lesser evil", an appendage to individuals, restricting their "autonomy"; now it appears to be something that every individual carries within him, in outline, something he must affirm if he is to affirm himself. The state may appear, in some aspect or other, to exercise "coercion from above", but even so it is only manifesting the divinely willed, creaturely form of the "we" (Rom 13); individuals have to fit into it willingly "from below" if this form is to fulfill its immanent purpose. According to Hegel, the union of both aspects—"law" operating from above, morality from below—is what characterizes the state. On the one hand, as an "institution", it has a coercive character, but, on the other hand, it is sustained by the attitude of its citizens, yet the institution is not simply the product of the attitude of its individuals.[110]

---

relationship of tension in the single, primary phenomenon of the revelation of being. Language is not a mere means of communicating with an environment that is opened up to us or presses upon us, an a posteriori adjunct to the lonely and inarticulate *cogito/sum*. Primarily it has its roots in the spirit's "we"-awareness. Accordingly it will persist in constant tension between the (inherited) expression of common human experience and the (creative) expression of ever-unique individuality. However, this tension rests on being's most fundamental, unarticulated self-presentation as true and good, which represents a supralinguistic, primal "word". This "word" is not uttered by me, for being presents itself to me as that which is ever-greater, but it is *understood* by me, insofar as my existence (my "being there", *Da-sein*) always implies the inner assimilation of what is presented to it. Of course, if this primal word is to show itself to be such, it needs the medium of articulated language that is a feature of shared humanity. On language as the opening up of the individual standpoint to new perspectives, facilitating an "infinite conversation on the part of an ideal community of interpretation", cf. H. G. Gadamer, *Wahrheit und Methode*, 2d ed. (Tübingen: Mohr, 1965), passim [*Truth and Method*, Sheed and Ward]; also "Replik" in *Hermeneutik und Ideologiekritik* (Suhrkamp, 1971), 313f.

[110] Cf. Walter Schulz, *Philosophie in einer veränderten Welt* (Neske, 1972), 732ff., esp. 736. The transition from the political structure of the state to that of humanity, if it is even possible, is an extremely difficult one, as the present time makes evident. From below, the relation of the individual to the whole is abstract, from above what is seen as indispensable becomes ideological, and this inevitably produces a counter-ideology in its turn, so that with the increasing

As far as philosophical reflection is concerned, therefore, individuality and community are originally intertwined, that is, in that originating act whereby, in its self-giving, the "Unconditional" causes "conditioned" dimensions to spring forth in itself and in others. While such reflection may presuppose a more profound level of consideration of the nature of the individual's spiritual being than actually existed prior to Christianity, it does operate within the framework of a "natural" anthropology, that is, assuming that the *theion* is open to view, implicitly given to every human being who attains human self-awareness.

All the same, this "openness to view" remains veiled, because it consists in participation in being-in-its-totality, which can only be seized in the cosmos of inanimate, animate and thinking beings. However, both as individuals and as a community, human beings incline to equate the *theion* that reveals itself in being-in-its-totality with the universe of beings, the cosmos; they take the latter as their standard, even understanding the hypercosmic as a dimension of the cosmic. Thus, for the third time, it emerges how vexing the question of death is, which arises in this context too. Again death shows itself to be an insoluble complex of problems, threatening and besetting the unity of the human being in ever new ways. It threatens the unity of spirit and body that actually constitutes the individual, the unity of personal and generic sexuality and now the unity of an individuality that has direct access to God while at the same time being bound to the community. Nothing is more understandable than the religio-philosophical attempt to overcome the paradox of death by regarding one element in man, the spirit (which is also *"forma corporis"*), as the essential determinant of the human being, and the body as an accessory that can be jettisoned: this is the Platonic solution and that found in Indian thought. In this view, furthermore, the "soul" acquires the dignity of something that originates in the world of the eternal, of the *theion*; in Plato it is gifted with an eternal, individual consciousness, but it becomes so "monadic" that its essential link with the earthly sequence of generations and with the

---

unification of humanity even profounder divisions into "blocks" seems unavoidable. On this topic, see Claude Bruaire, *La Raison Politique* (Fayard, 1974).

"bodily" community is lost from sight.[111] In India the individual, in contemplation, can bid farewell to the community
—utterly or almost entirely: even while alive he can seemingly
reduce his own humanity to that part which belongs to the
theion. Here the community forfeits all claims upon the individual; the part it played in awakening and shaping him is
regarded as a side issue of little significance. This dualistic
splitting of the human being (which aims to rescue at least what
is essential, what is hypercosmic in him) is and remains an
extreme solution, an emergency solution, so to speak. It is
proposed in the face of the greater opposite danger, which arises
where the *theion* is subsumed in the cosmic, namely, that of
surrendering the individual's continuing existence beyond time:
here the individual is seen as an ephemeral and untimely offspring of the universe, dissolving into the latter's elements.

In all three of the anthropological tensions we have examined,
death remains the great question mark that cuts across them. It is
symptomatic, showing that what we have here is not an in-
herently natural tension but a hiatus, a wound, that cannot be
healed by the available resources of cosmic anthropology alone.
It is foolish to accuse pre-Christian anthropology of failing to
solve the problem of man; if we look at the material at its
disposal it is clear that no solution proposed on the basis of man
can solve the problem, except by neglecting some essential
aspect.

3. *The New Christian Reality*

In seeking an understanding of himself, however ambivalent it
might be, pre-Christian man, or rather, prebiblical man, could
somehow have recourse to the cosmos in which, and behind
which, were the primal wellsprings of divine life. The moment
this hermeneutic aid was withdrawn, a fundamentally new
period dawned for man's understanding of himself and for
anthropology. In the present context we are not interested in the

---

[111] This is the place to mention the "communist" features in Plato's ideal
state, which are hard to reconcile with the nobility he affirms in the individual
souls.

facts of biblical revelation in themselves—as in the next volume and in the volumes on the dramatic action—but in their effect on our picture of man, who will have to step forth as an actor on the theodramatic stage. The dimensions of the human being are changed, not only partially—for example, with regard to the limited world of biblical believers—but progressively and totally. The "in-breaking" of the new reality—it can be described purely negatively as the "desacralizing" or "demythologizing" of the cosmos—shows itself to be an active principle operating on the whole of history; it is anticipated by certain "undermining" processes in the ancient world, intensified through the presence of the Jewish element and even more by the Christian element (the first Christians were initially regarded as "atheists"), and is shown to be irreversible even in times when Christianity no longer dominates man's understanding of himself. Post-Christian anthropology differs essentially from pre-Christian, "natural" anthropology because of the presence (or former presence) of the Christian element. We shall demonstrate and reflect upon this fact in the remaining pages of this volume.

On the one hand, the transition between the pre-Christian and the biblical and Christian world is abrupt, even if it does not break down all the bridges to the past. The first sentence in the Bible, read against the total content of what it has to reveal, announces a sovereign freedom on God's part that is entirely different from that found elsewhere in the history of religion. It proclaims the creation of the world in its entirety—heaven and earth—out of nothing by the power of God's word and puts an end to the tendency of cosmos and physis to merge into the *theion*. Both cosmos and man are now on the same side: they are creatures vis-à-vis the God who creates them. This axis determines the entire, new system of coordinates and cuts through all the "similarities" between God, world and man. "What is the difference between the *theion* and that which is (only) like it? The difference is precisely that the one exists uncreated and the other subsists on the basis of creation."[1]

Does this mean that the uncreated Creator is remote and absent from his world and from man who inhabits it? Both Old and New Testaments constantly affirm the contrary, initially in

[1] Gregory of Nyssa, *De hom. op.* 16 (PG 44, 184C).

a naïve way (for example, the way God "comes down" in Genesis) and then with growing reflection. We discern this progress, for instance, in the psalms that speak of creation and in the Torah, celebrating God's presence in the cosmos and in the world of men, which proclaim his glory; in the Wisdom literature, which ponders God's immanence in creation by his all-pervading "wisdom" and "spirit"; and finally in the Letter to the Romans, which shows man that he can rationally behold God's "eternal power and *theiotēs*", manifested in the created world (Rom 1:19f.). What we have, therefore, in the place of God's cosmic immanence, is not his one-sided transcendence; but God's transcendence is understood to be absolute in such a way that, for that very reason, he must be close to and immanent in his created world. As far as man is concerned this means, however, that, while he also encounters God in the realms of nature and of the world, he can no longer take his own standards from anything within the cosmos but only from the God who stands "over against" him. He is face to face with his Creator, which implies that he can no longer use God in any way as a measuring rod for himself, for man: he himself must submit to being measured and judged by God.

Nor does God's immanence in the world on the basis of his inhabiting the biblical heaven permit an exception to what we have said. This "heaven where God is" is not some place within the cosmos which men could discover. At least, it becomes less and less so in Jewish-Christian reflection. It is not something man could use as a norm for his own conduct, irrespective of God himself. He cannot contemplate his "heavenly idea" without first being obliged to look toward God. The system of coordinates known as "heaven and earth", within which man finds himself, goes right through God's sovereign will, as the first half of the "Our Father" shows:

> Our Father who art in heaven
>   Hallowed be thy name ⎫
>   Thy kingdom come   ⎬ on earth as it is in heaven.
>   Thy will be done   ⎭

Creation "out of nothing" points to God's absolute freedom,[2] that is, to his *aseity*, his self-sufficiency, which in turn means

---

[2] It is true that, in the countless creation myths of the nations, we encounter a

that, in order to conceive himself, he did not need to conceive a non-ego, a world.[3] Even less was he compelled to create a world in order to prove his full omnipotence to himself or to show himself to be Love.[4] From now on the creature sees its origin in this abyss of freedom and not primarily or adequately in a divine idea that possesses an independent existence in God, independent (wholly or relatively) from his freedom. There is no appeal from God's freedom to this "idea": it is nothing but the blueprint of the creature which God has freely set before him. For that very reason, as we have seen in detail, the "image of God" in the creature consists decisively in its *autexousion*, in the created mirroring of uncreated freedom. This self-determination cannot be conceived as separate from spirit (rationality).

Thus the "image of God" in man loses all objective visibility and ascertainability. Nor can its "content" be one-sidedly deduced from what man is by "nature" as opposed to what he is according to his "spirit", for this "nature" is entrusted to him by the Creator as an inseparable part of his self. As for the criterion for using or not using this nature, it is made plain to man in the very act whereby the Creator hands it over to him. It is by looking toward infinite freedom that finite freedom sees how it can and should realize itself in its finitude, its natural state.

The biblical revelation, however, does not only open up the profound abysses of uncreated and created freedom. They only open to allow "mysteries" to come to light, mysteries which

---

divine act which, if reflected upon, would reveal a certain freedom on the part of the creating divinity; it could be inferred from a certain awareness of contingence on man's part (on the myths, cf. the already-mentioned introduction to the Genesis creation accounts by Claus Westermann, *Genesis* 1 (Neukirchener Verlag, 1974; English trans., SPCK). But in fact there is no explicit reflection on this freedom. Man's questioning begins with the idea that the world must have come from some primal source and is satisfied when it can point to such a source.

[3] As A. Günther assumed. For him, the idea of the world is "the necessary shadow cast by God's idea of himself". *Thomas a Scrupulis* (Vienna, 1835), 142f.

[4] This is the ultimate consequence of Leibniz' notion of the necessary existence of the best of all possible worlds; it also follows from Hegel's demand for the "idea" to be realized and for love to be "taken seriously". We have already illustrated the consequences of the biblical idea of creation (right up to modern voluntarism) in the section on "the dawn of infinite freedom" (above). Here we are concerned with the anthropological effects.

can only be seen in these abysses; they show the true nature of the idea of man, as seen by God. The tensions in human nature which we have already examined in the foregoing, and which already provide a wealth of dramatic material, are once again stretched to the breaking point by the idea that is now being made manifest.

a. The Heightening of the "Natural" ("Pre-Christian") Tensions

1. When absolute, divine freedom creates over against itself a world with a free man within it, the intention cannot be simply to leave things like that. For, given a share in the act of real being, man and the world have been entrusted with the first word of a message. And, biblically and theologically speaking, the message does not end with the first word. For the first word is the constitution of a rational and free subject, which as such has been made receptive to further words and capable of responding to them. True, this first word does contain an inexhaustible message insofar as being (*esse*) is always richer than any particular totality of entities (*essentiae*) realized by it; *yet this "richer" realm apprehended by the spiritual being does not actually fulfill but rather holds out a promise.* And what it promises is not something recognizably definite (for such are the entities): what it does is simply to remove limitations, since no limited entity can appropriate it for its own ends, and points in the direction of a realm that is limitless. The latter would have to be free from the limitations characteristic of entities, but that does not mean that it would have to be indefinite; after all, the very definiteness of entities and the "I"-ness of spirits come from the richness of being. So all the particular entities that participate in being are given the gift of a promise; and this promise comes from a Giver who, far beyond any gift separate from himself, is able actually to give himself. The realized entities are filled with as much being as they can contain, but in being thus filled, insofar as they are spiritual, they also have access in principle to a self-disclosure on the part of absolute Being. However, it is no longer a question of the latter constituting ("natural") subjects; now, in a "supernatural" way, subsistent Being opens up to them its own free inner life.

This fulfillment, if it occurs, cannot be a mere speaking in transient words. Natural, finite subjects would understand such "words", reaching them from the realm of the absolute, even less than a man understands a foreign language. God's language is not that of his creatures; if they thought they understood anything, they would have transposed it into purely creaturely categories. If God wishes to communicate himself to his creatures, we must presuppose that, when he speaks, he opens up his own absolute being, communicating it and enabling us to commune with it [mit-teilt]; with this in view, he enables the created spirit to grasp this communication, this communing, as what it is and what it intends, namely, participation in the Absolute. The Absolute bends down toward the creature, but it only reaches the creaturely level, substantially, by lifting the latter up, beyond itself and its entire natural substance, to its own level, giving it access and citizenship in the sphere of the Absolute. In other words, if it is to be a self-communication of the Absolute, it must be both ontological (substantial) and verbal (addressing the mind, explicatory): "participation in the divine nature" without verbal communication is just as unthinkable as verbal communication without substantial participation. Or, from the perspective of the creature, if man is destined to share the divine nature, he must also be called to it in a way that is recognizable as such.

Plainly, such self-communication of divine life is an utterly free act. The only comparison available to us is the free self-opening of one human subject to another, where the person addressed has no inherent right to the knowledge thus imparted. But this analogy too fails at the crucial point: even information freely shared between equals cannot be compared with God giving creatures a share in his inner life, a life which, to them, is "fundamentally foreign" and an inaccessible mystery. In fact, when they are made the recipients of such communication, they experience for the first time what the "glory" of absolute freedom can be, and they experience it more and more deeply, the more they are initiated, through God's "Word", into the divine nature.

It is when creatures are thus lifted above their own creaturely nature to one that transcends them absolutely that they become aware of the yawning gulf between them and experience their own creatureliness for the first time. Faced with the abyss of divine freedom that opens up in the Word of God they become aware, for the first time, that their whole being is drawn from the abyss of nothingness by this freedom. In this light, everything previously known to them appears new. In God's revelation, in the biblical word and in the revelation that comes through Being, the creature is denied every possibility of gaining security for himself and defining himself except in God's free purpose. All cosmological and trans-cosmological primal matrices fade away, and even the womb of nature is no longer self-subsistent but, like the individual, has to acknowledge that its origin is not in itself. The only "substance" from which the creature can trace its origin—as we heard from the Greek Fathers—is the will, that is, the freedom, of God. So, at the very moment when the creature addressed by God is lifted above itself, up to a nature that is essentially foreign to it, hypercosmic and absolute, it plunges down into a hypocosmic abyss, which, however, is shown to be none other than the same abyss of God's freedom and power that lifts it above itself.

We do not have to adumbrate the theological implications of this. For the present we are only concerned with the *heightening* of the creature's inner constitution, whose finitude is now explicitly stretched between the poles of nothing and infinity, or rather of "nothingness" and "God". The creature cannot resist this heightening, which is imposed on it by God's freedom. After all, the creature's own freedom was always dependent, for its fulfillment, on absolute freedom. But now he is given access by God to the inner sphere of divine life, so that he may live and move in it. This is something the creature would never have dreamed of; he would never have postulated it for himself, either subjectively or objectively. At the very moment when God freely discloses himself to him and utters his inner word, man the creature—discerning his own nothingness—knows how little claim he has to such initiation.

When the word of God goes forth, the creature is given insight into God's purpose in creation and realizes something entirely new: God undertook that first communication of his being, whereby finite, self-aware, free beings were created, with a view to a "second" act of freedom whereby he would initiate them into the mysteries of his own life and freely fulfill the promise latent in the infinite act that realizes Being. This "second" act does not need to be temporally distinct from the first: the final cause, since it is the first and all-embracing cause, includes all the articulations of the efficient cause—that is, the world's coming-to-be and God's becoming man. To that extent, any "claim" the creature might make on God (assuming the word has any meaning) would always come too late, in view of the total gift already made and the response expected, namely, total gratitude.

It could be objected that there is little significant difference between this heightening of the creaturely tensions by the fact that man is both "created from nothing" and yet "called to share in the divine life"—and the pre-Christian situation, in which the individual is referred to a cosmic/hypercosmic norm. The difference, it could be said, is simply that the prevalently natural relationship has now become an emphatically free and personal one. This is not completely false, and it shows that the positive side of the *analogia entis*, that is, that the being [*Sein*] of the primal origins and the being [*Sein*] of the effects are to some degree comparable, is preserved in both views. On the other hand, in the biblical and Christian model of the world, the negative side of the same analogy—the "greater dissimilarity" —acquires quite a different force, since everything the creature can ever come up with in terms of similarity with the Creator rests upon the irreducible opposition of "out-of-itself" and "out-of-some-other" ("out of nothing"). It would be important always to keep this in mind in the Christian milieu (and even more so in the post-Christian), when the aspect of "likeness"— right up to "participation in the divine nature" and being "born of God"—transcends everything pre-Christian man normally[5] dared to hope for. While the creature is elevated into kinship with God at the level of being and of consciousness, in Christian terms he is never substantially divinized by it. Rather, he lives in the paradox of nearness and distance at the same time. The more the creature is found worthy of intimacy with God, the

---

[5] Normally: divinization after death was reserved to specially chosen individuals.

more deeply he becomes aware of God's uniqueness and incomparability, without his reverence turning into an inhibiting fear which would refuse the proffered intimacy.

2. The free self-communication of God (the essentially Unique and Incomparable) to man, if it actually comes about, has a second result: since the word which God addresses to man is always, in addition, the gift of a sharing in God's nature, the individual who receives the word acquires a new quality: he becomes a *unique person*. This category only comes to light in the biblical-Christian dispensation; in pre-Christian times even the man designated a "hero", or the individual who, as king, represented the macro-ego of the people before God, was not a person in this sense. The "person" only shines forth in the individual where the absolute Unique God bestows an equally unique name on him (unique because it is chosen by God), a "new name which no one knows except him who receives it" (Rev 2:17). The "new name" (Is 62:2), the "different name" (Is 65:15), the change of name (Gen 17:5; 32:28ff.; Is 60:14; 62:4; Hos 2:3; Jn 1:42): these all point to the fact that the man concerned, who was hitherto an individual of the species at the natural level, is now entering a "supernatural" and direct relationship with God and so receives a personal call and corresponding endowment. This event can take place during the person's lifetime, as in many episodes in the Bible, but it can also occur "in the womb" (Jer 1:5; Is 49:1; Gal 1:15; cf. Lk 1:41; 2:21). Something of the radiance of God's freedom and uniqueness falls on the essence and countenance of the chosen one, lifting him out of the purely natural species. It sets him apart for a face-to-face meeting with God; yet this does not transport him from the world but equips him to undertake a God-given task among his human brethren. Vocation, qualitatively speaking, always means being equipped for a task in the world; the substance of the task is part of God's plan for the world.

Here we are reserving the concept "person" for the supernatural uniqueness of the man who has been called into a relationship of intimacy with God; every human being can share this distinction to some degree. But this does not mean that we are taking back anything we said earlier about the hypercosmic aspect of every man, who is a spiritual subject. It is a question of terminology whether we grant the term "person" to the latter or only to the man who is called through grace; in the first case, one would have to distinguish between two forms or grades of personhood. Anton Günther, with his abrupt opposition of the nature-principle and the spirit-principle in man, drew the boundary line incorrectly; for if, in his view, nature consists in its living activity, right up to the forming of concepts, to the "complete systematic model of the external world",[6] but does not reach as far as the "idea", that is, insight into the causes of phenomena, he is arbitrarily separating elements of human knowledge that belong together. One can ask, of course (as Alois Dempf does) whether a double ground of individuation must be assumed, even in the natural spiritual subject: "a material one, as in all the other living entities, bearing the external features, and a spiritual one, bearing the person";[7] this would correspond to the inseparable cooperation, referred to earlier, in the generation of a new human being: that of the parents in the fruitfulness of the species and that of God, who administers the spirit-principle of direct access to him. However, this twofold principle of individuation is not like "nature" and "the supernatural", for both sides converge in the forming of the one spiritual subject; it is the entire spiritual subject that is the "natural" presupposition for conception in the full sense, that is, that supernatural giving of a name, that supernatural calling which fashions the person. Historically speaking, as we have likewise already shown, these two aspects can only be expressed inadequately in the categories of "image and likeness" as interpreted by the Church Fathers; for the latter always think of the natural and the supernatural as a unity.[8]

[6] *Süd- und Nordlichter* . . . (Vienna, 1832), 143.

[7] *Theoretische Anthropologie* (Berne: Francke, 1950), 139.

[8] Thus the tension between the chance-aspect of the sexual cause and its spiritual product is increasingly felt in the Christian and post-Christian eras. Listen to what Ernst Jünger has to say in connection with a projected book on death: "Any writing on death would have to begin, perhaps, with a chapter stressing the fortuitous nature of our individual life. We would not exist if our father had married a different wife and our mother a different husband. Even presuming the existence of this marriage, we ourselves have come from one cell out of millions. Thus we are transient combinations of the Absolute. We are like

Nor, finally, do we need to go into the relationship between this personalizing of the human spiritual subject and the innermost mystery in the God-who-reveals-himself, the mystery of his threefold life. Here it is sufficient to say this: if man is to be given the new name that comes directly from God and enabled to share in God's own, personal life, there must be some "place" in this life, some point of insertion, where this giving of the name occurs ("You are my son, today I have begotten you": Ps 2:7), together with the imparting of the divine Spirit ("The Spirit of the Lord is upon me, because the Lord has anointed me . . . and sent me": Is 61:1); and all this takes place in a mysterious, pulsating vitality, of which the creaturely community, at whatever level, can only be a pale reflection. And yet, insofar as the spiritual subject, dignified by a personal "name", does not cease to be a member of the species, even his natural form of community is made to share in this eternal vitality. Otherwise the person sent out into the world could in no way carry out his mission.

3. It also follows from what has been said, however, that the new immediacy and intimacy between the called person and the personal divine life gives a new quality to every turning aside, every refusal. Prior to Christianity it is possible to speak of human guilt in a variety of ways, guilt in the sight of the gods and of the community; but as yet there is no awareness of what the Bible calls *sin*. The boundary may seem to be a fluid one in that even a hero or king can transgress against his god. But for the most part such transgressions have only a partially ethical character; they are more like infringements of ceremonial rules

---

lots drawn, and the winnings indicated thereon in destiny's characters are paid out to us in earthly currency, in pounds, with which we are to do business and make a profit. We should conclude from this that, as individuals, we are imperfect; and that as far as we are concerned, eternity is neither appropriate nor bearable. What we need to do is turn ourselves back into the Absolute, and this is the opportunity offered us by death. . . . We become death's initiates." *Strahlungen* (Tübingen: Heliopolis, 1949), 186.

This kind of resignation calls for the context of a much more acute consciousness of the "Category of the Individual" which in Sören Kierkegaard does not refer primarily to individualism, but to the awareness of being chosen, of an apostolic existence (in contrast to personal genuis).

and agreements, violations of etiquette and often purely worldly trespasses (the stealing of a herd belonging to the god, and so forth) which must be punished. They may even be unconscious faults and incursions into the god's realm of competence or the arousing of a god's jealousy with regard to a third party (Hippolytus), and so on. Corresponding to this "cosmological" character of guilt, its atonement is also very often sub-ethical, indeed, frequently magical: the divinity in question is reconciled by particular deeds and credits.

Only where the biblical word of God is proclaimed to man as a "commandment" that addresses the very core of his personality does the desire arise within him to act against it: "Sin, finding opportunity in the commandment, wrought in me all kinds of covetousness" (Rom 7:8). The commandment is a function of the relationship between One who specially chooses and one who is specially chosen, that is, ultimately it is the function of a love relationship in which God grants us a participation in his own sphere, reserved to himself: "Be holy, for I am holy" (Lev 19:2). Participation in this sphere of divine holiness deepens as the Old Testament moves toward the New; and at the same time a shadow deepens: the shadow of what is called "sin", becoming a wounding of the heart's mystery of God himself. Vast abysses open up in relationship between God and man, and their presence and causal activity produce the dimensions and intensities of theo-drama. The latter, however, in contrast to the horrors of Greek tragedy, which come about because of the cosmic aspect of the gods or of an avenging fate, will remain in the relative hiddenness of the new relationship between God and man. What is visible and expressible in the Cross of Jesus, with regard to sin and the judgment on sin, is little compared with the vast implications of the event.

b. The New Tensions Are Confirmed in the God-Man

What follows is only the barest outline, since it is really the subject of the next volume. The world is qualified by the biblical assertion that it has been created "from nothing" and is called to participate in the divine life: this seems to rob anthropology of all foothold within the world (but God alone), while it slides hither and thither between nothingness and infinity.[9] But it gains a new foothold, as it were, a concrete system of coordinates, in the central figure of biblical revelation, the God-man Jesus Christ.[10]

1. In the first place, Jesus Christ is the proof that the supernatural "heightening of tension" in man (who is already stretched in tensions of many kinds) does not inhumanly tear his existence apart. Jesus Christ proves that existence in this tension is livable, in fact, that it is the solution to the riddle of the "Old Adam" and brings release from his torment. In him, true humanity is revealed, not only the humanity of man but also the humanity of God (*apparuit humanitas Salvatoris nostri Dei*: Titus 3:4). Of its very nature, however, this humanity cannot be earthly in a closed sense, for what is at stake is to give a final solution to the question of death, which cuts across all the structures of man. And the question of death cannot be answered from outside but only from inside, all the more since it is bound up with the whole problem of the world's sin vis-à-vis God.

The anthropological foothold gained in Jesus Christ throws up a new problem, however, which will lead, through the ways and byways of Christian theology, to that confusion characteristic of the post-Christian era. The "New Adam", henceforth the exemplary man, seems to call into question the fundamental rhythm of the *analogia entis*: similarity within an ever-increasing dissimilarity. On the one hand, with regard to his divine person, the similarity ("image and likeness") becomes an equality: the Son shares a unity of nature with the Father, in the Holy Spirit who is common to both. Accordingly it is impossible to see, on the other side, how we can still speak of ever-greater dissimilarity, particularly as it remains questionable whether the seed implanted into the Virgin's womb by the Holy Spirit of God can be described as "created" in the proper sense of the word. Or should we say that this "seed" refers not only to what replaces the male contribution to the generation of a human being but

---

[9] Cf. the experience of Pascal: *The Glory of the Lord* III ("Lay Styles"), 188–205.

[10] *Theologie der Geschichte*, 5th ed. (1962).

also, in this unique case, to the unique contribution that God makes to the coming-to-be of the "spirit-soul" of Jesus?

At all events it is clear that the Son accepts all that is involved in adopting human nature (*genomenos*: Phil 2:8; cf. Heb 2:17; 4:15), including, no doubt, existing in relation to God in the analogy of being. And when, in his temptations, he quotes the words: "You shall worship the Lord your God and him only shall you serve" (Mt 4:10), he does so, not for the sake of others, but very definitely for himself as well. Anyone who confesses the full humanity of Jesus must necessarily allow that, having "become" man, he stands within the *analogia entis*. And anyone who professes to believe in the full divinity of a person will have to admit that the person simultaneously transcends the analogy; or, more precisely, that he stands on both sides of the analogy, *that the analogy goes right through the center of his consciousness*. Now the difficulty will be to explain what the situation is of the man who is made to share in the privilege of Jesus' divine Sonship, what is involved in being "born of God" (Jn 1:13), and how Jesus can truly call those who belong to him his "brothers" (Jn 20:17; cf. Rom 8:15–17; Gal 4:6; Heb 2:10ff.). The difficulty can be overcome by reference (again) to the fact that the greatest intimacy can be united to an ever-growing reverence; but this mystery, which henceforward determines all anthropology, will become the latter's greatest temptation: man can imagine that the dimensions opened up to him by free grace are his by nature, are postulates of his; as for the distance between himself and God, which pre-Christian man took for granted, he can jump over it and settle down in God's realm as if it were his own.

2. Furthermore, the soteriology linked with the name of Jesus has significance for anthropology (and here too the briefest mention must suffice). In the Son, the word of God (a word in human form) enters the human community in order to save and rescue it. He enters it both as an individual who bears the destiny of all (just as the individual contributes to the destiny of the species) and as someone absolutely unique, the Father's Word in bodily form, authorized to bear in himself the destiny of all, representing them and so making atonement. What we have already said about the priority of the "we" in the human "I" is

important at this point. Since we share a world with others, there is in every human subject a formal *inclusion* of all the other subjects (who are materially *excluded* because each one is "for himself"). The a priori of the "we" is the anthropological point of departure for christological representation [in the sense of "being-for-others"], although the latter is something totally new and qualitatively different from it.

Once again, this mysterious point of Christian faith seems, from an anthropological standpoint, something very vulnerable and too easily misused. For it implies nothing less than an intervention in the "private sphere" of the individuals who make up the community: when, in the presence of God, their guilt is borne by another on their behalf, something in them is changed, without their knowledge; something that they alone —one would have thought—are authorized to change by making a free decision with regard to God. But there is a prior question: Are men actually capable of making this change? Or, in their situation, as sinners before God, have they so entangled themselves that they just cannot do what they ought? And there is a second question: Who but God alone can break their bonds? And he must do so by his forgiveness, which cannot be merely verbal but, as we have said, must allow the sinner a certain participation, grant him a new freedom. In this case, must not the word of forgiveness addressed to the sinner be at the same time a judgment on sin, so that the same Word which proclaims and imparts God's forgiveness also, in his human form and on his brothers' behalf, takes over the judgment that hangs over them?

A judgment such as this, however, can only take place in a dying and a death that cut the judged man off from the living God: Jesus dies on our behalf, abandoned by God, under the "curse" (Gal 3:13), "made to be sin for us" (2 Cor 5:21). He identifies himself with all that is anti-God in the world, as it were, with the second chaos, brought about by man in his freedom. He infiltrates the entire chaotic realm brought about by created freedom, in order—as the forgiving Word of the divine Father—to cut it loose from man and let it return to its nothingness. But also, descending into this second death, the product of freedom, he gives a new value to the first, that is, the natural death of the individual within the undying species, the death which is all of a piece with sexual generation and birth, the death which arises out of the disproportion between spirit and body. Now the Father makes it plain that this Jesus who died for the world's sin was his (the Father's) forgiving Word; he does this by showing this Word to be alive, by raising the incarnate Word bodily from the dead. This gives a new center to all natural anthropology: the event of Christ's Resurrection. Not only are sinners inwardly liberated from the inability to turn to God and given the grace of faith, hope and love for the God who forgives them and makes them sharers in his life; the internal complex of problems associated with the "Old Adam", who was hindered at all points from attaining his own fulfillment, is transcended in the "New Adam". "What is sown is perishable, what is raised is imperishable" (1 Cor 15:42).[11] The Resurrection not only guarantees redemption: it enables the natural man to be whole.

3. A final christological aspect follows from what has been said—not by human logic, but by Christo-logic. The unique "I" of Jesus Christ possesses his milieu, his "we", to such an extent that he can rule over it and draw his brothers' sins upon himself. He does not do this solely as the Word of God (logos asarkos) but as the Father's Word-made-man (logos ensarkos). Thus we discern the possibility and appropriateness of his Eucharist. It is only by having a body that he can die the death of the sinner; accordingly, it is only because he has a body that he can put himself in the place of his sinful brothers or, rather, draw them into the sphere of his own nature, which is simultaneously divine, spiritual and physical. That calls for this kind of "fluidizing" or universalizing of his "flesh and blood", which thus recapitulates the dimensions of the Word of God that he is and the dimensions of his mission to all men.

And once again this mystery of faith has a retroactive effect on "natural" anthropology. First, it removes the tragic side of individuation in corporeality. In Christ we are not only for one

[11] Cf. Gustave Martelet, *Victoire sur la mort. Eléments d'anthropologie chrétienne* (Lyons: Chron. soc., 1962); also his *Résurrection, eucharistie et genèse de l'homme. Chemins théologiques d'un renouveau chrétien* (Desclée, 1972).

another, as brothers; we are also members in his eucharistic Body. The interplay between us is not simply through the meeting of minds, our bodies being hermetically sealed off from one another: there is a sphere—far beyond sexual union—in which our bodies, too, communicate with one another. Not in a biological medium, but a pneumatic one, grounded in the Lord's Resurrection and his eucharistic state.

One final thing: the God-man is able to permeate the world he shares with others [*Mitwelt*] from within, without getting too close to the freedom of individuals. (For he is God's bodily Word, and God cannot get too close to anyone, since he is more internal to every man than each man is to himself.) But the God-man does not thus permeate the world for himself: in his Eucharist he gives us a share in it. So, in the field of anthropology, something entirely new comes into being: not only can people do things externally on behalf of one another, one person taking a burden from someone else; now it becomes possible internally as well: in Christ's Eucharist a person can share in bearing someone else's guilt or handicap. The *communio eucharistica* becomes—"analytically", as it were—the *communio sanctorum*. And the form of exchange in the latter is entirely marked by that of the former and inherent in it. This means that, for its part, it is proof against every subjective indiscretion or objective infringement of the other's sphere of intimacy. At most, the person who offers to share, with Christ, in bearing the burden of his brothers, will know that his offer is meaningful and fruitful; he will not know how and where it has its effect. His offer of himself, together with that of the Son, enters into the Father's forgiving word.

Initially, all these christological new departures seemed to signal a heightening of tension, a stretching, an explosion of the proportions of the human being—which, indeed, they are. In the end, however, it transpires that, in addition, they always fulfill what was fragmentary in the pre-Christian dispensation. Formerly, in the face of all anthropological tensions, the watchword was "moderation". Now, in Christianity, it is replaced by other words: gratitude, humility, hope, boldness. Man discerns dimensions in himself which, if he did not know that he could fulfill himself in God, he would despair of fathoming.

c. The New Rhythm

The Word of God in Jesus Christ becomes man in a fully bodily sense, and man exists in the threefold rhythm we have described. Consequently, wherever human existence includes an either/or, Jesus Christ can only enter the human sphere at the one pole, in order, from that vantage point, to go on to fulfill the other pole. This becomes concrete in the man/woman relationship: because of the natural, relative priority of the man (given an equality of both persons), the Word of God, on account of its absolute priority, can only enter the world of the human in the form of a man, "assimilating" the woman to itself (Eph 5:27) in such a way that she, who comes from him and is at the same time "brought to him" by God, is equal to him, "flesh of his flesh". This shows us that even in the first tension, that between spirit and body, a new rhythm has become established.

1. In natural anthropology there was a twofold and contrary rhythm: the body (nature) rises to spirit, and the spirit (which is the goal and rationale of "evolution") descends into the body (nature). Insofar as this twofold rhythm is an integral part of nature, it is not destroyed but overlaid by a primacy of the descent: from the world of the divine, the purely spiritual, into what is human and fleshly: "The Word became flesh" (Jn 1:14); "You are from below, I am from above" (Jn 8:23); "I have come down from heaven . . ." (Jn 6:38); "he emptied himself, taking the form of a servant, being born in the likeness of men" (Phil 2:7). The descent clearly takes the path toward enfleshment, incarnation. It is the path toward what is distinctively human in general, since "God is spirit" (Jn 4:24); furthermore it is the implanting of the divine seed deep in the human field, so that, instead of sprouting superficially and then withering (as just one more human concept among thousands), it should inform the whole substance; and finally, it is a movement that runs counter to all the sinful tendencies toward dis-incarnation, in which man would like to be "like God".

Since God, the Absolute, is essentially "above" and can only encounter his creature by freely bending down to the latter's level; and since, moreover, in this "inclination", absolute love cannot gain anything for itself but condescends freely and "for nothing", it follows that the "descent" is primary in the whole incarnational movement. Agape is not forced to come down by any longing or any avid, godward "ascent" on the part of Eros; it is not the relative opposite of Eros. Nor can we say that this descent sets itself a relative limit, a point at which it changes into the ascending movement of body toward spirit. The descent goes from the act of incarnation right down to the "obedience unto death, death on a cross" (Phil 2:8), and continues downward in the "descent into hell" in solidarity with all those who are lost to time. It goes farther: from the obedience of the Cross to the atomizing of his bodily being, shared out in the Eucharist. None of these forms of descent is revoked in the Resurrection on the third day and in the Ascension. Bodily Resurrection and Ascension are not dis-incarnation but a transformation of the entire human form, spirit and body, into the pneumatic mode of existence. The divine Pneuma is the power behind this transformation, making sure that the definitive descent of the Word becomes sacramental, for all times.

This is what comes about in the bodily life of the Church, effected by the personal Incarnation of the Word. In virtue of his physical nature, the Son can fashion mankind as his "body" (1 Cor 12:27) by means of his Eucharist (1 Cor 10:16f.): he pours his "fullness" into a vessel, which is formed by this very act of pouring (Eph 1:23). Thus the movement toward enfleshment is completed by becoming ecclesial, and even cosmic (*ibid.*),[12] whereas it was initially in the human figure of Jesus Christ that "the whole fullness of deity dwelt bodily" (Col 2:9). From the purely anthropological perspective, the spirit's rootedness in the flesh implies that the latter is permeated by spirit and lifted up into the sphere of the spirit; accordingly, in the new supernatural rhythm in which God becomes incarnate right down to the lowest depths and out to the farthest bounds, the physical is "divinized", permeated with God's Pneuma, transfigured and "transferred" (Col 1:13) into the kingdom of the Son, and hence of God. The Platonic Eros, striving upward from the bodily to

---

[12] H. Schlier, *Der Epheserbrief* (1957), 96ff.; F. Mussner, *Christus, das All und die Kirche*, 2d ed. (1958); Allan D. Galloway, *The Cosmic Christ* (London: Nisbet, 1951).

the spiritual and divine, is overtaken in the event of Agape and brought to share in a fulfillment that goes far beyond its own upward thrust; but this cannot take place unless it, too, is con-crucified together with the love of Christ.

2. In the rhythm of the sexual, too, according to the natural order, the new unity of procreating love and death comes into clearest focus. For now it is no longer a question of the closed anthropological cycle of the sexes that lies in man's animal and generic nature and—bafflingly—is linked with human guilt; now a purely personal love comes from above and enters into the generative chain, in order to undergo a death that is primarily equally personal and free, and by so doing to rob death (entailed by membership of the species, tainted by guilt) of its sting and its victory (1 Cor 15:55).

A process that encompasses and transcends the closed worldly cycle cannot be simultaneously subject to this cyclic law: it can only take place in a suprasexual (but not sexless) way. The reciprocal fruitfulness of man and woman is surpassed by the ultimate priority of the "Second Adam", who, in suprasexual fruitfulness, brings a "companion", the Church, into being. Now the "deep sleep" of death on the Cross, the "taking of the rib" in the wound that opens the heart of Jesus, no longer take place in unconsciousness and passivity, as in the case of the First Adam, but in the consciously affirmed love-death of the Agape, from which the Eucharist's fruitfulness also springs. The relative priority of the man over the woman here becomes absolute, insofar as the Church is a creation of Christ himself, drawn from his own substance. All the same, the first account of creation is over-fulfilled here, for in the mind of God the incarnate Word has never existed without his Church (Eph 1:4–6).

The suprasexual (and not sexless) relationship between the incarnate Word and his Church is a genuinely human one; human beings can be enabled to participate in it. Consequently the sexual man/woman fruitfulness need be no longer the exclusive model of human fruitfulness. On the contrary, this form of fruitfulness is seen to be the purely worldly metaphor of a unique fruitfulness that bursts through the cycle of successive generations and of which Christ says: "He who is able to receive this, let him receive it" (Mt 19:12). This unique fruitfulness is signed with the sign of the Agape-death, which is the ultimate bodily form adopted by the spiritual Word of God. The natural process whereby a man "leaves father and mother and cleaves to his wife" (Gen 2:24; Eph 5:3), which adds a new member to the sequence of generations, is changed: now a man steps out of the cycle of generation itself (Mk 10:29f.) in order to enter the unique, supratemporal, sexual relationship between the New Adam and his "Spouse" (Rev 21:9). Thus man is enabled to transcend the sexual—as a function specific to earthly existence —in favor of a form of existence in which God's Agape, which also reveals its nuptial aspect (sealed in the death on the Cross), becomes the all-inclusive total meaning of life.

3. We have already seen the direction in which the relationship between individual and community is transcended in our discussion of the *communio sanctorum*. The individual is transformed by being personally addressed by God, by being called and sent forth; the transformation is perfected in the Incarnation of the Word, because now God's utterly unique Word is an individual. And this transformation brings about a total restructuring of the community itself. The individual's dependence on the community is no longer merely the expression of the superiority of the continuous species over the transient individual; it is more: it is the expression of a universality which indwells the individual as such. His call and mission lift him out of the quantitative series of individuals within the species and make him qualitatively unique; and this results in an enrichment of all through his unique quality. Paul, in his doctrine of the charisms, has illustrated this qualitative aspect by pointing to the different organs in a living body. This image means more than the members' need to serve the whole and integrate themselves into it; it means the enrichment of the whole through that special gift which the member brings to it, which it does not possess already or *eminenter*. In pre-Christian times, roughly speaking, the totality of the *polis* or empire is greater than the sum of the parts. This view can be maintained, in Christian terms, insofar as the Church is "greater" because she is as such the mystical Body of Christ, integrating individual persons into the living organism of Christ. But the charisms are not allotted

to individuals through the Church's mediation but—for the Church's sake—given directly by God (Rom 12:3), directly by the risen Christ (Eph 3:8, 11). The individual is given a uniqueness that comes from the absolute uniqueness of God and Christ; it cannot be deduced from the community or found to be there antecedently, although the community can count on this uniqueness as something that enriches it and is specifically designed for it. As for the individual who has been chosen by God for a unique gift, this means that he is more profoundly drawn into the community, expropriated for its sake and obligated to it.

This confirms the principle already put forward that, in the "heightening" of the natural tension between individual and community, both poles are given greater emphasis: precisely because the individual is now more truly unique, the community is more closely knit. Notice that there is a christological basis for the intensification of both poles. What we have is not a "spiritualization" of the relationships, such as was proposed (by the Scholastics) to explain the communion between the created pure spirits.[13] It is rather that the whole rests on the Logos' becoming flesh and on the continuing communication of the members, through the Eucharist, in the bodily organism of the Church. It also rests on the fact that his enfleshment of the Logos is an expression of his self-emptying, his refusal to cling to the uniqueness of his "divine form" and his will to enter into the "form of a servant" of the mere individual, for the benefit of the "many" (*schēma hōs anthropos*: Phil 2:7). The incarnate Logos gives those who "receive him" and "believe in him" a share not only in his uniqueness but also in the unique surrender of his uniqueness "for many": it is this that builds up the unique body of the Church.

In the reciprocity between the uniqueness of the person and the uniqueness of his self-giving for the sake of the community, the Christian rhythm between the individual and the community becomes a concrete metaphor of trinitarian life within God, inscribed in the very structures of the creaturely tension between individual and species.

The absolute uniqueness of God (who is simplex, "one-fold")

---

[13] Thomas, *S. Th.* qq 106–7.

can only be shared by the creature in a bifurcation of the principles of unity: first, unity of being in the multiplicity of existent beings, and then (in the physical realm), unity of the species in the multiplicity of individuals. This splitting of the One was a basic problem of all Greek philosophy from Plato's *Parmenides*, via Aristotle,[14] to the end of the patristic period[15] and Thomas' *De Ente et Essentia*. In pre-Christian times there was bound to be a tendency to exclude the *atomos eidos*—since it was subrational—from the sphere of what was worth knowing, indeed, knowable at all; the movement of the One was seen as stretching from being-in-its-totality right down to genus and species.[16] In Christianity, by contrast, it is precisely the apparently irrational unity of the person, as an image of God's oneness, that comes into focus but in such a way that now even the community made up of individuals acquires a character that is personalized throughout. There is something ultimately incommunicable about the created individual (since it is created, it cannot have control of its own being),[17] and consequently the species retains impersonal features; but when we come to Christian participation in the divine life, something of this restriction is lifted. The person's self-surrender to the community can so personalize the latter that it is no longer an extrapersonal principle of unity beside and above the unity of persons but is integrated out of these surrendered unities, just as God's unity of nature is not something in addition to the interplay of relations between the divine Persons. At the same time, however great the "similarity" between God and the creature in the Christian order, it does not abolish the "greater dissimilarity", which consists in the fact that the created persons remain individual substances, each of which is an image and likeness of the Absolute Substance.

[14] Cf. the quotation from *Metaphysics* XI, p. 387 above.

[15] Cf. the chapter "Die Verwandlung der Eins" in *Kosmische Liturgie. Das Weltbild Maximus des Bekenners*, 2d ed. (1961), 100–109.

[16] p. 366 above.

[17] August Brunner, *Dreifaltigkeit. Personale Zügänge zum Mysterium*, Kriterien 39 (Einsiedeln: Johannes Verlag, 1976).

4. *Man without Measure ("Post-Christian")*

a. Gnostic Escalation

The biblical perspective, fulfilled in that of Christianity (in the Incarnation of the Word of God), has loosed man from nature. Since nature, like man, is created and so contains no *theion* in its essence, man for his part may not make any "graven image" out of it, neither an image of God nor an image of man, for man is created according to the image and likeness of God, who is free and invisible. The God who has dedivinized nature appears in Jesus Christ as the normative image (*eikōn tou theou*: 2 Cor 4:4; Col 1:15).

What then if man, no longer accustomed to taking his standard from the cosmos (now emptied of the divine), refuses to take it from Christ? This is post-Christian man, who cannot return to the pre-Christian fluidity that once existed between man and the cosmos but who, in passing through Christianity, has grown used to the heightening of his creaturely rhythms and wants to hold on to them as if they are his personal hallmark, a gift that now belongs to him entirely. This will be the general characteristic of the post-Christian era, however manifold and contradictory its concrete expressions may be.

Naturally there will be attempts to return to the pre-Christian age, as in the Renaissance. If we examine the latter more closely, however, it splits clearly into two: there was a Christian movement, which wanted, through a revitalization of the ancient languages, to liberate the original spirit of the gospel from the rank undergrowth of late Scholasticism (Erasmus) or to use the intimations of Plato and Plotinus as a kind of sounding board for Christian theology (Ficino) or (like many of the great painters) to bring out the incarnational aspect from behind the artificial sacralizing and angelizing of Byzantine art; and there was a minority that cultivated a forced kind of paganism and adopted an explicitly anti-Christian stance. Even the new model of the world constructed by Bruno, with its infinity-based pathos, is only conceivable in the wake of Christianity. In *The Glory of the Lord*, [vol. V] we presented a whole modern movement under the heading "The Realm of Metaphysics in

Antiquity".[1] Most importantly, we saw that everything that, in modern times, sails under the flag of "Eros" (allegedly based on Plato's *Symposium*) is in reality a secularization of Christian Agape. This is most evident as early as Gottfried von Strassburg and the medieval world around him, where Eros claims an absoluteness that unmasks it as a deliberate imitation and replacement of the incarnate, crucified and eucharistic love of God. The fatal character of courtly love [*Minne*] is borrowed from the Christian *mysterium*.

> Whoever is struck by love, with whatever consequences, love is experienced right from the outset as death; it is determined by death and wrested from death, lasts irrevocably until death and leads to death. Love is deadly, because it so changes the lovestruck person that he dies to his old life.[2]

The topic is pursued via Kleist's *Penthesilea*, Hebbel and Wagner, to Claudel's *Le Soulier de Satin*. We shall meet that paradigmatic "man of antiquity" in modern times, Goethe, in a different connection; here we must mention Hölderlin, whose infinite longing for Hellas (indeed he positively resuscitates the old gods) is ultimately explainable as a yearning for the genuine nearness of a loving God in the world, for the intimacy of the mystery of Christ. This is demonstrated by his late works.

Like Hölderlin in his *Empedokles*, all the great anthropological systems will take their standard from the figure of Christ: this is the point of departure which cannot be circumvented if we are to set out for "new shores". It will be opposed, of course, by sheer materialistic evolutionism, which binds man exclusively to the natural framework and denies that the spirit has any independence. But the question is: Where, in the world of antiquity, did *materia* ever possess such an immeasurable, creative urge? Where did it ever produce, out of itself, such an ambitious ascending thrust? There is nothing comparable from Democritus to Lucretius; and in the meantime a whole divine world of "ideas" has been covertly incorporated into it, together with the divine creative power. All the same, a serious an-

---

[1] *Herrlichkeit* III/1, part 2, 2d ed. (Einsiedeln: Johannes Verlag, 1975), 599–787 (*The Glory of the Lord*, V: *The Realm of Metaphysics in the Modern Age*).
[2] H. Rolf, *Der Tod in der mittelhochdeutschen Dichtung* (Munich, 1974), 380.

thropology cannot be pursued on a purely naturalistic basis; the
great systems to which we have referred—Scheler, Plessner,
Gehlen, to whom we would have to add others, such as A.
Portmann and K. F. von Weizsäcker—all show, in different
ways, that man cannot be reduced to subhuman nature. Either
two contrary principles are at work in him: material necessity
and spirit (Scheler), or man occupies a position outside the
whole of nature (Plessner), or his very structure has a retroactive
effect, transforming all the natural presuppositions of his being,
so that man can construct his institutions out of himself, like the
snail its house (Gehlen); man is by no means just one stage in a
developmental continuum of animal organization (Portmann,
Wilder-Smith). A. Dempf often hailed the biological approach
of these thinkers as a fruitful new departure in anthropology;
this is justifiable provided that its inadequacy is pointed out.
The honest recognition of persistent problems is one of the most
positive things in these systems.

In the long run, however, people cannot rest content with
unsolved problems. Faced with man's ambivalence and all the
suffering in the world, they try by means of *speculation* to "get
behind" the Christian mystery of the God-man who, in pure
freedom and love, was crucified for us; they apprehend the
abyss which the Cross opens up between sheer divine love and
sheer God-forsakenness, but they attempt to trace it back to a
source in the Absolute, so rendering it accessible to reason. This
suppression of Christian faith by speculation begins as early as
the second century in the grand manner of post-Christian
Gnosticism; the dichotomy imported into the Absolute becomes a complete one in Manichaeism, which experiences
periodic revival through the Christian and post-Christian centuries. But this speculative rhythm between heaven and hell can
also have a retroactive effect on Christian theology: the great
shadow that arose from Augustine's later works and, in the
form of predestination, darkened the Middle Ages, the Reformation, and Jansenism might not have settled at all if Augustine
had not been a Manichee in his early period.

In Scholastic speculation, too, reason systematically tries to
penetrate the very heart of God—which, in Christian terms, can
only be open to a loving faith—and seems to conquer it for

anthropology.[3] Here too, human thought is fascinated by the idea that the world and man have developed out of God. In the context of Gnostic or Cabbalistic cosmogenesis and anthropogenesis of this kind, antiquity's "reserve" in the face of the *theion* is lost, and the natural awareness of the *analogia entis* is weakened or entirely extinguished (Spinoza). Given the Christian assertion that man in Christ "is born of God", why should he not be ultimately of divine nature himself? Maybe, through a long Odyssean process, he will once more become the God he once was—and, even in his alienation, has never ceased, at a deep level, to be? The many forms of post-Christian Titanism, which dare to regard man as originating in a divinity that has (demonically) split (Jakob Böhme and those who came after him, right up to the Romantics, to Baader, Schelling and the Russians) and destined ultimately to redeem this tragic God, are all inconceivable apart from their passage through Christianity. But they all also lead to its total perversion.

b. Titanisms

According to the Titanic principle (in the modern sense), man simultaneously contests the divine legitimacy of the "new God" (Zeus or Christ) and claims this divinity for himself on the basis of his equality with God. Thus He-who-is-eternally is reduced to the level of an ossified relic of the past; in his place the Eternally-becoming, the authentically living force, is enthroned.

In its tendency toward straightforward intelligibility and utility, the Enlightenment, which, for that whole period, "naturalized" the Christian faith, seems far removed from all Titanism. Yet it is far more than latent within it. It is astir along the path that leads from Shaftesbury to Herder, and from Lessing (with his *Faust*) to Goethe: the whole age is under the sign of "the Prometheus principle".[4] Such a principle is unknown in the ancient world, in spite of Aeschylus, just as the

---

[3] This is one of the great themes of Gustav Siewerth's systematic study of the history of ideas.

[4] I attempted to illustrate this in the first volume of my *Apokalypse der deutschen Seele* (Salzburg: A. Pustet, 1937). However, the study lacks a number of important "Prometheus" texts.

Faustian dimension is unthinkable then. In both sides of its dialectic, the latter contradicts the Delphic *"Gnōthi Sauton"*, both in demanding that the moment be eternal, fulfilled and divine and in requiring that the man who strives and is eternally dissatisfied should be regarded as redeemed in virtue of that striving. The Faustian, Promethean attitude, which dominates the Age of Idealism (up to the middle of the nineteenth century), draws its nourishment from the anthropological "heightening of tension" introduced by Christianity.

What is given through grace, imparted from above—the gift of being a child of God—man accepts by reaching above himself. It can be clearly followed in the way in which, in Kant, the "gratis" quality of the Christian God's self-giving love—which is the very opposite of an external law imposed on human freedom from outside—becomes transformed into self-legislation on the part of practical reason. That God, since he is the Absolute, is also the Non-other, more interior to me than I am to myself; and that his unfathomable love in the act of creation, as in redemption and the outpouring of the Spirit, both grounds and fulfills the freedom of the creature—none of this can any longer be appreciated by Kant's anthropology. Nonetheless, over Kant's *Anthropology* (1798), which is an empirical science aiming to mediate "knowledge of man as a citizen of the world", there hovers a *Metaphysics of Morals* (1797), which contains a regulative principle for practical conduct; it is governed by an absolute principle that, while it cannot be established in terms of realization or nonrealization, in its unconditional nature can only have been borrowed from Christian theology. According to this principle, man, if he is to act ethically, must liberate the maxims of his action from all individual motives, so that he is in a position to understand them as a "general law", Kant even says a "general law of nature".[5] Separated by a chasm from the empirical man and not directly verifiable in his conduct, this absolute principle of practical reason hovers over him yet without being divine;[6] all reason can do, to be ethical, is to seize it as its own and identify itself with it. Only thus, provided with a

---

[5] *Grundlegung der Metaphysik der Sitten* (1785), 52 (Weischedel IV, 51).

[6] "A metaphysics of morals of this kind, so completely isolated, unmixed with anthropology, theology, physics . . . is not only the indispensable substratum

standard "from above", can the human race hope to make some progress in humanity;[7] similarly all politics should be subject to the dictates of the principle of ethics.[8]

The Kantian dualism in man between his empirical nature and his "pure powers" could not be sustained; Fichte interprets the possibility of self-legislation as that act (*Tathandlung*) in which the empirical ego assures itself of its absoluteness, the vanishing point toward which, through action, it moves in self-realization. But as we have already shown, Idealism and *Lebensphilosophie* show their origins in Christian theology in that reason cannot catch up with the deepest layer of man, be it act or will or drive; what is ultimate in man is so absolute that it cannot be mastered by the categories of reason. The topic persists in many metamorphoses: from the late Schelling to Schopenhauer, to Feuerbach's philosophy of Eros, to Nietzsche's will-to-power (which here is clearly only a variant of Schopenhauer's blind will-to-life), and thence to the *élan vital* of Bergson, Scheler's powerful "necessity" (*Drang*), Simmel's fluid life-force and Freud's libido. It is possible to see with one's eyes how the Promethean tendency, which was primarily concerned with spiritualization (the union of the limited "I" with the absolute "I"), logically turns into the Dionysian, because the absolute "I" possesses a suprarational, natural vitality to which the *ratio*, together with consciousness in its limitedness, must surrender. This brief summary cries out for detailed treatment of the differences between these thinkers, since each of them has a specific emphasis; all the same, the crucial axis goes right through post-Christian thought at this

---

of all certain theoretical knowledge of duties but also something of the greatest importance in genuinely fulfilling its prescriptions" *Ibid*. (Weischedel, 38–39).

[7] "In what order should we expect there to be progress toward the better? By things proceeding, not *upward from below*, but *downward from above*." *Streit der Fakultäten* II, 10 (Weischedel VI, 366).

[8] "Genuine politics cannot take a single step without having first paid homage to morality." *Zum ewigen Frieden*, Appendix (Weischedel VI, 243). Schopenhauer clearly recognized the theological a priori in Kant's ethics: "Kant borrowed this imperative form of ethics, tacitly and unobserved, from theological morals. The latter's presuppositions, i.e., theology, lie at the root of his ethics, and they are inseparable from it, alone giving it significance and meaning. They are implicit within it; consequently, at the end of his system, it was an easy matter for him once more to develop a theology out of his morality." *Über die Grundlage der Moral* (1840), *Werke* (Insel), III, 515.

point. Again, it is only logical that the Dionysian, in which the "I" is fulfilled only as it submerges in the life enveloping it, produces the theme of "Eros-Thanatos", which, in this intensity, was unknown to antiquity and could only reach such a pitch under Christian provocation—"Dionysus and/or the Crucified!" Freud, in his pessimistic objectivity, raised the topic, and many have followed him.[9]

In all forms of Titanism, ultimately, the person is sacrificed. It burns to glowing ashes in the belly of the Moloch of the Absolute, be it the "will" or "life" or "death". This is also what happens in Hegel, even though in him alone reason, spirit, remains the all-embracing reality. Hegel is able to describe in the most graphic terms the lower levels of individual existence, of the subjective spirit linked to a body, of the "heart" with its anticipatory intimations, of a consciousness initially imprisoned within itself; but in the end, after all, the individual standpoint must be abandoned, for reconciliation is brought about by the objective Spirit, and it allows no absolute claims to challenge the all-embracing reality. The claim of the individual man, Jesus Christ, cannot be ultimate in the Hegelian system but only symbolic. But the principle of the system itself is drawn from Johannine theology.

Feuerbach opposes Hegel, going so far as to assert that man's sense-bound nature, his finitude and mortality, is what is absolute and immortal. "Man pursues everything, even what is most finite, as if it is infinite",[10] so that "the present's 'other world' is already to be found in 'this world' " [das Jenseits der Gegenwart schon in das Diesseits fällt]. The "psychic human sacrifices" that Christianity demanded are thus no longer necessary, since there is nothing more real, more total and more fulfillable than earthly existence, to be projected into some yonder realm: "Every existent thing has the purpose of its existence within its existence. . . . Being is completeness, fulfilled potential. Life is being's self-realization."[11] "The Christian wants to be God, for he says explicitly that the divinity is his pattern

[9] On the sequence of the Prometheus, Dionysus and Thanatos principles, cf. the three volumes of the *Apokalypse der deutschen Seele* (1937–1939).

[10] "Die Unsterblichkeitsfrage vom Standpunkt der Anthropologie" (1846), *Werke*, 2d ed. (Bolin/Jodl, 1960), I, 113.

[11] *Ibid.*, 121, 131, 156.

and prototype";[12] now this is possible directly in Eros: "Man together with man—the unity of 'I' and 'thou'—is God."[13]

Marx's idea of positive humanism is the transposition of this anti-Christian system into social terms. The guiding idea, the absolute freedom of man in community, is the result of a confluence of ideas stemming from Hegel and Feuerbach. Sartre, finally (and again in an open campaign against Christian theology), proclaimed this absolute freedom as the raison d'être of finite existence. Here, at last, the "gratis" quality of the divine self-giving in Christ, this eternally overflowing love, is perverted into meaningless "superfluity" and hence absurdity. Where dependent being [An-sich], which is nothingness [Nichts], aspires to self-sufficiency [Für-sich], there can only be contradiction, the contradiction in which being's being consists in negating, in the freedom to put a question mark over everything. This means that every positive, loving relationship to one's fellow man, who represents an attack on my freedom, is fundamentally and finally destroyed. Freedom and betrayal go together; many of Nietzsche's ideas were already tending in this direction.

The practically endless attempts to take the Christian heightening of tension in created nature and reduce it to the dimension of anthropology—attempts which only contradict one another because they are situated in a circle around the Christian center —will only be alive and of interest as long as they manifest the element of protest. Once separated from what they are resisting, they collapse, because they draw their power to transcend (into the nonhuman, which as such cannot be nature and so can only be a nothing) solely from themselves, and so are bound to ruin the finite human being. Christianity adopted antiquity's philosophy of the human spirit—openness to all being and hence to the transcendental qualities of being: unity, truth, goodness, beauty—and brought them to full development; this was only possible because, in ancient thought, the *theion* was seen together with being, even if only analogically. Post-Christian thought, which rejects this view as allegedly "Christian", will also want to reject antiquity's openness to

---

[12] *Ibid.*, 274.
[13] *Grundsätze der Philosophie der Zukunft* (1843), 60. *Werke* II, 318.

being-in-its-totality (or, like Heidegger, it will exclude the *theos* as a Christian element). Thus it will narrow the True and the Good, within a purely anthropological perspective, to plain "interest". Interest, however, while it is an accompaniment of the Good, is not its center. And it is impossible to abstract from the latter for the sake of "pure" cognition.[14] For the True is "in its way an aspect of the Good" (Thomas) because, in both aspects, being shows itself to be self-giving (and hence profoundly Beautiful).

We must add a word about the post-Christian parodies of the "Body of Christ", the Christian Church. We made only brief reference to the latter's constitution; it will have to be unfolded in the next volume. The Church has been given the (sociologically difficult) task of testifying through what she is (not only through what she says) to the absoluteness of God's loving care for the world in Christ. She has to claim catholicity, that is, totality, while being one social edifice among others. This task, from the human point of view, is a heavy burden, bound to attract to the Church and her representatives the odium of an arrogant absolutism; and it becomes all the harder in modern times, against a background of relativizing historicism and Hegelian tolerance. And yet, in the post-Christian age, political edifices arise in competition with her; they claim the right, theoretically and practically, to administer the totality of salvation and truth, and they do so explicitly as one sociological part or "party" (*pars*). They also use force to implement their program (methods to which the Church herself, contrary to her true mission, once resorted), and, from their secularized standpoint, such use of force acquires an appearance of legitimacy. For, in the plan of "positive humanism", the common good is the freedom of mankind, which is to be pursued in all circumstances and hence with all available means.

The belief that this common good can be implemented using post-Christian, immanent resources, is sustained by the "hope principle"—which again shows us that an element of biblical and Christian "absoluteness" has been sequestered by the anthropological approach. At this point, however, a face looks out at

[14] Jürgen Habermas, *Erkenntnis und Interesse*, 2d ed. (Suhrkamp, 1973).

us from beneath the costume of post-Christian anthropology, a face not mentioned hitherto. Now we come to it explicitly, at the end of this volume, before going on to describe it in more detail in the next volume: it is the face of a biblical anthropology that is not Christian but Jewish.

c. The Other Face

We cannot fail to notice this face: it is too distinctive, too present to us. It comes *before* the Christian interpretation of the world and of man and has always been held to be its foundation; together with the "pagan" stream, it is one of the two main currents that flow together in the primitive Church, and theologically it is the more important. But it also exists *after* this Christian interpretation of the world, just as, after a building has been demolished, its foundations come to light once more; it reminds us that Christian anthropology comes from farther back than many people would like to admit. All the same, it is unwilling to appear on stage as the prologue; it prefers to see itself as the legitimate tragic hero, after the departure of the usurper. Thus Jewish anthropology has its own way of coming to an understanding with the post-Christian anthropology we have described. Indeed, one wonders whether the Jewish dynamism (which, in its "messianism"—according to its own view of itself—was and continued to be primarily infrahistorical) was not bound to come into its own at the very point when the Christians' transcendent expectation of the kingdom of God lost impetus and when man began to take upon himself the attainment of the kingdom of heaven "here on earth". Whenever Christians feel the desire to join in mankind's common efforts toward a better future, they return to ponder the Old Testament impulses in this direction. Those movements that place the community—the "nation", the "class" or "humanity" —above the individual are often of Jewish origin, such as that *Lebensphilosophie* to which we have referred which locates the entire hope and future of everything that lives in the driving life force, whereas all established forms already bear within them the seeds of ossification and demise. Thus Jewish anthropology will also be emphatically sexual insofar as the sexual is the basis on which the tribe, the coming community, is built.

On the other hand, its attitude to the body-spirit problem cannot be unequivocal. Convinced of the mortality of the individual and of the earthly immortality of the race, it is unacquainted with the prebiblical flight from the body and clings to the bodily reality of the present as long as it lasts. On the other hand, Israel's God did not become flesh and manifests himself in the spiritual word of commandment and promise; the wise of Israel live by pondering and interpreting this word. There are attempts to incarnate the coming reality in the here and now: in Hasidic mysticism; but it too is intimately related to Cabbalistic Gnosticism.[15] Man, both bodily and spiritual, is pulled in two opposite directions; he can only commend himself into the hands of the invisible God, entrusting to him that personal wholeness and totality which is beyond his ken. As yet, the Jew has not been granted the picture of the Risen Christ, the attained totality, the "pledge" of a totality that still awaits us.

However, most things remain in a state of flux; but it is a different flux from the "pagan" one, which alternated between *kosmos theion* and man. Judaism hovers in an openness that is unfulfilled. In what sense is the Jew a person? Certainly, the great ones, chosen from among the people to be its prophets and leaders, are persons. But what of the individuals of the nation? They are not persons in the New Testament sense. In what way, for the Jew, is the sexual, in its orientation toward the species, transcended in the direction of the personal? The Jew regards the "Song of Songs" as a nuptial hymn celebrating Yahweh's union with his people, but does this also actually become a physical union? Or is everything caught in a seemingly endless alternation between election and remote banishment? In the post-Christian age it is quite easy for this alternation in which Israel lives to fit in with the chiaroscuro of a persisting anthropology; both form the most diverse hybrids, in which Judaism's prophetic intensity tends to come to the fore. This is true even when the Jewish

[15] Cf. Chaim Potok, *The Chosen* (1967).

element appears in a liberal, unbelieving, atheistic form: as far as the individual is concerned, it is Israel as a nation which counts.

We shall have to return to this in more detail. It is mentioned here lest our theological "analogy of anthropology"—natural, pre-Christian; biblical and Christian; post-Christian—should lack one of its essential elements.

We have presented the main characters of the theo-drama: God and man. Two things, equally important, have emerged from their confrontation: God is not simply the "Other" (the "partner"); he is so high above all created things that he is just as much the "non-Other". This means that, in spite of this and because of this, man cannot be traced back to God, deduced from him, in any respect and at any level. God has given him a genuine, spiritual freedom which, because it has been really *given*, cannot be "upstaged" by God's infinite freedom but has to fulfill itself in its proper area (in God, where else?). The primal drama is played between divine and human freedom.

However, then we saw what a precarious being man is, how he is pulled by tensions this way and that, what a "sphinx" he is to himself. We saw how inevitably, purely anthropologically speaking, he must be drawn into confusions and entanglements. We saw how the whole structure (again speaking in purely human terms) seems to be doomed to tragedy. Indeed, since man cannot in any way reflect on himself from outside the ongoing action, he is already deeply involved in this tragedy.

From the Christian point of view, however, the list of characters is not yet concluded. As yet, we have not spoken specifically of the main actor, the "Mediator between God and men". And he does not stand there on his own: he is explicitly the principle of world history and of creation in its entirety, which means that all the other characters, which are dependent on this principle (that is, on him), must be taken together with him. From the perspective of theology, we have said, anthropology could be and ought to be treated as a function of Christology; and we have endeavored to do this in one respect. In another respect, it was right to discuss the "first Adam", who became a "living being" before the "last Adam", who will become a "life-giving Pneuma" (1 Cor 15:45).

The next volume will give more substance to this first part. Accordingly, in order to portray the characters, it will have to anticipate even more of the action. All the same, the action itself must remain the unforeseeable event resulting from the interplay of characters; we are all involved in it, but we cannot anticipate its outcome.

INDEX OF PERSONS